PURE

The Sexual Revolutions of

Marilyn Chambers

BY

JARED STEARNS

HEADPRESS

A HEADPRESS BOOK
First published by Headpress in 2024, Oxford, United Kingdom
< headoffice@headpress.com >

PURE
The Sexual Revolutions of Marilyn Chambers

The Publisher wishes to thank Jen Wallis

10 9 8 7 6 5 4 3 2 1

A CIP catalogue record for this book is available from the British Library

ISBN 978-1-915316-19-6   paperback
ISBN 978-1-915316-20-2   ebook
ISBN NO-ISBN   hardback

HEADPRESS. POP AND UNPOP CULTURE

Exclusive NO-ISBN special edition hardbacks and other items of interest are available at
HEADPRESS.COM

For Daniel, Dave, and Jeff,

who got me through this

and

for Willa,

who'll one day learn just how

revolutionary her grandmother was

TABLE OF CONTENTS

Photo gallery located between pages 94 & 95

ACKNOWLEDGMENTS

THANK YOU TO MY AGENT, Jane Kinney-Denning, who immediately saw the potential of this book and took a chance on a first-time biographer. We took a leap of faith together, and your guidance and support through this process has been invaluable.

The aphorism "sex sells" is only accurate to a degree. Including the word "porn" immediately triggers conscious and unconscious opinions and feelings. This is particularly true in the United States, where violence is revered and romanticized, and sex is often considered obscene and intolerable. Numerous publishers turned down this book.

David Kerekes and the Headpress team are progressive. They, too, saw the potential of this project. They saw beyond the "porn star" label assigned to Marilyn Chambers and were as enthusiastic as I was about telling her story. I am so grateful for their open-mindedness and fervency. It's been a joy working with them.

A heartfelt thanks to McKenna Taylor, who, in addition to becoming a dear friend, entrusted me with the awesome responsibility of telling her mother's story honestly and accurately. Her blessing of and cooperation with this project only encouraged me to produce the best book I could to preserve her mother's legacy. I am beholden to and honored by her trust and support.

I needed to tell Marilyn's story as truthfully as possible. People's memories are strange amalgamations of facts and fiction, a combination of what is true and what one believes or wants to be true. If something seemed unlikely, I did my best to back it up with additional sources, preferably from Marilyn herself. Fortunately, she gave hundreds, if not thousands, of interviews in her lifetime. However, when she died unexpectedly in 2009, she took with her countless secrets and stories.

PURE
The Sexual Revolutions of Marilyn Chambers

Thank you to those who generously gave their time and shared memories of Marilyn, including Liz Boyd, Liberty Bradford, Meredith Bradford, Bill Briggs, David Cronenberg, "Godfrey Daniels," Frank Durant, Norman Gaines, Edmund Gaynes, Howie Gordon (aka Richard Pacheco), Marty Greenwald, Jane Hamilton (aka Veronica Hart), Xaviera Hollander, Charles Jay, Peggy McGinn, Legs McNeil, Herschel Savage, Jann Smith, Crissa Stapleton, Jules Tasca, Jan Welt, and Dan Woog.

Some of these people have never before spoken on the record or shared intimate details about their relationship with Marilyn. Thank you for trusting me. There was a common theme among many of those whom I interviewed: they all loved and cared deeply for Marilyn as a human being. Their continued love remains palpable.

I'm blessed to have a fantastic group of close friends who've supported me throughout this project from inception to completion. Four people, in particular, deserve special mention: Daniel Schrimshire, Dave Ford, Jeff Mock, and Mark Cox. Each offered support unique to his personality and, in the process, learned far more about Marilyn Chambers than he ever dreamed or probably wanted.

Daniel's calm, loving presence soothed my neverending anxieties and distracted me from my thoughts. Dave took many frantic phone calls and offered his pearls of wisdom. He's a much better writer than I am, so I asked him to read every chapter of this book and provide feedback. He graciously did so. Jeff texted me every single day (seriously) and kept me laughing. He often gently reminded me to take breaks, relax, and practice self-care. And Mark, my beloved British bombshell and fellow collector, not only shares a deep passion for film and pop culture but also provided some of the archival materials for this book.

Thanks also to Royce Conner, Marcus Ewert, Dave George, Rocky Graziano, James Neal, Jeffrey Schwarz, Simon Sheridan, Jen Wallis, Joe Webster, Gareth Wilson, and my psychiatrist.

The Biographers International Organization (BIO) has been an invaluable resource, especially for networking with other biographers. Even though I was the new kid, my fellow biographers always treated me as an equal and enthusiastically supported my efforts. These wonderfully creative souls include Ellen Brown, Diane Diekman, Danny Fingeroth, Beverly Gray, Carl Rollyson, and Sydney Stern. Other BIO members who supported this project are Cathy Curtis, Vanda Krefft, and Billy Tooma.

Finally, to my family—Mom, Dad, Kim, Mike, Colin, and Callie—thanks for the love and support and for putting up with my idiosyncrasies all these years.

"To the pure, all things are pure, but to the defiled and unbelieving, nothing is pure; but both their minds and their consciences are defiled."
Titus 1:15 ESV

"The image I want to project is one of being wholesome, clean, and all-American."
Marilyn Chambers, 1973

INTRODUCTION

TRY SEARCHING FOR MARILYN CHAMBERS on IMDb.com, the Internet Movie Database. You won't find her. The search results offer several films with Marilyn's name in the title. To view her IMDb profile page, you have to click on one of those results, then click on Marilyn's name.

Now try searching for any mainstream Hollywood actress such as Charlize Theron, Margot Robbie, or Scarlett Johansson. Their IMDb profile is right at the top of the search results. You can even search for "the Munchkins," and the IMDb profile comes up for The Singer Midgets, their official credit in *The Wizard of Oz*.

So why doesn't Marilyn Chambers's profile page appear in the IMDb search results?

Because the algorithm classifies her as a "porn star." Just like the people who've programmed them, algorithms have excluded those who've made their living in adult films, even if it's only a small fraction of what they've accomplished in show business.

It's laughably ludicrous.

Long before the Internet became the master of our lives, and even before home entertainment like DVD and VHS, the easiest way to see a pornographic film was in an adult theater. In the early seventies, it became fashionable to do so. Dozens of X-rated films were made during this time, but history has boiled it down to three hardcore movies of historical import: *Deep Throat*, *The Devil in Miss Jones*, and *Behind the Green Door*. Just as one never forgets their first sexual experience, neither do they forget the first time they see X-rated material. For an entire generation, namely baby boomers, Marilyn Chambers became the first adult film actress they witnessed passionately, joyously, and freely expressing her sexuality on film. Mass mixed-gendered audiences went to see *Behind the*

PURE *The Sexual Revolutions of Marilyn Chambers*

Green Door, the 1972 film in which Marilyn starred, by the millions.

Adult film stars were outlaws. These people dared to say and do the things many wished they could in public or private. In many cases, the performers got into the business as an act of rebellion, not to get rich and famous. Many, like Marilyn, came from affluent or middle-class backgrounds. Participation in adult films wasn't just a part of the sexual revolution; the act itself was revolutionary.

Marilyn never set out to be revolutionary, but it was part of her DNA. Her lineage can be traced to the American Revolutionary War. An ancestor, Jesse Briggs, was a Private, 4th company, who served from February 1777 to December 1779.[1] Briggs fought for freedom and independence on behalf of his country. Marilyn fought for freedom and independence as an empowered, sexually-liberated woman in a misogynistic, sexist world.

From the moment she became famous until her untimely death in 2009, Marilyn spent most of her time defending herself—her choices, her profession, her marriages, her very existence. Perhaps she wouldn't have had to do so much explaining if she were a man.

In the twenty-first century, fame and celebrity are quantifiable. Popularity is measured in followers, likes, clicks, and views. We're so conditioned to it that it can be challenging to grasp how famous and popular Marilyn Chambers was. She was so prominent in the seventies and eighties that one needn't have seen one of her films to know her name. She was written up in newspapers and magazines like any other movie star. Often, the press didn't know what to make of this beautiful, wealthy woman who made no apologies for being a sexually adventurous and celebrated luminary.

'Marilyn Chambers, X-rated star of porno flicks, says except for her sexual proclivities she's just your average 26-year-old successful actress,' wrote Vernon Scott for United Press International in 1980. 'Of all women who perform the sex act on camera, Marilyn is perhaps the best known[.] [Her] reputation as the darling of sexually explicit films is based on her only two X-rated movies, 'Behind The Green Door' and 'The Resurrection of Eve.' But Marilyn's off-screen life is something else. She is, after all, a star of sorts and lives like one. She and [her husband-manager Chuck] Traynor make their home on a ranch in the mountains not far from Las Vegas, Nev. Her home is tastefully appointed and expensively furnished. Because she owns percentages of both her porn films, Marilyn has amassed a considerable fortune.'[2]

In many ways, Marilyn Chambers could have only become famous in the seventies. The sexual revolution began in the late sixties and fused with the concurrent civil rights, women's, and gay rights movements to form a molecular

INTRODUCTION

powerhouse of righteousness, anger, and freedom. The sexual revolution reached its zenith in the early seventies when X-rated films became the *cause célèbre*. Marilyn Chambers was at its center, driving difficult and complex conversations about sex, sexuality, women, race, obscenity, and First Amendment rights.

Marilyn Chambers was decidedly of her time, but her importance resonates decades later. However, since a few of her movies required her to have sex on screen, her contributions have been roundly ignored.

When she became famous, Marilyn Chambers ushered in a new strain of celebrity: the porn star. There was no such thing as an actor known primarily for their work in adult films before Marilyn and contemporaries like Linda Lovelace, the star of *Deep Throat*. A half-century ago, the phrase "porn star" was often used as it is today: largely as a pejorative. There are so many misinterpretations and preconceptions of what it means to be a "porn star."

This is not a book about a porn star. It is not a book to argue for or against pornography. It is, however, an attempt to change the perception of what a "porn star" actually is. Marilyn Chambers was a human being. She was a daughter, wife, and mother. This is the story of a woman, an entertainer, an actress, and a movie star who happened to make adult films.

To that end, I've consciously considered referring to Marilyn throughout this book as an actress, entertainer, or, where necessary, an adult film star. The phrases "porn star," "porno star," or "porno queen" only appear when someone refers to her as such, when she uses them herself, or when it's vital to the narrative.

Marilyn Chambers made several attempts to tell her life story. Each one reached different stages, but none came to fruition. Doubtlessly disappointed, she tried again. In a way, it was apropos of the life she led. In her professional and personal life, there were many times when things could have gone differently and more in her favor.

In the early nineties, Marilyn worked with writer Andrew M. Finley on a treatment for her never-published memoir, *The Hard Way*. They characterized it as 'a poignant tale of overindulgence (in an era that encouraged it) that ended in renewal. Marilyn was very ambitious. She wanted power, money, and fame and knew every step of the way what she was doing. Definitely a woman with a mind of her own, she was a feminist in many ways, giving it back to men the same way they gave it to her while never allowing herself to be forced or coerced by anybody at any time. Like Mae West said: 'Goodness had nothing to do with it!' But somehow, she ended up consciously relinquishing the mastery of her life to men.'[3]

This characterization is accurate to a degree.

Marilyn was a formidable presence, an industrious, sexually forthright, smart woman. Feminists and women's rights groups of the seventies and eighties denounced her, as they did many women in the adult film industry. Despite their grievances and misgivings, she was a feminist. As a woman in the unforgiving industry of show business, she faced misogyny and sexual harassment both publicly and privately, like so many women before and since. During interviews, she often flustered male reporters who expected her to be stupid and inarticulate.

"Always give people what they don't expect," was a piece of advice hammered into her by Chuck Traynor, her second husband and manager. It was a mantra she used throughout her life.

Chuck was one of the masters of her life. He exerted such a hold and control on her life and career that she never recovered. He took advantage of her financially. He verbally and emotionally assaulted her. He was physically violent with her. There were other verbal, physical, and emotionally abusive relationships with men after Chuck. Often, she fought back. In one case, she burned to the ground the home she was sharing with her vicious boyfriend. She always found the strength and courage to leave.

Her parents were devoid of almost any physical or verbal expression of love or affection. In many ways, the joyous mein of her sexual self was an attempt to fill the void left by her parents.

"You certainly have to be an exhibitionist as an actor, but in porn films, it has to be to an extreme," Marilyn said. "I did all kinds of things, and it was always like, 'Look at me, Mom and Dad! Look! Look!' I always wanted to be reassured that I was wanted and that I was doing well. I went way overboard and provided a lot of embarrassment to my parents, of course."[4]

She believed in fate. She believed in astrology. She practiced hypnotism. She believed in an afterlife. She sought guidance. When she got clean and sober and participated in twelve-step programs, she gave herself to a higher power. She was always seeking the truth, and shared her wisdom and experiences with others who needed help. More than anything, she craved approval—as a woman, a mother, an entertainer, and a human being.

She was, in many ways, the quintessential movie star. She had glamour, a perspicuous persona, and a bankable box office name. Her story has many of the same peaks and troughs as other movie stars. In the 1954 version of the film *A Star is Born*, Norman Maine (James Mason) tells Esther Blodgett (Judy Garland) upon hearing her sing for the first time that she had what the renowned nineteenth-century actress Ellen Terry called "that little something extra." In the

INTRODUCTION

twenties, that little something extra might have been called "it," like Hollywood's original "it girl" Clara Bow. Whatever the phrase, the meaning is star quality. That you've-got-it-or-you-don't charisma and aura that helps make some people famous. It's something that can't be taught. It goes beyond personality, talent, and physical beauty. It's chemical. Marilyn Chambers had a "little something extra" and a whole lot of "it."

PROLOGUE

MARILYN CHAMBERS WAS NERVOUS. SHE always got nervous before an audition. But instinct told her this time would be different. She gazed in a nearby mirror and checked her hair and makeup. She didn't need much makeup. She was tanned, toned, and knew she looked good. She was never smug about her beauty, though.

It was 1978. Just five years prior, she became an international celebrity—not only as the star of the hit pornographic film *Behind the Green Door* but also as the model holding a smiling baby on the boxes of Ivory Snow detergent. She managed to turn that notoriety and controversy into a career in entertainment beyond X-rated films.

No other actress known primarily for her work in adult films—not even her biggest rival, Linda Lovelace—had successfully crossed over into the mainstream. Marilyn Chambers was the first. She had just completed a six-month run in a Las Vegas staging of Neil Simon's play *Last of the Red Hot Lovers*. A recently-released horror film, *Rabid*, directed by David Cronenberg, was a box-office hit and had earned Marilyn good notices. She cut a disco record, wrote a monthly sex advice column and two books, and headlined a short-lived off-Broadway musical.

But she wanted one thing most of all: a Hollywood breakthrough. She yearned for a brilliantly-written script and a skilled director who could draw out of her a riveting performance that critics and the movie-going public couldn't possibly ignore. She wanted credibility as a serious actress, and she needed that validation. She knew she had the talent; she needed to find the right project to exploit it.

She thought the moment had finally arrived when she heard about the casting call for a film called *Hardcore*. It was a Hollywood movie, written and directed

PROLOGUE

by Paul Schrader, and produced by Columbia Pictures. Schrader had recently scored a huge hit as the screenwriter for Martin Scorsese's 1976 film *Taxi Driver*.

Hardcore was about the world of porn films. The role Marilyn wanted was that of a porn star. Sure, it was typecasting, and almost too obvious, but there was no onscreen sex. It was a straight dramatic role.

The film was about a pious businessman whose daughter goes missing on a church trip. A private detective hired to find her discovers she's been kidnapped and is starring in pornographic films. Her father, played by George C. Scott, goes on a quest to find her, traipsing through the supposedly dark and dingy world of porn filmmaking. He befriends Niki, the porn star role Marilyn hoped to get, who helps him and becomes a surrogate daughter during his search.

The role had grit, and she'd work opposite Scott, an Oscar-winning actor.

The casting director called Marilyn into the room. Marilyn took a deep breath and introduced herself. She read some prepared lines. When she finished, she exhaled and smiled at the casting director. He stayed silent as he considered her. Finally, he spoke:

"I'm sorry, we can't use you," he said.

Marilyn's eyes widened, and her mouth was agape. She'd been rejected for parts before—that's part of the business—but she knew she nailed this audition.

"I don't understand," she said. "Why?"

"We're looking for a porn-star type," he replied. "You're not it."

Marilyn always maintained a level of professionalism. Not this time.

"What? Are you out of your mind? I *am* a porn star."

"But you're too clean, too wholesome," the casting director said.

"And that's why I'm probably the biggest porn star there is!" she said. "That's the whole point. I'm the girl next door."

He didn't buy it, and thanked her for coming in.

Hollywood wouldn't cast her in roles because she was a "porn star," but when she auditioned for the role of a porn star, she was considered too wholesome to be one. It was the paradox of being Marilyn Chambers. An extraordinary stroke of luck catapulted her to stardom. Then, by creating the persona of "Marilyn Chambers"—a glamorous, twenty-four-hour-a-day sex queen and all-around entertainer—she maintained fame and success few other performers in the adult industry, men or women, had achieved. But for Marilyn, porn was a means to an end; she wanted to be a serious actress.

"In Hollywood, they still think sex is dirty," she said. "They're afraid of it. They were afraid to show people that a porn star was smart and had talent, and could act. That works against what society thinks."[5]

PURE *The Sexual Revolutions of Marilyn Chambers*

Marilyn took a most unusual road to stardom. Born Marilyn Briggs in 1952, she was an upper-middle-class WASP girl from Westport, Connecticut, who grew up in a house where sex was taboo. As Marilyn Chambers, she became the world's most famous sex star and revolutionized the adult film industry and show business. By the late eighties, she was tired of playing the role of "Marilyn Chambers." However, after more than a decade, she had no other identity. She spent most of her later life trying to figure out who she really was.

"I was Marilyn Chambers seven days a week, all the time," she recalled two years before her death in 2009. "Then, as I got older, I had to become me. It was...difficult to make that transition into what I really was. Everybody goes through the 'Who am I?' and discovering yourself, but mine came a little bit later and after coming off of a very big run. You know, it was difficult to be 'Marilyn Chambers' twenty-four hours a day, seven days a week, and come down off of that and be somebody else."[6]

The essence of Marilyn Chambers never left her, but neither did Marilyn Briggs. The closest she came to realizing her purpose was when she became a mother. Still, she wondered if Marilyn Chambers would be remembered. Had she, as Marilyn Chambers, contributed anything substantive to popular culture?

There's a simple answer: Marilyn Chambers wasn't just part of the sexual revolution; she *was* the sexual revolution.

How and why people, particularly women, enter the adult film business has always fascinated us. Why do they do it? What was their childhood like? Usually, the questions are tinged with pity, such as, How did they end up there? What could have happened? Marilyn was no different in asking many of these questions.

"I have had a lot of questions about my own life, but I had a great childhood," she said. "Something interjected in there, though, to propel me in that direction, whether it was outside forces or inner stuff. It would be very interesting to explore. Why or what is the type of person who is able to do this? What drives them to this? It's a very similar background. It's a pattern. It would be interesting, but it wouldn't be pretty. If you look at the volume of people who pass through the adult film world, if you look at the statistics of people, there are very few—a very small percentage—that are still okay and around. You have to get through it and be a survivor. I'm a survivor."[7]

Chapter 1

THE SHOW-OFF

---

*"I probably had the best childhood. If I could go back and change anything,
I wouldn't. I would consider it very 'normal,' whatever that is."*
— Marilyn Chambers, 1983[1]

FIFTY-TWO MILES NORTHEAST OF NEW York City lies the affluent suburb of Westport, Connecticut. A one-time farming community, the area's landscape changed during the Industrial Revolution, and it began to attract people from the city. Fashionable Westport drew artists and writers in the 1950s, who appreciated its easy access to the city by train or car.

Dan Woog, a lifelong Westport resident who went to high school with Marilyn, said the area's large number of artists—illustrators, advertising creatives, musicians—gave it a bohemian feel. "It had [a] vibe that other suburbs, which also had people commuting in to New York, would not necessarily have had," he said. Politically, Woog added, Westport had a balance of progressive and conservative factions.[2]

William Henry Briggs, Jr. was one of those advertising creatives. He was a successful executive and president of Monroe F. Dreher, an advertising agency on Madison Avenue in New York City. One of his big accounts was Avon, the beauty and cosmetics company. He'd take the 7:00AM train from Westport every morning and return home after 8:00PM.

He and his wife, Virginia ("Ginny") Isabelle Richardson, moved their family from Providence, Rhode Island, to Westport six months after their third child, Marilyn Ann Briggs, was born on April 22, 1952. The couple's two other children, Bill and Janice ("Jann"), were six and five years older respectively.

Ginny possessed a rectitude and frankness that Marilyn inherited. An austere woman, she exhibited characteristics typical of many New Englanders, including a reserve that bordered on emotional coldness. In the post-World War ll era, women were expected to leave their jobs and return home to rear children. Ginny continued to work. She wanted to be a doctor, but her Scottish father wouldn't allow it. Ginny was resilient and driven and eventually became a nurse. That's as much as her father would oblige.

On the day of Ginny's wedding to William in 1943, her mother asked William, "Do you know what you're getting into marrying her?" Ginny was strong and did not want to be a housewife. Perhaps inauspiciously, that's what William was looking for in a mate.

"My parents were very different personalities, [and] probably should not have been married," Jann remembered. "My father wanted a homemaker. My mom wanted to travel the world and work and read books. She didn't want to play golf with him. She didn't want those things. She wanted to go to Europe every year and look at museums and cathedrals and things like that. He had no interest in that. Yet they were incredibly loving parents. And I never saw my parents fight. Not once did I ever see my parents fight. My mom slammed a few doors in her life, but I'm a door slammer, too."[3]

The Briggs family was financially comfortable and considered upper middle class. Ginny kept her job as a nurse because she enjoyed working. This was somewhat unusual for Westport suburban families of the fifties and sixties.

"Many of the fathers were absent fathers," Woog said. "Perhaps a little more so in Westport because the commute was longer and jobs were higher power. The mothers were raising kids more or less by themselves. There was sure a decent amount of drinking and pill-popping by the mothers, which we really didn't know about. Probably many of them [if they had been] born twenty or thirty years later would have had high-powered careers themselves. But they weren't; they were raising kids in the suburbs."[4]

In Marilyn's later life, she often described the relationship with her mother as "oil and water." However, Marilyn was similar to her mother, particularly in her assuredness, honesty, and independence. These similarities often led to a magnetic repulsion.

'My parents understand that I've always had a strong will and that no one has ever told me how to live my life,' Marilyn wrote in her 1975 book *My Story*. 'My mom once told me, 'Marilyn, you'll never stop doing the unexpected, will you? No, you won't.' She answered it herself, and I was glad because it told me that she understood and perhaps even liked the idea that my life would be full of surprises for her (and for me, too).'[5]

Marilyn's father tended to be almost as emotionally reserved as her mother. Jann said her parents hugged the children when they were little but never said 'I

THE SHOW-OFF

love you.' For Marilyn, the youngest, this was especially difficult.

"That hurt Marilyn a lot," Jann said. "Although she told me one time he said it to her—but I don't know."[6]

Marilyn knew from an early age that she wanted to be an entertainer. She would often break into song and put on shows with kids in the neighborhood. William encouraged this creative expression when Marilyn was a child. In doing so, he provided Marilyn with some of the validation and approval she craved. However, when Ginny saw Marilyn performing in the family's living room, she would scold Marilyn and tell her to "stop showing off."

'I've always been a show-off, and I think [my siblings] resent that a bit, and that's just a carryover from childhood days,' Marilyn said. 'My sister would probably say she's the black sheep of the family (I guess because she's the middle child and the middle child's always supposed to be the 'different' one), but the truth is I'm the one who sticks out. I was a show-off, and I got attention, and I loved it. It has to be in you, a part of you, or you can't make it. It was always a part of me, and my brother and sister resented it a little.'[7]

Jann said she had many conversations with her brother and sister about the dysfunction within their home when they were adults. 'We liked our life growing up,' she said. 'We didn't want to see that maybe it wasn't as perfect as we thought.'[8]

Woog, Marilyn's childhood friend, said some Westport families seemed affectionate while others did not, a dichotomy typical of the area and the era. "I don't think it was different from much of the rest of the country. If you look at *Leave It to Beaver* or *Ozzie and Harriet*, you don't see the parents hugging their kids. You don't see them saying 'I love you' to their kids. And I don't think it was much different in Westport."[9]

Jann characterized the family as "close," but more in proximity than in emotional support. The family almost never went on vacations together. Ginny and William vacationed separately from one another. William went golfing every year, and Ginny took solo trips to Europe. The children were never invited. They found their parents' separate vacations strange but never asked about it. It simply wasn't discussed.

"You never had the sense that hers was a family that did things together," said Darryl Coates Manning, a school friend of Marilyn's.[10] And indeed, there was truth in that.

"My dad was the school of silence," Bill Briggs recalled. "He did not talk. It was a lot of grunting but not a lot of communication there."[11]

Nevertheless, Marilyn felt a special kinship with her father. In fact, she fell in love with him. Until his death in 2000, she tried to please him and win his approval. This infatuation led her to seek the approval of nearly every man (and some women) in her personal life. Her professional life afforded her much of the male approval she sought by being revered as a sex goddess.

Marilyn offered a raw summation of her life to *GQ* magazine in 1987:

> I was born and raised in Westport, Connecticut, a suburb for executives who worked in New York City. My name was Marilyn Briggs. I was a cheerleader in high school. My mother worked as a nurse, and my father was an ad exec in New York City. He worked on the Avon account. My parents were not into being affectionate. I craved that. Mostly from my dad. He was a handsome man. A silver fox. I had this mad sexual fantasy about him. It really was incest. But it was all right. Sometimes fantasies are okay if you leave them fantasies.
>
> When I was 18, I wrote him this love letter, but he never responded. I was crushed when I learned he had a girlfriend all those years. I was 21, playing the Riverboat Room in New York, when he walked in with his girlfriend. It shocked me even then that he wasn't perfect. All my life, I have tried to please my father, but I never could…There's something in me that doesn't please men. I don't know. Maybe that's why I worked so hard at it all these years. Maybe that's why I always need a man to take care of me. To be Daddy's girl.
>
> Sometimes I don't want to think about it.
>
> You know, my father is divorced from my mother now. He lives alone in an apartment. He told me for the first time only recently that he has kept my love letter in his dresser drawer all these years.[12]

It was known around Westport that William had at least one affair and probably more. It's not known if Ginny was aware of any affairs. If so, she didn't say anything. She was image-conscious and wanted it to appear that the family was happy. Whether or not Ginny knew about William's affairs, she likely unconsciously saw Marilyn as competition for William's attention and approval. And Marilyn worked hard for that approval.

As a student at Brown University, William had been a track captain. So Marilyn became an athlete, too—and a good one. She started diving and gymnastics at seven and excelled at both. She was also fiercely competitive. She earned numerous gold medals, particularly for diving. Every time she won a gold medal, she gave it to her father, hoping he'd say anything positive to encourage and validate her. She won far more medals than words of praise.

When she was thirteen, she participated in a challenging competition. She asked her father to go, but he had a golf game, he told her. Ginny dropped off

THE SHOW-OFF

"Ginny" Briggs with her children (l-r) Marilyn, Bill, and Janice outside their Westport, Connecticut home in the early 1960s. *Photo courtesy of Bill Briggs.*

Marilyn. Neither parent was in the audience to watch their daughter perform six difficult dives. Marilyn thrived on the concentration needed to perform and the adrenaline that came with it, but on this day felt "troubled." 'I had a lot on my mind and kept wishing my dad could be there to see me,' she wrote years later. 'It really hurt, and I don't think he ever knew that.'[13]

She wanted badly to win the meet but came in second place. When she returned home, her father sat in his big leather chair.

"Did you win?" he asked her bluntly.

She showed him the silver medal. She was disappointed but still proud of her accomplishment.

"Why didn't you get first?" he asked her.

Without saying a word, an infuriated, wounded Marilyn turned on her heels and marched out of the room. "I'd have come in first if you had been there, you son of a bitch!" she thought. In a way, it was a moment of clarity. Whether she placed first or second or didn't win a competition, he'd never give her the approval she craved. That didn't deter her from seeking it or hoping it would happen. She didn't want to believe he wasn't capable of showing support.

'I don't think he really expected me to get first, but he didn't want to show me he was really impressed by the silver,' she said. 'Although I knew secretly he was, it was never expressed. It was the same as never telling his kids he loved them in actual words—he just assumed we knew it. But we needed to be told that.'[14]

William's brother Jimmy often stood in as a father figure for Marilyn. He gave her verbal praise, would drive her to and from meets, and stay to watch her compete. ("I found out later that he was also a fan of my films," she said. "Figure that one out.")

As it happened, William wasn't singling Marilyn out by forgoing her meets and matches. Jann recalled that he didn't attend her athletic competitions and that it was also unlikely he showed up at Bill's.

Ginny, too, was only marginally involved in her childrens' lives. Although she'd drive her kids to athletic events, she didn't stay and often neglected to pick them up.

"It was like she forgot about us," Jann said. "She forgot that she was supposed to be there. If she were working or something, she'd say, 'You have to get a ride home,' or whatever."[15]

When that wasn't the case, they naturally expected her to pick them up. Yet many times, she left them stranded. If they didn't have a dime to use a pay phone, they'd have to walk or find other means of transport.

WHEN MARILYN WAS THREE, she cut off her hair the day before a family photo was taken—an act of defiance and a plea to be recognized. When Marilyn was four, the family agreed to be photographed by an artist friend of William's who would use them for an illustrated magazine advertisement. The artist believed the Briggs family represented the typical, good-looking, white, upper-middle-class fifties family.

Marilyn wore brand new Mary Jane shoes, which she adored. They were a welcome change from the usual, worn hand-me-downs she had to wear. She described the event:

> I think I was in trouble that day because I was feeling really vulnerable and sad. I remember that vividly. So [the artist] gave me [a] little dog to play with, which I instantly latched on to. Then he took the picture of this pouty little innocent doe-eyed girl. I don't know if I'd just been punished for something that I did. I think I had been. It seems like I was always being reprimanded for talking back or something.
>
> I just remember that day with my family all together. My dad looked so

THE SHOW-OFF

handsome, my mom looked really pretty, and you know what? I didn't feel like I fit in at all. For some reason, I didn't feel a part of the picture. I wanted to, but I just couldn't get into it. I just remember loving my daddy a lot.[16]

Around this time, she invented an imaginary friend named Brocky.

"I don't know what it was, but it was her friend," Jann remembered. "And he was a big part of her life. I call him 'him' because, I think, of the name Brocky. But I don't think it was ever defined whether he was a boy or a girl. He was just her buddy. She went everywhere with him, but mostly she just talked to him."[17]

Marilyn insisted the family cater to Brocky. She'd often say, "Oh, you can't sit here; Brocky's sitting here," if they attempted to sit beside her. So they'd sit in another seat. If she was served a glass of milk and said Brocky wanted one, too, her mother would pour a second glass. The family went along with it and never told her Brocky wasn't real. However, when the family was out shopping and Marilyn picked out a shirt for Brocky, Ginny got frustrated and told her she would not make any purchases for Brocky.

"It was the weirdest thing that you could almost even picture him sitting next to her," Jann said. "She'd just be chatting away with him. I think it was her way of not being alone."[18]

Their conversations were simplistic: "What will we do today, Brocky?", "What do you want to have for lunch?" It's unclear if or how Brocky answered, but in addition to filling a void of loneliness, Brocky may also have given her encouragement and positive reinforcement. Then one day, he simply disappeared. Marilyn stopped talking to him or about him.

"She turned a corner in her childhood, like, 'Okay, I don't need him anymore,'" Jann said.[19]

MARILYN WAS FORTUNATE TO recognize her gifts and talent as an entertainer from an early age. Whether she realized it or not, the conflicted relationship with her parents only stimulated her to pursue her interests even more. Her dream was to become like Ann-Margret, whom she saw in the film *Bye Bye Birdie*. The film's soundtrack, and that of *West Side Story*, were played continuously on Marilyn's record player. She memorized every lyric and sang along to the records, often spending hours acting out scenes in her mirror.

"I remember my sister and a friend walking in on me one day and making fun of what I was doing," Marilyn told the *Los Angeles Times* in 1977. "Usually that kind of thing discourages a child, but it made me more determined. Everybody thought I was just showing off. I wanted to show them that I could make it in [show] business. My family just couldn't relate to my aspirations."[20]

In school, she signed up for every theatrical production.

"You know, she was always bouncing around the house, just always," Jann remembered. "Just dancing, singing. If there was a play at school, she was [in it]. She was the lead in *The Sound of Music*. This was even in elementary school!"[21]

A *Westport Town Crier* newspaper photo from March 19, 1964, shows an eleven-year-old Marilyn belting out a tune in the school's production of the musical *Oliver!* Marilyn played the role of Nancy, a character who, despite her profession as a thief and prostitute, was virtuous, kind, compassionate, and honorable.

When the Briggs family had visitors, William encouraged his three children to perform for them—like a truncated, Connecticut-style Von Trapp Family.

"We would stand up there, the three of us, and sing to whoever was visiting my parents: my grandparents, aunts or uncles or their neighbors," Jann recalled. "My dad would say, 'Okay, why don't you sing in beautiful harmony together.' It was great. But then Marilyn would take a step forward and say, 'Well, *I* could also sing this.' I don't think it's quite right to say [she was] self-absorbed, but she was."[22]

Marilyn would gather her siblings and neighborhood kids and put on plays that she would direct, produce, write, choreograph, and star in. Marilyn was persistent in putting on play after play, and Jann admits to sometimes being exasperated by her younger sister. As Jann and Bill entered their teens, the age gap caused a rift between them and Marilyn.

"She was kind of a pest," Jann said. "I think partly because my brother and I are only twelve or thirteen months apart. We were just like twins and so close. And then she comes along and just wanted to be a part of it."[23]

Jann and Marilyn shared a bedroom, but after one heated argument, they demanded to be split up even though the house had no additional rooms. "We weren't speaking, so we didn't even want to look at each other," Marilyn remembered. A rope was strung across the room between their beds. Blankets were draped on them. If anything fell on the other side of the line, each sister would scream at the other. One day, they couldn't remember what the fight was about and reconciled.

'We had good times when we were kids,' Marilyn recalled. 'Good times fighting and good times making up. A more normal childhood you couldn't ask for. I wouldn't have traded it for anything in the world.'[24]

The sentiment was real. Marilyn's feelings about her childhood never wavered throughout her life, but the details were often painted a bit more sanguine than was true to obscure the cracks in the portrait.

THE SHOW-OFF

Three-year-old Marilyn on a New England beach in 1955. *Photographer unknown*.

Her siblings moved out of the house when Marilyn was about twelve. Her parents worked, and after school, she was by herself. She had many friends, was popular in school, and participated in extracurricular activities. (By the time she was sixteen, she had 'won more than 35 City, State, and Regional Diving Titles, and was being touted as a contender for the 1968 Olympic Team.'[25]) When it came to familial bonding, she was left to her own devices.

Liz Boyd, a close friend of Marilyn's since kindergarten, spent much of her time at the Briggs home and got to know the entire family well. While William and Ginny might not have been around after school, Liz quickly points out: "I was there!" Still, she admitted that William and Ginny "weren't really demonstrative; you know, [the] hugging, kissing kind of people. When I think of Ginny, I think of the word 'stoic.' Because she did smile—she had a beautiful smile—but she wasn't a happy-go-lucky kind of person."[26]

For example, when Liz was an adult, and Ginny phoned Liz's parents, Liz happened to answer. "I said, 'Oh, hi, Ginny!' She said, 'It's Mrs. Briggs.' But I loved her dearly, and I loved [Marilyn's] dad."[27]

Liz's memories of the Briggs family, particularly her friendship with Marilyn, were recalled in warm, rich detail. "When I was there, her dad was sitting on the couch or [his] chair. I [can] see the lamp, the ashtray, the Chesterfield cigarettes, and his drink—bourbon on the rocks, or whatever it was. I was too young to really know or care [about that]. [He was] always watching TV, and Mrs. Briggs was around. [If she wasn't] farting around in the kitchen, [she'd be] doing something in the dining room."[28]

As kids, Liz and Marilyn were virtually inseparable. They got into normal "shenanigans," as Liz described them, common with young and adolescent girls. There was the time they stayed up until 2:00AM trying to teach themselves to whistle by putting both fingers in their mouths. "Our cheeks hurt so bad, and I just remember us laughing and thinking it wild we stayed up so late," she remembered. "We eventually got it, though."[29]

She recalled that as young girls, the two often role-played and dressed up. In one case, they dressed up as nuns in a school. 'It was theater,' Marilyn remembered. 'That theatrical childhood that leads to a career in show business. Playing 'nuns' was acting out a fantasy.'[30]

"My memories are that if she wasn't at my house on the weekend, I was spending the night at her house," Liz said. "We spent a lot of time together. We were like Laurel and Hardy. She was skinny and taller; I was a little shorter. I have very wide hips, and Marilyn never had any wide hips. I have curly, frizzy hair; she had straight hair. And we always wanted to shave our heads, make wigs, and trade hair."[31]

While Marilyn daydreamed about becoming a famous entertainer, her brother succeeded in becoming one, after a fashion. Bill played keyboards in the garage rock group The Remains. The band toured New England, earning a loyal fanbase and becoming popular on the nightclub circuit. Several songs were regional hits but they had yet to make it nationally. In 1965, they signed with Epic Records and secured two high-profile television appearances: one was on the Top 40 teeny-bopper show *Hullabaloo*; the second was on TV's highest-rated variety program, *The Ed Sullivan Show*, which drew an average of thirteen million viewers every Sunday at 8:00PM.

While recording their debut album, the foursome was given the opportunity to tour as the opening band for another foursome: The Beatles. The Remains played a three-week stint on The Beatles' final US tour in 1966. By the time it was over, The Remains had disbanded, and their debut album, released the same year, drew little notice.

'I was very proud of my brother when his band was doing well,' Marilyn wrote in 1975. 'He was cutting records, traveling, and making a lot of money, and I was

THE SHOW-OFF

thrilled that he was my brother and I could walk around and tell people that, but I felt a little tinge of envy too.'[32]

UNSURPRISINGLY, WILLIAM AND GINNY never talked about sex with their kids. Human anatomy was something one learned in biology class. Teachers may have discussed the mechanics of sexual intercourse dispassionately, but the more intimate details were learned from friends, hearing about their experiences, or by sneaking a look at adult material in the house. William subscribed to *Playboy* and read it openly at home but never let the children see it. That didn't stop Marilyn from trying to get her hands on it.

'I was kept in the dark about sex from the very beginning,' Marilyn wrote in 1980:

> I was always extremely curious, or should I say obsessed, with the mysterious and forbidden thing adults only whispered about. Hell, my father used to keep *Playboy* locked up in his combination briefcase, and it was all my sister and I could do to try and figure out how to pick the lock and just see what we were missing! My mother even ripped up a copy of *Peyton Place* that my sister and I were eagerly reading out loud to each other with a flashlight. But being the determined 'perverts' that we were, we painstakingly pasted every last torn page back together and finished reading a mediocre sex novel. Thus, I think if I hadn't been made to feel so damned repressed about the normalities of sex and particularly nudity, it wouldn't have taken me this long to stop feeling drastically guilty for sexually enjoying myself.[33]

Marilyn attended Staples High School in Westport. Her high school years were formative and mostly positive. During this time, she began to realize how physically attractive she was. Men took notice of the five-foot-seven, toned, willowy blonde, and she took notice of them. She wasn't just cute or pretty; she was developing a rare kind of beauty.

"By her senior year, she was wearing much tighter and more revealing clothing and had kind of moved to an embrace of her sexuality, and was comfortable in it and in displaying it," said Dr Robert Selverstone, a psychologist who was a guidance counselor at Staples High at the time. "I remember Marilyn walking outside between buildings and male students, and even teachers, watching her. There was an awareness of herself and her sexuality. There was an aura of her sexuality."[34]

As a teenager, she started drinking, mostly beer, and smoking cigarettes. She also experimented with drugs, mostly marijuana. She was the head cheerleader but was kicked off the squad, along with other cheerleaders and football players, after another student caught them drinking beer. The incident bothered her parents more than it bothered Marilyn, but she didn't tell them the whole truth. She claimed she told them she was removed from the squad for not wearing underwear—as if that were somehow more chaste.

Cheerleading, she said years later, was a "kind of exhibitionism." Admittedly, she was an exhibitionist from an early age. She would get a thrill, particularly during diving competitions, from having nothing but a bathing suit—a thin piece of fabric—covering her body. All the while, she was elevated on a diving board, a kind of pedestal for all to see. In her teens, she explored her sexuality willingly. In high school, she passed a class she was failing because her male teacher noticed she wasn't wearing underwear.

She was not, however, particularly promiscuous. She'd flirt with boys and go on dates and enjoyed being a "cock tease" in her words—getting the young men excited but withholding intercourse. She built her idea of physical affection around the notion of sex and sex itself.

"Was she any more promiscuous than anyone else when we were growing up?" wondered classmate Darryl Coates Manning. "Probably not. But I think because of who she became, more men talked about having been with her."[35]

After she became famous, Marilyn said, "A lot of guys I knew from high school would say, 'Yeah, I fucked her,' but sorry, guys. That's just not true."[36] She lost her virginity at sixteen in the backseat of a car to a young man several years older who had just returned from Vietnam. The tale was greatly exaggerated for comedic and erotic effect in her 1975 book, *My Story*.

"She had an overwhelming need for attention and great gobs of it," recalled Cal Neff, who was a Staples High senior when Marilyn was a freshman. The two dated briefly in the late sixties. "I mean, she just doted on anyone who paid any attention to her at all. And, of course, it was inevitable that the male animal was going to look at something so young and nubile. Anyway, we went to a party one night, and she went off with somebody else, and that was pretty much the last time I was with her."[37] During her senior year of high school, she was nominated for homecoming queen, but she was not chosen. Instead, her classmates awarded her the auspicious honor of "best student body." However, the sting of not being crowned homecoming queen stayed with her, and she referred to it often in interviews over the years.

THE SHOW-OFF

"I DON'T THINK ANYONE who knew her back then was surprised when she started doing adult films," recalled Steve Miner, who knew Marilyn when she was fourteen. "What I remember is someone who was determined to make something of herself and her life. Somehow that ambition, combined with her relentlessly adventurous spirit and impatience with anything, or anyone, not moving fast enough, led her to make many bad choices."[38]

The implication is that getting involved in adult films was one of, and led to many other, so-called bad choices. At best, this is an oversimplified rationalization. As much as puritanical Americans would like to believe, adult films didn't lead Marilyn to ruin. Scores of people who enter occupations perceived as reputable make terrible choices. Of course Marilyn made mistakes and poor choices throughout her life. But she was a woman who, at a young age, recognized her sexuality—and its power.

After Marilyn Briggs became Marilyn Chambers, the sex star, stories proliferated in her hometown about how she had been promiscuous while living there; dated many men; and cavorted around nude at parties, among other things. These memories are likely great fabrications with only a kernel of truth. The mother of one of Marilyn's friends remembered Marilyn and several other girls attending a sleepover at the mother's home. The girls were about thirteen or fourteen years old. There was a strict "no boys allowed" rule. At one point, to check on the girls, the mother went through the garage and into a backyard to peer through a large picture window, looking into the living room. "There, out on the grass in the dark, she found half a dozen adolescent boys from the neighborhood staring through the same window, and facing them a few feet away on the other side of the glass, 13-year-old Marilyn, stark naked."[39]

Another classmate, three years Marilyn's senior, remembered meeting Marilyn at a party. The classmate claimed the two began kissing and caressing each other before disrobing and having sex on the floor in front of the other partygoers. Only after her death in 2009 did he relay this story to the press.[40]

WHEN SHE WAS ABOUT fifteen, Marilyn began to take seriously the idea of becoming an actress. The first step, she thought, was to become a model.

'I've always been in a rush to grow up, all my life, and modeling seemed to me to be going into another world, a very grown-up and mature world,' she said.[41]

The fashions of Twiggy, the rail-thin model who exemplified the British mod scene of the mid sixties, were on their way out. By the late sixties and early seventies, the healthier, sunkissed, all-American girl was the type of model agencies sought. Marilyn was almost too perfect.

Although William was a high-powered advertising executive, he refused Marilyn assistance in securing modeling jobs. Nor did he introduce her to any contacts. Neither he nor Ginny were thrilled about their daughter's ambitions, but Marilyn was stubborn. Furthermore, she thought becoming a model—a profession directly connected to her father's—would please him.

She worked up the courage and finally told him of her aspirations.

"Don't do it," he said. "You're not pretty enough. You'll never make it." Marilyn was devastated. "I know he did that to deter me from that cutthroat, horrible business, but the way he did it was wrong," she said. "I didn't think he loved me if he could say those things."[42]

Her mother didn't offer much help or support either. "Go to college, dear," she said. "Choose a career like nursing you can always fall back on, dear; marry a nice boy and have children, dear."

Nevertheless, she persisted.

She scrounged together the money to have professional photos taken and put together a portfolio. Then she looked for work in New York, often sneaking out of school to take the train or forging her mother's signature on an early-release permission slip. She got an appointment at the Ford Modeling Agency, a top international agency. But a representative told her she was "too fat," and her face was "too flat," lacking necessary angularity. She was humiliated. When she mentioned this to her father, he said, "Well, you *are* too fat." Maybe he was right about this whole modeling thing, she thought.

Then she got an appointment at Wilhelmina Models, another of New York's premier agencies, run by former Dutch model Wilhelmina Cooper. Cooper recognized Marilyn's potential. "God, Wilhelmina was just so nice to me," said Marilyn. "She accepted me, and she signed me. I was thrilled."[43]

Marilyn landed several television and print ads for Clairol, Pepsi, and other companies, while she was still in high school. The agency would call her once or twice a week with job opportunities. None of the jobs were glamorous. She said the Clairol haircare product she used for the advertisements made chunks of her hair fall out in the sink. She spent more time on photo shoots waiting for technical adjustments than doing actual modeling. But she learned her craft, and it provided a foundational work ethic.

Tired of the Westport-Manhattan commute, Marilyn moved to the city after graduating high school in 1970. She shared an apartment on Third Avenue and East Thirty-Third Street with another model. The work wasn't enough to make a living in New York. With not much money for food, "There were a lot of 'ketchup soups,'" she recalled years later. Between modeling gigs, she took acting classes at the Neighborhood Playhouse and tried unsuccessfully to secure roles in off-Broadway shows.

Finally, two promising opportunities presented themselves. First was the chance to audition for Procter & Gamble, one of the largest consumer goods manufacturers in the United States. They were looking for a new model to be the face of Ivory Snow, a powdered laundry detergent. Hundreds of young women were auditioning, but Marilyn thought she had just as much chance as the other contenders. The second opportunity happened unexpectedly.

While living in New York, she dated a man who was actor George Segal's stand-in on the set of the film *The Owl and the Pussycat*, which starred Barbra Streisand. He invited Marilyn to the set for a tour, which thrilled her. She eagerly absorbed the behind-the-scenes activities. He left her alone for a few minutes to attend to some business, and almost immediately, a man approached her.

"Are you an actress?" he inquired.

Perking up, she smiled and said, "Of course!"

"I might have a part for you," he said. "Can you stick around a while?"

Playing it cool to conceal her excitement and assuming the hauteur of a movie-set regular, she told the man she could stay for a bit.

'The truth was I could hardly call myself an actress,' she recalled. 'But when a guy on a movie set with a cigar in his mouth asks, you immediately pretend you're Bette Davis.'[44]

The man identified himself as George Justin, the associate producer.

"Two hours later, he introduced me to Director Herb Ross, then took me upstairs to casting," Marilyn told reporter Richard L. Lewis. "He talked to me, and another [girl] then left. A few minutes later, he called the other girl out, and I figured that was it. Then Justin returned to the room and told me I had it. I was going to be in the picture!"[45]

She went to work that night and for the next four days. She was even given ten lines of dialogue.

"It was like Lana Turner at Schwab's drugstore," she recalled, referring to the legendary Hollywood myth that a producer spotted a young Lana Turner at Schwab's soda counter and made her a star. Even years later, Marilyn recalled the moment with a hint of dubiety.

Then more good news came: Procter & Gamble had selected her as a finalist for the new Ivory Snow box model.

PURE *The Sexual Revolutions of Marilyn Chambers*

IVORY SOAP WAS INVENTED in 1879 by James Norris Gamble, the son of one of Procter & Gamble's co-founders, and named Ivory by Harley Procter, the other founder's son. It was the first branded product the company ever mass marketed. Its famous tagline, "99 $^{44}/_{100}$% pure," was in use since the early 1890s. More than seventy years after Ivory soap was invented, it remained the backbone of P&G's brand. Ivory Snow was marketed to mothers as safe and gentle enough to wash a baby's clothes.

As the sixties drew to a close and the first wave of baby boomers came of age, the executives at P&G wanted to update the product's branding.

'They wanted the 'now' generation housewife and mother,' Marilyn said. 'And so they took a lot of test shots with a lot of girls and then took more shots of us holding babies.'[46]

As a finalist, three male P&G executives took Marilyn, then just seventeen, to lunch. They impressed her with their dashing three-piece suits, clean-cut appearances, and seemingly kind manners. It's possible, even likely, that one or all of the men made a pass at her, and one did make an inappropriate comment.

"[L]ittle did naive Marilyn know that everyone's always trying to get into my pants," she said later of the lunch. "I'm thinking like, 'Oh, gee, they really like me!'"[47]

Whether or not anything untoward happened at the lunch, it was true they liked her. She got the job as the new face of Ivory Snow. Next, P&G decision-makers had to audition infants to find one whose face would adorn the box with Marilyn's.

'I think I held a hundred screaming, crying, wet-diapered babies and another hundred smiling, cooing, laughing babies,' she said. 'I love babies...but I didn't love them enough to enjoy sitting through all the photo sessions. Sometimes I'd begin to think my dad was right, that the world of modeling was pure insanity and masochism.'[48]

She tried to remind herself that this was a job, she was a professional model, this was a paid gig, and she was fortunate to get this opportunity.

In the photo, which was shot in 1970, Marilyn smiles and holds a laughing baby. It was a happy-suburban-housewife version of the classic Madonna and Child image. Howard J. Morgens, P&G's CEO, remarked that Marilyn 'looked like the Virgin Mary.'[49]

During a moment of downtime in the shoot, the photographer, described by Marilyn as "a really old, old ancient man," began chasing her around the studio, trying to force himself on her.

"I was running around, going, 'What are you doing?! Get out of here!'" Later, she said, "That old Ivory Snow photographer was disgusting. It was gross—this

THE SHOW-OFF

seventy-year-old guy right on me! I couldn't believe it. I was so disillusioned that this was what this business was all about. I was totally freaked out. Here I am posing for this 99 $^{44}/_{100}$% pure box, and what's going on in the backroom was disgusting."[50]

Marilyn earned $2,000 for the job, equivalent to more than $15,000 today. P&G paid half up front, the rest to follow when the box went into production. They informed her it would take approximately two years to phase out the old box and get the new box on the shelves. She took the money and tried to forget about her encounter with the photographer.

She couldn't have known she had just taken the most important photo of her career.

Chapter 2

THE PROPOSITION

R AY STARK WAS ONE OF the most powerful men in show business. In 1957, he co-founded Seven Arts Productions, producing classic films like *West Side Story*, *The Misfits*, *Lolita*, and *What Ever Happened to Baby Jane?* Nine years later, he set up his own company, Rastar Productions. The first film made was *Funny Girl*, an adaptation of the wildly successful Broadway musical. Stark produced both and was instrumental in helping cast a relatively unknown Barbra Streisand in the lead role. After the success of *Funny Girl*, they collaborated on *The Owl and the Pussycat*.

Pussycat generated considerable buzz during its production and was an attempt to spice up Streisand's image. She played a prostitute who tossed around four-letter words. She even filmed a topless scene but nixed it in the final edits.

George Segal plays a bookish writer down on his luck. One night, he complains about his noisy, sex-worker neighbor (Streisand) to his landlord, who evicts her. She confronts Segal. He feels guilty and allows her to stay in his apartment for the night. In a nod to the screwball comedies of the thirties, the two contrasting characters spend the next twenty-four hours bouncing around New York City, getting into trouble.

The screenplay by Buck Henry was adapted from a two-person Broadway play by Bill Manhoff. Henry expanded it to include characters such as Segal's best friend Barney, played by comedian Robert Klein. Marilyn played the role of "Barney's Girl," a girlfriend of Klein's character. Her scenes with Klein consisted mostly of the two in bed. "She came in—a beautiful girl, high school senior, eighteen-years-old, named Marilyn Briggs. So she did it," Klein recounted in a 1989 interview on the talk show *Later with Bob Costas*. "And we had underwear on. There was no sex or lovemaking. And she went, 'Ooh, my father will kill me

26

when he sees this.' And I said, 'Why? There's no nudity or anything.'" She told Klein her father was "very strict."[1]

Klein said it wasn't until years later that he learned the person who played his girlfriend became Marilyn Chambers. Then, in a grotesque admission, he smugly stated, "Actually, I slept with her." It was a thoughtless and misogynistic comment to make. It's difficult to imagine him saying the same of a young Meryl Streep or even an unknown actress. But for Klein, Marilyn's career as an adult film star precluded propriety.

When Costas pushed for details, Klein chalked up his behavior to being young, foolish, and single.

"What's wrong with that?" he asked. "She was [of] legal age. She was very gentle, seemed like a sweet person. Over the years, I was told by Buck Henry there was a scorecard. Many of the people associated with that movie had a similar experience. She said in a *Playboy* interview that I had been very kind to her. Technically, it was her first movie."

Then, looking at the camera, Klein wagged his finger and said, "Since then, some naughty things! Let's put it this way: I'm glad you're not my sister. But it's your business."[2]

Marilyn also faced harassment from the crew during her bedroom scenes.

"All these union guys are just standing around, standing up on the rafters, and they're whistling and going, 'Hey, honey, want to meet me after?'" she recalled. "It's just so obnoxious and sleazy."[3]

She never shared the screen with Streisand or Segal, but she had plenty of time to get to know them—or try to.

Segal sensed she was nervous and went out of his way to make her feel comfortable. "I'll always be grateful to him for explaining what was happening around me and translating the director's words into common language I could understand," she said. Of Streisand, she recalled: 'I met her, yes, but I still don't know what to say about her. I ran up to her the first day of shooting and told her our birthdays were the same, and she just looked at me and didn't seem too impressed. [*Ed. Note:* Streisand's birthday is April 24, two days after Marilyn's.] I talked to her a few more times—*to* her, not *with* her—and she wasn't very nice to me. She sure knew what she wanted. She also knew what she didn't want—me appearing too pretty or too naked.'[4]

Marilyn lamented the irony that she was made to wear two body stockings, underwear, and a bra, all in an attempt to give the illusion that she was nude in bed, under the covers. She put the blame squarely on Streisand.

'Barbra didn't want me nude from the waist up 'cause she had a scene where

Early modeling shots such as this helped Marilyn get signed in the late 1960s to Wilhelmina Models, one of the premier agencies in New York City. *Patrick Zack*.

she was supposed to be nude from the waist up,' she said. 'She didn't want any competition from the other girls in the film because she had a bed scene to play, and her bed scene had to be the *shocker*!'[5]

The Owl and the Pussycat was released in New York City in November 1970. Although Marilyn was on screen for only a few minutes, she worked enough days and earned the screen time required to apply for membership of the Screen Actors Guild. Her acceptance into the actors' union was a pivotal moment for Marilyn. It validated her dreams of becoming an actress and encouraged her to continue pursuing them. At just eighteen, she had a part in a major Hollywood film—one that became a box-office success. She was a legitimate film actress in the eyes of the industry. But her parents remained unimpressed.

Maybe they were right. It was an unpromising sign that her name wasn't listed in the credits. She was inexplicably credited in press materials as "Evelyn Lang," not Marilyn Briggs. Adding insult to injury, her ten lines met the proverbial cutting-room floor.

"[It] didn't matter," she said, putting a positive spin on it. "At least I was there."[6]

Stark arranged for Marilyn to travel to Los Angeles and San Francisco for a brief publicity tour. Actress Roz Kelly accompanied her. Kelly had a more prominent but still relatively minor role in the film. It was an unusual move. Why would a major producer ask two unknown actresses, one of whom was credited under a stage name and didn't speak a word, to participate in a publicity tour for an important Hollywood production that was already a hit at the box office?

On the one hand, it was something of a novelty. The young actresses attracted attention from the press. However, there was a more malefic motive for sending Marilyn to the west coast. The first stop was Los Angeles. Marilyn stayed at the Beverly Wilshire Hotel in a luxury suite. Champagne on ice awaited her, and bouquets of fresh flowers decorated the corners of the suite. She was awed and overwhelmed.

No sooner had she arrived at the hotel when the phone rang. It was Stark. His voice was brimming with excitement. He told Marilyn he'd been anxious for her to get to Los Angeles. In fact, he'd been thinking about her ever since they met in New York. Could he visit her hotel suite? He added that he'd love to discuss with her some acting opportunities he had in mind for her. Could he visit? Just for a moment?

Of course, she replied. She knew a good opportunity when it presented itself. She hung up the phone and began to freshen up. She wondered what opportunities he had in mind. They couldn't be insignificant, she thought. This man helped put Barbra Streisand on the map. He wouldn't have sent her on this trip in the first place if he didn't believe in her and hadn't noticed a glimmer of something when she was on set and on screen. He must have sensed how badly she wanted to become an actress. And he'd been so nice to her in New York, nicer than Streisand.

Stark arrived at her suite. They exchanged pleasantries, and Marilyn thanked him again for the role and for sending her on the press junket. It was simply incredible, she said, and the hotel was so opulent. Not bad for an upper-middle-class girl from Connecticut, she joked. She was just biding time. She hoped he couldn't tell how nervous she was and wouldn't read her overenthusiasm as desperation. Finally, he got to the point of the meeting.

He wanted to make a proposition.

She smiled and listened intently.

He'd like to help her get set up in Hollywood. He'd give her an apartment, a car, acting lessons, and spending money. He'd guide her career. Ensure she'd be successful. He could, and would, get her roles on television, in films, in theater, anything she wanted.

Marilyn tensed. There's a catch, she thought.

In exchange, she would be his mistress. However, it was of the utmost importance that no one must know. He was a married man, after all. And she mustn't under any circumstances date another man. She was his, and his alone.

He finished speaking and let the words hang. Marilyn, no longer smiling, needed a moment to consider his proposal. Stark was in his mid fifties. Unlike her dashing father, her fantasy lover, Stark was overweight and not especially handsome. He reminded her more of her grandfather.

Marilyn replied cautiously. She was flattered, she told him. She thanked him. It was a groovy offer, but she'd like a chance to consider it, really consider it.

Stark stayed quiet for a moment. Of course, she could take time to consider it, he said. She should think it over carefully, though. He could do a lot for her and her career. There was a subtle implication that should her answer be in the negative, he could do permanent damage to her career. He said he'd see her the next evening at the *Pussycat* premiere. Then he excused himself. As he left the room, he said, "Think it over, Marilyn."

This could be a huge break, she thought. His promise was not a hollow one. In Hollywood, she knew, knowing the right person was as important as possessing beauty and talent. Sometimes it was more important. It might be worth it if she had to sleep with this guy and fake it a few times a week. She wouldn't be the first starlet to take advantage of the casting couch.

However, something he said gnawed at her. She was to belong to him. He wanted to own her. Like a piece of property, easily disposable and replaceable. He'd undoubtedly demand to know where she was going and with whom; he might even hire people to follow her to ensure she didn't violate the agreement. If she were on set, he'd almost certainly have friends keep an eye on her. Ultimately, she'd end up cooped up in a swell apartment. She might have money and a car, but what if a great guy came along? What if a better opportunity came along? Could she get out of it? Would he let her get out of it? What happened if he grew tired of her and the work dried up? There was always a younger, prettier up-and-comer. He could drop her when he met someone else and promised her the same things.

She was depressed. Now she knew why she'd been asked to join this press tour. It had nothing to do with talent. He wanted to use her—to fuck her—in exchange for roles. And potentially, probably eventually, to fuck her over. The ice in the champagne bucket had melted, and the fresh flowers, now wilted, seemed somehow to mock her diminished demeanor. She plopped down on the couch. "How perfect," she muttered.

After Los Angeles, the tour moved north to San Francisco. It was a transformative experience for Marilyn. The magical, mystical elements of the city enveloped her like its famous fog. She knew instinctively this was where she belonged.

"I fell madly in love with San Francisco, and I wanted to stay," she said.[7]

Marilyn and Kelly were brought out to the Bay Area to open a new movie theater at the Stonestown shopping center in the city.

Reporter Robert Taylor covered the event for the *Oakland Tribune*. 'Nobody at the charity opening had heard of either one of them, but Roz and Marilyn played their starlet parts to the hilt, wearing campy old thrift-shop clothes, cracking jokes and stretching into pin-up poses for pictures with the charity ladies' husbands, some of them standing on a curb to look taller,' he wrote. 'For lunch at the elegant old Fairmont Hotel the next day, Marilyn, the more demure of the two, wore a white open-weave jumpsuit unbuttoned dangerously low.'[8]

Marilyn told the press she was actively seeking an agent and reading scripts. Even though her role was small, she hoped *The Owl and the Pussycat* would be a springboard to better offers.

Robert Sylvester's 'Dream Street' gossip column in the New York *Daily News* featured a small photo of Marilyn with the caption: 'Marilyn Briggs has no speaking lines in 'The Owl and the Pussycat,' but she can whisper sweet nothings in my ear.'[9]

A newswire service even picked up her Lana Turner-esque discovery on the film's set. In a typical evaluation of the young actress' merits that would later come to define nearly every article written about Marilyn Chambers, reporter Richard L. Lewis wrote:

> What a film to wind up in—with Barbra Streisand and George Segal—and, it didn't really matter that all she did was stand, or lie around in the nude with nary a word to recite.
>
> This is her acting debut, despite the fact the lines she spoke in the film wound up on the editor's floor. She plays Robert Klein's friend for the night, whose evening is jarringly intruded upon by Miss Streisand and Segal, who have been evicted from their respective apartments. And all Marilyn is supposed to do is stretch out on the bed, sit up, or stand up startled. The impression is that she is naked, but Marilyn confides: 'I really wore flesh-colored body tights. Actually, I was supposed to be topless,' she added with youthful candor, 'but Streisand was nude, and I guess she didn't want anyone else exposed.'
>
> A press agent winced and wished she had been less candid.[10]

The article noted that while Marilyn moved to New York after high school, she had no ambitions to be in the movies, which was untrue. 'She was never even in a school play,' Lewis, the reporter, falsely claimed.

'Her parents weren't too happy about her move to New York, a teenage girl into the jungle of cold, hard-hearted humanity,' Lewis wrote. 'They wanted her to go to college like every well-intentioned parent hopes for their children. But Marilyn proved strong-minded. 'I just told them no, that I wanted to do this thing in New York,' she explained. 'They said yes, which startled me. I could see myself running off in the night, but it wasn't necessary.''

By the time the tour ended and Marilyn was back in New York City, she had decided to move to San Francisco. First, she agreed to help some Westport friends with a film being made by one of them, a neighbor named Sean S. Cunningham.

Cunningham was a budding filmmaker, and was putting together an exploitation movie called *Together*. Marilyn was one of many friends and neighbors who appeared in the film.

Like other genre films, exploitation movies were generally inexpensive to produce and usually turned a tidy profit. In the late sixties and early seventies, the term "sexploitation" was applied to low-budget films heavy on softcore sex. They usually included full-frontal nudity from the actresses and bare-bottomed actors. Often a couple was shown making love, but no penises or penetration were visible or allowed to be shown.

Marilyn, a self-proclaimed "hippie chick," moved from the East Coast to San Francisco in 1971. *Nick Cinardo*.

PURE *The Sexual Revolutions of Marilyn Chambers*

Together was a sexploitation film disguised as a documentary. It chronicled the coming-of-age feelings about sex for young people in their late teens and early twenties. An actor portrays a psychologist who frankly discusses with patients his detailed research findings concerning young people and sex. A voiceover narration attempted to tie everything together. A patient named Mary Greenwood, played by Marilyn, "belongs to a generation that enjoys unprecedented sexual freedom," the narrator intoned.

Marilyn is photographed in natural light, a breeze often ruffling her silky blonde hair. She looks wholesome, natural, ravishing.

In voiceover transition scenes, she walks wide-eyed through the woods, frolics in a meadow plucking flowers, and strolls along a beach. She is alternately fully clothed, wearing a bikini, topless, or nude. It's at the beach that the camera goes in for a close-up. She engages the audience in scripted, ironic, and prescient dialogue: "I've slept with too many men. I've even been in love with some of them. The problem was just that I didn't really know myself before." Her work with the psychologist and learning about her sexuality has changed her for the better, she says. "Everything has become completely different. I didn't know that you could do something fantastic in sex. That's an incredibly great feeling."

Other young people share their experiences, but the camera rightfully spends most of its time on Marilyn. Sometimes, the mishmash of scenes makes it feel like you're watching boring home movies of a stranger's family. Coarse language is used as a means to entice. In a close-up shot of Marilyn's face, she smiles sweetly and says, "Kissing a man's cock is beautiful because it's giving." She then lets out a brief, breathy, nervous laugh and turns her face from the camera.

Then, in another close-up and with the same sweetness, Marilyn says, "I have a cunt. I'm not ashamed of it. I like it."

The moments encapsulate Marilyn's dualistic appeal—shy yet blunt—and foreshadowed her successful career in adult film. It's at once shocking, seductive, repellent, and alluring to see the dazzling, sun-kissed young woman utter words like "cock" and "cunt." Which was the point. Without realizing it, Cunningham gave the world its first glimpse of the woman who would become Marilyn Chambers.

The only noteworthy thing in the film is a beautifully photographed slow-motion scene in which a fully nude Marilyn does several dives into a pool.

"Roger Murphy, one of the cameramen on *Monterey Pop*, shot this amazing footage of her repeatedly diving into a pool," remembered editor Jan Welt. "It was like [Leni] Reifenstahl's *Olympia*, only better."[11]

Welt, who worked as an editor on three of Norman Mailer's films, saw the footage being put together by the film's assistant editor (and future horror auteur) Wes Craven.

"I was walking back to the editing room one day and saw the footage and walked in and said, 'Listen, I need to edit this footage. Let me do this,'" he said. He edited the sequence and, at Cunningham's request, provided the film's narration.

"I'll never forget the day [Marilyn], this beautiful eighteen-year-old blonde, first came to the studio," Welt said. "Almost immediately, she was accosted by [an associate of mine], 'Buzz' Farbar, in the elevator. He could not contain himself; he went over, grabbed her, and kissed her."[12]

It was the Ivory Snow photoshoot all over again. Marilyn pushed the lecherous older man off her and tried to laugh it off.

Cunningham approached Boston-based Hallmark Releasing about distributing *Together*. George Mansour, who booked theaters for Hallmark, didn't like the film, telling Cunningham it was "pretty crude and stupid." However, he believed people would pay to see it. The film had a scene with a nude Black man. Mansour told one of Hallmark's executives, "You know, there's a big group of people out there who have never seen a big Black dick before. We can exploit this."[13]

"Sean did something really smart where he made a lot of money with this silly film," Marilyn remembered. "He bought advertising time on local television stations, and the ads would announce a special sneak preview at 10 a.m. for all the housewives. They'd see this film with a Black man and white woman, and she was holding his huge schlong in her hand. There was another scene where the Black man got an erection but no sex. The housewives would tell everybody about this scene, but when it played its regular run in the theaters, the scene would be cut out. That's the power of advertising."[14]

Cunningham's plan worked. 'The film wasn't consciously made for women, but women patrons outnumber the menfolk two to one in Providence and Hartford theaters where it has already opened,' *The Boston Globe* noted.[15]

Variety, one of Hollywood's premier industry publications, was unimpressed with the film. 'This is another of those pornos that pose as a serious study of sex in order to justify prurient peeking,' the review ran. 'Distinguishing features include better-looking girls and boys and little hard-core cavorting. Backed by heavy radio promo, [the] film is attracting [a] wider audience than [the] usual sex stuff.'[16]

Marilyn even called the film a "rip-off that made about six million bucks."[17] She earned $250—nearly $2,000 in today's money—and spent a week in a closet doing voice dubbing. Despite the poor reviews, the film did well at the box office during its initial release. It was even picked up for international distribution in the UK and Australia under the title *Sensual Paradise*. Marilyn didn't receive an on-screen credit, but her image and name were used in publicity photos and advertisements. Some ads called out her appearance in *The Owl and the Pussycat*. However, a production assistant was not too pleased about *Together*. Her name was also Marilyn Briggs. As *Variety* noted:

> The Dec. 29 DAILY VARIETY review of 'Together', a Hallmark-AI porno starring 'Marilyn Briggs', has caused embarrassment to a Hollywood film production assistant with the same name, Marilyn Briggs. The latter is a purty [sic] (36-24-36), green-eyed brunette who has enough dates, thank you, and is NOT the lady (wow!) in the pic.[18]

It's nearly impossible to see the film today. A preservation master of the film is housed in the archives of the British Film Institute. As additional material for the film is scarce or nonexistent, it's held in deep archival storage so it's preserved for the future. Therefore, the film is not available to view by historians or the general public. Not that Cunningham would mind. The director apparently loathes the film and has prevented its release since it left theaters in the mid seventies. (A bootlegged, German-dubbed version of the film is available if you know where to look.)

DURING HER TIME IN New York, Marilyn broadened her ongoing sexual explorations to include women. In her book *My Story*, she goes to great lengths to make her first time with a woman read erotically. It's likely an exaggeration, but she confirmed parts of the story more than twenty-five years later. The experience was with a married woman in her thirties who strongly resembled Sophia Loren. (Marilyn considered Loren "the sexiest woman" she'd ever seen.) The two met at a modeling gig, and the woman, who recently had a baby and lived with her male lover, invited eighteen-year-old Marilyn over for dinner. After dinner, while the man watched, the two women had sex.

"I was an absolute nervous wreck," Marilyn said. "But it was an unbelievable sexual experience that I will never forget. It was my first time with a woman, and, fortunately, it was a beautiful thing."[19]

The encounter made her consider and question her sexuality. Was she a lesbian? Was she bisexual? Would people somehow know she had been with a woman? And if they found out, would they still like her?

"I didn't know it was okay to be bisexual," she said nearly thirty years later.

THE PROPOSITION

"Now, I do; then, I didn't." Then she added, without elaborating: "I went through some pretty traumatic things at that point."

One of those things was likely Stark. She owed him an answer. She had time to think about the proposition. She arranged to meet with him. She thanked him again for his offer but politely declined.

Stark was not used to not getting his way. He was furious. How dare this little nobody turn him down. She just blew the best thing to ever happen to her.

He replied with the most clichéd retort: "I hope you're not thinking of working in this town again." Bitterly, he stalked out of the room.

"I wanted the parts so bad I could taste them," Marilyn said. "But I didn't want it that way. I've seen it happen so many times. I would feel guilty. I'm very open sexually and very honest with myself. Sometimes I feel the entertainment business has nothing to do with talent. It's your name and who you know. You have to get a name; some gimmick."[20]

Still, she wondered if she made a big mistake turning down Stark.

It seemed he wasn't the only producer who propositioned Marilyn. In a 1974 interview, she said she encountered, "a lot of [New York] producers, and all this crap that all they want to do is sleep with you if you want to get a part. Yeah, that thing still exists. That really kind of got me down. It's a really sleazy, sleazy, under-the-table deal, all these guys in pin-striped suits and ties saying, 'Hey, well honey, want to do a fuck film?'"[21]

The timeline of Marilyn's move from New York to San Francisco is fuzzy. She gave conflicting accounts. In one version, she headed back to Los Angeles from San Francisco after the *Pussycat* publicity tour ended to audition for film and television roles. She was unsuccessful, so she returned to New York. The Los Angeles auditions were coordinated with or without Stark's help; both variations were given during interviews. In another version, she moved back to New York immediately following her time in California before quickly returning to San Francisco. In a different version, she returned to New York, tried to continue modeling and expand her acting career, and finally moved to San Francisco.

In some versions of the story, she traveled solo from New York to San Francisco in a rental car. In others, she traveled in a U-Haul with acquaintances from Connecticut; in a rental car with a small group of strangers; or in a car with members of a San Francisco-based band called It's A Beautiful Day, whom she had met either in New York or San Francisco during the publicity tour. In yet another version, she landed first in Los Angeles (or a Malibu beach) and hitchhiked to San Francisco.

Whichever version is accurate, what's true is that she relocated from New

York to San Francisco in mid 1971. ('Goodbye cockroaches, hello sunshine!' she wrote about the move.[22]) She didn't know a soul when she arrived in San Francisco. She had no job, no apartment, no friends.

It didn't matter. This was her declaration of independence. She set out to conquer San Francisco. At nineteen, she believed she was worldly-wise and a seasoned professional. She had a successful modeling career; had appeared in two films, one of them a popular Hollywood production; gone on a publicity tour; and explored and expanded her sexuality in ways never anticipated. Now she was driving across the United States of America, the land of opportunity and fresh starts.

She'd never done anything like this before. She was free and untrapped. The freedom emboldened her. She was sure of her future and knew exactly how it would happen. She was wrong.

Chapter 3

"NOW CASTING FOR A MAJOR MOTION PICTURE"

███████████████████████

BELOVED *SAN FRANCISCO CHRONICLE* **COLUMNIST** Herb Caen, whose perspicacious observations of the wonders that made San Francisco the nonpareil of American cities, once proclaimed it to be a

city of the world, worlds within a city, forty-nine square miles of ups and downs, ins and outs, and going around in circles, most of them dizzy. A small 'd' democrat city run by big-buck conservatives, a place where the winds of freedom will blow your mind and your hat off, where eccentricity is the norm and sentimentality the ultimate cynicism. Cable cars and conventions, boosterism living uncomfortable with sophistication, a built-in smugness announcing simply that we are simply the best.[1]

This was the San Francisco that greeted Marilyn upon her arrival in 1971. Just four years prior, the city became the epicenter of the twentieth-century sexual revolution in the United States. As many as 100,000, mostly young people, descended upon San Francisco in 1967 for its famed Summer of Love. The first of the baby boomers were now of legal age. Many of them rejected America's involvement in the Vietnam War; they were suspicious of anyone involved in the government ("Don't trust anyone over thirty" was a famous phrase); they were anti-capitalism; and, most notably, they expressed a sexual liberation not seen in the country since the twenties. This time it was much more explicit. It was counterculturalism at its finest and freest.

'The hippie 'scene' on Haight Street in San Francisco was so very visual that photographers came from everywhere to shoot it, reporters came from everywhere to write it up with speed, and opportunists came from everywhere to exploit its drug addiction, its sexual possibility, and its political or social ferment,' wrote Mark Harris in the September 1967 issue of *The Atlantic*. 'Prospective hippies came from everywhere for one 'summer of love' or maybe longer, some older folk to indulge their latent hippie tendencies, and the police to contain, survey, or arrest.'[2]

The Summer of Love popularized hippies' behaviors, characteristics, and fashions.

'It was easy to see that the young men who were hippies on Haight Street wore beards and long hair and sometimes earrings and weird-o granny eyeglasses, that they were barefoot or in sandals, and that they were generally dirty,' Harris noted. 'A great many of the young men, by design or by accident, resembled Jesus Christ, whose name came up on campaign pins or lavatory walls or posters or bumper stickers.'[3]

Marilyn considered herself a "hippie chick," the term she used most frequently to define that period of her life. She certainly adopted some of the more trendy hippie fashions and characteristics, but she always remained slightly more sophisticated. However, it wasn't uncommon to see young people from affluent, upper-middle-class backgrounds like Marilyn's leave their homes for San Francisco.

In the mid sixties, The Beatles transformed every conceivable aspect of art and popular culture in the Western world. Hollywood took a hard right. Beginning with 1967's *Bonnie & Clyde*, films of the late sixties and early seventies were made by a new generation of writers and directors unafraid of frank, dark, and disturbing themes. The advent of television had hastened the dissolution of the traditional studio system and the strict production code that had ruled and guided films since the thirties. Independent films rife with gratuitous violence and blatant sexuality became cultural touchstones—influenced by social and political currents, including the sexual revolution, the Vietnam War, the Manson murders, and the women's and gay liberation movements. Films such as *Midnight Cowboy*, *Bob & Carol & Ted & Alice*, *Easy Rider*, *The Boys in the Band*, and *The Godfather* were controversial but also enormously popular; critics lionized many, they won international acclaim and were honored with Academy Awards. In 1972, *Last Tango in Paris* became a scandalous arthouse hit. The film's most infamous scene shows its star, Marlon Brando, anally penetrating leading lady Maria Schneider using butter as a lubricant.

Old-time Hollywood executives couldn't ignore the changes; these films raked in hundreds of millions of dollars at the box office.

"NOW CASTING FOR A
MAJOR MOTION PICTURE"

'THE 1970S IN SAN Francisco were flamboyant, alive, full of color and passion, marked by dark periods and electric highs,' wrote reporter Amy Graff. 'To grow up in San Francisco in this prismatic era was extraordinary. The Summer of Love was over, but the free-loving hippie spirit prevailed, and bohemians, buskers, bongo-drum players, and jewelry makers thronged the city.'[4]

In many ways, San Francisco was the perfect place for a nineteen-year-old aspiring entertainer. The city had a thriving arts scene in the seventies. However, most of it centered around music, comedy, and performance artists. Film and television productions were primarily concentrated 350 miles south in Los Angeles. The most notable exception of the era was 1968's *Bullitt*, starring Steve McQueen. *Dirty Harry*, starring Clint Eastwood, was released when Marilyn arrived in the city. It was filmed on location and became a box-office sensation. Its success helped shift some attention to San Francisco as a go-to location for film and television. However, to say San Francisco was a hotbed of film and television production in the early seventies would be largely untrue except for one type of film: pornography.

On February 24, 1970, the first publicly-screened hardcore pornographic film in America played in San Francisco at a North Beach Movie theater. *Pornography in Denmark*, directed by Alex De Renzy, was billed as a documentary; a documentary could be argued as having educational value, thus affording a legal loophole in showing so-called obscene material. By late 1970, there were twenty-eight adult theaters in San Francisco, including The Screening Room, owned by De Renzy.[5] Every single one faced continuous police raids. On December 2, 1970, the First International Erotic Film Festival occurred at San Francisco's Presidio Theater.

Dianne Feinstein, president of the city's Board of Supervisors, was angered by the growing acceptance and proliferation of adult material in San Francisco.

Of the erotic film festival, she told KPIX television reporter Ben Williams: "The thing that I regret, Mr Williams, is that this whole field is jeopardized right now because of the irresponsibility of certain money-hungry people—people from outside of the state, from the east coast, and Los Angeles—who are capitalizing on sickness to sell their very depraved wares, and make a fortune out of it."[6]

She acknowledged, however, that there could be certain softcore pornographic films permissible to view by the general public if they contained "a certain amount of taste—and plot." It remained unclear who would be the judge of such taste.

'The year 1970 will go down in history as the year the lid came off, the year when women began going to stag films in great numbers, when erotic films

41

became Big Business, when thousands of San Franciscans shelled out millions of dollars to watch sex on stage and some of the bluest movies [were] ever made,' the *San Francisco Chronicle* proclaimed.[7]

Hippies and other sexually-liberated young people may have been the featured performers in many hardcore films, but they rarely purchased the product. 'A 1970 study led by a Cal State professor found that the majority who patronized San Francisco porn theaters and bookstores had white-collar jobs with college degrees,' wrote reporter Greg Keraghosian. 'Middle-aged men were the target demographic at most theaters, but women took an interest too. Les Natali, a former psychology major who managed De Renzy's Screening Room, said 30 percent of the customers at his North Beach Theater were women— many of them tourists.'[8]

In January 1971, *The New York Times* labeled San Francisco "The Porn Capital of America." Feinstein agreed, but she wasn't happy about it. She vowed to shut down the city's numerous adult bookstores and theaters.[9]

Today, a sidewalk plaque outside the location of the original Screening Room commemorates the historical significance of San Francisco's contribution to the adult film industry.

'I WANTED TO CHANGE everything, to start anew, to leave the old Marilyn Briggs behind,' Marilyn said about her arrival in San Francisco. 'I was naive.'[10]

The first thing she did was cut her hair short. This time it wasn't the day before a family photo, and she was an adult now, but the decision was no less defiant.

Marilyn quickly learned the City by the Bay was not "the entertainment capital of the world" she believed it was. She auditioned for nearly every theater, dance, and singing group in San Francisco, Oakland, Berkeley, and other Bay Area locales. Rejections prevailed.

'I found it terribly frustrating,' she said. 'Worse than going from modeling agency to modeling agency in New York. I felt like a high school girl trying to break into someone else's clique.'[11]

However, just as she knew San Francisco was where she was supposed to live, she was also sure about her ambitions. It was the waiting and wondering that left her discouraged.

Within a few months of living in San Francisco, she met a man who was to become her first husband.

Douglas Joseph Chapin remains the most mysterious man in Marilyn's life. Those who knew him remembered him as sweet, gentle, and quiet. Yet no one

"NOW CASTING FOR A MAJOR MOTION PICTURE"

The WESTPORT NEWS, Wednesday, November 29, 1972

Mr. and Mrs. Douglas Joseph Chapin

-Marin Photo Service

Newlyweds to reside in San Francisco

Mr. and Mrs. William H. Briggs, r. of Marc Lane, Westport, announce the marriage of their aughter Marilyn Anne to Douglas oseph Chapin. Rev. James Martin fficiated at the outdoor ceremony eld on August 26, Mt. Tamelpais, 1arin County, Calif. Mr. Chapin is 1e son of Mrs. John McPhee, unnyvale, Calif., and Mr. Wilbur 'hapin, Chicopee Falls, Mass. cottish bagpipers, including the room's stepfather, John McPhee, 1layed the wedding music and 'piped'' the bridal party following he services. The reception and a 1uffet luncheon were held at Alpine .odge, Mt. Tamalpais.

Mrs. Calvin B. Smith, sister of the bride, of Sacramento, Calif., and Miss Jane Vanderlip, San Francisco, attended the bride. Mr. Scott Langmach of San Francisco was best man for Mr. Chapin and escorting the bridal party were Capt. Calvin B. Smith, brother-in-law of the bride, William H. Briggs, III, brother of the bride, and Andrew Chapin, brother of the groom.

The bride wore a very old gown of white cotton eyelet with the three-quarter length sleeves and the ankle length skirt edged in a ruffle of the same material. Her headpiece was a circlet of red roses and baby's breath with matching velvet ribbons and she carried a nosegay bouquet of the same flowers. Mrs. Smith was gowned in a full-length blue organdy flowered in white stitchery with short capelet sleeves. Miss Vanderlip's gown was a similar style in green organdy flowered in yellow. Both wore circlets of fresh flowers and baby's breath and had matching nosegay bouquets.

Mr. and Mrs. Chapin took a camping trip through the Sierra Mountains. They are at home at 1060 Hampshire Street, San Francisco, California.

Marilyn and Douglas Chapin were married atop California's Mount Tamalpais in 1972. Their brief relationship was marred by the notoriety of Marilyn's appearance in *Green Door*—and a man named Chuck Traynor. *Marin Wire Service photo/The Westport News.*

43

could remember anything noteworthy he said or did. He simply existed.

"I don't even know what he did," said Liz Boyd, Marilyn's childhood friend, who visited the couple in San Francisco. "I mean, he was a nice guy, very quiet. He was there, [but] he just kind of let us be to ourselves."[12]

Marilyn described Doug as a true hippie—photos from when the two were together supported that assessment, at least in appearance. Doug wore his dirty blond hair long, just slightly beyond shoulder length. He had a long, full, scraggly beard. His blue eyes were deep-set and piercing. Marilyn said he lived in a commune when she met him in 1971 and remained steadily unemployed. Doug's hippie appearance starkly contrasts with a high school yearbook photo from 1963, showing a handsome, unbearded young man with his hair cut short and combed to the side.[13]

He was born in November 1945 and grew up in western Massachusetts.[14; 15] His high school yearbook notes that he planned to join the service after graduation.[16] It's unclear when or how he landed in the Bay Area. However, his mother had remarried and resided in Sunnyvale, about forty miles south of San Francisco. Doug was of Scottish heritage and proud of it. For money, he played bagpipes on the streets of San Francisco. It was through his playing that he and Marilyn met.

Walking along the street one day, Marilyn heard the faint but distinct sound of bagpipes and followed it. When she turned a corner, Doug was sitting cross-legged on the cement playing the instrument. She was smitten.

'I'd always heard that crap about two people being in the right place at the right time, and suddenly it wasn't crap,' she said. 'He stopped long enough to tell me that his name was Doug and invited me home with him. So I went home with him. And stayed for two years.'[17]

They lived together in a Victorian-style house on Hampshire Street in the Potrero Hill neighborhood of San Francisco.

'The first year was super,' Marilyn remembered. 'We were like little kids, flower children grown up, bopping around the hills of San Francisco, spending a lot of time in bed, enjoying living. Then one day, we joked about getting married. It was silly talk, but suddenly we found ourselves committed to it.'[18]

They married on August 26, 1972, atop Mount Tamalpais in Marin County, just north of San Francisco, on the other side of the Golden Gate Bridge. Her parents traveled from Westport to attend the wedding. Her siblings flew in, too. When the couple decided to marry, Marilyn broke the news to her mother over the phone. "Hi, Mom. I'm marrying a bagpipe player." There was a stony silence. "Mom, you there?" Finally, her mother spoke.

"NOW CASTING FOR A MAJOR MOTION PICTURE"

"Does he play professionally, Marilyn?" ("Sure, Mom, he's first chair in the San Francisco Symphony's bagpipe section," she thought.)[19]

Marilyn explained how they met. He played bagpipes because he enjoyed it. She even gave him money the first time she heard him play. No, he didn't have a job, but he was looking. Besides, it didn't matter. He worked on cars occasionally (when the spirit moved him), played the bagpipes (when he felt like it), and the pair were in love.

Her parents were understandably concerned and resisted the idea of marriage for about a week. After all, they wanted the best for her but shouldn't have been too surprised. 'They were beginning to realize their little girl was a little screwball,' Marilyn said. 'They also realized I was going to do it anyway, so they figured they'd better give me their 'blessing,' as it is called. My God, Doug and I had lived together for a year, what was the difference now?'[20]

Doug had an easygoing attitude. Everyone liked him. They liked him so much they wouldn't tell him he had any faults. Marilyn certainly didn't, although she secretly wished she could force him to decide what he wanted to do with his life. She had ardor for her career and wanted him to have the same. He needed a steady job so they weren't always struggling and on welfare. They had to keep the dog fed. They had to pay rent. Bagpipe playing wasn't cutting it. But not having a real job was part of being a hippie in San Francisco, so she said nothing; she enjoyed pleasing her man.

With no offers from theater groups, agents, or film or television opportunities, Marilyn relegated herself to a series of odd jobs: hostess at the Shandygaff Cafe on Polk Street, administrative assistant in a dental office, an employee in a health food store.[21] When money was tight, she danced nude in a place she called a "dump." She was an excellent dancer but saw the job simply as a means to an end.

'Anything to stay alive, to keep the body in shape because even though times were rough, I had ambition and plans for the future,' she said. 'I just didn't know how they were going to work out, what was going to turn the key to open the door to a career. If someone had said sucking cock on screen would do it, I would have laughed at him and then slapped him. Funny how things turn out.'[22]

Marilyn checked the newspaper daily for jobs. On March 13, 1972, she spotted an advertisement in the *San Francisco Chronicle*. It read: "Now casting for a major motion picture."

She knew instinctively this was the moment for which she had been waiting. She phoned the number listed in the ad.

"I'm sorry, but all the roles have been cast," said the woman who answered.

"No, wait! You haven't seen me yet. Please let me come down and audition." She was practically screaming into the receiver.

"OK," said the woman. "But it probably won't do you any good."

Marilyn wrote down the address, thanked the woman, and hung up. She grabbed her modeling portfolio and quickly made her way out the door of her apartment.

All the unmarked warehouses on Tennessee Street looked the same, but she finally found the Stage A building. A host of people were milling about, sorting through applications, building sets, and chatting. Marilyn sensed this wouldn't be like any other audition as she entered. Something about the vibe of the place was weird. Not in a bad way, just strange. Maybe she was just nervous.

She approached a table near the front and explained that she had spoken to a woman about an audition. She was handed a green form and asked to fill it out. She found a seat and placed her modeling portfolio beside her. The first few questions were all standard, such as name, contact information, and previous experience. Near the bottom of the form, one question startled her. It read: *Balling or non-balling role?* She wrote in the word 'non-balling.' Wait a minute. Certainly, this had to be a typo, she thought. They can't mean what she thought they meant. They probably meant to type "bowling or non-bowling." That had to be it. She crossed out the word 'non,' so it simply said 'balling.' She could handle a little bowling, she thought.

She returned the form to the person at the table. They scanned it and said, "So you'll be fucking in the movie?"

"What? No!" she said. "Is that what kind of a movie this is? No way. Nudity is okay, but I'm not screwing on film." Dejected and angry, she gathered her materials and started for the exit. The woman on the phone was right. Coming down to the audition didn't do her any good.

Art Mitchell was sitting in the second-floor office he shared with his brother Jim. He noticed Marilyn as she was leaving. She bore such a striking resemblance to model and actress Cybill Shepherd that he did a double take. She was not like any of the other girls who came to audition for the brothers' films. What was she doing here? At that moment, he knew the slender blonde, steps away from walking out of their lives forever, was precisely the girl they needed for their next film. He had to act fast.

"Hey! Hey, you!" he shouted after her. Everyone stopped what they were doing to look at Art's head poking out of the office window. "The blonde girl. Wait! Don't go. Come back!" Everyone turned to look at Marilyn.

She kept walking.

"NOW CASTING FOR A MAJOR MOTION PICTURE"

Art raced from the office, down the stairs, and started to chase her. "Hey! Come back." She turned around. Who was this corny-looking guy? He was dressed in a Brooks Brothers sweater vest, kept a well-maintained beard, and looked like somebody from Westport, not a sleazeball who made fuck films.

"Are you here to audition?" he asked.

"I was, but I didn't know it was *that* kind of movie," she replied. "The ad in the *Chronicle* said nothing about the movie being X-rated."

"C'mon upstairs," he said gently. "My brother and I would love to talk with you. Please? Just for a few minutes. You're exactly what we're looking for."

She was dubious but charmed by his demeanor. Yet there was no way she was going to do a porn movie.

"What could it hurt?" he asked. "It'll just take a few minutes. We just want to talk to you."

Out of all the people in the place, he was the least weird, yet it seemed he was in charge. She had to admit she had nothing else going on, just more housework and wondering when her big break would come. She agreed and followed Art upstairs, and he introduced her to Jim. The brothers dressed and looked so similar that she assumed they must be twins. She took a seat on the sofa. Jim asked to see her portfolio. She handed it to him, and he flipped through a series of professional modeling headshots. When he finished, he looked at Art. They didn't say a word. Jim turned to face Marilyn.

"You just happen to be who we're looking for," Jim said.

"Oh, really? Wow!" Marilyn said.

"Marilyn, you're the girl next door," he continued. "You're the face every guy dreams of shoving his cock into. But he never does because he can't find you! You're fresh air and apple pie."[23]

She was slightly startled by his candor but found it refreshing, unlike anything she'd experienced at other auditions. But the idea of having sex on camera was just too naughty. A respectable upper-middle-class girl from Connecticut didn't do that, "hippie chick" be damned. Then again, she moved to San Francisco to escape New England's puritanical, restive atmosphere. And these two men treated her respectfully, unlike those producers in New York who behaved like pigs.

"I don't have anything against sex films," she said, lighting a cigarette. "I just don't want to be in one."

"Listen, you're classy, and this is going to be one classy film," Art said. "We're putting everything we have into it. Let us just explain the concept and tell you the story. The whole thing is a fantasy."

PURE
The Sexual Revolutions of Marilyn Chambers

He said the film was *Behind the Green Door*, based on an anonymous short story. She had never heard of it.

"We've been pretty successful making hardcore films," Art said. "This film is our shot at breaking through to a mainstream audience. So it's not like we're asking you to star in a fuck film. This is going to be a real movie about real sex."[24] (*Green Door* was the brothers' 337th film in just three years—their first feature-length one.[25])

Jim and Art Mitchell were well known in San Francisco when *Green Door* went into production, particularly by law enforcement. The O'Farrell Theater, the flagship adult theater they owned, was raided countless times by police since its opening in 1969. X-rated films lensed by the brothers were confiscated. The brothers, as well as patrons, were often arrested and charged with obscenity. The brothers took it all in their stride. They were masterful self-promoters and believed in the old saying, "There's no such thing as bad publicity." Any press they received from raids on their theater would only generate public interest. Moreover, they fought every charge on First Amendment grounds—and won. They were likely the first pornographers and perhaps the first independent filmmakers who fought to successfully protect their works in the judicial system. The brothers grew up in Antioch, California, about forty-five miles northeast of San Francisco. Their father was originally from Oklahoma, and the brothers were self-proclaimed "Okies." Despite their striking similarity in appearance, Jim was, in fact, two years older than Art. In the sixties, Jim attended San Francisco State University, where he took a couple of classes in filmmaking. It wasn't long until he realized producing sex films might be the ticket to a lucrative career. He recruited his brother into the venture. The two surrounded themselves with close friends and family to help.

"Art and I would make a beaver film for, say, a hundred bucks," Jim said. "You'd pay a girl twenty-five dollars, buy forty worth of film, and still have thirty-five for processing and incidentals. When you had it done, and if it was any good at all, you could easily get two hundred bucks, so that was pretty nice. We didn't really know much about filmmaking, but there wasn't a lot of product around."[26]

With each film they made, they pushed the envelope. The idea, Art said, was "always to come up with a better fuck film."[27] Now, they were ready for a full-length pornographic feature film. They wanted to make it look modish, imaginative, and professional, resembling real cinematic art. Marilyn was intrigued. However, despite what Jim said, this was a fuck film. Ever since she could remember, her parents firmly reinforced that sex was private, even dirty, and not to be discussed. She thought she'd break out in hives or go crazy if she tried to have sex on film with lots of people watching. This wasn't legitimate. This wasn't even Hollywood.

Still, she liked the brothers. They were friendly and had an easygoing style. Art talked about his daughter and being a dad. She felt comfortable. So when they asked if she would disrobe so they could take some Polaroids, she didn't hesitate. There was no casting couch bit; that was almost too obvious for a film like this. They were professionals.

It's entirely possible this film could be a stepping stone to something bigger, Marilyn thought. The brothers said as much. No one had made a feature-length narrative film with hardcore sex before, they told her, and the timing seemed right. It appeared they were running a major operation here. They were serious about their business; their business just happened to be pornography. And from the sound of it, she was the whole movie. Maybe she could make this movie so erotic that Hollywood producers would have to take notice. If they even saw it. Could these guys distribute the film properly? She didn't want to make it and have it play in a single San Francisco theater that no one attended. The brothers were nice enough, but maybe they were just blowing smoke. Then again, if a Hollywood producer did see it, he might oust Marilyn from Hollywood for good.

And what about her parents? Their little girl would be up on the screen, doing unspeakable things. It likely wouldn't win their approval. Their image of her and as an upstanding family would be shattered, and Marilyn would be the family's shame.

She hesitated. "Well, it sounds interesting," she said. "How much are you paying?"

"For you? Maybe twenty-five hundred," Art said. "That's five, maybe ten times more than we've ever paid a lady before."

"No way," Marilyn said flatly. "I want at least twice that much, probably more. And I'd have to have a percentage of the profits. Not the net—the gross."

The brothers were gobsmacked. Who did this girl think she was? Some Hollywood rich kid? Their leading man, George S. McDonald, had made at most $350. The guys were planning to use him for *Green Door*, so if they paid her more, they'd likely have to pay him more too.

"You know something?" Art asked, his voice brimming with anger. "Girls, great-looking girls, have been happy to get fifty dollars to fuck in our movies."

"That was them, not me," she replied. She reminded them of her credentials. She was a professional. "I know how it works."

"Well, listen, it's been nice talking to a real live actress," Jim said sarcastically. "Tell you what. Give us your number and, as we say in the business, 'We'll call you.'"

She was miffed, yet a sense of relief filled her. She just couldn't do a sex film. She was hip, but that was the limit. She excused herself and left.

Back at the apartment, Doug was gone. She went back to scrutinizing the want ads. About an hour later, the phone rang.

"Marilyn?" the voice asked. "This is Jim. Listen, we've thought it over. You're the girl we want, and we're prepared to give you everything you asked for."

"Well, I... " she said haltingly.

"So Art and I will be right over with the contract," Jim said. He confirmed the address, and they hung up.[28]

They had called her bluff. Now she had to do it. She didn't even have the opportunity to respond, and they were about to walk through her front door.

It all happened so fast. Marilyn's head spun as the brothers entered her apartment, shoved the contract before her, and handed her a pen. True to their word, they had included a generous sum of money and percentage points from the film's total gross. She signed her name on the dotted line.

"Had I had the chance to really think about it," she recalled years later, "I would have said 'no.'"

However, she was proud and stubborn (a true Taurus, she liked to think), and she wasn't about to let these two guys think she wasn't up to it. The brothers seemed sincere in their goals, and she was resolute in making this the most erotic motion picture ever.

DOUG WAS APOPLECTIC WHEN Marilyn told him over dinner that she had signed on to do a pornographic film.

She tried to keep her composure as she explained this wasn't one of those nasty old stag films. "It's a fantasy," she told Doug. "It's going to be very classy." She was trying to keep the topic light so Doug would stay calm. She was already doubting the agreement, but if she played it cool, maybe she could convince him—and herself—that it was no big deal.

"You'll like the guys doing it," she continued. "They want me to bring you down to the sound stage next time I go so they can meet you."

"But why?" Doug protested. No matter how classy the brothers made it seem or how respectable she thought it would be, it was still a fuck film, he told her.

"Well, the money's good, and I think I could do a good job," she said. He wasn't the breadwinner in the family, she thought. If the film made a profit, they could live comfortably off the residuals. There was a moment of awkward silence, and she blurted out, "And so what?"

"Look, it's your body, your decision, your life," Doug said. "All I'm saying is, think about it first, OK?"[29]

"NOW CASTING FOR A MAJOR MOTION PICTURE"

She said she would. She couldn't help it. This opportunity could jeopardize her marriage, her relationship with her family, and her career.

THE SHORT STORY UPON which *Behind the Green Door* was based has an ambiguous history. Historians and scholars of erotic literature agree it was an underground piece of erotic fiction written anonymously and passed secretively among friends in the form of tattered and stained mimeographed copies. Sometimes titled 'The Abduction of Gloria,' its original author or authors are unknown. The story is about a woman who's taken against her will to a secret location and forced to perform various sex acts. One scholar noted that 'Behind the Green Door' and another erotic short story called 'The Young Stenographer' were 'perhaps more universally known than any other individual pieces of English language prose erotica.'[30]

"Behind the Green Door'...is so widespread, in a multiplicity of versions...and... appears to be most frequently encountered by college students and servicemen,' wrote Frank Hoffmann in his book *Analytical Survey of Anglo-American Traditional Erotica.*[31]

Indeed, Art first read the story in college in the early sixties and said it was about twenty typed pages. When he and Jim were ready to make a feature-length film, Art suggested 'Green Door.' Marilyn claimed service members passed the story around while they were in the trenches; every guy who read it would add his part to the story.

'An account of what might be termed the ultimate one woman-multiple men orgy, it is not properly a traditional story,' Hoffmann noted. 'However, it is shot through with popular beliefs regarding the sexual organs and responses to sexual activity.'[32]

Even though the story was well-known, the brothers found it difficult to locate a copy in the Bay Area. They went so far as to put an ad in the *San Francisco Chronicle* that read "$25 and business opportunities for a copy of The Green Door." They received a few leads but no actual manuscript. Finally, a friend of theirs came through. Her mother in Wisconsin had a copy in a trunk and made a handwritten copy for the brothers.[33]

Art and Bill Boyer, who often wrote screenplays for the brothers, adapted the story into a rough script; it was more of an outline than an actual screenplay.[34]

The phrase "behind the green door" first made its way into the public consciousness in 1956, courtesy of the number one song The Green Door, performed by Jim Lowe. Coincidentally, the song was a favorite of Marilyn's

PURE The Sexual Revolutions of Marilyn Chambers

"BEHIND THE GREEN DOOR" starring Marilyn Chambers

Marilyn strikes a pose in a promotional photo for the Mitchell Brothers' 1972 hardcore classic *Behind the Green Door. Mitchell Brothers Film Group.*

father. The early rock and roll tune, written by Bob Davie and Marvin Moore, has the narrator wondering what's happening at a noisy, raucous secret club into which one must enter through a green door. Much laughter emanates and he wishes "they" would let him in, so that he can see what he's missing.[35]

Marilyn Briggs was about to discover the mysteries hidden behind the green door—and come out the other side as Marilyn Chambers.

Chapter 4

BEHIND THE GREEN DOOR

■■■■■■■■

PRINCIPAL PHOTOGRAPHY FOR *BEHIND THE Green Door* began soon after Marilyn signed the contract in March 1972. In addition to Studio A on Tennessee Street, filming would occur at the swanky Alta Mira Hotel in Sausalito and the O'Farrell Theater in San Francisco. The O'Farrell, the first adult theater the brothers owned and operated, was their flagship location. They would soon open ten more adult theaters throughout California. The two-story electric blue brick building, located at the southeast corner of O'Farrell and Polk Streets in downtown San Francisco's Tenderloin district, had served as a restaurant and a Pontiac dealership before the brothers rented it in 1969. They fixed it up with hand-sewn drapes by Art's wife Meredith, plush carpeting, comfortable seating, ornate chandeliers, and a projection booth. There was even a suggestion box in the lobby. As operators of an X-rated movie theater, the brothers knew the police would inevitably raid them. So, they ensured the place was classy and attractive. The films were shown on the ground floor, and the brothers' offices were on the second floor. The theater's doors opened on Independence Day, 1969—a conscious decision by the brothers who firmly believed in First Amendment rights. Before filming, Marilyn insisted that every actor and actress participating in a sexual act get tested for venereal diseases, regardless of whether or not she was having sex with them. Several years before *Green Door*, one of the Mitchell brothers' actresses knowingly gave gonorrhea to numerous cast and crew members because she was annoyed she didn't have a more significant part in one of the films.

"I could tell after talking with her a few minutes that she was totally into the film," co-star George S. McDonald said about Marilyn.[1] He had been working with the Mitchell brothers for several years and starred in hundreds of their eight- and sixteen-millimeter films, but he knew *Green Door* would be his last. He was ready to retire.

BEHIND THE GREEN DOOR

"Marilyn seemed more professional than any other girl that I had worked with in any prior film," he said. "She also loved to drink beer and smoke marijuana. Even first thing in the morning, when everyone was struggling over coffee, she would have a can of beer in her hand."[2]

The Mitchell brothers gave everyone contracts, including the extras, and paid them more than they ever had, but the actual payments were deferred for six months. Most people in the business then were in it to make a quick buck, so this strategy proved to be a tremendous headache for the brothers. Two months after the film was completed, people called asking if they could get their money.

Contracts also committed people to make the film. *Green Door* was scheduled to shoot for four weeks with virtually no days off—a more extended production schedule than usual for adult movies of the time.

"Before, you were never sure that if someone said they would be there, that a week later they would be there," McDonald said. "At least by signing a contract, they had a legal and moral obligation to be there for the start and the finish of the film. A problem in the porno industry is that if you give people a chance to think about it, they'll often have second thoughts and back out. Before, if you got someone to agree to be in a fuck film, they were on such a short production schedule that the producers would probably use the person that day or on the next."[3]

Still, some participants, like McDonald, were concerned. How could someone be legally held to a contract when their job was technically illegal? Throughout the sixties, the Supreme Court ruled that most pornography was legal—except hardcore. Participation in or possession of hardcore "pornography"—which was often called an "obscenity"—was illegal. However, state and local interpretations of what was considered pornography varied widely.

"Obscenity is a matter of geography," stated Stanley Fleishman, an attorney well-known for defending First Amendment obscenity cases.[4]

The brothers mapped out nearly 600 shots for the film. They rented the Alta Mira Hotel for outdoor shots and hired a hair and makeup team. A motley crew of lighting, sound, and cameramen was on hand as well as the usual group of extras and actors in Mitchell brothers' films. They even secured Oakland Raiders defensive end Ben Davidson for a small non-sex part as the big, burly sex club security guard. Davidson was a prominent local celebrity, and the brothers paid him $500 for his cameo.[5] They thought this was a great gimmick and knew his name would help sell tickets.

Art started directing the film, with Jim producing, but it quickly became problematic. Before *Green Door*, the brothers had their shooting pattern down:

set up the shot, shoot it, print. This was their chance at the big time, and Art insisted on take after take. The camera angle on Marilyn was correct, and then it wasn't. McDonald's expressions were too serious or not serious enough. Some of the efforts backfired. Marilyn was made to wear a black wig, defeating the purpose of showcasing the all-American blonde girl next door. According to Marilyn, the lighting was set up incorrectly, making one of the original sets look like a morgue. To make matters worse, nearly all of the footage from the first day's shooting at the Alta Mira was exposed in the lab and scrapped. Even after the film was reshot and completed, a crucial fifteen minutes had burnt in the lab. No one can remember what part of the story the footage contained.

Jim stepped in to take over directing. He changed McDonald's character from an advertising executive, as originally written, to a truck driver. "The next time we shoot, show up in Levi's," he told McDonald. "And think of some trucker dialogue." When they resumed filming, Studio A was transformed into an exotic sex club, with drapes, Persian carpets, and large, overstuffed Victorian sofas.

There wasn't much of a script, but when Marilyn reviewed it, she noticed one glaring omission: she didn't have a single line of dialogue. Wasn't this a mistake? "I'm an actress, remember?" she asked the brothers. They told her it would be an even greater challenge as an actress to communicate everything through her eyes, face, and body using no dialogue. "They were right," she admitted. "Words would have blown it as far as I'm concerned."[6]

Despite being a narrative feature, the plot is tissue-paper-thin and somewhat nonsensical. The film opens at a truck stop diner with a driver recounting a recent sexual experience to other truck drivers. He tells them about a beautiful woman he saw on a stopover at a hotel. Although they never speak, her face is etched in his memory. Unbeknownst to him, that same woman, a wealthy socialite named Gloria Saunders, is kidnapped later that evening, blindfolded, and taken to an elite sex club in the North Beach neighborhood of San Francisco. (Jim and Art played the kidnappers.) Frozen with fear, she is led by a soft-spoken woman into a cool white room, much like a doctor's office. The woman reassures her that she won't be hurt. She instructs Gloria to lie on an examining table. She explains that she was in the same position as Gloria once and that a "kind woman" helped her relax and prepared her for "the most extraordinary experience" of her life.

"It was a cold, cold instance for me," Marilyn recalled. "It was a stark white room, and the woman was very nervous. And I was very nervous, and this was one of the first scenes we did, and I felt very uncomfortable."[7]

As Gloria lies on the table, the woman begins massaging her feet and moving her way up to her breasts while speaking softly; essentially, she's hypnotizing

BEHIND THE GREEN DOOR

Gloria. Serendipitously, the truck driver has paid admission to the same sex club and is escorted to his seat. As guests arrive, they are treated to a bizarre and creepy mime act. Once Gloria has been massaged and hypnotized, she is led into the club through a green door by six women clad in black hooded robes. An announcer's voice booms over the public address system, explaining to the audience what's about to happen:

> Ladies and gentlemen, you are about to witness the ravishment of a woman who's been abducted—a woman whose initial fear and anxiety has mellowed into curious expectation. Although, at first, her reactions may lead you to believe that she is being tortured, quite the contrary is true. For no harm will come to those being ravished. In the morning, she will be set free, unaware of anything except that she has been loved as never before. Perhaps you'll recognize one of your friends in the role of victim. Remember, you are sworn to observe silence. If you break this rule, you will be dealt with severely. So, with the knowledge that you are powerless to stop the performance, just relax and enjoy yourself to the fullest extent.

The women disrobe a reluctant and shivering Gloria and make love to her, at first caressing and kissing her all over her body and eventually laying her down to perform cunnilingus. This is the first onscreen sex act, arriving twenty minutes into the film.

"Six women, wow!" Marilyn said. "It frightened me, but it turned me on. I was the total receiver. I wasn't to give anything. Being in that position, it's a lot easier to enjoy yourself, for sure, if it's, like, the first time. Especially with women, there's no taking of a certain side, the masculine or the feminine. You don't have that split-second to decide which role you are assuming. It's just right there for you, and all you have to do is say, 'Far out!'"[8]

After several minutes, a spotlight is turned to the green door, and from behind it steps a Black man, deliberate yet decisive in his movements. His face is covered in tribal makeup. He's shirtless and wearing a necklace adorned with what appear to be the teeth or claws of a large jungle cat. He's dressed in white leggings with the crotch cut out, revealing a large, semi-erect penis. As he steps through the door, you can hear a male audience member exclaim, "Wow!"

The women beckon him over to Gloria, who lies spread-eagled on the floor. His movements are purposeful, considered yet carnal, like a slow-motion ballet. He finally approaches Gloria, and the women hold her down. She resists slightly.

"I was embarrassed!" Marilyn said. "It was supposed to be subtle. I'm kidnapped and in shock. I'm supposed to be rich and sophisticated, and, gosh, going to a swingers' party was something I knew about but figured I was just too cool for. The whole point was to be, not overly rebellious, but to get into it. I'm here anyway, so don't fight it and enjoy it. My character finally realizes that."[9]

The Black man crouches down to perform cunnilingus. A close-up shot of Gloria reveals her to be frightened, even slightly repulsed, by the sex act. As he moves to penetrate her, the image cuts to the audience members beginning to touch themselves and others. While Gloria and the Black man are having sex, the camera stays mostly on their faces and eyes. Gloria begins to moan, and in doing so, it becomes clear she's starting to enjoy what's happening to her.

As the man's rhythm picks up, so does the music: a driving drum beat and pulsating bass line that perfectly accentuate the increasingly frenzied sexual experience. He brings his face as close to hers as possible. A close-up shot of Gloria's face shows her eyes to be closed, and as the man continues pumping, she opens them slowly. They make eye contact and hold each other's gaze. At that moment, Gloria lets go. In doing so, the scene and film itself become a palpable, carnal experience. The close-up is a single take lasting two minutes and ending with her climaxing. Thirty-five minutes into the movie, *Behind the Green Door* is finally a sex film.

"It had to turn from fear to lust, and I made sure that that happened," Marilyn said. "That whole thing with looking into [each other's] eyes, I didn't want it to happen because I was kind of scared, but then it was really sexy. It really turned me on. It was that moment [when] my life changed. Right then. You saw it. I'm an actress, and I'm a professional. But when the actual sex happens, then it becomes a real thing. You cannot hide what sex does to you. It becomes real. It becomes *you*."[10]

For the nameless Black stud role, the Mitchell brothers tapped Johnnie Keyes, a former boxer and stage actor who appeared in the West Coast touring productions of *Hair* and *Jesus Christ Superstar*. Marilyn met Keyes for the first time one afternoon in the second-floor offices of the O'Farrell Theater.

"I thought she was a cute little mama, you know," Keyes recalled. "She had a pleasant little naiveté about her."[11]

In approaching his role as the Black stud, Keyes said, "I just regressed myself, like I had just come out of the jungle, my natural trip, and nature just took over. I became what you saw. When I walked through the green door, I had become just a magnificent animal, a leopard or something."[12]

Keyes displayed a lot of stamina. When they filmed the first take of their intercourse scene, he lasted forty-three minutes without stopping. Marilyn had several orgasms. After her final one, she fainted.

"I'm looking down at this woman, her eyes rolled back in her head, and I thought, 'What the hell? I just killed a white woman! I'm going to jail. I just killed a white woman with my dick!'" Keyes said.[13]

Several crew members carried Marilyn off the set and laid her down. They gave her smelling salts. When she came to, she was bewildered. A relieved Keyes walked over to her and said, "Marilyn, are you alright? What happened?"

"I don't know," she replied hazily. "I can't remember. The last time I came, I just went somewhere else, and I don't know what happened."

After pausing momentarily, the film resumed its schedule.

Upon its release, *Behind the Green Door* 'likely became the first American feature-length hardcore film to include a major interracial sex act.'[14] Underground stag films included interracial scenes, mostly with white men and Black women. Still, at the very least, *Green Door* was the first mass-distributed film including an interracial sex scene to reach a mixed-gender audience.

"That made the myth of the Black dude with the big dick in white society; it made it real," Keyes said.[15]

The scene wasn't without its share of controversy. Keyes got death threats from the Ku Klux Klan and needed a security detail briefly after the film's release.

"I got death threats from all kinds of people who were upset about watching me fuck Marilyn Chambers," he said.[16]

After Gloria climaxes, a strange trapeze-like mechanism is lowered from the ceiling. Metal rings adorn the ends of six lengthy, tentacle-like arms, connected into three pairs by a single piece of flat wood shrouded in fabric. Once it's in position, a trio of men sit on the pieces of wood. Gloria is positioned to face one man, with the others to her left and right. A fourth man stands behind her. As one man vaginally penetrates Gloria, she performs oral sex on another and strokes the third and fourth men with her free hands. The camera cuts between Gloria and the audience members, who are now fully engaged in sexual activity.

"You know, it's funny," Marilyn said later. "People always see what they want to see. And people always insist that I'm the one on the trapeze. No, wrong. I'm the one that's holding everyone up on the trapeze. That was probably one of the most difficult days of my life because I had to prop myself up on the person below me, and I was really straining every muscle in my body. It was quite a day."[17]

The trapeze scene was shot in one fourteen-hour day.

When the man penetrating Gloria is close to climaxing, the shot turns to slow motion. An ominous electronic music score pulsates as the man pulls out to ejaculate. Still in slow motion, the scene changes to a shot of Gloria's face in the bottom left corner of the screen and a penis in the upper right, with semen dripping onto her face. In perhaps the film's most famous sequence, Gloria's face is seen at the bottom of the screen in a mirrored image as an endless psychedelic slow-motion stream of men ejaculate onto her. The technique, called polarization, displays the images as film negatives awash in reds, greens, and oranges. One scholar wrote that the scene was reminiscent of an animated Jackson Pollock painting.[18] It's a repetitive, six-minute come shot set to a creepy and haunting experimental soundtrack. The scene took about five hours to film, with three cameras from three angles.

'When the director explained the scene to me, I said, 'Oh no! You're not going to let him do that!" Marilyn wrote. 'I thought it was degrading to have six or seven guys coming all over me. I felt humiliated as an actress and a person to have to get into a back-breaking position (so the camera angle would be just right) and stay there while one guy after another worked his cock over my face. That's why the sequence seems so real—it was! It's exciting because it's honest.'[19]

Despite any humiliation she endured physically and psychologically, the cast and crew remained entirely professional, beginning with the Mitchell brothers.

'Never once did they try to make me. Nor did they once think of me as Sally Slut. I was a hired actress and treated as one. They respected me, and they, in turn, were respected by me.'[20]

In an overhead shot of the orgiastic crowd, the truck driver notices Gloria and recognizes her as the woman he saw at the hotel. He breaks free from his sexual activity, dresses, and runs over to her. He throws her over his shoulder like a cartoon caveman and escapes through the green door. What he is escaping from is unclear, as is his motivation for "rescuing" Gloria.

On the first take, McDonald said he "pushed the two girls off, grabbed my pants and managed to get one leg in them, hopped across the stage, picked up Marilyn in a hero's sweep, and as I ran through the door, I was in such a hurry that I banged her head into it."

"'CUT!' said the director. "Let's try again, but take it a little easier with the star this time."[21]

After he carries her through the door, we're inexplicably back at the diner. When the cook asks the driver what happened next, he smiles and leaves. "Some other time, Gish," he says and walks out. Next, images of him and Gloria having sex are superimposed over shots of him driving his truck, as if to suggest that this is what happened after he took her through the green door. The scene dissolves into their lovemaking, but neither climaxes—implying that what happens behind

BEHIND THE GREEN DOOR

the green door is perpetual sex, an incessant fantasy. The film ends.

Even though Marilyn read the script and had a general idea of what would happen, she told the brothers that she didn't want to be told if any surprises were in store. She was already nervous and knew that would appear on the screen, but she wanted to ensure her reactions were genuine, especially if something unplanned happened.

"That's why I think the film hit," she said. "I lost my inhibitions on-screen at the same time Americans everywhere were losing theirs."[22]

The brothers' longtime cameraman, Jon Fontana, recalled shooting "something like thirty-six hundred to five thousand feet of film" in one day, the equivalent of two-and-a-half to three hours.[23]

The filming of *Green Door* had more in common with a mainstream film than people realized and was less like anything the Mitchell brothers had previously attempted. It took time to set up shots and lighting, position the actors, and memorize dialogue.

"There's a definite concentration level that has to be maintained," Marilyn said. "It's not turning yourself on sexually so much as it is turning yourself on mentally."

Then there was the X factor of the male star's ability to perform on cue. It wasn't the orgiastic free-for-all that some may have imagined.

'The atmosphere must be relaxed and informal so the sex scenes will 'happen' and have the look and feel of reality, but everyone realizes they are doing a job for which they are paid,' Marilyn said. 'Usually everyone goes their separate ways after a day's shooting unless they're married or living together or something because they don't have the sexual hang-ups of most middle-class people (and most people working on fuck films are pretty much middle-class or come from that kind of background). They don't get all hot and bothered by what was filmed that day and run out together and have a wild orgy that tops anything yet seen on camera. Johnnie Keyes didn't mean anything to me, sexually, off-screen. He was just another actor, a co-star, a co-worker, a nice guy.'[24]

By the time filming was nearing completion, Marilyn was mentally and physically exhausted. They had shot scenes twelve hours a day for thirty days straight, and Marilyn was in almost all of them. On the last day, she was to film her scene with McDonald. He arrived at Stage A at 8:00AM to find Marilyn standing barefoot in the dressing room with her hair in curlers, full makeup, and wearing a robe. She had a cigarette in one hand and a beer in the other.

"She [was] burned out," McDonald said. "She had done all the sex scenes for thirty days except ours. She's still trying to keep it together, and she's just as sweet as can be to me that morning. Marilyn was, far and away, the sweetest lady I ever had to work with on film."[25] Their scene, which featured several optical effects the Mitchells were trying for the first time, was complicated and took two hours to complete.

Behind the Green Door looks nothing like the professional pornographic films made today. In many ways, it plays like an experimental art film made by a first-year film student. But it's a perfect time capsule of seventies independent filmmaking. It's highly stylistic, and there's a hypnotic quality to it that's both bewildering and erotic. That might explain its appeal. It's simply unlike any other sex film made before or since. It tapped into the zeitgeist of a generation with its explosive and often controversial sex scenes. Whether or not the Mitchell Brothers succeeded in changing public opinion about X-rated features as an art form is irrelevant; there's no question that they believed they were making a statement.

Marilyn ultimately believed in the film, but it took some convincing.

"Frankly, I had my doubts that I could do [*Green Door*] to start with," she said. "Art and Jim Mitchell had no doubts, but I did. I was a little hesitant—because, at first, I didn't want to make it too dirty. But I think it helped make me a better person. I'm more honest with myself about life. I don't feel hung up as much as I was before."[26]

ON JUNE 12, 1972, as *Green Door* was in production, another hardcore pornographic film debuted at the nondescript World Theater in New York City's Times Square. Originally called *The Sword Swallower*, its director, Gerard Damiano, later gave it a more appropriate and prophetic title: *Deep Throat*. The comedy featured a clever gimmick in which a woman's clitoris is at the back of her throat. The only way she can orgasm is if she engulfs a man's entire penis in her mouth, all the way down her throat. The release of *Deep Throat* was a watershed moment in adult films, popular culture, filmmaking, and politics. It changed the face of pornography forever and would become one of the most successful films ever made. It would act as a lightning rod for controversy long after it left theaters. Its star, Linda Lovelace, became a household name, something never before achieved by an actress in a blue movie.

"How far does a girl have to go to untangle her tingle?" was the film's titillating tagline.

"This is a male fantasy," author Erica Jong said in the documentary *Inside Deep Throat*. "It says: 'I like to get my cock sucked. I really get off on it. Therefore, she must too.' Look, men want to believe that the clitoris is in a woman's throat because if they believe that the clitoris is in a woman's throat, then they can believe that by thrusting their penis into a woman's mouth, she gets as much pleasure as they do. Guess what? It's not true!"[27]

By January 1973, the film played in more than seventy theaters nationwide and grossed more than three million dollars ($21.5 million in today's money). Shot in Florida over six days and made on a shoestring budget of about $25,000 (nearly $185,000 today), the film would eventually go on to gross anywhere between $30 million and $600 million worldwide (between nearly $200 million and $400 million when adjusted for inflation), depending on the source, making it one of the most profitable films in the history of motion pictures.

"*Deep Throat* succeeded commercially, at least in part, because the government went after it," said attorney Alan Dershowitz. He had represented lead actor Harry Reems in successfully appealing his conviction for distribution of obscenity just for appearing in the film. "The government became the driving force behind the public relations."[28]

The film became a litmus test for what constituted obscene material in the legal sense and became the subject of numerous First Amendment cases. Local authorities confiscated it at theaters nationwide, and theater owners were arrested and jailed. News

Unpublished photos from a modeling session circa 1973. *Photographer uncredited.*

of these arrests only added to the hype. At the World Theater in New York City, where it premiered, the film drew 'an average of 5,000 people weekly, including celebrities, diplomats, critics, businessmen, women alone and dating couples, few of whom, it might be presumed, would previously have gone to see a film of sexual intercourse, fellatio, and cunnilingus...*Deep Throat* has become a premier topic of cocktail-party and dinner-table conversation in Manhattan drawing rooms, Long Island beach cottages, and ski-country A-frames,' wrote Ralph Blumenthal in *The New York Times*. 'It has, in short, engendered a kind of porno chic.'[29]

The phrase "porno chic" defined the era: a glittering, fleeting moment when pornographic films went mainstream and reached a mass, cross-generational, mixed-gendered audience. They earned a certain degree of respect from the general population—including the artistic community, especially among filmmakers—that had not existed before. At the very least, if the films weren't respected, mainstream media had a 'willingness to advertise and review pornographic cinema.'[30] Indeed, no less august a publication than *The New Yorker*, spurred by *Deep Throat*'s popularity, was moved to include porn films in its cinema listings.

In the sixties and seventies, visiting an adult theater was the easiest way to see an X-rated movie. This act was often illegal in many parts of the country. The clientele was mostly men. Since moviegoing was a public act, they often wore large raincoats to appear anonymous and allow discreet access to their genitals while they watched the film, which gave rise to the phrase "the raincoat crowd." Short films, called "loops," "stags," or "smokers," like those made by the Mitchell brothers, were still available to purchase at adult bookstores.

Deep Throat changed that. With celebrities like Johnny Carson, Ed MacMahon, director Mike Nichols, Truman Capote, Jack Nicholson, Warren Beatty, Barbara Walters, and even Jacqueline Kennedy Onassis lining up to see the movie, porn became a social event. It also brought a lot of women into adult theaters, as well as young couples. While the "porno chic" period only lasted a few years in the early seventies, it changed pornographic films forever and essentially established adult films as a viable industry. Its reverberations would continue for generations.

"I find the term 'porno chic' mildly offensive because it's like anything else chic, you know, it's decadent America," said Jon Fontana, the cameraman on *Green Door*. "As far as a fad, it's all synthetic demand. The fad was created, and now what matters is how to sustain it. It's gone from being a fad to being a way of life for a certain person to go to pornographic movies two or three times every year. And to please those people, we've started looking for acting ability as much as sexual ability. We're trying to get into drama and see what we can do with it. There's no doubt we're in the entertainment business[.] The change is because we *are* entertaining, we've improved, we've got longevity and tenure. We're just another institution now. As for Truman Capote and people like that paying transitory tribute to something, who really gives a shit? You just know that next year they'll be on to something else."[31]

For all its hype, *Deep Throat* is a dreadful movie. Critics savaged it. Nora Ephron, the journalist and screenwriter perhaps best known for the Academy Award-nominated screenplay for *When Harry Met Sally...*, wrote, 'I have seen a lot of stag films in my life—well, that's not true; I've seen about five or six—and although most of them were raunchy, a few were sweet and innocent and actually erotic. *Deep Throat*, on the other hand, is one of the most unpleasant, disturbing films I have ever seen—it's not just anti-female, but antisexual as well.'[32] One of the problems was that although Lovelace's oral talent was impressive, she was a terrible actress. She had a prettiness about her but was rather homely, and even when she is supposed to be in the throes of sexual ecstasy, there's an inherent darkness and sadness about her.

Just five days after *Deep Throat* opened in New York, a break-in occurred at the headquarters of the Democratic National Committee inside the Watergate Building in Washington, D.C. Although the break-in barely made a ripple in the news cycle when it happened, two dogged reporters at *The Washington Post* believed the crime was more significant. As it unfolded, the story had deeper political ties, possibly even a connection with President Richard Nixon. Bob Woodward, one of the reporters, contacted a source with intimate knowledge of the inner workings of the White House. The source was on "deep background," a journalistic term meaning the information provided could be used without attribution, including anonymity.[33] A *Post* editor nicknamed the source "Deep Throat" because of the film's popularity. The phrase "deep throat" became a noun and a verb and was too provocative for the media to ignore. However, were it not for Watergate, the film *Deep Throat* would likely have been largely forgotten—swallowed by history.

Lovelace graced the cover of *Esquire*, became a punchline on popular network sitcoms like *Sanford and Son*, and hobnobbed with Frank Sinatra, Liza Minnelli, Hugh Hefner, and Elvis Presley. Never far away was her possessive husband and manager, Chuck Traynor, who acted as production designer and location scout on the film.

Chuck had already developed an unsavory reputation while making the film. He was incredibly polarizing. People liked him, or they didn't. There was no in-between. He could be charming and friendly, especially with women, but he was controlling and often displayed an explosive temper. He freely admitted to physically abusing Lovelace when he felt like it.

"I've often tried to pinpoint the psychology of Linda," said Gerard Damiano, the film's director. "She seemed to have a distinct sadomasochistic relationship with Chuck, to the point where he constantly dominated her. They were never anywhere where she wasn't holding him or touching him. There was always a physical closeness and contact. There was this strange need all the time. And she was never out of Chuck's sight. But as close as they were in the daytime, I knew Chuck would bang Linda off the wall all night. The next day she'd appear on the set black-and-blue."[34]

Damiano followed *Deep Throat* with another feature-length hardcore film, *The Devil in Miss Jones*, starring Georgina Spelvin. It, too, became a box office hit. Unlike *Deep Throat*, it received excellent critical reviews.

"I saw *Deep Throat*, and I thought it was funny," Marilyn said. "It was a new thing, and I liked it. As to what kind of an actress Linda was, I don't think there was much in the film to show off her acting ability."[35]

Adult actor and director Fred Lincoln said more bluntly: "Linda thought they liked her acting! Jesus Christ, instead of being a masochist, she was a fucking idiot!"[36]

"THE MOST INFAMOUS STORY ever told—eight months in the making!" the advertisements screamed. *Behind the Green Door* was ready to be unleashed on the public. Before the film's release, Marilyn and the brothers discussed how she would be billed. Most actors and actresses in adult films didn't use their real names (George S. McDonald was an exception), mainly because they wanted to protect themselves and their families from public ridicule. Marilyn certainly understood that. She was already worrying about having to tell her parents about the film.

She was comfortable using her first name, but she didn't want to use her real last name. Neither did she want one of those silly names some adult actors used, like Anita Dick or Ben Dover. The brothers claimed to have come up with the surname "Chambers." Marilyn claimed she suggested the name Fiona Chambers after a beautiful girl she admired back in Connecticut.[37] Somehow, Fiona seemed unsuitable, but Chambers had a nice ring. It was euphemistic enough but not garish. Regardless of who originated the name, it was agreed she would be billed as "Marilyn Chambers."

BEHIND THE GREEN DOOR

Marilyn relaxes in Cannes, France, where *Green Door* was screened to rave reviews at the prestigious Cannes Film Festival in 1973. *Jerry Bauer.*

Both Marilyn and Linda Lovelace used their real first names. It marked the first time an adult star had an identity. Both women freely gave their given names in the press. (Lovelace's real surname was Boreman.) Never before in American popular culture had actors become famous for appearing in adult films and using their actual names.

Green Door opened with great fanfare in August 1972 at the O'Farrell Theatre. As with the film production, no expense was spared on the premiere. Invitations were printed on the highest-quality bond paper and mailed to famous and infamous Bay Area politicians, journalists, artists, writers, and scene-makers. Klieg lights and a red carpet were placed outside the theater. A local television reporter stood under the marquee and explained to viewers the goings-on. "Marilyn Chambers, the star of the film, arrived just moments ago in a stretch limo," he announced. "And it's no stretch of the imagination to say she left the crowd wanting to see more, which they undoubtedly will."[38]

The brothers, dressed in tuxedos, welcomed nearly 200 guests inside the theater. Servers passed around trays of champagne. Plenty of marijuana was on hand, and some guests briefly disappeared into the restrooms to snort cocaine.

PURE   *The Sexual Revolutions of Marilyn Chambers*

A couple had sex in one of the aisles while they waited for the film to begin.

The film was supposed to start promptly at 9:00PM. It still hadn't started by 10:00PM, but none of the guests seemed to notice or mind. Upstairs, Vince Stanich, the projectionist and longtime crewmember of the Mitchells, was in a panic. The film was still at the lab.

"They're going crazy at the lab, trying to add things at the last minute to the soundtrack," Stanich said. "Every time I call, they say, 'Don't worry, the film is on the way.' But the film ain't here, and it ain't gettin' any earlier."[39]

Stanich quickly loaded it into the projector from the 'Reel No. 1' canister when the film finally arrived. Someone flicked the lights off and on, and the audience gathered in the theater to take their seats. McDonald, who never liked watching himself on screen, stayed in the lobby, nervous as hell. Approximately seventy minutes later, the film ended, and the audience poured into the lobby. Everyone congratulated McDonald. "You were great!" "Fabulous!" "It didn't make sense, but I loved every second!" He was confused. Why didn't it make any sense? The usher explained that Stanich was rushing to load the film into the projector; he showed the reels out of sequence. It didn't matter. The audience loved it.

Because of the porno chic fad and the public's demand for and fascination with artistic pornographic films, for a short time, venerable Hollywood publications like *The Hollywood Reporter* and *Variety* reviewed these films; major newspapers did, too. John L. Wasserman, a critic for the *San Francisco Chronicle*, wrote that the film was 'rather feeble in the story department, mediocre of dialogue and downright pathetic in the recording of human voices. But in terms of lighting, photography, technical experimentation, and erotic content, it stands pretty much alone.'[40]

Reviews of *Green Door* and other X-rated films of the era reflected the disdain and condescension of critics. For example, the *Chronicle* rattled off a list of sexual acts featured in the movie. Still, it made a point that it avoided 'the likes of bestiality, necrophilia, sodomy, child molestation and other aberrations practiced by perverts, weirdos, maniacs, and your neighbor.'

But credit was given where it was due, and *Green Door* was a most unusual film that tried hard to be aesthetically original and inspired. 'The highly effective slow-motion footage, the hypnotic soundtrack, the process shots, and the bow-to-Fellini grotesqueries are all standard in the literature,' Wasserman wrote. 'But they are used, and used effectively, and that has not been done before in this persecuted little orphan of the film world. [It provides] a pervasive element of weirdness that is reminiscent of no less than [Luchino] Visconti's *The Damned*.' The *Chronicle* had little to say about Marilyn in its initial review—'[she] brings

BEHIND THE GREEN DOOR

a fine body and extraordinary commitment to her work'—but they would soon give her, and the film, much more ink.[41]

Both *Variety* and *Chicago Sun-Times* film critic Roger Ebert made similar remarks in their original reviews. 'Unlike the crones who used to populate pornos, Chambers may be remembered as the fresh-faced 'innocent' in *Together*. In that one, she was bare a lot but never went all the way. In this, she does everything quite realistically. Unfortunately, she never has enough to say to judge whether she qualifies as an actress,' wrote *Variety*.[42] Ebert was nonplussed about viewing *Behind the Green Door*, especially after seeing *The Devil in Miss Jones*, which he considered the most erotic of the fashionable adult films to date.

'It doesn't work even though it has high-quality camera work, imaginative use of music and visual effects, and Marilyn Chambers,' he wrote. 'She is the most beautiful porno actress yet. And there's no denying that in the movie's trapeze scene, she qualifies as the busiest actress in porno history. But the movie doesn't succeed in overcoming its explicit sexual content. It gives us too many close-ups without context; too many joyless couplings without dramatic meaning. Pretty as she is, Miss Chambers gives no clue in the movie as to whether she can act.'[43]

One of the film's more high-profile reviews was from Arthur Knight, a critic for the serious-minded *Saturday Review*.

'In San Francisco, probably the most permissive city in the United States at this moment, customers are currently flocking to the O'Farrell for *(Behind) the Green Door* [sic], a film produced by that city's venturesome Mitchell brothers,' he wrote. 'The Mitchells have gone all out in this episode. The girl, lulled by six girls in nun's attire, is mated with a strapping Negro. She performs multiple sex [acts] with athletes suspended from trapezes, meanwhile inspiring the onlookers to do likewise. It is sex as ritual, sex as fantasy—sex as it could be only in the movies.'[44]

The film even attracted the attention of journalist (and later noted molecular biology historian) Horace Freeland Judson, who wrote in *Harper's*, 'An example of how to build a fantasy is *Behind the Green Door*. The idea of this one is that a young woman is kidnapped to be the central figure in a ritual sexual performance before an audience at a secret club. The woman was played by Marilyn Chambers, a cool patrician blond model. The camera dwells as much on her face and [Keyes's] as on their connection; it's evident that Miss Chambers works for her orgasm and that she gets it.'[45]

The trapeze scene, Judson noted, was too awkward to be pleasing, but meanwhile, below them, the orgy has exfoliated into wall-to-wall flesh. The variety of people is a welcome change: beautiful people, young people, thin people, old people, homosexual and lesbian people, ugly people, perfectly ordinary people in several colors, a bald little man whom we repeatedly see nibbling at a woman's right nipple, the enormous fat lady whom we glimpse doing obscure but evidently pleasing things in the middle distance whenever the camera pans past her, every imaginable act being performed in multiple versions—except, I was interested to note, no anal intercourse. The orgy is the culmination of the film. It has been directed with vivid and amusing imagination.[46]

Judson saw something in *Green Door* that no other critic captured. He perfectly encapsulated the essence of San Francisco in the seventies: the celebration and normality of the diversity and lovingness of humankind. Judson viewed the film through the Mitchell brothers' lens. He also described the potential of adult films of the era. If filmmakers retained a 'vivid and amusing imagination,' the porno-chic period might have been more than a fad. Al Goldstein, co-founder and editor of *Screw*—a hardcore, influential, New York-based weekly alternative newspaper— was usually a man of Rabelaisian language and demeanor. Never one to shy away from blatant misogyny, he actually found the fantasy of *Green Door* off-putting.

'Even my sexist perversities don't encompass this deviant line of misguided sexuality,' he wrote in *Screw*. 'The inertia and the slowness of the film and the fat, ugly grotesques were repugnant aesthetically and sexually. *Green Door* is more in the line of anarchy than eroticism, more like a teenager's fart than a film molded with pride and craftsmanship. So in spite of the ballyhoo for *Green Door*, I must say that it was a bumbled piece of smut.'[47]

Still, he was impressed with the trapeze sequence ('includes print reversals, special optics, slow motion, and Stanley Kubrick-like photographic tricks') and the beauty of the film's leading lady.

'[T]he only reason I would suggest that SCREW readers view this effort is because of Chambers' great body and the optics, which are wondrous to behold,' he wrote.[48]

By the time *Green Door* premiered, the brothers' initial investment of $18,000 ($131,000 today) had ballooned to $60,000 (nearly $437,000 today). In its first year, the film played primarily in three of the Mitchells' Bay Area theaters and a few select theaters nationwide. In the Mitchell-owned theaters, the film played continuously on a loop. After playing for about ten months, the film had grossed approximately two million dollars (a little more than fourteen million dollars today). The brothers recouped their losses. And Marilyn earned some money in residuals.

None of them knew they were about to luck into one of the most profitable and notorious promotional opportunities in film history.

Chapter 5

"99 $^{44}/_{100}$% PURE"

UPON *GREEN DOOR*'S RELEASE, THE most common question Marilyn received from reporters and general passers-by was: "What does your family think?" Her coy response was often, "Think about what?" It was a gentle tease and a chance to deflect from answering it.

"I'll never forget that first day when we actually shot the hardcore footage," Marilyn said. "I walked out onto that stage and thought to myself, 'Oh, God, this is really humiliating. What have I got myself into? What am I doing here? This is a sex film, Marilyn.' It was the stark realization as I was being led on stage that 'Oh, no, my mother's going to see this!'"[1]

She broke the news to her parents soon after *Green Door* premiered. They were horrified.

"I'll never forget the look on their faces when I told them," she said. "Oh my God, Marilyn! You've ruined our image!" her mother told her.

"What image? What do you mean? It's me who did it, not you," she replied.

"Our friends are appalled; that's what I mean!" her mother said. "We keep hearing, 'Oh, you poor things, you're going to have to live with this!'"

Marilyn knew they wouldn't understand. They made it about themselves.

One rumor that filtered back to her was the story of her father's business buddies taking him to see *Green Door* shortly after it opened in New York City without telling him who the star was. He "freaked out," as Marilyn put it.

"I don't know if he walked out, but I heard that he really wasn't ready for it," she said. "I don't know if that story's true, but I could see it happening. I really do think he's seen the films since then, probably alone."[2]

It's unclear if he saw them, but Marilyn likely wanted him to.

"You see, the thing is that [my parents] have always preached to me all my life: Be honest, be honest, be honest," she said. "So, here I am being honest and—

they're afraid of their image, or what their friends will think, or whatever. And this, to me, is just a lie, and it's a contradiction of everything they've tried to teach me."

Even with the spot in *The Owl and the Pussycat*, Marilyn's success was met with a lukewarm response from her parents. What she was doing was not reliable work, they told her. When she was about to move to California by herself, her mother said, "Well, good luck. I've always wanted to do this all my life. So, I'm glad you can do it."[3] It was a typically tepid response, supportive on the surface but revealing her mother's own thwarted ambitions. When Marilyn struggled in San Francisco, her parents would say, "We told you so. Why don't you come back home where you belong and start college?"

Marilyn was convinced that nothing she did would ever meet their approval. She would never receive the warmth, love, and affection she expected or needed. So she became determined to defy them. She resented their hypocrisy. Although they had instilled in her a sense of authenticity and honesty, when she set out to pursue her dreams, they tried to dissuade her, often in brutal terms, or worried that she ruined *their* image. That was one of the reasons she decided to move to San Francisco, marry Doug, and do *Green Door*.

When asked if her parents were involved with her career, she replied tartly, "I try to keep them out of it entirely. They're very straight. My father is the president of a company. He's very paranoid on account of that. He's afraid to be scandalized. So, I changed my name. 'Marilyn Chambers' is my screen name. That much I can do for them. But they're not happy with what I'm doing. They don't agree with it at all. They really think it's outrageous. They'd like to pretend that they don't know, but it's kinda hard with all the publicity."[4]

Marilyn said of her siblings' reactions, '[They're] of another generation, and that's the generation that reads *Playboy* but isn't ready to see their baby sister having intercourse or giving head on the silver screen. So I don't think they will ever quite understand.'[5]

Soon after Marilyn completed *Green Door*, Jann visited her sister in California. "She said, 'So I did this little film,'" Jann recalled.

When Marilyn explained what type of film she did, Jann was appalled.

"What? You're kidding me! Why would you do that?" she asked her sister.

"I was really kind of upset with her," Jann said. "But she explained to me that she would rather do this of her own free will. She said, 'I'm not ashamed of it. It's my job. This is business—versus the Hollywood casting couch.' And you know what? When she said that to me, I said, 'Okay, I can accept that.' But I was just concerned about her. That's all. You know, health-wise, and what it actually meant. She explained to me in detail—more than I probably wanted to know at the moment—[about] why it wasn't a bad thing."[6]

Bill can't recall any conversations he had with Marilyn about the film or her participation. It's possible they never spoke about it, he said.

During a rather revealing interview in 1973, when asked if she believed either her brother or sister had seen one of her films, Marilyn said that her sister had not, then inexplicably veered into Freudian territory when discussing her brother.

"My brother, I don't know. Maybe," she said. "I've had fantasies about my brother, for God's sake, all my life, about screwing him. If he wasn't my brother, I would have picked him up in a second. But, in actual fact, I don't ever see him. I don't ever talk to him. He's very uncommunicative. But I believe he'd think it was cool. He'd probably think it was far out."[7]

Marilyn's parents refused to acknowledge her new career.

"My mother didn't want to talk about it," Jann recalled. "How do I put this? Talking about Marilyn's career wasn't something we did. I could talk about it with [Marilyn]. I could talk with my brother. But it wasn't something I felt [my parents] wanted me to talk about. If they wanted to talk about it, they would have asked me. That's kind of the way things rolled."[8]

When Jann saw her parents, her mother often asked if Jann had spoken with Marilyn and how she was doing. But there were no questions about "Marilyn Chambers."

"I talked to my parents every week," Jann said. "And they would come out to see us, we'd go back east...and they would come out to the West Coast. At least my mom did, at least once or twice a year. I think it hurt Marilyn sometimes—that [our mother] would always see us and not see her."[9]

WITH *GREEN DOOR* WRAPPED up, and playing in several of the brothers' Bay Area theaters, Jim and Art decided to shoot another feature-length hardcore film starring Marilyn. One day in late 1972, Jim, Art, and Marilyn were at the O'Farrell Theater discussing preparations for their next movie, *Resurrection of Eve*. Then Marilyn casually made an announcement: "Oh! I forgot to tell you guys. A couple of years ago, I shot a photo for the cover of the new Ivory Snow soap box. It's just been released." It was on her mind because she had recently received the second part of her payment in the mail.

In lesser hands, an announcement like this might have been ignored or not adequately exploited, but the Mitchells were skilled marketers. They were well connected with the San Francisco and New York press and realized the potential of a publicity bonanza.

PURE

The Sexual Revolutions of Marilyn Chambers

Meredith Bradford, Art's wife, remembered the night Art came home and excitedly told her about the Ivory Snow box.

"It was manna from heaven," added Liberty Bradford, Art and Meredith's daughter.[10]

"We knew it was big," Art said. "But we didn't want Procter and Gamble to pull out of it immediately. So we all decided the thing to do was wait, like, at least six months to make sure they had the box out everywhere."[11]

But they couldn't wait six months. The film's box office receipts in San Francisco had started to dip, and it was underperforming in New York City, despite $15,000 ($105,000 today) in advertising. The brothers had bills to pay. In April 1973, roughly four months after *Green Door* debuted in New York City, the brothers took the Ivory Snow story to the press, including nationally syndicated columnist Earl Wilson and a reporter at *Playboy*. Everyone turned it down. "They didn't get it," Art said.

Finally, Tony Mancini of the *New York Post* agreed to run the story over the wires. He called Marilyn in California to get a quote. The story ran on May 3, 1973, and the response was explosive. "Mrs. Clean is a Porno Cutie," read the New York *Daily News* headline. "All In a Lather Over That Soap Box," read another. The story appeared in newspapers and television news reports nationwide and even in parts of Europe for the next few days. Even the decorous *New York Times* included a blurb in their "Notes on People" column. The plan worked. It was an avalanche of free publicity. Ticket sales soared.

"They don't fuck [with] that box," Art

said. "That box is their baby. They went through two years of backroom bullshit to finally agree that that was the look they were going for, the young blond mother image."[12]

The executives at Procter & Gamble were deeply embarrassed when they learned of the story.

"A young woman named Marilyn Briggs submitted several photos to us in 1970, and we bought them for $1,000," one P&G official told the *Daily News*. "One of the pictures was used for our Ivory Snow boxes. We have no knowledge of her activities since then. Procter & Gamble has no further statement."[13]

Indeed. While their version wasn't exactly true—Marilyn was selected by P&G executives from hundreds of models and posed for the photo—they admitted that the young woman on the box was the same woman starring in an X-rated film.

Marilyn countered, "There was nothing in my contract with Procter & Gamble that said I couldn't do dirty movies."

Despite the embarrassment, the free publicity boosted sales.

"A lot of people bought the product just to see her," said former P&G CEO Howard Morgens.[14]

With this unexpected publicity boost, and Marilyn's status as a household name, the Mitchells decided to make an intrepid move and enter *Behind the Green Door* into the prestigious Cannes Film Festival. They weren't sure it would be accepted; never before had a hardcore sex film been screened and reviewed at the festival. When it was accepted, the brothers were elated and figured that even if it was poorly reviewed, they could live with the fact that their film had played at Cannes.

The brothers and their wives, and Marilyn and Doug, traveled to France to attend the event. The film was screened out of competition, a common practice at film festivals that allows movies to be shown to an audience during the festival's run without being considered for any awards.

The three couples sat in the theater's balcony at the first showing.

"So here's this movie that, to me, makes no sense whatsoever," recalled Meredith Bradford, Art's wife. "And we're all up in the balcony, the six of us. It's the end, and Art's just going, 'Oh my god, what are they gonna do?' Because it was dead silent. All of a sudden, the audience burst into applause. It was endless. We thought, 'Is this a joke?' We had no idea what to expect. It was incredible."[15]

Pictured left: A beaming Marilyn holds a box of Ivory Snow detergent featuring her face. The contrast of the all-American girl cavorting onscreen in a hardcore sex film caused an international scandal in 1973. *Photographer uncredited.*

PURE
The Sexual Revolutions of Marilyn Chambers

Marilyn told the brothers she could speak a little French. As the ovation continued, Marilyn raised her hand to ask them to be quiet. She delivered a sweet thank-you speech in high school French, which brought even louder cheers.[16] The rest of the screenings were packed, and crowds waited to see this strange American sex film.

An American film critic who attended the screening wrote, 'The high-class porno flick...is, quite simply, about the most genuinely erotic—and well-made—example of the genre ever.'[17]

On their way back to the US from France, they stopped in New York before heading home to San Francisco. In addition to their triumphant appearance at Cannes, they had more news to share. Procter & Gamble had extended Marilyn's contract by ten years and paid her an additional $1,000. The company hoped to keep the contract extension and thank you payment quiet. The Mitchells and Marilyn felt otherwise. They contacted reporters about the news and held a press conference. *Variety* called the whole affair 'the biggest non-criminally angled publicity break for a porno feature in New York.'

The press dubbed Marilyn "The Ivory Snow Girl," and she was everywhere. Once they returned to San Francisco, they held a second press conference for the west coast reporters. During these press conferences, Marilyn was usually the center of attention, often with the Mitchell Brothers holding court in the background wearing t-shirts emblazoned with photos of the Ivory Snow box.

"We all got lucky on Ivory Snow," said Jim, in a whopping understatement.

During one of the press conferences, after Marilyn explained the concept of *Green Door* and the challenge of acting her part, a reporter asked, "It's quite a long way from Ivory Snow, isn't it?"

Marilyn considered the question for a moment and scoffed. "Well, I don't know about that."

"What do you mean?" the reporter asked.

"Well, I'm a clean-cut, wholesome American girl," she said. It was a sly undercutting of the long-held Ivory Snow brand image of wholesomeness and a statement that even the mother on the Ivory Snow box can joyously express her sexuality.

"Do you use Ivory Snow?" another reporter asked.

"No," she said. "It smells like diapers."[18]

The following day, in response to the press conferences, P&G told reporters they were "actively moving ahead to remove the photograph." But Marilyn's box would be in supermarkets for several months as they moved to recall and replace the boxes. P&G had no comment about the contract extension. A new box was redesigned in absolute secrecy and prepped for distribution in February 1974.

"99 ⁴⁴/₁₀₀% PURE"

"The current box is just not consistent with the image we are trying to portray," a company spokesperson told the New York *Daily News*. "But we didn't want to launch a mass recall in these days of paper shortages."[19] However, there was no shortage of paper flowing into the company's coffers. The press conferences made international headlines in print and on television and gave the group a chance to plug not only *Green Door* but the soon-to-be-released *Resurrection of Eve*. One reporter quipped that they should change the latter film's title to *Deep Soap*.[20]

"See, my image is clean, wholesome, all-American, Ivory Snow," Marilyn said. "That's what people want to see; that's their vision of a person maybe they'd like to go to bed with, a sexy person, right? So give it to them; that's what I figure. I'm a very simple person, you know. That's fine with me. I'm kind of straight to a certain extent. I believe in love. I don't think there's too many people that could say I'm disgusting and crude." Speaking of P&G, Marilyn said, "If they were smart, they'd play it up in a good way. They'd sell more Ivory Snow boxes. People who like the film can just buy Ivory Snow and wash with it—wash their souls clean."[21]

A year after it opened, thanks largely to the unexpected publicity bonanza, the film grossed over ten million dollars (more than $67 million today). It would continue to generate revenue for years.

ON JUNE 21, 1973, nearly a month after *Green Door* screened at Cannes, the Supreme Court handed down a landmark ruling in *Miller v. California* that offered 'a new set of guidelines on obscenity that will enable states to ban books, magazines, plays, and motion pictures that are offensive to local standards, even if they might be acceptable elsewhere,' wrote *The New York Times* in a front-page news story about the ruling.[22]

Chief Justice Warren E. Burger, writing for the majority, held that the First Amendment of the United States Constitution did not protect obscene material. The Court developed three guidelines for determining if something is obscene, which became known as the Miller test:

(a) whether "the average person, applying contemporary community standards" would find that the work, taken as a whole, appeals to the prurient interest;
(b) whether the work depicts or describes, in a patently offensive way, sexual conduct specifically defined by the applicable state law; and
(c) whether the work, taken as a whole, lacks serious literary, artistic, political, or scientific value.[23]

PURE *The Sexual Revolutions of Marilyn Chambers*

The New York Times explained, 'States have the right to assume, in the absence of clear proof, that there is a causal connection between pornographic material and crime and other antisocial behavior. There is no constitutional doctrine of privacy that protects the display of obscene material in public places, and governmental limits on this sort of display do not involve 'thought control.''

The dissenting judges saw this as a challenge to free speech and freedom of the press. They 'stressed the vagueness of any definitions based on local community views and predicted that citizens would be unable in the future to know whether they were running a risk of violating the law.'[24]

It wasn't just X-rated films like *Green Door* and *Deep Throat* that were the primary targets. Within days of the decision, the Supreme Court of Georgia affirmed a jury conviction under local obscenity law for theater owner Billy Jenkins, who showed the 1971 film *Carnal Knowledge* at a theater in Albany, Georgia.[25] The film, directed by Mike Nichols and starring Jack Nicholson and Art Garfunkel, was a critically-acclaimed major Hollywood production that featured a nude Ann-Margret but showed no explicit sex whatsoever and was a box-office success. Ann-Margret was even nominated for an Academy Award for the role.

Canadian film magazine *TAKE ONE* wrote: 'The decision cast a pall over the entire film production-distribution-exhibition (as well as the literary) scene. Here was a distinguished motion picture—lauded by eminent critics—its female lead (Ann-Margret) nominated for an Academy Award—clearly a film serious in intent—restrained in the treatment of its sexual theme—condemned by a know-nothing jury and a split Appellate Court.'[26]

As *The New York Times* wrote, the Supreme Court's ruling, 'taken at face value, threatens to make it difficult if not impossible for producers and distributors of national magazines and motion pictures to have any advance assurance that their products will not subject them to criminal penalties in one locality although they are unobjectionable in another.'[27]

It was not the first time the Supreme Court ruled on obscenity, nor was it the first time the federal government targeted pornography specifically. In the 1969 case *Stanley v. George*, the Supreme Court ruled on the right to privacy, maintaining that people could view and read items considered obscene or pornographic in the privacy of their homes.[28] The ruling limited the government's power to police the private possession of obscene materials.

In response to the court's 1969 decision, the President's Commission on Obscenity and Pornography, established in 1967 by President Lyndon B. Johnson, and funded by the United States Congress, examined the ruling in *Stanley v. George* to determine whether or not there were 'Constitutional and definitional

78

problems related to obscenity controls; with a particular focus on 'the effects of such material, particularly on youth, and their relationship to crime and other antisocial conduct.'

Completed and presented in 1970, the report 'found that obscenity and pornography were not important social problems, that there was no evidence that exposure to such material was harmful to individuals, and that current legal and policy initiatives were more likely to create problems than solve them.'[29]

Congress widely rejected these findings. President Nixon, whose administration assumed control in January 1969, issued a statement on October 24, 1970, that 'totally' rejected the report. It read, in part:

> So long as I am in the White House, there will be no relaxation of the national effort to control and eliminate smut from our national life. Pornography can corrupt a society and a civilization. The people's elected representatives have the right and obligation to prevent that corruption...Smut should not be simply contained at its present level; it should be outlawed in every State in the Union. And the legislatures and courts at every level of American government should act in unison to achieve that goal...pornography is to freedom of expression what anarchy is to liberty.[30]

The *Miller v. California* decision gave states greater freedom in prosecuting alleged purveyors of "obscene" material because a majority of the Court had agreed on a definition of "obscenity." Hundreds of "obscenity" prosecutions went forward after the ruling. The Supreme Court, which had reviewed many "obscenity" convictions (over sixty appeared on the Court's docket for the 1971–72 term, pre-*Miller*) now denied reviews of these state actions.

A companion case, *Paris Adult Theatre I v. Slaton*, gave states greater leeway to shut down adult movie houses. Almost immediately, theater owners across the country showing X-rated films were arrested by local authorities and had "obscene" materials confiscated. *Green Door*, *Deep Throat*, and *The Devil in Miss Jones* drew the lion's share of local and federal government crackdowns, but they were hardly the only adult films being made then. At a raid of a theater in Caldwell, New Jersey, in 1973, movies rated X—but only believed to be pornographic— were taken as well. One was Andy Warhol's *Flesh*, which contained numerous scenes of a nude Joe Dallesandro but no sex acts. The distinction also led to the popularization of categorizing films as "hardcore" or "softcore."

The Mitchells were busy editing *Resurrection of Eve* when the *Miller v. California* ruling was handed down. They called it "totally insane" and vowed to fight it. During an August 1973 television interview, a local reporter asked Marilyn whether the legislation would affect future films. "We really can't get too excited about it," she said. "More people are going to see [erotic films], for some reason, and more people are making them. It's supply and demand."

"You are an artist, after all," the reporter continued.

"Oh, yeah," she replied with a hint of uncertainty.

"And this is a whole genre of films," the reporter said. "What is your message as an artist?"

"Well," she started, her eyes looking up as if searching for a response, "I think that this society today is becoming a lot more honest and liberated within themselves as people. And, uh, I think that being honest, as myself, to my audience, as an actress, is the main thing that I'm trying to be—is just myself. Because I enjoy acting, and I like to please an audience."

"Do you feel the films you're making are, in a way, political?" the reporter asked.

"Oh, definitely!" Marilyn said. "Because this is what's happening in our country today. The sexual revolution is here to stay. And it's about time people became more aware of themselves."

"Do you think your art can be appreciated only by big city sophisticates, or is it an art of the people?"

"It's an art of the people," she said. "If you have a small town...I don't think there's anything [the authorities] can do about obscenity and have things taken out of their town. Because if they did, they would have a lot of very famous novels [and] very excellent movies taken out, and [the people] wouldn't like that, I don't think. And they would fight to get it back."

"You really think so?" the reporter asked incredulously. "Why?"

"I just think people are a lot smarter than that," she said. "I give people a lot more credit than the government gives us as far as our feelings and what we believe in. And I think that people are going to speak their mind, and I think they're going to do what they have been doing all along."

"Which is?"

"Going to the movies they would like to see and read the books they would like to [read]," Marilyn said. "It's still going to be here; it might go underground again... But I'm not going to change my way, in any way, for the Supreme Court ruling."[31]

The Supreme Court rulings had the opposite effect on business for X-rated films.

"People are flocking to see erotic films because they're afraid the Supreme Court is going to ban them eventually," Marilyn said. "It seems like whenever *Deep Throat*, *Green Door*, and *The Devil in Miss Jones* go to court, ticket sales go up. If the court rules them not obscene, ticket sales go down because they're no longer curiosities."

New York Times columnist Robert Berkvist, disputing the paper's editorial on the subject, found the ruling ludicrous.

'It's hard to take the Supreme Court's obscenity ruling seriously in this city, where peeps jostle pornographic bookshops and every other movie house seems to be showing films with names like 'Lecher', 'XXX Adult Hits' and 'Selected Male Shorts'. Georgina Spelvin, star of the hugely popular porn epic, 'The Devil in Miss Jones', dominates more movie marquees than Garbo ever did.'[32]

Gerard Damiano, director of *Deep Throat* and *Miss Jones*, commented to Berkvist: 'The lowest echelon is thriving. This is a boon to them because restrictive laws make pornography glamorous, and these [filmmakers] are in a position to go underground. They've no traceable books, no nothing. The same thing happened during Prohibition when organized crime became very successful in the liquor business. Some things, like morality, can't be legislated. If you want pornography to die, just leave it alone, and it'll die a natural death.'[33]

By the time of the Supreme Court ruling, the Mitchell brothers had won some forty obscenity cases, all on the grounds of First Amendment rights. They had been fighting such cases since their theater opened in 1969, and they had lawyers they could trust. And with two hit films on their hands, they were raking in millions at the box office to cover lawyer fees. Still, when the ruling was handed down, Jim admitted to encountering "quite a bit of pressure" to keep their films in theaters without having the local authorities continually confiscating them. The brothers' plan, he said, was "to try to stay in business and make good sex movies, not prurient ones. We don't think any judge should tell people what to see. We think we have the right, under the First Amendment, to make movies and distribute them, and we're willing to go to jail on that. Our movies aren't obscene. Sex is the first big lie we all get told and taught. Judges feel guilty about sex. We don't."[34]

Making hardcore sex films was technically illegal. The only way a sex act could be inserted into a movie was if the film was packaged and marketed as educational, as filmmaker Alex De Renzy had done with *Pornography in Denmark* in 1970. But this was no guarantee a court of law wouldn't rule it obscene. Just as underworld crime bosses saw an opportunity to get rich during Prohibition, the mob ran a similar operation for hardcore porn. They would provide loans to filmmakers in exchange for a share of the profits. Damiano scored such a loan to make *Deep Throat*.

The publicity around pornographic films and the Supreme Court's ruling also brought unwanted attention from the feds. On six occasions, police in Hayward,

California, raided the Hayward Theatre, seized copies of *Green Door*, and arrested theater employees. A federal civil lawsuit was filed on behalf of the theater owners.

Marilyn and the Mitchells held a press conference on June 6, 1973, to discuss the recent raids on the Hayward theaters. "I will go all the way—testifying in court or whatever else is necessary so that my film can be shown in Hayward," Marilyn read from a statement. "I have a First Amendment right to my freedom of expression. My acting is very important to me. My film has never been found to be obscene by any court in the United States or anywhere else in the world. We just recently showed it at Cannes. The chief of police, his officers, or the District Attorney in Hayward are not the judges of my work. Why don't they want *Behind the Green Door* shown? Are they afraid of honesty [in] sexual matters? Would that destroy their community? One police officer in the raid of the theater in Hayward said it was 'his city.' I say it is time for Hayward to join the twentieth century and hope that my film, *Behind the Green Door*, will help it do so. There are lots of people there who want to see it."[35]

Hayward wasn't the only place *Green Door* was confiscated. The brothers were tried for obscenity in Los Angeles County District Court. When the jury found *Green Door* not to be obscene, the judge became enraged and lectured the jurors: "This movie would violate the community standards of Sodom and Gomorrah!"[36]

Those in favor of or against the obscenity ruling were often divided along generational lines. During a radio show in Kansas City to promote *Green Door*, an irate older man called in to castigate Marilyn.

"How could you say that oral sex was good?" he asked. "It's disgusting! It's dirty! My children are sitting here listening! We used to be a great fan of this disk jockey, and we think that you are sick."

Marilyn asked the man if he had ever tried oral sex. He said he hadn't. He and his wife had been married for fifty years and wouldn't dream of it. Marilyn told him he should try it because he didn't know what he was missing. She felt lucky because she got to try a host of sexual experiences.

"What is your husband going to think if you get knocked up by somebody in the cast?" he asked.

"Haven't you ever heard of birth control?" she replied.

"I mean, really, this guy was not hip," Marilyn told a reporter later when she recounted the story. "There are a lot of people in America like that. This kind of film is going to totally blow their mind out! It might snap them out and make it a reality for them. So many couples come to see *The Green Door*; it's amazing! I've heard a lot of people say, 'God, we went home, and we hadn't screwed for so long, and jeez, it was out of sight!'"

"99 ⁴⁴/₁₀₀% PURE"

But the older generation didn't always express repulsion. During a radio interview in Johnson County, Kansas City, one lady phoned in from a bridge party she was holding to tell Marilyn that not only was she going to drag her husband—which wouldn't be too tricky—but she was going to insist all her bridge partners and lady friends see the film.[37]

TO CAPITALIZE ON MARILYN'S newfound fame, the producers of *Together*, the 1971 softcore film in which Marilyn appeared nude, rushed the movie back into theaters. Only this time, it was billed as '*Together* starring Marilyn Chambers.' With a new publicity campaign using stills taken during the film's production, and even *Green Door* photos, Marilyn's innocent-looking, smiling face featured prominently on ads and posters. Hallmark Releasing owned the rights to the film, and since Marilyn didn't own a percentage and had already posed for photos during film production, there was nothing she or the Mitchell brothers could do to stop its release or the use of her name. It played in theaters nationwide for the remainder of 1973 and into the next year. Someone else made money from the Marilyn Chambers name. It was a scenario that would follow her for the rest of her life.

"*BEHIND THE GREEN DOOR* is kind of a male-chauvinist-pig fantasy," Marilyn said. "In a way, I thought it was degrading, but in another way, I enjoyed it."[38] On the other hand, *Resurrection of Eve* told a story from a woman's point of view. The film had its world premiere in San Francisco at the O'Farrell Theatre on September 13, 1973. Other premieres took place in New York and Los Angeles a few weeks later. The plot for the film was as complicated as *Green Door*'s story was simple. It has enough material for five different movies. Unlike in *Green Door*, Marilyn had dialogue in *Eve*. As one skin magazine put it: "After Garbo: Chambers Talks!"

The script was an original by Art Mitchell and Jon Fontana. The film opens with a woman named Eve (Mimi Morgan) kneeling on the sands of a beach and staring aimlessly into the distance. She's reminiscing about meeting a man called Frank Paradise (Matthew Armon), a radio DJ. She then recalls when she was twelve years old and was molested by a man her mother brought home. (This is shown as a flashback; the woman playing Eve in this scene is a different actress with her hair in pigtails to give the illusion she's younger.)

We see the adult Eve's relationship with Frank blossom. He tries to convince her to join a swingers' party, but she declines. Despite being interested in swinging, Frank has a jealous streak. When Eve is introduced to a boxer (Johnnie Keyes), Frank believes Eve is attracted to him and even fantasizes about Eve with Keyes. They argue, and Eve angrily leaves their home and drives away furiously. She's seriously injured in a car accident, with most of the damage to her face. Doctors save her, but they must perform extensive plastic surgery and give her a brand new face.

The surgery is a success, and we have a brand new Eve, played by Marilyn. She and Frank rekindle their romance, and he again suggests they join a swingers' party. Eve begrudgingly agrees to go to one but leaves almost immediately because she's sickened by it. Frank suggests they try another one, and she relents. This time, she's an active participant, and she enjoys it. They continue to attend group sex parties, but the roles begin to reverse: Eve feels liberated by the experience, but Frank starts to feel uncomfortable. She insists they go to another. At the final orgy, Frank watches Eve have sex with Keyes. He demands they leave and forget the group scene. But it's too late. Eve's resurrection is complete, and she ends her relationship with Frank.

Eve took approximately two months to film, twice as long as *Green Door*, and more than twice the footage was shot.[39] It was also the first time the Mitchells used thirty-five millimeter film. *Green Door* was shot on sixteen-millimeter film and blown up to thirty-five.

The final orgy scene was filmed two doors from the O'Farrell Theater at the famed Great American Music Hall. The Mitchell brothers, always looking for a publicity angle, invited the press to the filming of the orgy. The scene was chaotic, with over twenty actors, including Marilyn and Keyes, either engaged in various sex acts or relaxing on set. A bunch of extras in non-sex roles needed for atmosphere shots sat around tables waiting their turn; the crew and camera operators set up shots and adjusted lighting; various staff members flitted about wrangling extras or delivering messages to the crew. Astonished members of the press took all of this in. Reporters and photographers from *Playboy*, *Oui*, *Penthouse*, *Saturday Review*, *Adam Film World*, and CBS were on set. ABC sent an entire film crew because they were shooting a documentary on making a porno movie. Photographers got in the way of other photographers and even in the way of the cinematographers.

By any subjective standards, *Eve* is terrible, but it's great fun to watch. Technically, it shows the Mitchells' skills improved after *Green Door*. The lighting and camerawork are better, there are genuine moments of intended comedy, and a few of the sex scenes are genuinely erotic. However, the acting is uneven

"99 ⁴⁴/₁₀₀% PURE"

"Resurrection of Eve"

starring MARILYN CHAMBERS, MIMI MORGAN, and MATTHEW ARMON / Music by Richard Wynkoop

Resurrection of Eve, the Mitchell Brothers' follow-up to *Green Door*, benefitted at the box office from the notoriety of the Ivory Snow controversy. *Mitchell Brothers Film Group.*

and often laughably bad. Leading man Armon, a legitimate Shakespearean actor, is particularly wretched. But, like *Green Door*, the brothers took the film's production quite seriously.

"It's more story than we have ever done before...much more even than *Green Door*," Art said. "There's sex in the film, plenty of it, but we hope there's not a single sexual scene that shouldn't be there, that's excess, or that's boring, or that's just there to show some fucking. That's where we're at."[40]

Marilyn did her best, but the script needed to be less complex. The direction needed to be smoother and more cohesive. Because Art directed half the film, and cameraman Fontana directed the other half, the film is disjointed. The brothers did, however, invest in an original musical score, and the rock and blues creations of Richard Wynkoop rank as some of the best music in an X-rated movie.

Marilyn said she would have rather played Eve before and after her "resurrection." In fact, she should have played all three iterations of Eve. It would have given her more screen time and a chance to stretch her acting ability.

'My personal feeling is that the Mitchell brothers tried to cram too much into one film,' she considered in *My Story*. 'I think they write mainly for their own fantasies, what turns them on, what happened to a friend of theirs, drawing things only from their little family, the in-jokes that the audience really doesn't understand or care about. They're the opposite of someone like Gerry Damiano, whose movies are really very serious and require some heavy thinking on the part of the audience. I think both have their extremes, though, and I prefer something in the middle, like *Green Door*.'[41]

Still, Marilyn appreciated that the storyline was from a woman's point of view, something highly unusual for adult films of the period. '[Eve] comes off the winner in the end,' Marilyn noted. 'I've talked to a lot of men who didn't like the film because of that; their egos felt threatened. Men's egos, my God! They're so crazy, so fucked up! Why do they feel so threatened all the time? I really don't understand it. *Eve* shows that women have sexual feelings, too; they're not plastic. Women have sexual feelings that turn them on.'[42]

Art was particularly proud of *Eve*.

"That film can stand up to any criticism you'd want to me," he said. "It's a very personal film, and even I like it a lot. Plus, it gave Marilyn a chance to act. I thought it showed a lot of class not to have her say anything in *Green Door*. Since she was so beautiful and what was happening to her, just the amount of sex, was so powerful. Films should be bigger than life, and she really was. But *Eve* was much better. [T]he thing with *Eve* is that being beautiful in our society means power, real power. Marilyn just somehow sweeps people off their feet because she *looks* a certain way. That's really a strange phenomenon, but it's been with us forever. What the film was trying to show is how people can get their way just because of their looks, and most reviews I've read never pick up on that."[43]

Perhaps that's because Mimi Morgan, the actress who played Eve before her "resurrection," wasn't unattractive.

Although the box office take didn't match *Green Door*, the nationwide pornography controversy ensured ticket sales. Marilyn's face appeared on billboards in New York's Times Square, off Highway 101 in San Francisco, and on top of taxi cabs in Los Angeles. The Mitchells placed advertisements in newspapers nationwide and in Hollywood trade publications like *The Hollywood Reporter* and *Variety*, often touting *Eve* and *Green Door* as the 'double-bill of the year.' They even offered group rates and student and senior citizen discounts to see the films at their Bay Area theaters.[44]

Screw called *Eve* 'one of the all-time great sex films. It has a strong script, good acting, excellent photography, and tons of sex. Along the way, Miss Chambers demonstrates her remarkable talent for every form of fucking and sucking.'[45] ABC-TV commented, "Marilyn Chambers is the first hardcore film star who has radiated the old fashioned Hollywood style glamour."[46]

"I DON'T THINK THE movie offended me," Doug told *Interview* magazine about *Green Door*. "I didn't feel jealous because I didn't really have anything to be jealous about. Actually, it helped me work the jealousy thing out. We have a very stable sexual life which is the foundation for the rest of our life. We go out and enjoy ourselves in other ways too. The other part of our life couldn't exist without sex and vice versa."[47]

Jealous or not, the onslaught of publicity and the increased demands on Marilyn's schedule put a strain on her marriage. Doug was always a bit lazy, but now with Marilyn making enough money for the both of them—enough to enable them to move out of their shared apartment in San Francisco and into a small house in suburban Walnut Creek—he seemed more content than ever not to do anything. Yet, nearly a year after their marriage, Marilyn tried to downplay any turmoil in their relationship. "Oh, we had our ups and downs about it," she told one reporter. "Listen, I wouldn't do explicit sex if I didn't have him." Perplexed, the reporter asked her to explain.

"He's my moral support," she continued. "If I was on my own and screwing in pictures, I'd get discouraged and wouldn't want to come home. But when you're in love, you want to come home. During [the production of *Green Door*], we learned an awful lot about each other, and we became better lovers. It helped our marriage incredibly. In the beginning, of course, he wasn't anxious for me to have all that sex with different men, and he still has that attitude to an extent. That's great. I want to keep it that way. I don't want to lose him!"[48]

SHE MIGHT HAVE BEEN a sex symbol to many men and some women, but the sexism and misogyny Marilyn faced, even within the adult industry, was astonishing. When the Ivory Snow story was first revealed in newspapers, many reporters and editors felt it necessary to include her bust, waist, and hip measurements. Her interviews and profiles were almost always by men. Of the hundreds of interviews she did in 1973 alone, only one woman interviewed her.

Al Goldstein baited her in her first interview with *Screw* magazine in November 1973.

"You have been called a bitch by your husband," he said. "We want our SCREW readers to know that you can be a bit of a cunt. What is it that gives you this reputation?"

"I guess I can be a little bossy," she replied. "Men are incredible. I have to be really careful about what I say to them because I am a bitch, and I can be really nasty."[49]

The women's liberation movement was firmly established in the US when *Deep Throat* and *Behind the Green Door* became part of the public consciousness. While radical feminist groups like Women Against Pornography were not formally established until the mid seventies, there were always factions of feminists who specifically targeted pornography and the exploitation of women.

Susan Brownmiller, who became involved with the women's liberation movement in 1968, and fellow feminist supporter Sally Kempton, appeared alongside *Playboy* founder Hugh Hefner on *The Dick Cavett Show* in 1970. When Cavett asks Brownmiller what men are doing wrong, she replies, "They oppress us. They won't let us be. And Hugh Hefner is my enemy. Hugh Hefner has built an empire on oppressing women."

"I'm more in sympathy with the girls than they realize—" Hefner started to say before Brownmiller corrected him: "We're women. I'm thirty-five."

"I use 'girls' to describe women of all ages," Hefner said.

"You should stop," Kempton and Brownmiller replied simultaneously.

The confrontation culminated when Brownmiller turned to Hefner and said, "The role that you have selected for women is degrading to women because you choose to see women as sex objects, not as human beings. We're not bunnies;

we're not rabbits; we're human beings. The day you're willing to come out here with a cottontail attached to your rear end—" The audience burst into applause. Hefner said nothing and continued to light his trademark pipe. His expression seemed to imply annoyance and a realization that Brownmiller's point was correct.[50]

At the same time, some contemporaries of Marilyn's, such as Georgina Spelvin, Candida Royalle, Annie Sprinkle, Gloria Leonard, and Sharon Mitchell, declared they had willingly entered the adult film industry and considered themselves to be the real feminists.

"I was very angry about the lack of support from the feminist groups," said Royalle, who became the first female star to establish a production company making adult films specifically for women. "Because I considered myself a feminist, way back in the second wave and all of that. And I thought what I was doing was very important. That if women didn't create our own sexual materials and images, and ideas, that men would continue to do it for us. And I felt that pornography was not going to go away. And to try to make it illegal and censor it just pushes it further underground and makes the working conditions even worse for the people in them."[51; 52]

Spelvin, star of *The Devil in Miss Jones*, insisted that the sex in X-rated films was 'exciting, exhausting, energizing and fun, and self-satisfying, enabling her to claim, as she puts it, the 'Feministic Feeling of Empowerment."[53]

Sharon Mitchell, who made her first adult film in 1975, added: "I got to be an actress. I got to be nude. It was the perfect way to say 'fuck you' to the Catholic Church and my family at the same time and get revenge. It was ideal. I remember I had to wait a year-and-a-half, two years for my first movie to come out, and I saw my pussy sixteen feet high on the silver screen, and I thought, 'That's mine! That's wonderful!'"[54]

Marilyn was a bit more complicated.

"Women want to be equal," she said shortly before the release of *Eve*. "They don't want to be pushed around by men and treated like creatures of a lower order." Of the women in her industry—specifically, herself, Linda Lovelace, and Georgina Spelvin—she said, "We've assumed the roles of leaders in the area of sex films. We're bringing forth this concept of sex in films as an honest approach to life."[55]

However, she often said, "I'm not into feminism; I'm into being feminine." That comment can be interpreted as a savvy appeal to her primary fan base of straight men, as was her comment, "I think it's every woman's fantasy to be raped by a beautiful man, of course. The Women's League for Something or Other may kill me for saying that, but it's true."

PURE *The Sexual Revolutions of Marilyn Chambers*

Rich Moreland, in his book *Pornography Feminism: As Powerful as She Wants to Be*, writes, 'Women freely enter the business, take control of their sexual image, and often make decent money in the process. Georgina Spelvin and Marilyn Chambers are early examples of these empowered choices. Marilyn Chambers and Georgina Spelvin were feminist-like before any feminist label was applied to pornography's modern era. Marilyn had a liberating sexual attitude that accentuated a control of her career.'[56]

A *Los Angeles Free Press* reporter wrote that Marilyn 'brags about her dependence on men and cheerfully endorses archaic male-female roles in the face of feminist opposite. She's a deeply moral person and insists fidelity is the only way to go in a heterosexual relationship.' The writer noted that Marilyn quickly pointed out that any man was not exploiting her—she was only exploiting herself.

'In her own modest way, Marilyn has managed to exploit today's double standard for pleasure and profit,' continued the *Los Angeles Free Press*. "She has made the unrespectable respectable. More than any other porno star, including the *Deep Throat* lady herself, Marilyn has made fuck-films an acceptable topic of debate in mixed company. Everybody knows Marilyn is 'a high-class chick', and that's justification enough to patronize her films.'[57]

Marilyn's female peers always respected her because she was instrumental in bringing attention to the adult film industry and more than a touch of glamour. She was a pioneer.

"Marilyn was completely capable, but I do think she allowed the men in her life to run the show," Jane Hamilton speculated. Hamilton, who performed under the name Veronica Hart, was a friend of Marilyn's and one of the most successful and respected adult stars of the early eighties. "But, you know, I don't think she looked at [her work] from a feminist point of view. I think she loved being a star. I think she loved being famous. [Because of] who she was, people wanted to be with her. I think she enjoyed all of that. A feminist is not one of the things that comes to mind when I think of Marilyn. But everybody has different ways of doing things. I don't want that to ever sound like a put-down or derogatory because it's sure not. She was completely awesome, and I loved her dearly."[58]

While Marilyn never denigrated the adult film industry, in her later years, she often expressed some regret for being a part of it. She advised anyone interested in becoming a porn star to rethink their decision, or, at the very least, have a backup plan.

"99 ⁴⁴/₁₀₀% PURE"

BY LATE 1973, WITH the tremendous success of *Behind the Green Door*, *Resurrection of Eve*, and the publicity bonanza of Ivory Snow, everything seemed possible for the twenty-one-year-old Marilyn. Magazines and newspapers were touting her as "the Grace Kelly of porno flicks" and "the new Marilyn Monroe."

"The big [Hollywood] companies want me alright," Marilyn said. "But they want to cast me as a sex object. I'm not a total sex object or a dumb blonde. I'm an actress who will participate in sex on the screen if it is called for. It depends totally on the script."[59]

Producers for *Magnum Force*, the sequel to *Dirty Harry*, began filming in San Francisco in April 1973 and contacted the Mitchell Brothers about casting Marilyn in a small part. When she learned she was to play a free-spirited hippie who comes to a violent end, she refused.

"I'd get killed, fall out of seventeen stories, you know, it's just this blood-and-guts, cops-and-robbers stuff," she said. "That really turns me off. Plus, my part was supposed to be some chick that didn't have any clothes on, pretending to go down on this guy. That's a lot of shit. I don't want a part of that. I don't agree with that at all."[60]

One of the more intriguing offers came from Serbian director Dušan Makavejev, whose 1971 political satire *W.R.: Mysteries of the Organism* achieved international acclaim. That film featured simulated sex scenes, and Makavejev envisioned a movie with actual sex scenes starring Marilyn. There were even hints she was being considered for the next James Bond installment, *The Man with the Golden Gun*.

"What kills me is that [the motion picture ratings board] have the nerve to rate a film with sex as an 'X,'" Marilyn said. "A guy could be seen kissing a woman's breast, and it's rated 'X,' but if he cuts it off, the film is rated 'R' or 'P[G].' To me, that's sick."[61]

She had a point. Three of 1972's highest-grossing films included excessive and often bloody violence: *The Godfather*, *The Poseidon Adventure*, and *Deliverance*. The same was true for three of the top five highest-grossing films in 1973: *The Sting*, *The Exorcist*, and *Papillon*. None were rated X. *The Godfather* and *The Sting* were both honored with the Academy Award for best picture in their respective years.

In October 1973, Marilyn was invited to be a guest lecturer at the New School for Social Research in New York's Greenwich Village for their six-session series, Pornography Uncovered, Eroticism Exposed.

"This country has tremendous sexual hangups," Michael C. Luckman, the school's publications director and initiator of the series, told a reporter. "I dare say for most of the people here, it will be the first real confrontation with erotic expression."[62]

The standing-room-only crowd was treated to an erotic puppet show before a group of panelists, including Marilyn, offered their opinions and philosophies on obscenity laws. During the question session, one person asked Marilyn how it was possible to do thirty or forty takes for scenes involving sexual intercourse. Marilyn responded that even four takes of a scene were rare. As a follow-up question, the person asked, "So, how do you go about getting discovered?"

"The way you go about it...Come backstage," she replied with a wink.

Among the 500 guests in attendance were four police officers from the city's Public Morals Division. They said they were off duty.[63]

According to one estimate, Marilyn made at least $25,000 ($147,000 today) annually in residuals from *Green Door*.[64] The Mitchells convinced her to form a corporation, 'putting her in a better position,' *Variety* joked, 'to capitalize on her gross national product.'[65] In interviews, she took every opportunity to remind reporters and, more importantly, the public that she should be taken seriously as an actress.

"Jeez, someday I'd love to meet Ingmar Bergman and do something with him," she said optimistically in 1973.[66] She tossed out other names, primarily European directors with whom she'd like to work, such as François Truffaut.

"I'm in a position now to be able to choose what I want to do," she said. "And if I make the mistake of going and doing something stupid, then I'll blow it. Maybe I'm being naive, I don't know, but if I only settle for something really good, then they'll accept me for the things I do on screen, may it be sex or whatever."[67]

In retrospect, it's heartbreaking. Even though she had a look, the name, and the talent, Marilyn Briggs committed the cardinal sin in Hollywood: she had sex on camera—and she showed no remorse for it. She never set out to become an adult film star. The film was a stepping stone, as she had hoped, but when she became Marilyn Chambers, she sealed her fate in the eyes of Hollywood. She was aware of this and worried about it. She hoped she could overcome it.

"I'm just afraid that my past might restrict the roles I will be offered in the future, that my sex image will go against me," she said.

The Mitchell brothers acted as Marilyn's unofficial managers.

"She's part of the team now," Jim said about Marilyn. "She's not under contract to us or anything, but we've already been getting inquiries from people who want to see her in other films, and we're sort of doing an agent bit for her, just trying to get a good shake for her."[68]

Marilyn adored the brothers and thought of them more as family.

"99 ⁴⁴/₁₀₀% PURE"

"I'm sure there was some of the 'producer falls in love with the star' thing, but I never looked at them like that," she said. "I liked them, but I was never in love with them. I always thought of them as my older brothers. They always protected me from everything."

Meredith, Art's wife, agreed that the brothers' relationship with Marilyn was close and platonic.

"Their private lives intertwined," she recalled. "I'd go back to Cape Cod every summer—that's where my family is—with the kids. And one summer, Doug and Marilyn came, and we put them up in a motel. She went fishing on my father's tuna boat. They were really like close family. She was definitely part of the family for years."[69]

Occasionally, Marilyn babysat for Meredith and Art's daughter, Liberty.

The Mitchell brothers were ready to do another film with Marilyn after *Eve*, but she was restless. Sex films were okay, but the market was flooded with them in late 1973, and she was afraid of being pigeonholed. Legitimate offers were coming in, but they wanted to play up her sex goddess status. She had bigger ambitions and sensed the Mitchells couldn't help her. "They were always talking about some half-assed idea I knew wouldn't come off," Marilyn said. "'Flakes' is a terrible word, but they were, in a cute sort of way."[70]

On the other hand, Linda Lovelace, whom Marilyn considered her chief rival, was on to bigger and better things, at least according to reports. *Variety* wrote in late August 1973 that Lovelace would star in a song-and-dance revue to open in Florida and eventually move to the Tropicana Hotel in Vegas. There were rumors in the gossip columns that she was in rehearsals for a legitimate theater debut with scheduled tryouts in Philadelphia and even a potential Broadway run. That was on top of a $100,000 publishing contract from Pinnacle Books (more than $677,000 today); a $24,000, two-year contract for an advice column in *Oui* magazine (more than $162,000 today); television commercials and an endorsement of a new shampoo called Head; $300,000 for a new motion picture (more than two million dollars today); and a Linda Lovelace adult board game.

Why couldn't Marilyn do that? She was stuck at the Plaza Hotel in New York, doing more promotion for her two films, answering the same questions about Ivory Snow while Lovelace was preparing to hit the Vegas stage. There was even chatter that Sammy Davis, Jr. was fronting some money for the Vegas production.

"Were Linda and I rivals?" Marilyn asked. "Yes, because I felt I had more talent than she did. I was prettier. She had a big scar all the way down her middle. And I knew Chuck Traynor was behind her success."[71]

Marilyn had never met Chuck but had certainly heard of him. He had tried to reach her a few times only recently, but he couldn't get past the Mitchell brothers. He had some ideas for hooking up Lovelace and Marilyn in a project, but the Mitchells weren't interested. Chuck was their competition. Marilyn had two hit movies and was looking for other opportunities. She wasn't interested in another X-rated film with her biggest competitor.

Chuck didn't have the best reputation, but he was said to have masterminded Lovelace's career. He was responsible for all of her lucrative deals, at least to hear him tell it. If he was able to get Lovelace a starring role in a Vegas show, there's no telling what he might be able to do for Marilyn.

So when the phone rang one day, and it was Chuck Traynor—who had somehow managed to track Marilyn down at her hotel—she decided to listen to what he had to say. He was unexpectedly charming and disarming. Just the sound of his voice made her feel comfortable. He sputtered. He had some business ideas he wanted to run by Marilyn. They were projects he was working on for Lovelace. The only problem was she had left him and filed for divorce. She refused to honor any of the contracts Chuck signed on her behalf, claiming they were invalid. But he was still on the hook for them, and the producers wanted a return on their investments.

"Well," he said, "I think you'd be the perfect fit for these projects. I can do for you what I did for Linda. I can turn you into a superstar. Can you meet me in Los Angeles?"

Marilyn didn't even have to consider her decision before blurting out, "I'll be right there." She booked the first available flight from New York to San Francisco. She'd stop at home, grab some things, and tell Doug she would head down to Los Angeles for a brief business trip. She wouldn't have time to tell the Mitchells but let them know later. Nothing was set in concrete, yet she felt the same way when she saw that ad in the *Chronicle* over a year ago. Even though everything was happening so fast, she could tell Chuck was sincere, and from their brief conversation, she liked him. He could bring her career to the next level. She knew it.

"I'm going to be a superstar," she thought.

PURE

The Sexual Revolutions of Marilyn Chambers

Marilyn in an unpublished outtake from *Interview* magazine, 1973. *David Schoen*.

PURE
The Sexual Revolutions of Marilyn Chambers

Backstage at Marilyn's Riverboat cabaret show inside the Empire State Building, New York City, 1974. *Oscar Abolafia*.

PURE
The Sexual Revolutions of Marilyn Chambers

A moment of downtime during the filming of David Cronenberg's *Rabid*, 1977. *Cinepix.*

Marilyn flirts with actor David Morris during *Insatiable*'s infamous pool table scene. *Photographer uncredited/Miracle Films.*

PURE

The Sexual Revolutions of Marilyn Chambers

Marilyn and Chuck, circa 1979. *Photo courtesy of Mark Cox.*

PURE

The Sexual Revolutions of Marilyn Chambers

Marilyn Chambers

Live at the Jolly Trolley Casino

Nude

Starring in
Sex Surrogate

Show times 10 P.M. - 2 A.M.
Friday, Saturday and Sunday
March 16, 17 and 18 Only
$5.50 Includes 2 Free Drinks
Adults Only
Sex Clinic Follows Show

Promotional flyer for *Sex Surrogate*, Marilyn's 1979 one-woman show in Las Vegas. Due to its brief full-frontal nudity, the show was banned. *Photographer and designer uncredited.*

Marilyn Chambers & **LONE STAR** BAR RESTAURANT & DANCE HALL

Invite you to a nite with...

HAYWIRE BAND LAS VEGAS

At Lone Star Bar Restaurant & Bar
Thurs., Fri. 3340 S. Highland 9pm
& Sat.

Marilyn put together a band called Haywire to prepare for her role as a country singer in her film *Up 'n' Coming*. They played several club appearances in Las Vegas in 1982. *Designer uncredited.*

Marilyn did her own singing in the film *Up 'n' Coming*, 1983. *Billy Tinney.*

BOULEVARD THEATRE
at the RAYMOND REVUEBAR
Walkers Court, Brewer Street, London. W1. Tel. 01 437 2661

PAUL RAYMOND presents

Queen of America's Sex Films

MARILYN CHAMBERS

First and Exclusive   **British Appearance**

The Show that
**SHOCKED
Las Vegas!**

'SEX'
Confessions!

Written by Hollywood's
MEL GOLDBERG

**THE
ULTIMATE
EXPRESSION
OF SEXUAL
SENSUALITY**

Star of over 30
Adult Movies
"Behind the Green Door"
"Never a Tender Moment"
"Resurrection of Eve"

Plus

**The Hottest Look
at Sexual
Permissiveness
ever!..**

BANNED BY THE CENSOR

Written and Conceived by
VICTOR SPINETTI

After *Sex Surrogate* was banned in Las Vegas, Marilyn brought the show to Raymond's Revuebar in London, where it was retitled *Sex Confessions*. Barrie James Artists Associates.

Live-on-Stage

TWICE NIGHTLY 8·0 & 10 Mon. to Sat.

PURE

The Sexual Revolutions of Marilyn Chambers

Unpublished outtake from Marilyn's photo spread
in *Easyriders* magazine, 1980. *Billy Tinney.*

PURE
The Sexual Revolutions of Marilyn Chambers

Marilyn poses during the photoshoot for the *Insatiable* poster, 1980. *Tom Keller.*

PURE *The Sexual Revolutions of Marilyn Chambers*

Marilyn embarked on a two-year worldwide tour to promote *Insatiable. Photographer uncredited.*

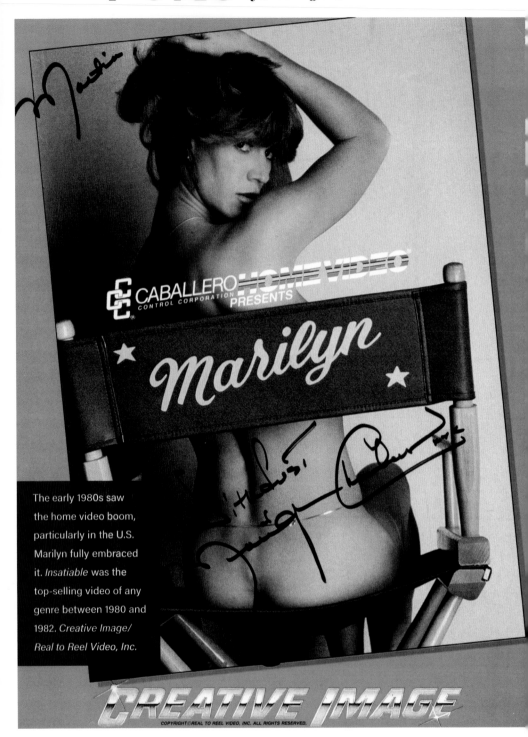

CABALLERO **HOME VIDEO** PRESENTS

Marilyn

The early 1980s saw the home video boom, particularly in the U.S. Marilyn fully embraced it. *Insatiable* was the top-selling video of any genre between 1980 and 1982. *Creative Image/ Real to Reel Video, Inc.*

CREATIVE IMAGE

PURE *The Sexual Revolutions of Marilyn Chambers*

JANUARY 1981 ⓒ 02574 $1.50

HOME VIDEO

MARILYN CHAMBERS
Video Sex Goddess

SEX AND VIDEO:
A SPECIAL REPORT

Molly Haskell on the Past and Present

Isaac Asimov on the Future

X-Rated Acts:
▶ **Videotaping in the Boudoir**
▶ **How the Mob Controls Video Pornography and Piracy**
▶ **How Sex Plays on Cable TV**

Test Report: Magnavox Camera

Home Video magazine declared Marilyn the "Video Sex Goddess" in 1981. She released six bestselling direct-to-video X-rated features in the early to mid-1980s. *Gideon Lewin*

71486 02574

PURE *The Sexual Revolutions of Marilyn Chambers*

Marilyn attends an erotic film awards celebration in the early 1980s. *Michelson/Globe Photos, Inc.*

PURE *The Sexual Revolutions of Marilyn Chambers*

An evocative photo of Marilyn and actress Cody Nicole while filming *Up 'n' Coming*. *Billy Tinney*.

Holding court with the press during the 1989 Cannes Film Festival. *Photographer uncredited.*

Marilyn wrote a sex advice column for *Club* magazine for more than a decade. Her photo was also featured on the magazine's cover and within its pages. *Photographer uncredited.*

PURE *The Sexual Revolutions of Marilyn Chambers*

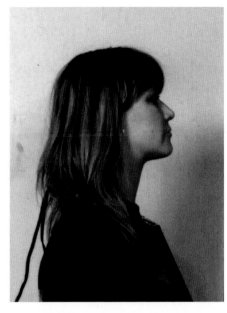

Marilyn's mugshot following her 1985 arrest in Cleveland. She was charged with pandering for prostitution during a live strip show. *City of Cleveland Police Department*.

Marilyn drastically changed her look for her softcore films that aired on cable television in the 1990s. *Photographer uncredited*.

Dark Chambers was the second of three X-rated films Marilyn made for VCA between 1999 and 2001. *VCA Studios Publicity*.

PURE
The Sexual Revolutions of Marilyn Chambers

Marilyn Chambers: Eternally pure. *1973/Photographer uncredited.*

Chapter 6

THE NEW MARILYN CHAMBERS

━━━━━━━━━

"I know it can't last forever. In this business, women get old when they're young, and either you get out, or you freak out like Marilyn Monroe."
— Marilyn Chambers, 1977[1]

CHUCK TRAYNOR WATCHED FROM A limousine as Marilyn stepped off the plane at Los Angeles International Airport. He first noticed her relaxed garb: ripped bell-bottom jeans, a t-shirt, and sandals. He made a mental note. She slouched, and her hair needed to be restyled. He continued to make mental notes about her appearance and demeanor as he watched her walk over to the area where the limousines were parked. He saw Marilyn in the same light as he'd seen Linda Lovelace: she was "a mess."

"I had seen those glossy stills from *Green Door*, the shots of her in the long, sleek black gown and white pearls around her neck, the elegant beautiful young chick," he said. "I expected her to be polished and classy, and all I'd have to do is start a promotion thing because I already had the contacts and friends in Vegas and wherever, and I'd just drop Marilyn in the slots and watch the jackpot money roll out. Boy, did I have another thing coming."[2]

Marilyn got in the wrong limo. Chuck laughed. He called out: "Hey, Marilyn! Over here." He smiled as she tried to determine who was calling her name. Finally, she saw him, apologized to the driver of the other limo, and scurried over to Chuck's, which had been sent by *Playboy* magazine.

"He didn't look at all as I had pictured him," Marilyn said. "I was expecting a real freak with long hair, for some reason, and he turned out to be pretty straight-looking."[3]

The limousine whisked them off to dinner, where they spent the evening talking and planning Marilyn's next career move. Marilyn stayed in L.A. for a week. She wanted to get a contract hammered out quickly. When she and

Marilyn evoked an old-style Hollywood glamour while still maintaining a sex goddess image.
Photographer uncredited.

THE NEW MARILYN CHAMBERS

Chuck came to an agreement, she flew her San Francisco lawyers down to southern California.

"I trusted Chuck, but ever since the film *Together*, I trusted lawyers more," she said, only half-jokingly.[4]

Her caution was not without merit. In addition to money she was never paid when *Together* was rereleased in 1973, and the financial involvement of organized crime in the adult film industry, Marilyn had every reason to make her contract with Chuck as airtight as possible. Moreover, Chuck had a reputation as a conman. More than one insider had described him as a "suitcase pimp," a term originating in the adult film business and referring to an unemployed boyfriend or husband of a female adult star who handled the woman's financial business. Marilyn had heard about this, but she saw (or desired to see) something different.

"He was the opposite of what I'd heard—that Chuck Traynor is a bastard and will ruin me," she said. "He was pleasant, intelligent, together."[5]

Chuck hoped to do for her what he couldn't do for Linda Lovelace: go beyond X-rated films and turn her into an all-around superstar entertainer like his buddy Sammy Davis, Jr. Despite his admiration for Marilyn's drive, savvy, and beauty, he knew he had work to do.

"We had to begin from scratch," he said. "All we had was a gimmick, this time Ivory Snow as opposed to deep throat, but we had things to do, singing lessons, dance lessons, acting classes, hairstyles to choose, dresses to be designed, arrangements to be written. I wanted people to recognize Marilyn every time she stepped out of the house. Who'd recognize her in jeans and a t-shirt?"[6]

In Marilyn, he saw a golden opportunity to play Pygmalion, the Cypriot king and sculptor of Greek mythology who fell in love with a statue he'd carved from ivory. In Chuck's mind, Marilyn would be the ivory sculpture he molded to perfection—and to his liking. But instead of coming to life, as in the myth, this "sculpture," though alive and breathing, would remain an object over which he could exert total control.

"You can only polish if the silver is good," Chuck said. "I'm around to remind Marilyn, 'Never believe your own hype.' If you get too swell-headed, then you get impossible to handle. You simply can't be an entertainer if you're the only person who thinks you're great. And that's the kind of person I look for—someone who can handle that aspect of fame."[7]

Asked if Marilyn was "hard to handle from the beginning," Chuck replied, "She was a very fast learner. If you explain to her why something works, she'll listen to you."

Linda Lovelace developed a huge ego as a celebrity, Chuck said. He didn't intend to let the same thing happen to Marilyn.

PURE *The Sexual Revolutions of Marilyn Chambers*

Marilyn Briggs became Marilyn Chambers when she made *Green Door*. The Ivory Snow scandal made her famous and turned her into a celebrity. A character splitting likely began around this time as she received enormous attention from the press.

According to psychologist Donna Rockwell, who co-wrote 'Being a Celebrity: A Phenomenology of Fame' for the *Journal of Phenomenological Psychology*, becoming a celebrity

...alters the person's being-in-the-world. Once fame hits, with its growing sense of isolation, mistrust, and lack of personal privacy, the person develops a kind of character-splitting between the 'celebrity self' and the 'authentic self' as a survival technique in the hyperkinetic and heady atmosphere associated with celebrity life.

Being famous is variously described as leaving the person feeling: 'lonely; not secure; you have a bubble over you; family space is violated; a sense of being watched; living in a fishbowl; like a locked room; and familiarity that breeds inappropriate closeness.' Yet, while the celebrity experiences many negative side effects of fame, the allure of wealth, access, preferential treatment, public adoration, and, as one celebrity put it, 'membership in an exclusive club,' keeps the famous person stuck in the perpetual need to keep their fame machine churning.[8]

Rockwell wrote, 'At the moment they are famous, celebrities have become a commodity, and their job is now to sell their 'image' to contemporary, celebrity-making media outlets. They are left alone to sort out the difference between image and self, between media creation and authentic being.'[9]

Instead, Marilyn consciously leaned into the media creation of Marilyn Chambers at the behest of Chuck Traynor. "Marilyn Chambers" became more than a persona; she became a character. Her authentic self became virtually imperceptible.

Norman Gaines, a friend of the couple, saw a change in Marilyn's body language when she played "Marilyn Chambers." She sat upright, almost stiff, he said. She was more aware of camera angles and how to hold her head and position herself in the best lighting. Gaines said it was obvious she was being an actress. When she wasn't playing "Marilyn Chambers," Gaines observed that she was much more relaxed.[10]

"I'm a sex object. I always want to remain a sex object because that's what I do best, on stage and off," Marilyn told *Man's World* magazine in 1976. The reporter asked if she favored the role because it had proven lucrative or because it was the real her.

"I assure you, it's the real me," she replied.[11]

It's not unusual for celebrities to create alter egos. Some do so to quell nerves before a performance and provide a level of confidence their actual selves don't possess. But they're usually able to differentiate between their alter ego and actual selves. In Marilyn's case, the alter ego of "Marilyn Chambers" became an all-consuming, pernicious affair.

Chuck was fifteen years Marilyn's senior. In him, she found the father figure she so deeply desired. He would love her and support her ambitions. He'd guide her career and provide plaudits. There would be no competition for attention from siblings or even from Linda Lovelace. Chuck's sole focus would be Marilyn, and he'd be available to shower her with attention. Most importantly, she believed he would take care of her. In actuality, it was subjugation. In time, however, Marilyn's fantasy would crash into cold, hard reality. Chuck would beat her, shout at her, shame her, feed her drugs, pocket most of her earnings, dominate every aspect of her life, and micromanage her days—including when she could use the bathroom. Chuck had booked Lovelace for several gigs, most notably a stint in Vegas, and he intended to replace her with Marilyn. When he realized Marilyn needed more training than he anticipated, he nixed the idea. Chuck told Marilyn it would likely take three years of hard work, commitment, and focus to be Marilyn Chambers twenty-four hours a day. How he arrived at three years instead of one, two, or even five is anybody's guess. It's also unusual. Three years is a long time in the life of a pop celebrity.

Marilyn was extremely disappointed, believing she was prepared to take the stage. But Chuck was right that her limited experience, though providing a solid foundation, required training and education to elevate her to stage-and-screen readiness.

The crux of Chuck's proposition seemed simple enough: together, they would create the persona of "Marilyn Chambers," a sex superstar. Marilyn was in charge of inhabiting the role and bringing it to life. Chuck would handle the business dealings and instruct her on what and what not to do. They would keep Marilyn Chambers a household name and cash in on her sex appeal but shift the focus of her career to more mainstream projects.

'Marilyn Briggs was part of my old life,' she said. 'Chuck and I said farewell to her, and I was glad to see her go.'[12]

Marilyn believed the image of the all-American girl next door would peak in the seventies zeitgeist—and she was right. Traditional society believed the girl next door never engaged in intercourse until marriage.

PURE
The Sexual Revolutions of Marilyn Chambers

"But the subtheme was always there," Marilyn explained. "Being the girl next door and being sexy at the same time was something that men could fantasize about. Until she married. That was always the happy ending. But the truth is that the fucking still went on. So there's no real contradiction between my sexuality in X-rated movies and the image of the healthy girl next door. The content of truth has been raised."[13]

Marilyn understood that moving from "porn star" to all-around entertainer would be tough, but she liked the challenge. And she knew the timing was right. By the end of 1973, the "porno chic" fad was essentially over. A-list celebrities no longer lined up outside theaters; *Variety* and *The Hollywood Reporter* stopped reviewing the films; the media decried the insta-fame of the adult movie actors; and suburbanites grew bored with the product. Still, in just a little over a year, three X-rated films became landmark cultural touchstones, altering the landscape of cinema and independent filmmaking, pushing the boundaries of art and sex, setting off debates about what is and is not "obscene;" and fueling the change in US obscenity laws. Their cross-generational appeal helped people to become more sexually aware and uninhibited.

"Let's face it, this is not 1935, and the days of the old Hays Office are fortunately gone," Marilyn said, referring to Hollywood's self-imposed guidelines for movies released between 1934 and 1968, which prohibited profanity, overt sex, and undue violence. "Moviegoers who would have blushed at porn scenes thirty years ago take them now as a matter of course. I am certainly not ashamed of anything I have done. If other people are ashamed, well, that's their problem, isn't it? I'm just afraid that my past might restrict the roles I will be offered in the future, that my sex image will go against me."[14]

Free-spirited though she sounds in such quotes, Marilyn suffered at home under Chuck's rigid adherence to traditional sex roles. A woman, he told her, should be proud of her home. She should be proud of how she lives and how her old man brags about her. She should want—and be proud—to keep him happy. He explained that if she isn't doing any of these things, she won't make it and isn't a true woman. Her husband's appreciation and approval are the reward.

"I know a lot of people in Hollywood, starlets, and so-called superstars, can't do anything around their houses because they work in movies," Chuck said. "Well, I always had the attitude, and I think I conveyed it to Marilyn as I conveyed it to Linda, that working on films and shows isn't work. Work is when you go out and lay concrete bricks like I've done, eight hours a day. That's work! Going and standing on a set someplace, or getting balled in a film, that's not work!"

THE NEW MARILYN CHAMBERS

And if the not-really-work in films dried up and Chuck had to go back to bricklaying, he "would expect Marilyn to go out and turn tricks."[15]

CHARLES EVERETT TRAYNOR WAS born on August 21, 1937. His mother, Elaine, was only seventeen.[16] His father, Everett Wiley, was also a teenager and uninvolved in Chuck's life.[17] Because Elaine was underage and unwed, her parents, Angelo and Teresa Traynor, sent Elaine from their home in New York City to stay with relatives in Connecticut until the baby was born. When she returned, Angelo and Teresa decided to raise Chuck as their own, refusing to acknowledge the baby was their daughter's—and allowing Elaine little say in the child's upbringing.

Elaine was devastated. Depending on which version of the story is told, she either started nursing school or became the girlfriend of a local mobster. If she started nursing school, she never finished. If she took up with a gangster, reports are that they set her up with a flower shop as a front for the gang's criminal activity. It's also been suggested by people who knew her that she did sex work.

In 1944, she became pregnant with her second child. Because she was still unwed, her parents sent her to Connecticut again to have the baby. When she returned in early 1945, her parents moved the family, including seven-year-old Chuck and his three-month-old half-brother Bernard, to Homestead, Florida, approximately twenty-six miles southwest of Miami. Angelo and Teresa allowed their daughter to raise Bernard but didn't want their new grandson co-mingling with Chuck. So Elaine and Bernard lived in one house while Angelo, Teresa, and Chuck lived around the corner in another.

"My parents were simple people," Chuck said. "My mom was a nurse, just like Marilyn's, and she remarried, and I really know my stepfather better than my dad. And they were really very hip people for their time; they took all kinds of trauma in stride—well, most traumas."[18]

Chuck was told the truth about his parents when he was in his teens. His grandparents offered no explanation. He was just expected to take the information and deal with it.

"They were really a nice family," said childhood friend Floyd Harden. "He was really close to his grandparents, and they treated him like a little prince. He was a really amenable person. He got along with all classes, really. You'd get to know him real quickly."[19]

In high school, he said a girl he had seen regularly told him she was pregnant. She was a migrant farmworker, but he didn't say where from. Chuck told his mother. She was livid. Chuck didn't want a child. He told the girl to go to Texas. He gave her $100 to get settled and said he'd meet her there in three weeks. She left, but Chuck never went to Texas.

"And I never heard from her again. Which was fine by me," Chuck said. "I really don't think she was pregnant at all. A lot of chicks would use that to get married, that's all."[20]

Chuck had wanted to be a soldier since he was a boy. He graduated high school in 1955, and when he turned eighteen that August, he enlisted in the Marines. He joined the 2nd 155mm gun battalion and, in October 1955, won a medal for marksmanship. In 1956 he married his first wife, Eula Joiner. It was a short partnership, and in early 1959, Chuck left the Marines and got a job driving a dump truck for the Three Bays Improvement Company in Florida. In June, he married his second wife, Mary Fowler. They divorced a year later.[21]

One day in the early fifties, the transient nature of Traynor's young life altered when he met a woman who would open his eyes to the world of art, entertainment, and pornography.

Bunny Yeager was a pinup model turned photographer. She would snap shots of scantily-clad women, often posed on the beach or with taxidermied exotic animals, and sell the pictures to men's magazines and photography publications. Her photos helped many young women earn a living, and turned one, Bettie Page, into a cult icon. Yeager befriended a young man named Hugh Hefner and convinced him to use her photos in his new magazine, *Playboy*. Her specialty was nude shots, including self-portraits. Nude photography of any kind, whether stills or movies, was illegal. Eventually, Yeager turned to filmmaking. Her first films were "nudie cuties," softcore flicks which showed half-naked women, often doing stripteases.

As a dump truck driver, Chuck regularly drove past the home of one pinup model, Maria Stinger. Since she posed nude, he assumed she must also walk around her backyard in the nude. One day, Chuck said he stopped at Maria's house and saw a woman unpacking some stuff from her vehicle. He approached her and introduced himself; he told the woman he'd like to meet Maria.

"You ever wanna be in a movie with her?" the woman asked. He enthusiastically agreed, and the woman introduced herself as Bunny Yeager. She told Chuck they were about to make a movie. "If you wanna be in it, I could sure use it," she said.

Yeager didn't recall it that way.

"Chuck Traynor said that when he was sixteen, he knocked on the door? No, I don't think so," she said. "Maybe he would've liked it that way. Maybe he called me up and offered up his services—I don't remember that."

But she remembered him fondly.

THE NEW MARILYN CHAMBERS

"I always liked Chuck," she said. "Very likable, very charismatic, very laid-back, easy to get along with, and quick to laugh."[22]

However it happened, Chuck began a career in movies as a nudist camp extra and performed simulated sex scenes with nude women.

"I thought they were going out, myself," Bernard said of his brother and Yeager. "They were more than just friends. But (Chuck) was kind of a scammer. He was always into something. I don't think he worked an honest day in his life."[23]

In 1961, Chuck married his third wife, Eileen Bourne, a frequent pinup subject of Yeager's. Bourne was an in-demand model for men's magazines and used the name "Cindy Lee." They were married until 1964.

Chuck obtained his pilot's license in the early sixties and earned money as a crop duster in Florida for companies like Minute Maid Orange Juice and the Ocean Reef Club. However, the toxic chemicals used for the job led to breathing complications and a nasty cough, so he had to quit. Yeager had taught Chuck some basics of photography, and he picked up work as a freelance photographer for local newspapers. Through Yeager's connections, Chuck also served as a crewmember on several exploitation films. He appeared briefly in the 1968 sexploitation film *How I Became a Nudist* (aka *Girls Come Too*) opposite Maria Stinger.

Chuck also learned how to operate a movie camera and was tapped to do occasional day work on the television show *Flipper*, which was filmed in Miami, Key Biscayne, and Nassau, Florida. One day during an underwater shoot on *Flipper*, a snapping turtle bit the middle finger on Chuck's right hand. The wound became infected and the top of the finger, down to the first joint, had to be amputated.

He paid about $2,000 (nearly $20,000 in today's money) for the rundown wreck of a raunchy topless beer bar on North Miami Beach at 123rd Street. The place was fixed up and renamed the Las Vegas Inn. It catered to bikers and construction workers. It soon went from a topless to a nude bar. This happened only after the door had been locked.

"Luckily, they never did it with any ATF [Alcohol, Tobacco and Firearms] agents in the place," Chuck said.[24]

As the Las Vegas Inn owner, Chuck had a steady stream of young women at his disposal. He believed all women were disposable if they weren't making him money. Soon exploitation filmmakers in Florida called upon Chuck to see if female employees wanted to be in their movies. Chuck provided access to his cadre of women for a fee and in exchange for roles for himself.

"The mind boggles at Chuck's skills as a lady wrangler," explained Tim Lucas, biographer of prolific exploitation director Joe Sarno. Sarno was one of the directors who went to Chuck for help finding models and actresses. "I don't mean to be unkind, but the women Joe had to use on these pictures, for the most part, were far below those he had been finding through New York channels. They were simply not attractive. Their hair was bleached and stiff with hairspray, and naturally, they couldn't act. One plump, dark-skinned actress could not even speak passable English. But Joe was in a jam, and he had to deliver. His Florida films are unquestionably the nadir of his career up to that point."[25] At his home in North Miami, Chuck typically had three or four women living with him, some as young as fifteen or sixteen. He perfected his manipulation of the opposite sex during this time.

"I saw that if a chick really dug you, there wasn't anything you couldn't ask her," he told *Rolling Stone*. "Well, it got to the point where all the women in the house were sleeping together with me and whoever came over to visit; some of them turned tricks, some of them just posed, some worked at straight jobs and gave all their money to me. It was like a commune. If one of them didn't like the arrangement, I threw her the fuck out."[26]

In November 1970, Chuck and another man, Robert Ingalsbe, were arrested on an abandoned airfield in South Dade. A group of hunters spotted the men lugging burlap sacks, which were later found to contain marijuana. Four hundred pounds of pot were discovered by law enforcement in the woods along the airfield, known to locals as a popular spot for drug running between Florida and the Caribbean. Chuck and Ingalsbe were charged with drug possession. Chuck's brother posted his bond. During their four-day trial, Chuck and Ingalsbe took the stand and told the jury they were scouting locations at the airfield for possible use by a parachute club. They claimed they stumbled upon the bags in the woods as they walked around the field. A narcotics agent approached them, they said, and asked them to help lug the bags to a waiting vehicle. The defense maintained it could have been any of the parties involved—including the hunters who identified Chuck and Ingalsbe—who were there to pick up the marijuana. The jury bought it, and the men were acquitted.[27]

In fact, Chuck, Ingalsbe, and a third unidentified man were smuggling pot to make extra money.

ONE OF CHUCK'S REGULAR biker customers was dating a woman in her early twenties named Linda Boreman. She was staying with her parents in Florida, recuperating from a serious car accident on a New York parkway. The accident caused severe injuries and left Linda with a large vertical scar on her torso which ran from just below her breasts to her bellybutton. Linda was friends with Patsy Carroll, one of the bar's topless servers. Carroll introduced Linda to Chuck. Chuck invited Linda to stay at his house.

"I viewed it as a good opportunity for me in a lot of ways," Linda said. "I wouldn't have my mother constantly telling me what time to be home and stuff like that. Chuck wasn't ugly, so I started dating him. At first, he was like a gentleman—a real human being, you know? He would open the car door for me and light my cigarettes."[28]

Since he was financially secure, Chuck often purchased Linda gifts such as clothing and jewelry.

Chuck's magnetism did not go unnoticed.

"These girls did fall in love with him, you know?" said Lenny Camp, a photographer who also worked as a location scout and set designer for *Deep Throat*. Camp recalled one young woman who was "madly in love with him. She was at his beck and call. She would do anything for him. *Anything*."[29]

Camp said Linda "followed Chuck around like a puppy dog."

But not everyone agreed.

"Chuck Traynor was a nickel-and-dime guy as far as I was concerned," said former FBI agent Bill Kelly, who investigated the people involved in the making of *Deep Throat*. "He wasn't big-league or anything. So I don't think I ever did a real extensive investigation on him. I considered Chuck Traynor a pimp. What else would you call him?"[30]

The Las Vegas Inn eventually became a front for Chuck's prostitution racket. He'd raffle off his female employees to patrons. Tickets went for as much as $700 apiece (more than $5,300 today). Customers who had raffle tickets marked one through seven would get their selection of one of seven women whom they could use for an hour in the bar's back rooms for anything they wanted. Sometime in 1971, the Las Vegas Inn was closed by the Bureau of Alcohol, Tobacco, and Firearms. By law, all bar owners in Florida had to have a "Person in Charge," whether a manager or server. This person must carry the P.I.C. card at all times. When ATF agents visited and found no employee in possession of the card, they shuttered the bar.

With his main source of income suddenly gone, Chuck needed cash. He had stayed in contact with Yeager and often recommended women for her to photograph. Yeager trusted his judgment until he brought over Linda.

"The trouble with Linda was that she was flat-chested," Yeager remembered. "Not that there's anything wrong with small bosoms, but what I'm thinking is, 'I can't sell her." Another thing—I didn't want to bring this up, but Linda had a scar all the way down the middle of her chest. But I shot her anyway, more as a favor to Chuck."[31]

During this time, Linda claimed Chuck would send her "out in the streets and pick up girls to get them to work for his prostitution business." Linda, admittedly, was not very successful. "I thought, unconsciously, 'Well, he's finally going to get rid of me,'" she said. "He told me that I was a failure at what I was doing, but he didn't get rid of me."[32]

Chuck thought his next logical step was to make pornographic films himself, with Linda participating. A South Florida woman named Vickie had earned local renown for her ability to perform a sex act dubbed "deep throat." It involved her taking a man's penis into her mouth and down her throat. This brought her lips to the base of his organ. Lenny Camp claimed Vickie showed Chuck and Linda one night. Chuck said he had already learned the technique in Japan while stationed there in the Marines.

"Ninety percent of what Chuck says is just total bullshit," Camp said. "The night I told him about Vickie and deep throat, Chuck just stayed in the corner. Vickie didn't perform deep throat on Chuck that night. No, Chuck was very, very, very shy as far as having sex in front of people—although he liked watching other people have sex."[33]

Linda, on the other hand, was highly sexed, Camp said. When Chuck and Linda showed up at Camp's door one night, he claimed Linda and Vickie began having sex with no prodding or suggestion from either him or Chuck.

"Linda did whatever she wanted," Camp said. "Chuck was trying to be like Hugh Hefner. Oh, he would have loved to have been Hefner. He thought he *was* Hefner. But Chuck was a superpimp; that's all he was. He put the talk on everybody. I mean, as far as he was concerned, it was whatever the girls could make and whatever he could get away with. That's all he wanted."[34]

According to Linda, her sex life with Chuck was lackluster at best. They would have sex once a month or every six weeks, and it was bad, she said. "At first, I thought there was something wrong with me," she said. "I guess a woman always figures it's her fault at first. I was so dumb."[35]

Her vibrator was her closest companion, she claimed.

"Did I fall in love with [Linda]? Love?" Chuck wondered. "I think I probably loved her somewhat... I mean, it probably wasn't like the way John Derek loved Bo Derek. Because, you know, they called me the John Derek of the porno business."[36] (Derek was an actor who began his career in the late forties. He was probably better known for his personal life and relationships with women. He became involved with and often married young starlets—most notably Ursula

Andress, Linda Evans, and Bo Derek—and became their husband and manager.)

Linda worked as a prostitute, which she said Chuck forced her to do. If she resisted, he'd beat her. The formerly gracious, congenial man had devolved first into verbal taunts and criticisms and finally into physical assaults.

When Chuck learned a friend was opening a bar in Aspen, Colorado, he decided to move there. Before Chuck and Linda left Miami, the couple were married. En route to Aspen, a car accident in Biscoe, Arkansas, landed them in a local hospital. The closest large city to Biscoe is Little Rock, but that was too small for Chuck. So they headed for New York, accompanied by their cat Hitler.[37]

Although there were hundreds of pornographers, performers, madams, adult bookstore owners, dancers, and others peddling sex in New York City, it was a tight-knit community.

"What's amazing to me was how quickly one got to know them all," Linda recalled. "They were all links on the same chain; you met one person, and he passed you along to the others. I swear, before the week was out, Chuck Traynor managed to meet every prominent pervert in New York."[38]

Linda supported herself and Chuck through sex work and by selling nude photos of herself to adult bookshop owners. Chuck took many of the photos. Some of them featured Linda solo; others featured her with one or more women. Chuck even appeared with Linda and another woman in a series of photos. The money was steady but not nearly enough to survive on.

Hundreds of porn films were made in New York City in the early seventies. Although it's considered a cliché, participants were young people looking for a quick cash score, including penniless artists. The short films, "loops," were easy to produce, cost little, and had a high return for the filmmakers and the adult bookstores that sold them. Customers needed an eight-millimeter projector to watch them.

Chuck and Linda made their first film with Bob Wolfe, one of the most prolific loop lensers of his days. Actor Rob Everett, who often appeared in films under the name Eric Edwards, participated as well. Linda and Everett hit it off and soon made dozens of loops for Wolfe. Everett's wife, Kathie, joined them. For the first loop, Everett remembered he received forty dollars (roughly $300 today), and Linda received fifty ($375 today).

According to Linda and Chuck, Wolfe suggested they shoot a film about Linda having sex with a dog. Traynor agreed, but Linda balked. She feared dogs.

Linda recounted in her autobiography, *Ordeal*, that the next morning Chuck told her she would be making the film whether she agreed or not. 'There would be a beating, I knew that much,' she wrote in *Ordeal*. 'For once, the prospect of a beating was not the worst alternative. Any beating, no matter how severe, would be better than being raped by a dog."[39]

The couple went down to Wolfe's studio, and Chuck led Linda into a room where Wolfe and his assistant were waiting, seated behind a table. Chuck joined them on the other side of the table.

"Okay, Linda," Wolfe said. "Why don't you get undressed, and we'll get on with this."[40]

Linda refused. She claimed Wolfe told her to think over her answer carefully. It was then that she noticed a small revolver on the table. Wolfe asked her again if she wanted to make the movie. She wrote that Chuck said, "Take off your clothes, cunt."[41] (In Linda's second book, *Out of Bondage*, published six years after *Ordeal*, she contradicted her story by writing that it was Chuck, not Wolfe, who threatened her with a gun.)

Chuck denied such a threat ever happened and claimed he was never on the set. Everett also characterized Linda's story as inaccurate.

"There was no gun pointed to her head; there were no people around other than Bob Wolfe and me," he said.

> There was no forcing her to do anything. Chuck wasn't even there, not on that particular set. He was more of a manager that came in to make sure everything was okay and then would leave. I've known Chuck Traynor for a long time, and I have never, ever seen anything other than a businessman in him. I've never seen any kind of malevolence in him. He was more involved in the business and getting his wife to do certain things. But I never *ever* saw any kind of abuse. I always felt that Linda was enjoying everything that she did in front of the camera. I never had a feeling that she was *not* enjoying herself. Even with the dog—and I was *in* that loop.[42]

The film was made and released under a few different titles. The most common was simply *Dog Fucker*.

Chuck soon hooked up with Lou "Butchie" Peraino (also known as Lou Perry), a member of the Columbo organized crime family who financed and distributed low-budget films. Chuck and Linda met director Gerard Damiano, who also worked with Peraino. Damiano wanted to do a feature-length hardcore sex film. First, he directed Linda and actor Harry Reems in some loops. During one of these shoots, he discovered Linda's ability to deep throat. Neither he nor Reems had ever seen anything like it. Damiano told Peraino about an idea for a feature film based around deep-throating, but Peraino didn't care for Linda. Damiano insisted, but Peraino incessantly criticized her. Chuck told Linda if she performed deep throat on Peraino, the matter would be closed. She did, and it was.

In January 1972, Chuck, Linda, Damiano, and Reems headed to Miami to film *Deep Throat*. Chuck was excited because he saw it as an opportunity to return to Florida permanently. He was supposed to be a location scout and find additional actors for the film, and he claimed he did. Lenny Camp disagreed.

"Chuck Traynor was nuthin'," he said. "He was less than nuthin'. He couldn't get anybody, couldn't get any locations. So they called me."[43]

At some point during the making of *Deep Throat*, Linda Boreman was given the stage name Linda Lovelace.

The beatings came regularly during the filming of *Deep Throat*, Linda claimed. In some scenes, dark marks on her body are visible. She said they were bruises. Many of the cast and crew corroborated Linda's story of physical abuse in that they *heard* Chuck beating her but never saw it. Other cast and crew members rebutted the claims. They didn't see or hear anything. Linda was a pathological liar and made everything up, they said.

AS THE REALITY OF Chuck's plan coalesced in Marilyn's mind, it became clear her marriage to Doug would only hinder her chances at greater success. Marilyn confided in Chuck. He made sure to use Marilyn's complaints about Doug to his own advantage. He convinced Marilyn that Doug was weak, submissive, and fragile, incapable of treating her with the care and attention she deserved.

"Living with Doug was enough to turn any girl into the dominant figure," Chuck insisted. "She was almost forced into that role of being overly protective of herself. No one had ever taken care of her. She had taken care of herself and her husband."[44]

She certainly was the breadwinner and the more ambitious of the pair.

Chuck entered Marilyn's life at a time of great vulnerability and pressure. Her star had ascended, but the Mitchell brothers weren't providing the career guidance she needed. Doug was merely along for the ride, an insignificant pawn in the intricate fame game. She asked herself how Doug would or could fit into the plans she and Chuck made. She concluded that he couldn't.

'Okay, he had been great for me,' she recalled in her 1975 book, *My Story*. 'Someone to come home to and be with, never standing in my way, letting me do whatever I wanted to do, but there was no future for us now. I didn't want to admit it, but I could clearly see it.'[45]

Marilyn's account of the dissolution of her marriage is the only version of the story that exists, and since she wrote it with Chuck's help, it's biased.

Marilyn had been in Los Angeles for little more than a week when Doug decided to visit. He had only heard about this mystery man who was determined to make his wife a superstar. By the time he arrived, Marilyn had moved into Chuck's Malibu home, and the two had become sexually involved. Although she had told Doug by phone that she was moving in with Chuck, he didn't seem concerned. If he sensed anything about Marilyn and Chuck's newfound intimacy once he arrived, he never let on. He liked Chuck. But for Marilyn, the spark with Doug was gone. He stayed for a few days and told her he would fly back to San Francisco, get the car, and drive back down to L.A. with some of her belongings. Then the two would get their own place. Too scared to tell Doug how she felt, Marilyn propitiated. She vowed to tell him it was over when he returned to L.A.

"You won't be married to Doug for another six months," Chuck told her when Doug left. She became defensive and insisted he was wrong, but instinctively she knew Chuck was right.

When Doug returned, he moved into the beach house, but Marilyn busied herself with career plans instead of ending her marriage. Doug didn't seem to mind, but his presence distracted her. Chuck tried to involve him in conversations about Marilyn's career, but he wasn't interested.

'He just sat around,' Marilyn said. 'He pondered what he was going to do with his life, just as he'd been doing since long before I met him playing the bagpipes on that street corner.'[46]

Finally, nearly a week after he returned, Marilyn confronted Doug. "There's no hope," she told him. "Our lives have gone down separate paths, and it's time to wave goodbye."

She lied and told him, "It has nothing to do with Chuck."

Doug stared blankly at her, processing what she said. She was choosing her career over him, and although she knew it was selfish, that was the truth, and that's what they had to deal with.

"I know you don't really want to move to L.A.," she said. "It's not your kind of place. You don't want to get involved in show business; it's not the kind of life for you. You'd be happier being a farmer in Oregon."[47]

After a stony silence, he said he agreed with her. He was hurt but thanked her for her honesty and said he felt free to go his way. The whole conversation went better than Marilyn expected. Then they held each other for a long time, the last time.

THE NEW MARILYN CHAMBERS

Marilyn's second husband, Chuck Traynor, managed her career beginning in late 1973. Traynor was previously married to *Deep Throat* star Linda Lovelace. *Las Vegas News Bureau.*

The next day, he said he felt lighter. "You know, I think this is the best thing that's ever happened to me," he told her. She was sad but unburdened.[48]

He gathered his belongings, packed the car, and drove back to San Francisco. They never saw or spoke to each other again.

'I guess I believe that when you walk away from something, you just walk away from it,' she wrote. 'You don't hang on to the knick-knacks and mementos, which will just make it more difficult for you. You keep the memories and [forget] the furniture.'[49]

It was a sentiment she expressed but never practiced. She never returned to her home in San Francisco, but she did have to go back to the city to tell the other men in her life—the Mitchell brothers—that their relationship, at least professionally, was over, too. Unlike Doug, they did not take the news so easily.

"But why *him*, Marilyn—of all people?!"

They knew of Chuck's reputation as a grifter, and as he had managed Linda Lovelace, he was seen as direct competition.

"Chuck says he can make me a superstar, and I believe him," she replied. "He's already got a lot of great things lined up for Linda Lovelace. She's gone now. I know I've got what it takes, but I need his help."

"You can't do that, Marilyn," Jim said sternly.

"It's already done," she replied coolly. "I've already signed the contract. Chuck is my exclusive agent and manager."

"He's a scumbag!" Art yelled, his voice filling with rage. "A fucking pimp! He'll ruin you, Marilyn!"

Marilyn stood firm. She insisted she and Chuck shared a mutual interest in turning her into a star. The brothers countered they had discovered Marilyn and had already turned her into a star. This angered Marilyn.

"Hey, it's not like I was some fucking charity case," she said. "You guys did pretty well selling Marilyn Chambers."

"You owe us, Marilyn," Jim said.

"You make 'owe' sound like 'own,' as in 'We own you, Marilyn,'" she said.

"You could have at least talked to us before you did this," Jim replied.

She told them it was just something she felt she had to do. It was her career, and she needed to do what made sense to advance it. And they could still work together, she said. They were like her own brothers; she wanted to remain friends. The brothers insisted she had betrayed them. They repeated: "You owe us, Marilyn."

"You'll have to talk to Chuck about that," she snapped, leaving the room.[50]

CHUCK USED HYPNOSIS TO teach Marilyn (and Linda) the "deep throat" technique. Within the first week of Marilyn's arrival, Chuck was hypnotizing her. Chuck claimed he learned hypnosis while he was in Honduras. He was a member of the American Institute of Hypnosis, a society founded in the mid fifties by pioneering hypnotherapist William Joseph Bryan, Jr. Most scientists agree hypnotherapy is a legitimate form of adjunct therapy when used correctly. It can be helpful with weight loss, anxiety, and stress, among other things.[51] However, some scientists believe hypnosis can be used for harm as well as good.[52]

Chuck said he could teach anyone the "deep throat" technique through hypnosis. In fact, he claimed he could hypnotize anyone, period—particularly women. It was a means to control. "The method I use in hypnosis is this: first, I have to establish total contact with the person," he said.

> She has to believe what I'm saying and really trust me. Now, of course, the first time I hypnotize her—I don't know if you've been hypnotized, but you're aware of everything that's happening—well, she wouldn't trust me the first few times. So we'd have to have several sessions where I'd be hypnotizing her and take her maybe to the second level and then bring her back out, telling her how good she feels and how rested and possibly that something would taste really good afterward. You know, just suggestions. Always positive suggestions, because that's the method I use.[53]

Marilyn was receptive to the idea of being hypnotized because she trusted Chuck completely. She, too, joined the American Institute of Hypnosis. She learned from Chuck how to hypnotize, become hypnotized, and do hypnosis on herself.[54] In one interview, she claimed that she and Chuck communicated through telepathy and practiced it regularly.[55]

"I normally use my finger against the temple after the first time and tell them, 'From here on, when I touch your temple and tell you that you're going into a deep sleep, then you will go into a deep sleep,'" Chuck said. "And the method works. I then reach a point, like with Marilyn or with anyone else, where they want to do it. They really want to do it."[56]

Linda, however, was put off by the idea of being hypnotized when Chuck first suggested it to her. The first time he did so, Linda said he told her he would use it to help her feel well-rested.

'He had me lie down on the rug and stare at something bright around his neck while he talked,' she wrote in *Ordeal*. 'I don't remember what he said, but in a couple of minutes, I was sound asleep. When he snapped me out of it, I was fully rested. All as advertised.'[57]

Linda said Chuck 'had a sure-fire way of telling when I was really hypnotized and when I was faking it,' but she never said what it was.[58]

'Sometimes I was able to remember everything Chuck said to me when I was under [hypnosis],' she said. 'Some of his suggestions I was powerless to resist, and some I just wouldn't do. To protect myself from a later beating—and Chuck would be furious with me if I didn't follow his post-hypnotic suggestions—I would always play along at least part of the way.'[59]

Chuck hypnotized Linda several times a week, she said. Even though she could sometimes remember everything Chuck said to her while under hypnosis, she also claimed there were groups of days where she didn't remember anything.

'Sometimes I'd wake up and have to ask what day of the week it was,' she said. 'The things I can remember are so horrible; I wonder what happened on those days that I can't remember.'[60]

Marilyn never made any such claims.

"Linda has tried to say several times, and it really wouldn't work, that everything she did, she did because she was in a state of hypnosis," Chuck said. "Well, doctors and psychologists, of course, that deal in hypnotherapy will tell you that you can't do this."[61]

CHUCK IMMEDIATELY CONCOCTED A plan to introduce Marilyn to the public as a mainstream entertainer. Within a month of meeting her, he'd booked her first gig. It was a burlesque revue called *Skin 'n' Grin*, which opened on December 5, 1973, at the Capitol Theater in Passaic, New Jersey. Marilyn was added as a last-minute attraction. She was given top billing and appeared in a twenty-minute song-and-dance act. Her set was preceded by variety numbers starring two male adult stars: Harry Reems, who co-starred with Linda in *Deep Throat*, and Marc Stevens, who appeared in a scene with Georgina Spelvin in *The Devil in Miss Jones*.

Promoters billed the show as "an entertainment event of unprecedented magnitude." Marilyn provided the advertised "skin."

"We felt the time had come to rescue burlesque from oblivion," producer and theater co-owner Al Heyman said. "And who would be better suited to do it than the men and women who put the skids on burlesque?"[62]

Marilyn's performance would help Chuck identify which songs and dances worked, which didn't, and which required more polish. Then they'd expand the act and take it to a formal cabaret in New York City—they hoped. Songs selected included covers of The Rolling Stones' Satisfaction and The Doors' Light My Fire. She also performed a rendition of the fifties hit Green Door. Chuck told a local newspaper reporter that the production cost for Marilyn's act alone was $40,000 (more than $260,000 in today's money).[63]

Marilyn also touted her Terpsichorean talents in a sexy number that left her in nothing but a G-string and bra. Assistant County Prosecutor John T. Niccolai warned theater owners that Marilyn would be arrested if she appeared nude on stage. "We don't want any Ivory Snow baths on stage in Passaic County," he said.[64]

About 1,100 people filled the 3,265-seat theater on opening night.[65] Thunderstorms, heavy rains, strong winds, and frigid temperatures didn't help the turnout.[66]

The Associated Press covered it, and the next day, the wire story was picked up by newspapers across the country. It's odd to think that a short set, performed in an inelegant burlesque show—in New Jersey, no less—by an adult film star who'd only become a household name eight months prior, would garner coast-to-coast coverage. It augured the type of attention the media give to instant celebrities today. Her performance was described as a valiant attempt at singing and dancing. Chuck, however, was discouraged. He recognized her potential, but there was something missing: consistency.

"Marilyn would appear on the stage...and talk about one thing, and she'd be someplace else," Chuck explained. "There was never any uniformity about her. I believe to create a superstar nowadays, a girl has to be immaculate. Not only does she have to look like a superstar, but she has to have a certain hairstyle. Sure, the press knows her, but people on the street have to know her, too."

Chuck pointed to Marilyn's cover image and photo spread in *SHOW* magazine, published three months before *Skin 'n' Grin*. She had a certain look, but she looked a different way in other photos. In addition to a new hairstyle, she needed new clothes and a car to draw attention. Chuck convinced her to buy a burgundy Jaguar.

"Yeah, it's an image thing," Chuck said. "It's a formula that stars used to use before everybody started thinking it's cool to be obscure. It's not cool to be obscure because if you're obscure, nobody knows you. In the good old days, somebody drove up in a chauffeured limousine, got out in a long flowing mink, and people knew it was a star. Well, I believe in the same formula. I think Hollywood is slave labor, but Hollywood hasn't created a superstar in several years. I've created two in two years, you know. Particularly with Marilyn."[67]

One reporter found Marilyn's new image off-putting.

'Personally, this writer believes that 'Skin 'n' Grin' could have stood on its own without Marilyn Chambers and her much-vaunted soapbox,' wrote one reporter.

She came in—in a chauffeur-driven limousine attended by a private task force of PR men, a choreographer, a musical director, and assorted spokesmen, all there to help Miss Chambers in her delusions of grand stardom. She even acted the part—snapping at reporters, ordering 'no pictures' to assembled photographers, while her manager threatened to pull Miss Chambers out of the show at a finger's snap if anyone so much as dared to pop a flashbulb during her act.[68]

While Chuck okayed mainstream press coverage of *Skin 'n' Grin*, he refused reporters from adult publications. This was part of his strategy to turn Marilyn into a "legitimate" performer. Adult publications would only reinforce the idea that Marilyn was an adult performer. However, the theater's owners and show's producers claimed Chuck promised them that Marilyn would help promote the show in adult publications. When she didn't, they stopped payment on her checks.

The couple filed a complaint in Passaic Municipal Court in January 1974, claiming the show's producers defrauded them for $8,564.53 'in payment of her services.'[69]

"She screwed me out of $1,500," said John Scher, one of the two theater owners named in the complaint. Scher pointed to the lack of adult publication press coverage. "We lost a fabulous amount of money. Tens of thousands of dollars because of her."

Scher claimed that he and his partners had 'footed all the bills and promotional fees' for the show and went on to charge 'that her attitude was so uncooperative and that the box office she did was so pathetic, that they want her to return the $1,500 in expenses they advanced her for the opening.'[70]

Scher filed his own lawsuit against Marilyn and Chuck for breach of contract. The theater issued four checks, Chuck claimed, all of which were returned for insufficient funds. Scher countered that the checks weren't returned due to insufficient funds. He and co-owner Allen Heyman made a business decision to stop payment.

Chuck admitted he forbade the adult press from attending opening night and interviewing Marilyn.

"She needed time to prepare herself," he said. "She was in no condition to talk to the press then. She had her hair in curlers."

Scher didn't buy it.

"They came to us and said we want to make her more than a porn queen," he said. "They ignored the porn press."[71]

The complaint against Scher and Heyman made its way before a Passaic County grand jury. The outcome remains confidential, as is common with grand jury reports.

The Capitol Theater was already in financial and legal trouble before Marilyn and Chuck's lawsuit. In October 1973, two months before the premiere of *Skin 'n' Grin*,

THE NEW MARILYN CHAMBERS

Scher and Heyman were fined $3,000 (more than $20,000 today) by Passaic County Judge William Woods after they pleaded guilty to allowing a boy under eighteen to attend an X-rated film at the theater. The film was *Behind the Green Door*.

MARILYN WAS BOOKED AT The Riverboat, a cabaret lounge in the basement of the Empire State Building, for a four-week engagement beginning March 7, 1974.[72] Charles McHarry, a columnist for the New York *Daily News*, claimed Marilyn would get $10,000 a week (nearly $60,000 in today's money), plus one dollar per customer for the engagement.[73] But Chuck told one reporter that Marilyn got $4,000 a week (more than $25,000 today), plus one dollar per head.[74]

Chuck told a *Rolling Stone* reporter that the cost of the production, including everything from costumes to personnel to his and Marilyn's hotel suite, ran to roughly $40,000 ($235,000 in today's money).

"We end up workin' for exposure," he said. "They've got a little dressing room there; you can't even change. They've got a big dressing room on the other side, but you have to walk through the audience to get to it. They're penny-wise and dollar-foolish."[75]

Marilyn found the seemingly endless rehearsals wearing.

'That's when I wanted to run away and hide and hope they'd never find me,' she wrote.[76]

Opening night was a relief. She was thrilled to be onstage to debut her new show.

Nearly two weeks later, Marilyn was invited to Hunter College in New York City to give a lecture about the "porno chic" fad, her show at the Riverboat, and her burgeoning career as an entertainer. About 100 people, mostly women, filled the auditorium. Marilyn also discussed her role as a feminist and her embrace of sexual freedom. After a brief speech, Chuck joined her onstage to answer questions from the audience.

"The first couple of questions, Chuck broke in and answered the questions," recalled Norman Gaines, a Columbia University student who had befriended the couple after seeing Marilyn in *Skin 'n' Grin*. "After the third question, a woman [in the audience] broke in and said, 'Excuse me! We'd like to hear what *she* has to say.' You should have seen the look on [Chuck's] face."[77]

Gaines said Marilyn did a thirty-minute question-and-answer session.

"And by the way, she was asked some very respectful and very progressive questions, mostly by women in the audience, none of whom [tried] to shame her, slander her, talk down to her in any way, or anything of the sort," Gaines said. "A lot were very curious about what it actually was like to do what she did—not just get fucked on stage, but the actual process of making the movie, how you got to that, and her relationship with the Mitchell Brothers."[78]

Gaines added that the audience was receptive to Marilyn's answers and enthusiastically applauded when she finished.

Chuck had little trouble drumming up promotion for the Riverboat, except for one medium: television. Although Marilyn had appeared numerous times in clips on television news broadcasts, she'd yet to be booked on a talk show. That's what Chuck wanted. The dream of nearly every celebrity was to be a guest on *The Tonight Show* with Johnny Carson. Especially for a new, young entertainer, sitting on the couch next to Carson was like having your name up on the marquee at Caesars Palace. Carson freely used Marilyn's name as a punchline during his opening monologues, but she wasn't allowed on as a guest.

The three major networks had morning, afternoon, and late-night talk shows. Producers tended to pass on booking Marilyn, even though doing so might have boosted a show's ratings. Sure, having a quote-unquote porn star on network television could upset middle-American audiences and make for some angry phone calls, but television was a business. Each network had shareholders to whom executives were beholden. Moreover, all money was made from advertising. And which company spent more on advertising than any other American company? Procter & Gamble.[79]

Finally, on August 1, 1974, Marilyn made her primetime network television debut on the syndicated talk show *Good Night, America*, with host Geraldo Rivera. It aired four months after she opened at the Riverboat, but her show was doing brisk business and her contract was extended. Marilyn sauntered onto the *Good Night* set in a gold lamé pantsuit and matching flats, with gold glitter sprinkled throughout her curly lion's mane hairdo. She was given nearly seven minutes of airtime chatting with Rivera. Relaxed and confident, she deftly handled Rivera's sometimes sophomoric humor and misogynistic line of questioning with quick wit, playfulness, and an ironic grin.

"How do old friends react to you now when they see you? Do they react to you in a typical kind of Hollywood sense, like, 'There's Marilyn, the star'?"

"Yes," she answered before he could finish the question.

"Or do they say, 'Ah, naughty, naughty, I know what she's been doing'?"

"No," she replied, letting out a breathy laugh. "I just think they wish they could be doing the same thing." She flashed a coy smile.

The audience laughed nervously and Rivera seemed genuinely surprised. "Do you really think that?" he asked.

"Sure, don't you?"

THE NEW MARILYN CHAMBERS

Her response left Rivera fumbling for words as the audience laughed and applauded. After discussing Marilyn's entry into the adult film world, Rivera asked about her "new career" in nightclubs. Before she could answer, he interjected, "You know, I read the strangest reviews. They said that you were really too good. They expected it to be more trashy. And they expected you to really, I think, repeat your performance in the triple X-rated movies onstage, and you were more legitimate, and your voice was pretty good."

"Well, I think people are going to be more critical of me because of my past," she said. "And it's kind of fun. I really am enjoying myself. I have a nightclub act, for those of you who don't know."[80]

Rivera interrupted and asked to see some of it when they returned from a commercial break. Singing and dancing to the instantly forgettable funk-rock tune What is Hip?, Marilyn did her best with what could have been a star-making showcase. She had energy and presence, but the song was a poor choice. After months of voice and dance lessons, this was her moment to show America her talents as an entertainer. She does a serviceable job. However, with the criticisms and skepticism she was facing, it wasn't good enough.

Still, her appearance must have eased the minds of some network executives. She was booked for several more talk shows after that, including the popular, nationally syndicated *Phil Donahue Show*. But it was still a hard no from Johnny Carson.

THE PRESS GAVE GENEROUS if often unflattering coverage of Marilyn's attempt to "go straight," as it was commonly phrased. A lengthy March 1974 article by the *Washington Post*'s Judy Bachrach painted an especially unfavorable picture of Marilyn and Chuck. Newspapers across America picked it up from the *Post*'s wire service, running it under headlines such as, "No-Talent Porno Queens are His Specialty."

Bachrach and Chuck were watching Riverboat rehearsals, where, as Bachrach noted, Marilyn was 'bumping and grinding and singing 'Satisfaction' in an uncertain warble.' When Bachrach asked Chuck about Linda Lovelace, he was quick to point out that he was responsible for Linda's success.

"Now Marilyn," said Traynor, indicating the star, 'she's different from Linda. She's got talent."[81]

However, just seven months before, when Chuck and Linda were still together, he told reporters, "Linda's very, very talented in two or three other ways than the film she has already done. She handles comedy very well."[82]

Now, he told Bachrach, Linda was "nothing more than a body with a name stuck on it."

'Chuck Traynor fairly swelled with pride as he looked about the nightclub and realized all he had done for Marilyn Chambers,' Bachrach wrote. "Oh sure,' he said, 'my dear friend Sammy Davis Jr. gave me a few pointers, but I was the guy who put this act together."

However, this particular rehearsal wasn't going well, so Joe Cassini, the choreographer, was 'going bananas.' Don Randi, the musical director, was 'privately cussing out the band,' muttering that 'they stink.' And Marilyn, 'weak from a cold, was wiggling her tiny fanny to 'Let the Good Times Roll."

Marilyn told Bachrach that she was confident in her talent, "but only Chuck knows how to bring it forth. Chuck changed my whole appearance.' Miss Chambers swallows her beer. 'He taught me how to be a lady.' And what is a lady? 'A lady,' says Miss Chambers gravely, 'A lady is someone who looks good. And doesn't speak unless she's spoken to."

Bachrach asked Marilyn if she felt jealous of Linda Lovelace, 'whose movie grossed $15 million more than hers, who was her predecessor in Traynor's affections?'

"Oh, no,' said Miss Chambers, vehemently shaking her pincurls, 'I'm not jealous of Linda Lovelace. And you know why?' Why? 'Because,' she replied simply, 'because Chuck never loved her."

When Marilyn took the stage two hours later, Bachrach wrote, the 'transformation was complete. She looked—and this is said with all due respect for her individuality—like Linda Lovelace.'

It's an astounding and confusing claim. Marilyn and Linda looked nothing alike. If Bachrach was trying to make the point that all porno starlets are interchangeable, it was lost.

The band was too loud...and the numbers too slow ... Miss Chambers danced in spangly bras and silver lamé jackets and flimsy pink pajamas, and people kept right on chewing and drinking. (She is still appearing, however; a spokesman at the River Boat [*sic*] said the run will last 'three or four more weeks.')

And a lot of the audience didn't like the show. A lot of them laughed at everyone and everything (except the comedian who preceded Miss Chambers.) Toward the end, a large man who said he had directed over 130 porno flicks lumbered over to a reporter's table. 'I want you to feel,' he said. Feel what? 'I want you to feel for that girl who's being exploited,' he said, walking away.[83]

THE NEW MARILYN CHAMBERS

It was a familiar, tiresome narrative. The one positive thing about stories like this is that it kept Marilyn's name in the press.

Marilyn (and Chuck) fired back at Bachrach in her book *My Story*.

'She's a very staunch women's libber, totally biased,' Marilyn wrote, adding that Bachrach showed up three hours early during the dress rehearsal:

> She was very put off that we wouldn't stop rehearsal for her, that we wouldn't take a break for her interview. I'm sorry, but the most important thing was the show, and she could wait. Judy talked with me for an hour, but I don't even think she stayed for the show. Maybe she hung around backstage for a few minutes after it started, but then she split. Judy did the interview with a chip on her shoulder, and in the interview, I told her the truth. I love men and depend on them, and that turned her off.[84]

Despite Bachrach's assessment, the Riverboat show received mostly positive reviews.

The New York *Daily News* wrote: 'Miss Chambers has a kind of girlish charm that is quite warming. She had little trouble in winning over her audience. She dances like mad, and when she gets her breath back, she sings. She moves like a go-go dancer, and her songs seem to suit her fine. The singer-dancer came through to this onlooker as a combination of Juliet Prowse and Ann-Margaret [*sic*] who needs only more experience to become a popular nightclub performer.'[85]

Syndicated columnist Earl Wilson, who turned down the opportunity to break the Ivory Snow story, gave Marilyn 'an A-plus for courage. Most of the girls were out to knife her for her figure. She can sure shake and wiggle and sings almost as well as other Instant Singers.'[86]

New York alternative biweekly newspaper *Good Times* wrote, 'It really doesn't matter, though, whether she can sing or dance. You should go see her because, very simply, she is the perfect woman. Forget her singing; her show is a visual extravaganza. Every move of her body commands your attention. Her final routine, performed in a G-String, was a sensual feast.'[87]

Norman Gaines, who saw Marilyn in *Skin 'n' Grin* and accompanied her and Chuck to her lecture at Hunter College, wrote in the *Columbia Daily Spectator*, 'Contrary to the stereotyped 'exploited female' movie star, Ms. Chambers was in complete control of the act, and all its musical elements. While her singing could use some improvement, the overall content of the show was excellent. Marilyn Chambers in her nightclub career seems to have a better basis for continued club performances than other film actresses-turned-entertainers such as Raquel Welch and Sally Kellerman.[88]

Gaines added that the Riverboat wasn't 'the ideal place to debut such a promising show.' He said the lighting system was poor, and the seating arrangement was terrible. Many tables were behind large pillars, obscuring patrons' view of the stage. Still, he urged readers to see the show.

David Tipmore of *The Village Voice* was unimpressed.

'Is audience anxiety the newest novelty in nightclub acts?' he asked. 'Does Marilyn Chambers think so? She seems to know the secret of making the crowd so worried and embarrassed *for* her that they'll do anything. Even clap.'[89]

The Riverboat appearance drew international press as well.

'The setting was, to say the least, a little odd,' wrote Alec Grant in the British magazine *Titbits*:

> For the singer on-stage in a New York night club in the basement of the Empire State Building was Marilyn Chambers, a star of hard-core porn films. And as she sang, danced, and shook her bottom at the audience, wearing only a G-string and tiny bra, the men and women from the stationary department of Macy's Store were applauding her act.
>
> And one of their leaders, a Miss Carmen Healy, said she thought Miss Chambers was 'a lovely entertainer' and might very well go to see one of her films. Which is quite a statement.[90]

'I was impressed with Marilyn from the start,' recalled keyboardist Don Randi, who was hired as musical director and arranger for the Riverboat engagement. Randi was part of the renowned group of studio musicians called The Wrecking Crew, who played uncredited on virtually every hit single of the sixties. Getting someone with Randi's credentials was a coup for Marilyn, and he was dazzled by her.

Randi praised her focus and work ethic. She took 'the preparation for the show very seriously because she wanted to prove she was more than an adult film actress,' he said. She had a good voice, he said, but she wanted to sing perfectly. She hired a voice coach to help her.

'[She] was a smash, and her show at the Riverboat went on for four months,' Randi wrote.[91]

During one performance, Marilyn felt her wig starting to slip. She reached up and made sure it was on more securely. She was pretty sure the audience didn't notice, but Chuck did.

'And, God, was he mad!' she recalled. 'It's a no-no to touch your wig on stage, and I soon learned that. It's not professional. Can you see Ann-Margret adjusting her wig in the middle of a number? Never. So I learned, I grew as the act progressed, and Chuck was always there to tell me what I was doing wrong.'[92]

When a reporter visited Marilyn backstage at the Riverboat and asked the seemingly non-sequitur question of who she'd like to be other than herself, she replied promptly, "Chuck Traynor."

"He's dynamite," she said. "He's a very, very intelligent person who knows about everything. He's got an instinct in him. I don't know what it is, but he's never wrong. I need to be dominated by a man."[93]

Marilyn expressed her desire to be dominated by a man so frequently, it's likely she believed it to be true. Long after Chuck was gone, she said it.

'There are different ways for a person to be dominant, but researchers consider social dominance to include traits like being authoritative, in control, and taking a leadership role,' wrote Gwendolyn Seidman, PhD, a professor of psychology and chair of the psychology department at Albright College in Reading, Pennsylvania. She continued:

> However, such traits are not normally associated with kind, caring people. Dominant people tend to be more self-centered and insensitive to others' feelings, not traits most of us seek in a romantic partner. For dominant individuals to be seen as desirable mates, they need to combine that commanding personality with other traits that show a willingness to be generous and helpful. Women want a partner who is competitive with others but treats them well. Anxious women appear to prefer dominant partners because they offer protection and *security*, while disinhibited, easily bored women seem to prefer dominant partners because they're *exciting*.[94]

Chuck could never be accused of being kind and caring, unless, as Linda Lovelace claimed, it was at the beginning of the relationship to establish control. Marilyn likely saw Chuck's dominance as protection and security. Apart from Chuck being a father figure, her reasons for desiring dominance are likely far-reaching. She never sought psychiatric help. There's no medical file to give an inkling as to what those reasons were. Her friends and family were at a loss for an explanation.

PURE *The Sexual Revolutions of Marilyn Chambers*

BY APRIL 1974, IT was reported that Marilyn's show at the Riverboat was doing 'the biggest business that the Club has done in the last three years.'[95] No figures were given, but it was noted by the press that the managers signed Marilyn for an additional three weeks, with an option to return in the summer for another four. The show's success drew more press notices, but many were hostile and flippant.

'Porno queen Marilyn Chambers whose tonsils you saw in closeup in such classy offerings as 'The Girl Behind the Green Door' [*sic*] and 'The Resurrection of Eve' [*sic*], has decided to show she has talent standing up too, and she debuted her singing-dancing act at the Riverboat,' columnist Dick Maurice wrote.

> Forget about the act (I'll give it four gargles) and just think of the interesting parts. A) She's supposedly a well-to-do girl from well-to-do parents in well-to-do Westport, Connecticut, and she never speaks about them in interviews on account of they ain't too proud of their kid. They'd prefer she was peddling dope or something refined like that. B) Her manager or agent, or whatever he is, is the newly divorced husband of fellow porno queen Linda 'Deep Throat' Lovelace. Guy's name's Chuck Traynor. With choreographers, singing coach, musicians, etc., the night club act cost $25,000 and better, and she should have given that money to the church.[96]

The Riverboat engagement coincided with a lavish ten-page layout in *Playboy* magazine, a first for an adult film star. After a successful cover and layout in *Genesis*, another men's magazine with a circulation of four million, she was asked by the editors to write a monthly sex advice column called "Private Chambers."[97]

In May 1974, Procter & Gamble released its revised packaging of Ivory Snow. It reiterated to the press that its current package, with Marilyn's photo, was inconsistent with the company's values. The new box also featured a mother and child, but it was created by sketch drawing. The boxes with Marilyn's photo were still in stores and would be phased out over time, P&G said.

'That P&G took this long to come up with a new package, after they first found out 11 months ago, shouldn't surprise anybody,' noted George Lazarus of the *Chicago Tribune*. 'P&G wasn't going to scrap 'Marilyn'—packaging costs too much.'[98]

Packaging costs undoubtedly factored into keeping the boxes with Marilyn in stores. Mass recalls are expensive, too. But sales likely wouldn't suffer if fans and collectors knew they had limited time to grab the most infamous laundry detergent box ever released.

THE NEW MARILYN CHAMBERS

With the release of the new box, P&G also took time to address Marilyn's comments on extending her contract. They said they didn't and paid her nothing more than the $2,000 fee she was initially contractually obligated to receive. Marilyn stuck with her story that P&G renewed her contract for ten years and paid her an additional $10,000 (nearly $63,000 today).

Another change P&G made was adding a morality clause to their modeling contracts. Models and actors were prohibited from appearing in anything "unsavory" when a P&G product was promoted. Other companies and agencies added the same stipulation to their contracts. Within the advertising and modeling industries, this was commonly referred to as the "Marilyn Chambers Clause."[99]

Although Marilyn's parents avoided discussing her career, on rare occasions, they would attend one of her shows if it wasn't X-rated. One night her father surprised her at the Riverboat. He wasn't alone. Marilyn was doubly surprised when she saw a woman who wasn't her mother on his arm. Marilyn knew the woman. It was a neighbor from Westport. Their long-term affair had been an open secret for years around town. William was often seen going into the woman's house. They had been circumspect in their actions initially, but only recently had they become more flagrant. The brazen act of William coming to see the Riverboat show unannounced and with his girlfriend left Marilyn devastated.

When the first run at the Riverboat ended in June, Marilyn took her nightclub act on the road to three states. The first stop was a two-week engagement at Lucifer's, a nightclub in the Kenmore Square neighborhood of Cambridge, Massachusetts. In their first three days in Boston, Marilyn and Chuck made five radio appearances, and spoke with an untold number of television and newspaper reporters. The price of admission at Lucifer's was usually one dollar but was bumped up to two dollars (nearly thirteen bucks today) for Marilyn's engagement. The club did steady business with both men and women. However, according to one person, Marilyn's entourage was discouraged that crowds weren't spilling out into the streets, given the press Marilyn and Chuck were doing.

A *Boston Globe* piece on the show focused less on the performance and more on attempting to psychoanalyze Marilyn.[100] The underlying questions in such articles often seemed to be: "Why did this woman appear in X-rated movies, and why does she believe she can do anything but appear in them?" Perhaps more to the point, the question was, "Who does she think she is?"

Globe reporter Otile McManus touched on all the usual topics unrelated to the show.

MONEY: 'Money, not sex, is Ms. Chambers' chief number,' McManus wrote. 'She is worth a half-million dollars [$3.1 million today], according to her agent, partner, and fiancé, Chuck Traynor, and [by June] she has already exceeded the $300,000 [$1.9 million today] which was projected as her 1974 income...He talked about several of the promotional deals they are considering. She talked about their $150,000 [$941,000 today] 'tri-level' house in Beverly Hills and her Jaguar XKE.'

HER PHYSICAL APPEARANCE: 'She is about 5-foot-five tall and looks like she couldn't weigh more than 90 pounds. To say she has a boyish figure is almost to put it mildly. She allowed how she doesn't look like Raquel Welch and added that she never will. 'You can't be sexy. If sexy is you, then it's you,' she said by way of explanation. 'I'd say being sexy is being young with a younger outlook.''

LINDA LOVELACE: 'A woman named Linda Lovelace represents [Chuck's] biggest claim to fame. He was married to Ms. Lovelace and is, he says, fully responsible for her performance in 'Deep Throat.''

SEX: 'Streakers are hardly titillating when you consider that Marilyn Chambers can be seen in theaters across the country performing explicit sex acts in movies like 'Behind the Green Door' and 'The Resurrection of Eve' [*sic*]... As Ms. Chambers talks about her ambitions and how healthy and liberated her attitudes towards sex are, one imagined her sitting pristinely in the waiting room of the Masters and Johnson clinic in St. Louis.'

COMPARISONS WITH OTHER FEMALE ENTERTAINERS: 'Traynor maintained there were differences between [Raquel] Welch and his fiancée, who will be listed in *Playboy* as one of 30 of the nation's wealthiest, non-college-educated young people. 'Raquel Welch can't really sing or dance. People come to see her because she is who she is. They orchestrate a show around her—a band, dancers—and the audience leaves thinking she's performed,' he said. 'Marilyn is really talented.''

Marilyn possessed talent as an entertainer beyond appearing in adult films. However, in Chuck's assessment of Raquel Welch, there seems to be some projection, jealousy, and confession. Marilyn had four screen credits to her name. None of these parts demanded classic acting techniques. The same could be said for Welch, a woman of great physical beauty but whose acting abilities were never exploited or used to their capacity, however limited. Neither was she an exceptional singer or dancer. However, she had starred in television specials and was a top Vegas headliner. While she never received glowing reviews for her acting, her live performances were well-received and did well at the box office.

But Welch never appeared in a porn film. So, she was granted the mainstream acceptance that Marilyn was not.

THE NEW MARILYN CHAMBERS

The cabaret show was a bright idea. It provided Marilyn an opportunity to display the areas in which she excelled. Yet her show, by all accounts, was very much like Chuck's description of Welch's show. People came to see Marilyn in part because she'd gained celebrity from starring in adult films. Traynor had wisely built a show around her, with a band, dancers, and songs. There was undoubtedly a curiosity in seeing an adult performer live in person—whether she was singing, dancing, or telling jokes—just as there was in seeing one of the most beautiful and photographed women in the world headlining at Caesars Palace.

UPCOMING PROJECTS: 'He talked about several of the promotional deals they are considering. 'For example, we've had an offer from 'Flooring Magazine.' It really is an in, hip magazine. They've used some in, hip people like Mick Jagger. People don't realize that John and Yoko don't live in a capsule. They probably have carpeting on the floor just like the rest of us.'[101]

CHUCK: 'If good marketing comes naturally to Ms. Chambers, it seems to be Chuck Traynor's raison d'être. He relaxed in their sixth-floor room at the Fenway Commonwealth Motel and talked about show business as if he were Bernie Cornfeld.[102] He's clad in studded blue jeans and a denim shirt slashed to reveal a gold chain hung with pendants. He talked with a Homestead, Fla., drawl. 'You can't even take it easy in this business. You don't have 15 years to make it. You got to make it happen now because it's happening now. If you're at nine and people lose interest, and you drop down to five, it's impossible to get back up to nine,' he said.'

Although the *Globe*'s McManus named a few of the show's songs, noted its lighting, and described one of Marilyn's costumes, he plainly thought those were secondary to considerations of money, looks, sex, Traynor, and more. As was common, the article ended with an insult:

> At least one couple at her Wednesday night performance didn't agree [she had talent].
> The woman suggested that beyond talent Ms. Chambers also lacked class.
> 'She can't sing; her dancing's nothing special. I don't know why anyone would pay to see her,' she said.
> Her companion nodded: 'She was better off with the soap flakes.'

Marilyn and Chuck next took the show to New Jersey's Cherry Hill neighborhood, in July, where one columnist offered a hostile critique. Before reviewing the show, *Philadelphia Daily News* columnist Larry Fields wrote that Marilyn wore a 'see-through blouse—only there wasn't much to see. Obviously, Marilyn, unlike Linda [Lovelace], doesn't believe in silicone.'

'Marilyn...proved to some 200 persons in the Chez Antonio lounge that she can do more than the things for which she was (and is) most famous,' Fields wrote. 'She REALLY can sing and dance, but not too well. She smiles a lot, wiggles her fanny a lot, and sings in a loud and frequently off-key voice. But she does what she does with considerable energy, sexiness, and, yes, charm.'[103]

Backstage Marilyn told Fields about an upcoming Vegas gig and a potential role in a Dino de Laurentiis film. She didn't name the Vegas venue or which film, just that both were in negotiation. 'In other words, nothing definite is lined up,' Fields wrote. Chuck, ever present as always, hovered by Marilyn's side during the interview. Chuck repeated the familiar line that Linda severely lacked what Marilyn had in spades: talent.

Fields noted that Marilyn interrupted the conversation with Chuck to ask permission to go to the bathroom. "Not right now," Chuck replied. Marilyn dutifully complied.

It's been reported by some, namely Gloria Steinem in her book *Outrageous Acts and Everyday Rebellions*, that Marilyn protested Chuck's instruction to not use the bathroom, and Chuck told her to "Just sit there and shut up." Fields allegedly objected, and Chuck interrupted him and angrily shot back, "I don't tell you how to write your column. Don't tell me how to treat my broads."[104] However, this back-and-forth exchange doesn't appear in the original article. It's a more-than-plausible scenario, but it seems unlikely that Fields wouldn't include it in his column.

Fields asked Chuck what kind of "magic" he had "to manipulate women like Marilyn Chambers and Linda Lovelace."

"I've got a lot of friends in show business," he answered. "And I know a lot about the business. I'm an entrepreneur."

'Most fellas who use women the way he does,' wrote Fields, 'might be called a different name.'

If Fields intended his piece to discourage people from seeing Marilyn's show, it didn't work.

'[N]ever underestimate the power of the press!' he wrote. 'Yesterday I wrote that porno movie star Marilyn Chambers is lacking a little something (like talent) at Pavio's Chez Antonio in Cherry Hill, where she is currently singing and dancing. So? So she's just been booked for a week-long gig at The Downingtown Inn starting next Friday.'[105]

Another reviewer attempted to be kinder, it seemed. The headline in the *Courier-Post*, "Soapbox Porno Queen Wows Pavio's Audience," would suggest the article accompanying it was a rave. Not exactly. The article began with customers griping about the unusually high $5 cover ($30 today). While the reporter, Lawrence A. Light, noted that Marilyn had filled the small bar to capacity

THE NEW MARILYN CHAMBERS

since her first appearance there, he quickly pointed out that she was backed by two 'conspicuously less pretty singers and an ear-jarringly loud rock band.' Light also wrote that Marilyn was so out of breath between dance numbers she could barely muster a "hello" to the audience. At one point during the performance, when she removed her jacket to reveal a see-through halter top, a regular male patron shouted at her: "Put the jacket back on!"

Light did not write what type of reaction, if any, Marilyn had to that comment. "She can really dance," Ronald E. Kyle, Marilyn's Cherry Hill-based booking agent, told the *Courier-Post*. "And she can sing...adequate."

The bar's ticket seller and bookkeeper admitted she was reluctant to book Marilyn at Pavio's because she was unsure what crowd she'd draw.

"But I was wrong," said the woman, who *Courier-Post*'s Light identified only as Rose. "We even had a man from the county prosecutor's office checking out her act."[106]

A reporter once asked Marilyn if she and Chuck saw themselves on some type of crusade. "Pioneers" was a better word, she replied.

"What we're doing has never been done before," she said. "In all his life, Chuck never followed what he was told to do or what was set down to do. And I've embraced that point of view—morally, legally, and every other way. And I think the result is that what may seem like a crusade to others is just an ordinary way of life to us. Once you've been there, it becomes old ground to you, no matter how exciting it seems to the next guy."[107]

THE NIGHTCLUB CIRCUIT WAS a promising start, but Marilyn's biggest goal was acting in a Hollywood film. She'd have to settle for dinner theater. It wasn't glamorous, but it provided an excellent opportunity to hone her skills and work alongside professional actors.

Jules Tasca's comedy *The Mind with the Dirty Man* opened at the Union Plaza Hotel in Las Vegas the week of September 30, 1974.[108] The play had previously been staged, without Marilyn, in Los Angeles, San Francisco, and Chicago. If the Vegas run was a success, there were talks of bringing it to New York. Marilyn was ecstatic at the prospect.

"At long last, I'll be starring on Broadway," Marilyn said, beaming. "That definitely proves there is a new and unrepressed attitude toward sex in this country today. About ten years ago, I would have been thrown in jail or burned at the stake."[109]

Marilyn played the girlfriend of a free-spirited young man rebelling against his parents. He purchases his small hometown's local movie house intending to turn it into a palace of pornography. The town council is upset; the president is the young man's father. The play tackled timely issues of obscenity, pornography and morality with comedic flair, never taking itself too seriously.

While a three-act straight comedic play seemed almost antithetical to flashy Las Vegas and its elaborate stage shows, it clicked with audiences and became an instant hit. It was booked for an indefinite run at the Union Plaza, playing two shows a night, six nights a week.

Critics took note of Marilyn, and she earned praise for her performance.[110]

The Hollywood Reporter commented that she was 'very promising and makes her role work surprisingly well.' Las Vegas columnist Forrest Duke said, 'Miss Chambers is a pleasant surprise, showing great flair as a comedienne.'

Playwright Jules Tasca was also pleased with Marilyn's performance.

"She had good comic timing, she held her own with everybody, and they were highly satisfied with the job that she did," he remembered.[111]

He spent a couple of weeks in Vegas when the show started and would have lunch with her, Chuck, and other cast and crew members every day. Her part, as originally written, was that of a free-spirited hippie. Along the way, he said it got changed by producers or mischaracterized in the press as a porn star because Marilyn was in the role.

"She was the draw," Tasca said:

> Everybody knew who she was at the time. Marilyn Chambers didn't come off the way people would think she came off. She was a very kind, soft-spoken person, even though she had a wild sexual desire. People enjoyed her company, who spent time with her at lunch, and things like that. She was not a primadonna. I didn't know what to expect. I have never seen *Behind the Green Door*. I didn't know what the hell she did or what she was doing. All I knew was that the reason they put her in the play was because she'd be drawing [audiences to] Vegas.[112]

Chuck, on the other hand, was not well-received by the cast and crew.

"We genuinely didn't like him because we thought he was taking advantage of her," Tasca said. "He was taking a cut of her money. He wasn't *doing* anything. He was just looking out for her because he was buying stock. He bought Marilyn Chambers. And he wanted to protect his investment. Usually, when he would say something, people started rolling their eyes and things like that. He wasn't well liked—but she was."[113]

Tasca said that despite being soft-spoken and congenial, Marilyn could sometimes be naughty.

THE NEW MARILYN CHAMBERS

One evening she was having dinner at a restaurant with a group of men: Chuck, Tasca, some cast, crew, and the husband of the play's co-star Jane Keane. After the meal, the men decided to have cigars. Tasca stayed behind at the table with Marilyn.

"Are you in trouble with the soap company at all?" he asked, making conversation.

"No," she replied. "But I *am* very highly sexed. That part is true."

"Oh?"

"Oh, yes. When I sit here with all these guys around the table, I fantasize about myself being under the table giving everybody oral sex."[114]

She might have sworn off adult films, but she still inhabited the character of Marilyn Chambers. All sex, all the time.

For example, halfway through its run, Marilyn and Chuck decided Marilyn should appear onstage with fewer clothes to maintain her sex goddess image. Maynard Sloate, the producer, strongly disagreed. Onstage nudity was against the law in Las Vegas. The Union Plaza could lose its liquor and gaming license if authorities found out. Sloate attended a Saturday night dinner performance in January 1975, and during a scheduled dance number, Marilyn appeared "with so little clothes on she might as well have been naked!"

"Her image doesn't concern me," he fumed to the *Las Vegas Sun*. "But the play does, and she is not going to shed her clothes."[115]

He ordered stage manager Paul Sziegty to instruct Marilyn that she was to wear the clothes called for in the script. Chuck got involved, and a lengthy argument broke out between the two men. Sloate intervened when the off-stage argument became noticeable to patrons.

"I think Sloate should get his head out of the sand," Chuck said.

"My head is not, nor has it been in the sand," Sloate replied. "When I say Marilyn Chambers will wear clothes during a performance, she's going to wear clothes."[116]

When a reporter asked Marilyn about the kerfuffle, she said: "I'm not ashamed of my body, and I can't understand what all the hang-up is regarding nudity. After all, it's an adult play in an adult town."[117]

Marilyn took many press photos for the play in the nude, but she relented and wore the costumes during the performance.

On December 2, 1974, Marilyn's divorce from Doug was finalized.[118] Marilyn and Chuck married in a small private ceremony in Sammy Davis, Jr.'s suite in Nevada three days later.[119] Davis served as best man, and his wife, Altovise, was the maid of honor.

Davis was well-known for his love of pornography. In his autobiography *Why Me?*, he wrote: 'I was intrigued by the porn world and wanted to meet Linda Lovelace, so I called her and got friendly with her and her husband, Chuck Traynor. I also became close to Marilyn Chambers.'[120]

"Marilyn had a special quality," Davis told *Gallery* magazine. "If Marilyn is going to continue in the field, and I don't say you have to do that the rest of your life, thank God we've grown beyond that. But I think Marilyn, Georgina [Spelvin], and Linda Lovelace should do one movie together. And I think it should be called *The Last Porno Movie*."

When asked who would direct, Davis quickly replied: "Me."[121]

Davis experienced a career renaissance in the early seventies. He had his biggest hit with the 1972 release The Candy Man, which topped the Billboard chart and earned a Grammy nomination. That same year he made a guest appearance as himself on a landmark episode of the culture-shifting sitcom *All in the Family*.

Davis served as Marilyn's main entree into elite celebrity social circles. He helped introduce her to old and new Hollywood stars she otherwise would not have met. At one of Davis's parties, she was in 'deep conversation at the bar' with actress Loretta Young—the princess of porn and the farmer's daughter.[122] Marilyn and Chuck regularly socialized with Davis. Being seen around town with a mainstream entertainer added credibility to Marilyn's image. Marilyn worked Davis's name into as many interviews as possible. She aspired to have a show business career like his, she said. Unfortunately, their friendship did nothing to help her career overall. Davis introduced Marilyn and Chuck to important people, but he didn't negotiate deals for them. Marilyn and Chuck had to do that themselves. With Marilyn's notoriety as an X-rated star and Chuck's polarizing personality, the meetings with VIPs likely proved more difficult than they anticipated.

It was through their friendship that Marilyn had a moment of reckoning. Davis was scheduled to guest host *The Tonight Show* and wanted Marilyn as a guest. Finally, she would appear on the most-watched late-night talk show in the country. Johnny Carson had never had an adult film star on the program. Her appearance on *The Tonight Show* would have been a first of its kind. The producers nixed the idea at the last minute, and Davis had to break the bad news to Marilyn.

"*The Tonight Show* wasn't ready for me," she said. "The pornography thing had a bad connotation, and now I was seeing the consequences. I was crushed, but it was also kind of hypocritical because everybody [famous] wanted to know me and meet me."[123]

Tracey Davis wrote in her book *Sammy Davis, Jr., My Father*:

THE NEW MARILYN CHAMBERS

He was friends with a lot of people, all sorts of people—Pop didn't discriminate for any reason. I remember stopping by his house with [my husband] Guy and finding one of the most surprising visitors of all. A very pretty blond woman was chatting with Dad. He introduced her. She was Marilyn Chambers, the porn star. She was so normal and really a lot of fun. After she left, Guy turned to me and said, 'She has sex on film. Wow. Can you believe it? What a trip.'[124]

A sign on the Davis family home greeted guests with the words: 'This house welcomes all colors, races and religions as long as they have peace and love in their hearts.'[125]

Marilyn and Sammy became both friends and lovers. Davis liked to lavish gifts upon Marilyn, particularly jewelry. Marilyn got her labia pierced with a ring, studded with twenty diamonds, that Davis purchased; he bought it to honor the body part that made her famous. In addition to writing her monthly sex advice column for *Genesis* magazine, Marilyn often appeared within its pages in photo layouts. Davis especially liked a photo in one layout, which had been taken at his home for the magazine. Marilyn wears nothing but an unbuttoned shirt. A belly chain—her fashion trademark—glints. She's drenched in sunlight, giving her an ethereal aura and a fulgent halo. The entire layout is beautiful, but this one shot Davis particularly liked. A copy was made for him. According to Marilyn, he hung it in his bathroom where 'he used to go jerk off while popping amyl nitrates.' It wasn't entirely a dismissive comment.

'That picture meant a lot to me,' she wrote. 'Actually, envisioning that scene in my mind sums up my life with Sammy. On one hand, he treated me like an angel. On the other hand (which was usually grabbing his dick), I was strictly a means of enabling his fantasies to come true. Add some drugs, and the picture's pretty much complete.'[126]

The Mind with the Dirty Man was a massive hit. Heralded as the 'sleeper of the year,'[127] it ran for fifty-two weeks—the longest-running play in Las Vegas history at the time. More than 175,000 Vegas visitors attended the performances.[128] The longer it ran, the more producers discussed bringing the show to Broadway. There were talks about adapting the play for film, too.

It wasn't rare for Marilyn to look out into the audience during the show and see a table of men ogling her. She enjoyed being desired. One night during the show's run, she was shocked to see a table of men and, among them, her father. Her mother wasn't there. It was her father and his friends watching a half-naked Marilyn onstage. Marilyn thought it was odd. He never mentioned he was coming to this performance. This marked the second time, after the Riverboat, that he showed up unannounced. She appreciated any time he attended one of her performances. It marginally made up for all the swim meets he missed. But it left her with a strange feeling. It brought to mind the story she heard about some of her father's New York friends taking him to see *Behind the Green Door* without telling him who was in it.

Marilyn took an eight-week break from *Dirty Man* in the summer of 1975 to do a publicity tour for her newly-released autobiography, *My Story*, and begin working on a second book co-authored with famed escort Xaviera Hollander.

'The public appetite for the life stories of porno stars seems insatiable,' wrote Michael Perkins in *Screw*. 'Even the biggest legitimate movie stars usually wait until they're in semi-retirement before they tell all to a ghostwriter, but porno stars can't afford to wait so long.'[129]

Indeed, books by adult stars briefly sprouted a subgenre that came to be known as "erotobiographies." Linda Lovelace published two. Harry Reems and Marc Stevens, Marilyn's co-stars in *Skin 'n' Grin*, also published books about their lives. *My Story*, Marilyn's tale, had three distinct voices: Marilyn's, Chuck's, and the ghostwriter's. Many basic facts and anecdotes are true, especially those told in Marilyn's voice. Some stories, like Marilyn's first sexual encounter with a woman and how she lost her virginity, are told with great exaggeration to titillate the reader. Chuck was given his own chapter to wax lyrical about how wonderful he was.

Marilyn dedicated the book to him: 'To Chuck, my Traynor, and constant companion. Thanks for making my life so beautiful! Lovingly, Marilyn.' It's unlikely Chuck would have allowed her to dedicate it to anyone else. Linda Lovelace dedicated her first book, *Inside Linda Lovelace*, to 'Chuck Traynor—the creator. L.L.' But her second, *The Intimate Diary of Linda Lovelace*, published in 1974 after their divorce, was dedicated to 'Chuck the Schmuck.'

My Story was published in paperback by Warner Books in June 1975.

'Her book is a good read...for a number of reasons,' read the review in *Screw*. 'One is that whoever wrote it (it's hard to believe she did) does a competent job of exciting a reader's page-turning mechanism. There's enough sex and enough of an inside glimpse of the fascinating (to outsiders) porno film industry to hook even reluctant readers.'[130]

The reviewer also makes an astute observation when assessing the juxtaposition of Marilyn's all-American upbringing and her image as the queen of X-rated films.

What's more intriguing is the thought that the product of such a background became a porno queen—which seems to me even more typically American, and not much of a contradiction at all... The product of that kind of background is geared for success from birth, and it doesn't really matter where that success comes from as long as it finally arrives.

Traynor is also typically American, but in a different way. He's an independent entrepreneur with an instinctual knowledge of women, which has taken him to the top of the list of great pimps. The pair are perfect representatives of the newest version of the American Dream.[131]

It did not go unnoticed by the reviewer that 'Marilyn's dependence on Traynor seems fully as great as Linda Lovelace's was.'

Other reviewers found the book an 'image-conscious ego trip.'

'It's the old Hollywood routine: fight your way up, discard those who love you but can't help you climb, work hard, cultivate a glamorous image, publish your autobiography (which contains the word 'I' a dozen times on each page) and try to achieve stardom—and hope you don't end up a suicide, like Marilyn Monroe, like many of the Hollywood survivors. Good luck, Marilyn Chambers, and you'll need it,' wrote *FLICK* magazine reporter Dick Valentine.[132]

It was risible to publish Marilyn Chambers's life story when she was barely twenty-three. She agreed. She told a friend two decades later, "They came to me to write my life story. I was twenty-one-fucking-years old! I didn't even have a life story at that point."[133]

But there was money to be made for Marilyn, Chuck, and Warner Books. And a book was another legitimate way to brand "Marilyn Chambers." Oddly, the mainstream press didn't review it. Warner Books was part of Warner Brothers, which most assuredly had a good PR department. The "porno chic" fad was over, but Marilyn was a well-known name. What the book lacked in mainstream reviews it made up for in sales. *My Story* sold several hundred thousand copies and went into second and third printings. Xaviera Hollander, born Xaviera de Vries in 1943, was a secretary in a Dutch consulate in Manhattan when she quit to become a call girl. It was 1968, and she went from earning a secretary's wages to more than $1,000 a night ($8,700 in 2023). A year later, she opened a brothel and became New York City's premier madam. She was arrested for prostitution in 1971. That same year she published her ghostwritten memoir, *The Happy Hooker*. It sold over twenty million copies—and thrust Hollander into the mainstream as an outspoken advocate for sex workers and sex positivity.

Attorney Paul Sherman, whose clients included both Hollander and Marilyn, had the idea for the two women to collaborate on a book: The Happy Hooker Meets the Ivory Sex Goddess. Neither woman had met the other, but they both liked the idea and made a week-long trip to Toronto to discuss their sex lives.

PURE *The Sexual Revolutions of Marilyn Chambers*

Their conversations would be recorded and then transcribed. Hollander came up with most of the questions, and did the transcription and first draft herself.

The ladies (and Chuck) holed up at the Four Seasons Motor Hotel on Jarvis Street.

For a book chronicling the coital concerns of two seventies sexual icons, it's incredibly dull. Hollander's voice dominates, and she comes off as impersonal. The book's aridity is probably one of the reasons it didn't sell. In fact, Hollander considered the book a turning point in her career as a writer.

"It was my own downfall for any book I tried to write and get published afterwards, as it was too superficial and basically boring, I hate to say," she said.[134] Nor did she have many kind words for Marilyn.

"In all the interviews I had with her, she never made me smile," she said.

> I was aghast at [how] she wanted to introduce the book to the public with a dedication to Chuck—who was her manager, abuser, and user at that time—by writing: 'To Chuck, My Traynor.' If that didn't show how dependent and enslaved she was to that horrid man(ager). I really could not get truly inspired to add some humor to that booklet. She was outright boring, far too skinny for my taste, and what I would call a working-class type, much like Linda Lovelace. So neither Linda nor Marilyn appealed to my good taste in women.
>
> At one point, for the record, Marilyn and I ended up in bed together. Now, I do know how to please almost any woman in bed as long as she is for real and not a phony so-called lesbian or even a bisexual, which [Marilyn] claimed she was, which she was definitely not. While Chuck was watching and cheering us on, she screamed for happiness, supposedly, but what I felt under my hands and mouth was a frigid woman putting on a great loud act for her man, an act of make-believe as she remained as dry as the back of my hand. And neither did I—who really loves women as well as men—get excited.[135]

Following her book tour, Marilyn returned to her role in *The Mind with the Dirty Man* in August 1975. The play was still the most popular and longest-running in Las Vegas. The mayor gave cast members the key to the city.

MARILYN'S BUSY SCHEDULE MADE it tough for her and Chuck to visit their families, but she spoke by phone occasionally with her parents and siblings and wrote frequent letters to Elaine, Chuck's mother. Periodically the couple visited Elaine in Florida. Family photos show a beaming Chuck standing beside his mother with his arm around her. From the tone of Marilyn's letters, it's clear she adored Elaine.

When the pair visited Marilyn's family, her siblings noticed a change in Marilyn's demeanor. She was aloof and restrained, especially when Chuck was around. It was difficult to determine if she was acting out the part of "Marilyn Chambers," like a character in a real-life movie, or if this was a new persona. There were likely several reasons, but one thing was clear: Marilyn behaved differently when Chuck was around. Not that he was especially social with Marilyn's family. "He didn't say much," Jann, Marilyn's sister, remembered. "He always reminded me of the word 'Svengali.' He kind of looked at you, just looked at you a lot, like he knew more than you did. [He was] sort of an odd personality and uncomfortable. I think that she just really, really, really talked him into coming because it was important. And he let her do it. It was all about what he let her do."[136]

Marilyn and Chuck were offered a drink when they visited Jann and her husband in Washington. Chuck didn't drink much, and he didn't let Marilyn have a drink either, Jann said.

"Then we were playing Trivial Pursuit," Jann continued, "and she pulled me out of the room. She said, 'I don't think this is a good thing for Chuck.'"

"Why?" Jann asked.

"He can't read," said Marilyn. "What do you mean?" a stunned Jann replied.

"He's illiterate," Marilyn whispered.

"How could he be illiterate when he's your business manager?"

"Well, he gets by," Marilyn said.[137]

Chuck didn't particularly like it when Marilyn was reunited with both siblings simultaneously.

"He was pretty standoffish," Bill remembered. "He would stand back and watch us interact. All three of us got together, and [he would] not say much. But he was controlling her, I could tell. It appeared that way to me. Also, I had heard stories [about him controlling her]."[138]

Marilyn made a fatal mistake when she put herself in the hands of an illiterate, abusive, opportunistic, misogynist. A once-promising career was derailed. It was a most abstruse interpersonal dynamic. Chuck ticked several boxes: he was a father figure who promised to guide and support her career. Yet there were classic signs of an abusive domestic relationship, including isolation and verbal and emotional maltreatment. There was even at least one instance of physical abuse to that point. He was a malevolent force.

For most people in an abusive relationship, simply walking away isn't that easy. For a public figure, it's even more complex. By the time Marilyn realized her situation, it was too late. She loved Chuck. He was a master manipulator hellbent on maintaining his lucrative possession. For her part, Marilyn was consumed by the "Marilyn Chambers" character. She had no other identity. There was no other option but to stay with Chuck and keep working.

Liz Boyd, Marilyn's childhood friend, recalled the first time she met Chuck, when he and Marilyn were in Westport one time. She visited them at their hotel.

"I went up to their room, and we chatted for a bit," Boyd said. "She told me to bring a bathing suit. Marilyn said, 'We're gonna go down by the pool, Chuck.' And he's like, 'OK, go ahead. I'll see you in a bit.' We walked out of a hotel room, and she stopped in the hallway. 'Holy shit, Liz,' she said. 'He never lets me go anywhere without him. He must really trust you.' She was just floored. She said, 'He never lets me out of his sight.'"

Boyd said she invited Marilyn and Chuck over to her house for a small party. Marilyn went, but Chuck stayed at the hotel. In fact, he never left the hotel room the entire time the couple was in town.

"It always made me wonder after that what the hell was he *doing*?"[139] Boyd said.

With each infrequent visit from Marilyn and Chuck, Jann noticed that Marilyn also became more of a diva. It was no secret Marilyn craved the spotlight, but her lust for attention bordered on obsession and correlated with a more defiant attitude.

"She was in this dynamic of 'I'm going to be a star. Chuck's the one that's making the star,'" Jann said. "It was much more 'It's all about me' than she had been before, and to me a little bit more narcissistic. I always felt like that's really not quite who she is. I think she liked it a little bit. But he definitely had control over her. And I never understood it. Never did."[140]

Drugs were prevalent in the marriage, particularly cocaine. Chuck didn't get whacked out on drugs. Nor did he drink to the point of drunkenness. If he had, his inhibitions would have been loosened and he would no longer be in control. He tried to control not only how much liquor and drugs Marilyn consumed, but when and where she did them. "He was feeding her drugs," Bill said. "I mean, she was willingly taking them, obviously, but he was supplying her with drugs, from what I could tell. She had a nice car and a certain amount of freedom, but I think he was trying to control the drug use. I think he was trying to control that. Like, have it not get too out of hand. She'd get together with me, and she'd break out the coke. And we'd be doing coke, and he would be scowling. It never seemed like a cordial relationship between the two."[141]

Bill described his sister as "happy-go-lucky." When she married Chuck and cocaine entered the picture, that plucky, bubbly young woman ceased to exist. For a woman in her situation it's almost a foregone conclusion.

In 1975, *Hustler* magazine asked Chuck if he and Marilyn wanted a family.

"Oh, yeah. Sure," he said. "Two girls."[142]

It was one of Chuck's few, if only public confessions that he desired children. He never considered himself a family man. On the other hand, Marilyn strongly desired a family. She just wasn't sure when.

Marilyn shared some devastating news during one visit to her sister's home.

"She was drinking at our house one night and got all weepy and stuff, crying in the bedroom," Jann recalled. She went to check on Marilyn and asked what was wrong. "And she said, '[Chuck] made me have an abortion. And I didn't want to do it. I don't know; I don't think he's ever going to let me have a baby.' I was just heart-sore for her. It took me a while to get her to calm down."[143]

Jann tried to comfort and reassure Marilyn, but she could no longer hold her tongue when it came to Chuck.

"I'm like, 'Well, it's not the end of the world. You can have a baby—but it should not be with him. Marilyn, why are you with him? Why?'" she said. "And I don't remember what the answer was, but they cut their visit short."

The next day the couple said they had to fly home for a gig.

"I think it was because he saw she needed me," Jann speculated. "I was nurturing, and he didn't like that. He didn't want to see her being nurtured by anybody else but himself."

Jann believes Marilyn had at least one more abortion with Chuck. "He didn't want her to have kids," she said. "He didn't want her to have a family. That was who he was."

It was never a pleasant experience when Marilyn and Chuck visited Jann or Bill. But even when Chuck wasn't there physically, which was rare, his presence loomed large. One visit to Jann's proved to be a breaking point for the sisters.

Marilyn began drinking beer early in the morning. The phone rang, and Marilyn answered it. Suddenly, Jann heard Marilyn screaming and crying from her room. She ran to her and asked what was going on. Marilyn was nearly hysterical. Jann grabbed the phone. It was Chuck. He called to tell Marilyn her cat had died. It somehow got trapped under the couple's home and froze to death.

"She was like a maniac," Jann said.

Then she started saying horrible things to me. I couldn't believe it. Then she said, 'You know, I could have your husband in a minute!' That was the last straw. I said, 'You need to leave. You need to leave right now.' She's screaming about her cat, and I said, 'I don't care about your cat, and I don't care about you.' It was very nasty. She pushed me over the edge. I turned to my husband and said, 'I'm going to take the kids to school. I want her gone by the time I get back. You need to take her to the airport. I need you to drop her off and leave her there.' She just pushed me right over the edge. Then we did not speak for a number of years. And that's too bad because she probably could have used me at that point. But she was drinking, and she was doing drugs. I told her she couldn't do it in my house [because] I had small kids. That was just not appropriate behavior. I think she was just really in a lot of pain, a lot of pain. And I think it was because of Chuck. He didn't have to tell her the cat froze to death under the house.[144]

The press was not unaware of Marilyn and Chuck's relationship either. One paragraph in a 1975 article by *Chicago Sun-Times* reporter Laura Green is heartbreaking:

'Traynor is Svengali to her Trilby. He is her mentor, leader, lover, manager, and only friend on the road. She has no personal life, no friends besides Traynor. The two live out of suitcases and rarely get home to their places in Los Angeles and the Nevada hills. 'Our lifestyle doesn't permit friends. Fortunately, Chuck's my friend,' she said.'[145]

The article continued: 'She laughs at the women who say she's being exploited for her looks and randy image, and her voice gets hard as brass. 'I own 90 percent of myself, and I expect to make $350,000 this year,' she said. [This is nearly $2 million in today's money.] 'I do what I want; they do what they want.''[146]

It begs the question: who owned the other ten percent of Marilyn Chambers?

MORE THAN THREE YEARS after they premiered, *Green Door* and *Eve* were still playing in adult cinemas nationwide, often on a double bill. The two films also went to Japan, with Marilyn in tow for a promotional tour. In the US, law enforcement still cracked down on adult theaters but not as much as during the "porno chic" fad. X-rated films continued to make a healthy profit. Still, after Watergate, which was the biggest political crime in American history to that point; the unprecedented resignation of President Richard Nixon (before he was impeached for involvement in the Watergate crimes); the 1973–1974 stock market crash; the official end of the Vietnam War in late April 1975; an ongoing oil and energy crisis; and the kidnapping of media heiress Patricia ("Patty") Hearst—after all that, somehow, the crime of publicly showing an adult film paled.

That's not to say the general public readily accepted the movies or Marilyn. In

THE NEW MARILYN CHAMBERS

early 1976, Marilyn was invited to participate in a panel discussion on women's sexuality in cinema. It was at the International Women's Film festival, held at Tulane University, in New Orleans, and sponsored by the French and Canadian consulates. The festival would also screen a new X-rated film, *Inside Marilyn Chambers*, directed by the Mitchell brothers. Just the invitation to attend the festival caused great consternation from other attendees—particularly Canadian filmmaker Micheline Charest, who was scheduled for the same panel discussion.

The panel 'nearly fizzled,' according to the Associated Press, 'as Parisian filmmakers Liliane de Kermadec and Dolores Grassian maintained a haughty distance from Marilyn and Brazilian cinematographer Anna Carolina confessed she was 'intimidated' by the microphones and packed auditorium.'[147]

Marilyn talked about her role in *Green Door* and told the audience it was meant purely as entertainment.

"It's a very submissive type of fantasy," she said. "It's one of my very favorite ones."

Charest, the Canadian filmmaker, went into a frenzy during the post-panel screening of *Inside Marilyn Chambers*. She "stalked out of the theater saying she was 'too angry to think clearly.'"

"If there weren't so much money involved in that kind of film, I might have some money to make films," she said.[148]

Charest was working on a documentary about the women's movement at the time. It's unclear what money had to do with it. The Mitchell brothers were independent filmmakers and used their money to finance their films. It wasn't their fault, or Marilyn's, that their films were making tens of millions of dollars. Nor was it anyone's fault that they had scored an unexpected publicity boost from the Ivory Snow scandal. Hollywood certainly wasn't doling out money to the Mitchells or Marilyn to make more films.

Marilyn's presence at the festival was deemed "most unfortunate" by a member of the French consulate. "The other women directors—what can they say now?" he asked.

Festival director Ron Weinberg said Marilyn served a purpose in participating, but even his reasoning was misguided at best.

"She's a catalyst who has helped the transformation of most first-run theaters into pornographic movie houses," he said. "It's an issue that has to be discussed. People no longer have the freedom to see what they want."

It's a ludicrous statement from a director of an international film festival. The issue of pornography was certainly a credible matter of debate, but by 1976 most first-run theaters were *not* showing X-rated films anymore. In asking Marilyn to participate and argue in favor of pornography, he put the "freedom to choose" of

PURE
The Sexual Revolutions of Marilyn Chambers

the cinema-going public squarely on the shoulders of Marilyn Chambers.

Weinberg also admitted that one of the reasons Marilyn was invited was to "provide certain guarantees" the festival would make money.[149]

As the Associated Press reported, 'About 1,000 students, faculty members, and curious local residents purchased $10 festival tickets [roughly fifty-five bucks in today's money] to see Miss Chambers. Some women shouted obscenities, and others sat in stony silence as Miss Chambers labeled men 'the dominant race.' Some men shouted. 'Take it off.' 'If [these women] don't want to be submissive, what do they want to be—dominant?" Marilyn posited.[150]

"BELIEVE ME, NEW ORLEANS wasn't ready for it," Marilyn said about *Inside Marilyn Chambers*.[151]

Neither was Marilyn. The film was made in 1975 by the Mitchell brothers without her knowledge.

Marilyn, Jim, and Art hadn't communicated much since parting ways in late 1973. The brothers were still smarting from her abrupt departure. Moreover, the only film they released after *Resurrection of Eve* was their 1975 epic, *Sodom and Gomorrah: The Last Seven Days*. It was advertised as having a $1 million budget (approximately $5.5 million today) and was the brothers' cocaine-fueled interpretation of the Biblical saga, with a subplot of extraterrestrial aliens observing Earth. It flopped spectacularly at the box office.

"We were friends, and business partners, which was a good marriage until Chuck took over the business aspect of my career," Marilyn said. "Then the friendship ended. I really don't know why it had to, but it did. They told Chuck I was nothing, that I had sucked off some spades on screen, and that was as much as I was ever going to be. They told him that I was washed up."[152]

The Ivory Snow scandal had significantly elevated the public attention for everyone involved, but it wasn't what made the films successful. It was Marilyn Chambers. The Mitchell brothers proved they couldn't make another hit film without her. Marilyn, however, was still making headlines (for better or worse) and earning some positive notices for her performances.

The brothers had hours of unused and behind-the-scenes footage from *Green Door* and *Eve*, most featuring Marilyn. They cobbled together some of what they considered the better clips, including alternate shots of several sex scenes, padded it with interviews from male co-stars like Johnnie Keyes, and called it *Inside Marilyn Chambers*. It had its world premiere on January 23, 1976, at several of the Mitchells' theaters.[153] It was billed as "The All-American

THE NEW MARILYN CHAMBERS

Girl Exposed!" with "the only other hardcore footage in existence of Marilyn Chambers" and promised to tell her "true story." There was only one problem: the story wasn't true. They made up details about her life, such as that she had graduated from Vassar College in Poughkeepsie, New York. That didn't matter to them. The film was the brothers' way of getting even for Marilyn's perceived betrayal—and make some money in the process.

Marilyn may have negotiated royalties for *Green Door* and *Eve* but did not own the copyright for either film. When she found out about *Inside Marilyn Chambers*, she was livid. A new hardcore film starring Marilyn Chambers, even if it were made up of footage from two other films, would not help her chances of landing any straight dramatic roles. The brothers didn't need her permission to use the footage, but they didn't even notify her of the film's release. Their behavior was similar to Marilyn's when she signed a contract with Chuck and then told the brothers about it. A lawsuit would only draw attention to the film, so Marilyn decided to contact the brothers. Maybe they would keep the movie under wraps if she could clear the air.

She pleaded with the brothers to not release the film. The brothers were set on releasing it, but they agreed to cut Marilyn in on the film's profits if she would appear in the film and help promote it. She begrudgingly accepted. She made several personal appearances at the Mitchells' theaters, including the O'Farrell in San Francisco and the Four Star Theater in Los Angeles. Before the film was shown, she signed autographs in the lobby, briefly chatting with each patron. Once the autograph session was completed, she retreated to the dressing room, where she changed into two *Inside Marilyn Chambers* t-shirts and two pairs of bikini panties. Before the film was shown, she paraded across the stage and entertained the audience with a striptease. The t-shirts and panties were given away to members of the audience. There she stood stark naked—the outside of Marilyn Chambers for the audience to ogle. Then the projector started, and the film, which Marilyn detested, began.

Charles A. Fracchia, a San Francisco historian and one of the founders of *Rolling Stone* magazine, wrote about Marilyn's appearance at the O'Farrell Theater to promote the film. He had first interviewed her during the production of *Eve*. In the three years since he noticed a remarkable transformation.

'The Marilyn Chambers on the stage, helping the Mitchells promote the film, was not the porn star of old, glorying in her All-American face and cheerleader's body, enjoying the flood of publicity accorded her when, after she made *Behind the Green Door*, it was discovered that she was pictured on millions of boxes of Ivory Snow with a baby in her arms, but also unsure of herself, insecure about her new position of adulation, and unhappy about various aspects of her life,' he wrote. 'Time had treated Marilyn well. Her body was at its lush prime. Her successful career was professionally managed. What has changed substantially in Marilyn during the past few years is her 'rap.' During her days as a porn actress, Marilyn would speak of little else than how pornographic films should be allowed, were good for society, etc. She has not changed these opinions, but she has expanded her philosophical repertoire. She has become much more willing to discuss other aspects of her life and ideas.'[154]

Unfortunately, Fracchia neglected to mention any of the aspects, ideas, or philosophies.

Whenever Marilyn was in San Francisco, Meredith Bradford, Art's wife, went to the O'Farrell to catch up with her old friend. But there was something peculiar. The effervescent Marilyn was no longer.

"She kind of changed a lot after she met [Chuck]," Meredith recalled. "She just closed down. She would just glaze over; she just didn't want to talk. I didn't understand her situation at the time, but she was a lot different. She just wasn't forthcoming the way she had always been in a personal conversation."[155]

Word of Marilyn's pre-film stage appearances made its way to law enforcement, and in some cases, rumors made their way to Chuck and Marilyn that police officers would be sent to theaters to detain Marilyn if and when she disrobed completely. At one theater in Carmichael, California, about eleven miles from Sacramento, Chuck spied a man in a red jacket and felt certain he was an undercover cop. Marilyn performed her show as usual, ending it in the nude. The man in the red jacket stood up and started walking down the aisle toward the stage. Marilyn froze. Chuck grabbed her by the arm and pulled her offstage.

'The agile Miss Chambers made a quick getaway out a rear door wearing only a few goosebumps under a black cape thrown hastily over her shoulders,' wrote Wayne Wilson in *The Sacramento Bee*. 'Their fears apparently were unfounded. No attempt was made by law enforcement to inhibit the very personal appearance of the girl from 'Behind the Green Door.''[156]

Inside Marilyn Chambers, which cost $25,000 to produce (more than $137,000 in today's dollars), earned $40,000 (nearly $220,000 today) in its first two days of release. Like the one in Carmichael, the crowds were 'surprisingly young, surprisingly open, and surprisingly mixed sexually.'[157]

'Contrary to rumors, it will not be Marilyn Chambers' last porno flick,' *The Bee* noted.[158] It was an unusual mixed message, most likely from Chuck. Chuck was possibly reconsidering an exit from X-rated films after seeing the 'large and appreciative' audiences at the personal appearances and the healthy box office performance of *Inside Marilyn Chambers*.

Naturally, a prominent, positive write-up in *The Sacramento Bee* was enough to provoke anger and pity from the public. Several days after the article ran, the newspaper's editors included a letter from a reader:

'The story you published about Marilyn Chambers is a sad one, indeed,' wrote Mrs. James Barry of Sacramento. 'I find it really sad that a former Olympic diver has reached such a low that she makes pornographic movies and exhibits her nude body to anyone who has the price of a ticket. The Bee gave her story a large, prominent write-up and published a large picture of the young woman. Such publicity can only encourage this person and others to continue in this degrading way of life.'[159]

During her appearance at a theater in Los Angeles, Marilyn wasn't so lucky in avoiding the police. She appeared on January 30 at the brothers' Four Star Theater on Wilshire Boulevard. She performed her usual show, and while she was not taken into custody, police officers in the audience reported her so-called offenses, including public nudity, and filed charges.[160]

Marilyn failed to appear for trial in Los Angeles on those charges. A Municipal Court judge issued a bench warrant for her arrest. Her lawyer told the court, "She was somewhere in the Nevada desert and cannot be found."[161]

In August 1976, 'a three-judge Superior Court panel halted legal proceedings' against Marilyn, the Associated Press reported. 'The panel Friday withdrew a bench warrant for the arrest of the 24-year-old Miss Chambers and also stayed further proceedings against the star of erotic films until a hearing is held Sept. 24 on whether she must appear in Municipal Court in person.'[162]

The charges were dropped two years later, according to United Press International, 'after the city attorney's office admitted its staff had simply lost track of the case. Municipal Court Judge David Rothman tossed the case out— he says too much time has elapsed since the alleged incident, that the theater in question has closed, and that Miss Chambers no longer is engaged in live performances that 'create a public nuisance.' Prosecutors told the judge they wanted her to repeat her dance in court—as evidence.'[163]

SCOTT MANSFIELD WAS A successful model, actor, and musician when, in late 1975, he decided to write, produce, and direct an erotic musical revue called *Le Bellybutton* and bring it to Broadway. It would be more daring than *Hair*, he claimed, the enormously successful musical paean to the sexual revolution, noted for its infamous scene where the principal cast appears onstage fully nude.

One of the keys to achieving commercial success for Mansfield's show was casting Marilyn Chambers in the lead.

With *Dirty Man*, she had earned some credibility as a reliable stage actress and comedienne. Her cabaret shows proved she could carry a tune. And she was a name that would attract attention. Before the show even went into rehearsals, the press made it clear that she would appear fully nude onstage in her Broadway debut.

Alongside Marilyn would be five men and four women actors-dancers-singers. They were unknowns, Mansfield said, "but they'll be people with legitimate experience. We have some real Broadway dancers."[164]

Mansfield wanted a cabaret-style theater rather than a traditional one with raked seating rows. He settled on the Diplomat Cabaret Theater inside the Diplomat Hotel on West 43rd Street in New York City. The hotel management agreed to adapt their ballroom into a tabled 500-seat theater—an agreement they would renege on before the show's slated opening in late March 1976. It was never outfitted to function as a traditional theater. Rows of straight-backed chairs were arranged on the dance floor surrounding a platform stage.

Alan Kootsher, an actor in the show, said the theater was "literally like going to a high school play with rows of chairs."[165]

Alcohol was served, and guests could move freely about the ballroom during the show—like dinner theater without the dinner. And the acoustics were abysmal.

As in *Dirty Man*, Marilyn insisted on having more nudity in the play, and convinced producers to push the show's opening to April 2 so she could work up a solo nude dance for the production.[166]

About a week into production, Associated Press drama writer William Glover did a lengthy profile of Marilyn that was carried in newspapers nationwide.

"I was lucky to come along just when I did," she told Glover, who described her as "a most happy show-off."[167]

'The revue opened at the Diplomat Cabaret, a suddenly renovated ballroom in a rundown hostelry a half-block off Broadway,' Glover wrote. 'This is not exactly in the same league with playing the Palace, but the blue-eyed and hoydenish 23-year-old feels she has traveled a lot further up the prestige ladder than such celebrated sister exhibitionists as Linda Lovelace and Georgina Spelvin.'[168]

Glover commented on the ineluctable presence of Chuck, described as a 'heavyset, quiet type who's always nearby.'[169]

Producers charged 'unprecedented Broadway prices (the top is $20)' (roughly $110 today) for *Le Bellybutton*, according to one newspaper.[170]

THE NEW MARILYN CHAMBERS

Marilyn didn't seem too sure as to what the show was about.

"It's the type of thing which could possibly take place in the 1980s," she guessed. "It's a nostalgia trip back to the seventies. It's about sex and sexual perversions and whatever, so it has a certain amount of shock value."[171]

However, Marilyn said the show was far superior to other popular adult musicals of the time, such as *Let My People Come*. It had "a little more production value," she told reporter Michael Musto.

'As an example, she cited a rape scene which is done to ballet,' Musto wrote. '*Le Bellybutton* has sex, but not all kinds and it's only used in context—but it's still a lot more sensual than most nude shows around.'[172]

When the show wrapped in New York, she planned to take it to London, Los Angeles, and Las Vegas. After that, she would star in *Inside a Doll's House*, a softcore film version of the Henrik Ibsen play.

Musical theater scholar and historian Elizabeth L. Wollman concluded in her book *Hard Times*:

> Although starring in a live nudie musical as a means of getting out of the hardcore racket might not seem like the savviest of career moves, Chambers's attempt to headline in an adult musical in New York City made good sense. Because of their association with the musical theater—and thus with a middle-class, middle-aged audience—adult musicals never carried the same stigma that hard-core films did. In sharp contrast with the porn scene, adult musicals were, for most actors, indeed stepping stones. A Broadway show was thus rightly viewed by Chambers as a step in the right direction.[173]

As Marilyn told *TIME* magazine that year, the show was 'lucrative in the way of experience.'[174]

Edmund Gaynes co-produced *Le Bellybutton* with Mansfield. He made no secret of the fact that he and Mansfield were out to create a blatantly commercial show.

"Scott was trying to do a ripoff of *Oh! Calcutta*, basically," he said, referring to the popular, risqué, sketch musical comedy in which the actors often appear nude. *Oh! Calcutta* enjoyed a lengthy Broadway run in 1976, the same year *Le Bellybutton* premiered. "There was some clever stuff...a lot of nudity, a lot of jokes, a lot of music. Scott's intent was trying to make money. That's what his thinking was. Certainly, this [show] was not something I would have ever done, but hey, it was there; I wanted to get into producing, I was an actor, and it was like, 'Okay, why not?' Shows like this were trendy, and people were trying to

Wearing her trademark belly chain, Marilyn rehearses for her Broadway musical revue, *Le Bellybutton*, which closed after twenty-six performances. *United Press International Photo*.

figure out an angle to see if they could make some money."[175]

Gaynes claimed the show did poorly, in part, because "it opened during the newspaper strikes, very common in New York in those days, and it didn't get reviewed. There was no Internet. It was just that newspaper coverage. So we struggled along for four weeks with the strike."[176]

However, no major New York newspaper strikes occurred between 1962 and 1978. In fact, because of the Diplomat Cabaret Theater's location, it technically opened on Broadway. The geographical location helped what would otherwise be considered an off-off-Broadway show. Box office listings ran consistently in the "Broadway" column of *The New York Times*.

The show didn't even attract celebrities to boost its appeal. The most notable attendee was singer Tiny Tim.[177]

Marilyn appeared on at least two New York public access television shows to promote the musical. Efrom Allen, host of *Efrom Allen's Underground TV Show*, told her he kept his expectations low when he attended a performance of *Le Bellybutton*.

"I'll be honest with you," he said. "I said, 'OK, here's Marilyn Chambers; she's playing it for all she can get. I don't know if she has talent or not.' But when I walked in there and saw you get up there, you lit up the stage, everyone knew you were there, and you were good."[178]

Allen's show was live, and they took phone calls from viewers. Marilyn answered a series of banal questions and stripped nude. About thirty minutes into the program, a caller phoned to say he was a big fan of hers but was disappointed in *Le Bellybutton*.

"I thought you were very good, but I thought the show was mediocre," he said. "I hope to see you in some better things in the future."

"OK, thank you for your opinion," she replied curtly.

The comment made her uneasy, and the caller pushed by bluntly asking if *Inside Marilyn Chambers* was a rip-off.

The next caller said he worked for one of the major networks and recently saw her in person when she did a morning talk show.

"You're a lovely, beautiful, attractive girl—and a fairly good actress," he said. "And I have what I think is a valid question. Why do you find it necessary to do porno when you could have done *Zhivago* or that type of thing?"

She tried to explain that she hadn't done an X-rated movie in three years and was busy with a nightclub act, a Broadway show, and a legitimate stage play in Las Vegas.

"I think I can call myself a legitimate actress," she shot back.

Although her face remained expressionless, she bolted upright in her chair and grew increasingly agitated. When the caller asked why she "felt it necessary" to remove all of her clothing, she succinctly replied, "Because I was asked to, and I enjoy it." Then she flashed a wicked grin.[179]

Le Bellybutton was an Equity production, but according to Kootsher, Mansfield had no experience directing a high school musical, let alone an off-off-Broadway show on Broadway proper.

"He was so gung-ho on this thing," Kootsher said. "I mean, he was a nice guy, but there really wasn't a whole lot of direction to the scenes. I mean, in retrospect, I was terrible. I was just doing what I thought I should do. [T]hings were not so much choreographed as—we'd just sort of move around."[180]

Kootsher thought Marilyn was not a strong enough personality to carry an entire show. "Marilyn was not an actress," he said. "I mean, if you've ever seen a movie with her in it, you can see that. So to me, that had a lot to do with why the show closed. The surrounding cast made her look good, but she was horrible."[181]

While Kootsher found Marilyn friendly and pleasant to work with, Traynor cast a pall over the production.

"*She* was fine," Kootsher said,

It was her husband, or manager, Chuck Traynor, who was—pardon my French—a real prick. He was—you know, 'She's a star, and this isn't right, and that isn't right.' She kinda let him do all the talking, and I don't know how much of it was him, but she was nice, and she didn't play the star bit with us. But if you got close to her, it was 'Don't touch her, don't go near her.' He was just really protective of his property. And she was his property in every sense. Traynor visualized himself as bigger and better than he was. She was quiet, and I think that was probably why Chuck was the way he was—I think they both knew it. I think [the show] was a vehicle for them to hopefully make more money, but I think she felt very self-conscious because she knew she wasn't an actress.[182]

Perhaps she simply knew the show's material wasn't good and didn't want to admit it.

Mansfield told one reporter he wrote some of his best songs for *Le Bellybutton*. After hearing them, one is left to wonder what he considered a bad song. The music of *Le Bellybutton* is uninspired and unmemorable. However, sheet music, which was expensive to produce, was created for two featured songs: Marilyn's Theme and Jenny. Although a formal soundtrack was never recorded, a bootleg version of a performance has circulated for years. The one bright spot is the breezy pop tune Gotta Get Back to You, performed by Marilyn. Clocking in at less than two minutes, it sounds like something Nancy Sinatra would have recorded in the late sixties, with harmonized background vocals and an electric keyboard. The hook is an irresistible earworm, and Marilyn's vocals—as much as can be determined on a well-worn, muffled bootleg—are solid.

The comedy was even worse than the music, particularly the dirty old man character who appeared throughout the play and in blackout scenes between musical numbers. He wore a long overcoat and flashed the audience repeatedly. In one blackout, he appeared on a balcony above the stage. "Hey, folks! Wanna see Marilyn Chambers' box?" He whipped open his overcoat to flash a blow-up still of the Ivory Snow box. He did, however, score the biggest laugh of the evening when he first appeared onstage a few minutes after the lights went out. He flashed the audience, then quipped, "Betcha didn't think you'd see a cock this early in the evening, did ya?"

Ahead of one performance, Marilyn received an anonymous death threat. Someone called into the theater and said he was an instrument for God's retribution against Marilyn for her sexual sins. The show that evening went on as planned, but security was beefed up.[183]

Despite the buildup, and advertisements in every major New York newspaper, critics ignored Le Bellybutton. The box office numbers were dismal, as the show played to twenty-five percent capacity. It closed on April 25, 1976, after just twenty-eight performances.

Since the success or failure of a show like Le Bellybutton rested largely on its star, the musical flop sent an unwelcome message to theatrical producers—not to mention Marilyn and Chuck—that Marilyn could not carry a Broadway show. There was, however, an even bigger project on the horizon—one that might change everyone's minds.

The day before Marilyn's twenty-fourth birthday, and four days before the final curtain closed on Le Bellybutton, Variety announced on its front page that Nicholas Ray, the highly-regarded director of Rebel Without a Cause and other films of the fifties, was returning to filmmaking after being out of action for more than a decade. He had already selected his leading lady: Marilyn Chambers. Ray's last major studio film was 1963's 55 Days at Peking. Ray suffered a heart attack during filming, and Guy Green and Andrew Marton helmed the film through to completion. The film, starring Charlton Heston, Ava Gardner, and David Niven, was a dud. However, Ray was a celebrated auteur in the late forties and throughout the fifties and early sixties. He peaked with In a Lonely Place (1950), starring Humphrey Bogart; Johnny Guitar (1954), starring Joan Crawford, and *Rebel Without a Cause* (1955), starring James Dean. The mercurial director suffered from alcohol and substance abuse, and by the mid sixties, he was unfit to work and uninsurable.

He struggled to secure financing for his film projects after *55 Days at Peking* and worked primarily on scripts. At the encouragement of his friend Dennis Hopper, whom Ray directed in *Rebel Without a Cause*, the filmmaker began a second career as a professor at Binghamton University's Harpur College of Arts and Sciences in upstate New York. From 1971 to 1973, he gained a devoted following of young student filmmakers and earned a reputation as a cult figure in cinema. When his contract with Binghamton wasn't renewed in 1973, Ray returned to New York City and continued to teach acting and directing at the Lee Strasberg Institute and New York University. But he never stopped tinkering with ideas for films and scripts.

A return to features after a thirteen-year absence by one of Hollywood's most inventive and respected filmmakers was newsworthy. The fact that his leading lady was an actress most famous for adult films added to the hype. Soon after the announcement, Rip Torn was announced as the leading man opposite Marilyn. Ray had directed Torn in the 1961 epic *King of Kings*. The writer Norman Mailer, known as much for his brawling nature as for his brilliant work, became attached to the project as an actor. With this powerhouse team in place, the film, called *Murphy*, seemed destined for success.

The script was written by Jan Welt. He had edited the slow-motion footage of Marilyn diving into the pool in *Together*. It was he who recommended Marilyn for the role. Welt also served as a producer.

"I thought, 'What's a good move politically and financially?' And then I remembered Marilyn," he said. "It was firmly believed by Nick that she had it in her. And I could see it and agreed, and Rip did, too."[184]

A full-page ad in the April 30, 1976 issue of *Daily Variety* congratulated Marilyn on signing on to star in the film. For the first time in motion picture history, an actress known primarily for her work in hardcore X-rated films was selected by a preeminent director for a mainstream dramatic feature.

Ray had seen neither *Green Door* nor *Eve* or even *Inside Marilyn Chambers*, but he was confident in his leading lady's abilities. He caught a performance in *Le Bellybutton* and signed her, unusually, without a screen test. When asked about this, he replied: "I have a camera in my head."[185] He also recognized that signing Marilyn was a casting coup and would be good for publicity. On an early spring day in April, the two walked across New York City's midtown to discuss the film and get to know each other. In essence, this was Marilyn's audition.

THE NEW MARILYN CHAMBERS

"I see in her no lack of concentration," Ray told *Variety*. "She is from an upper-middle-class Connecticut family, and I believe she can make the transition from porno into legitimate film work. I also believe she will eventually be able to handle anything that the young Katie Hepburn or Bette Davis could."[186]

Talk about pressure. Nonetheless, it was a huge boost for Marilyn's credibility as a serious actress. Ray optioned Marilyn for two additional films. (Two publications wrote that Marilyn edged out Bette Midler and Diane Keaton for the role.)

Financing was secured, and the budget was set for $500,000 ($2.7 million in today's money). Filming was tentatively scheduled to begin in June in New York City. Pre-production began soon after Marilyn signed her contract, which included script readings with Torn and Mailer at Ray's New York office on the corner of Broadway and Canal. Marilyn, Ray, Torn, and Mailer also met at Marilyn and Chuck's Manhattan apartment for rehearsals. At one meeting, Marilyn remarked that, when photographed, blue was her most flattering color.[187] This rattled Ray. He detested the use of blue and preferred reds and yellows when lensing a film. (Just picture James Dean's iconic red jacket in *Rebel Without a Cause* or Joan Crawford's banana yellow western shirt with blood-red scarf tie in *Johnny Guitar*.) He gave the idea some thought. To Marilyn's delight, the movie would be photographed in various shades of blue. Ray even changed the film's title from *Murphy* to *City Blues*.

Almost immediately, things started to fall apart. Ray began drinking champagne at breakfast and fell asleep in his soup at lunchtime. His behavior went largely unnoticed by many or was ignored. Drugs soon entered the picture.

"Nick easily found all the herbs, liquids, and powders he claimed he wanted to quit, and he went for them all," said Susan Schwartz, Ray's fourth wife, and widow.[188]

Still, Schwartz said, Ray kept working on the *City Blues* script, scouted locations, talked with the actors, and planned his vision. Sadly, it was all a grand delusion. The starting date for filming kept getting postponed, and the coup de grâce came in August.

The film was originally funded with tax shelter laws in place. A tax shelter is a way for individuals and companies to reduce the amount of taxes paid on income. The laws governing these tax shelters can differ by state and at the federal level. There was news of a potential vote by Congress on a bill that would eliminate tax shelters. The vote never took place, but the news was enough to unnerve financiers who no longer felt the tax shelter situation was stable enough to protect precarious investments, such as filmmaking. The money dried up. However, the Hollywood trade publications wrote that the project was still happening and that Torn, Mailer, and Marilyn were firmly committed.

In mid August, Mailer withdrew from the project because he 'devotes the month of August to his family, shunning writing and other chores, including acting.'[189] It was reported that the budget had ballooned from $500,000 to $1.5 million ($2.7 million to $8.2 million when adjusted for inflation). Ray said he still hoped he could begin filming later that month.[190] In September, he fell down a flight of stairs. The injury, a recent separation from his wife, the precarious state of the *City Blues* project, and continued poor health spurred the sixty-six-year-old director to make a change. He remained in detox for two months.

Welt continued in earnest to find the money to produce the film. Investors weren't interested. When Ray was released in November, *City Blues* was no longer considered a viable project. Marilyn and Torn moved on to other projects. A once promising and potentially great piece of filmmaking had gone horribly awry. Marilyn's big chance became her career's most profound loss.

TAKE ONE magazine caught up with Chuck in late 1976 and asked him about *City Blues*.

'Traynor stressed that *City Blues* had been a viable, well-financed project and that Ray had attacked it with a tremendous amount of vigor,' the film magazine reported.[191] Chuck said that Marilyn had been promised $60,000 (nearly $320,000 today) and five percent of the gross. On signing, she received $10,000 ($53,000 today). While she was no longer under contract, she was still interested in the project and would be in the film if her schedule permitted.

"That's the story of my life!" she lamented years later. "That kind of shit kept happening to me throughout my life. It's bad luck, I guess."[192]

After the devastating outcome of *City Blues*, the movie offers were few and far between. According to Chuck, Marilyn was scheduled to do two films between 1975 and 1976: *Arkansas Wipeout*, co-starring Keenan Wynn, and a horror film entitled *Pick Axe*. Both these titles appeared in promotional materials, including her biography in the program for *The Mind with the Dirty Man*. Marilyn spoke about the Keenan Wynn project during interviews. She mentioned a three-picture deal she took instead of an offer from Gerard Damiano to do another X-rated film for $200,000 (approximately $1.1 million in today's money). However, there's no proof that these films were any more than ideas, vague promises by producers or directors, or outright lies. Moreover, no production notes or materials could be located for *Arkansas Wipeout* or *Pick Axe*. Chuck also claimed Marilyn auditioned for a role in Dino de Laurentiis' big-budget remake of *King Kong*, released in 1976. The part went to actress Jessica Lange in her film debut. The *King Kong* audition is far more plausible and was likely a casting call, which would have drawn thousands of actors to best Fay Wray's performance in the 1933 original.

Chuck was likely playing "the Hollywood game." It's a well-worn industry trick used for decades by managers, agents, screenwriters, and actors: always claim you're busy, even if you're not. No one wants to cast an out-of-work has-been, especially if that person became famous for making pornographic films. As Marilyn's manager, Chuck had to prove that Marilyn was a valid and valuable commodity. One way to do this was to make it appear like she received countless, lucrative offers in various mediums and was constantly demanded by producers, directors, and studios. Chuck always tossed out random financial numbers. There was no way a reporter could verify them in those days; contracts were confidential. Name-dropping was okay, as long as it couldn't be traced. Even today, celebrities appear on talk shows and mention an in-the-works project about which they say they cannot speak.

Chuck was a "supermanager" and "superhustler," as Marilyn described him.[193] He knew how to talk a good game, but, occasionally, people saw through his façade. *Los Angeles Free Press*, an alternative weekly newspaper, devoted a cover story to Chuck and Marilyn's claims under the headline "Marilyn Chambers: the facts behind the fiction." Mitch Morrill, the reporter, didn't believe a word Marilyn said during the interview, which went double for Chuck, so he fact-checked their claims. Chuck told Morrill that he and Marilyn were in L.A. to tape a syndicated television special for NBC. The network said there was no special. The local NBC affiliates had no specials planned either. Morrill called ABC and CBS.

'They haven't taped a special with Marilyn Chambers, and they don't intend to,' Morrill wrote.[194]

Marilyn told Morrill she received a percentage of *Green Door's* and *Eve's* receipts. She claimed it was ten percent. Morrill spoke with Jim Mitchell, who said she had ten *points* or a third of a percent.

'She didn't make $1.4 million,' he wrote. 'Her share of *Behind the Green Door* was $25,000.'[195]

Chuck and Marilyn said she had a contract with London Records. A representative for London Records denied the claim.

"Not with us," the rep told Morrill. "We're not even discussing a contract. No way! What does she do?"[196]

'There's a reason Marilyn Chambers and Chuck Traynor felt that they had to con me,' Morrill wrote. 'Maybe they're having financial troubles, or maybe she's just a 22-year-old girl who's found she's not as young, not as pretty, as she used to be. For the past ten months, she's played a fairly unimportant part in a minor play in a medium-sized hotel in the middle of Nevada. She's not a big star; she may never be one, and maybe pretending is easier than trying."[197]

Morrill did the right thing by trying to verify the facts as told to him by Chuck and Marilyn. It's admirable. Few other reporters went to such lengths. However, his final summation of Marilyn, which is sexist and ageist, soured an otherwise interesting piece.

The only kernel of truth in Marilyn and Chuck's otherwise bogus claims was about cutting a record. Record companies first approached Marilyn in 1975 after the success of her Riverboat engagement. She had a name, but they weren't entirely sure what to do with her.

"They just wanted to put something out fast to capitalize on the name," she told the *Los Angeles Times* in 1977. "One company wanted me to listen to some Janis Ian-type stuff. I wanted to keep my image spicy. Jerry Love and Michael Zager came to us last year in New York with a song I really liked. It was sexy, and that's my image. I thought, 'This is the one.'"[198]

The song was an up-tempo disco tune called Benihana. Marilyn cut it in two weeks for Roulette Records, the record company she signed with in February 1977. A single would be released first; if it did well, she'd record an album.[199]

In the seventies, it seemed anyone who was a personality cut a pop record—even if they couldn't sing. Most of them couldn't. Burt Reynolds, *The Brady Bunch*, *Laverne & Shirley*, Telly Savalas of *Kojak*, *Wonder Woman*'s Lynda Carter, John Travolta, Vicki Lawrence, and even Muhammad Ali released music. Occasionally there was a hit like Lawrence's number-one song The Night the Lights Went Out in Georgia, but most were seen, even then, as novelties. Disco was especially popular. (Ethel Merman even recorded an entire album of Broadway show tunes set to a disco beat.) The music wasn't usually demanding of singers; it was more notable for the hooks and arrangements. The Andrea True Connection scored a massive disco hit in 1976 with More, More, More. What most people didn't realize, though, was that Andrea True was a porn star. She had been in dozens of adult films when she recorded the song. She never hid her past and openly discussed it with the press, but her past didn't impinge on her song's chart success. It hit number one on Billboard's disco chart and four on the pop chart. If one adult film actress could score a hit song, maybe another, more famous one, could too.

Benihana came about when Zager, a songwriter and producer, had an idea of doing a song for the Japanese hibachi grill restaurant chain of the same name.

"We went to [Hiroaki 'Rocky' Aoki, the founder of Benihana] and said we had an idea that would promote his chain and that we wanted to record a dance track called 'Benihana,' which means 'little flower' [in Japanese]," Zager recalled. "We wanted him to finance it, and if it became a hit, he'd get free publicity. I thought we should get a beautiful Japanese pop star to sing it and hopefully promote it into an album. Rocky said he had Marilyn Chambers in mind for it—but I had no idea who she was!"[200]

All Aoki told Zager about Marilyn was that she was beautiful and could sing. By the time the two met, Zager had learned about Marilyn's work in adult films.

"He sent her up to our office, and she *was* stunningly beautiful!" Zager remembered. "She was wearing this wild outfit, and you could see right through her shirts and pants. And she had been walking down the street that way with her husband. It was unbelievable! She was absolutely breathtakingly beautiful—just gorgeous—and she was a very nice girl."[201]

Taking a cue from Donna Summer's orgiastic Love to Love You Baby, Marilyn mustered all the moans, groans, and heavy breathing she could for Benihana.

"We brought in a sax player to play at the end of that record," Zager said. "And we turned the lights down in the studio for Marilyn to do that [orgasmic] part of the song. From what I remember, we told her to do all that moaning while he was playing—and [as a result] he could hardly play! It was really quite funny."[202]

Marilyn's voice is light and airy, and it warbles unevenly in several places. (It was twenty years before Autotune, a software that alters a singer's pitch, became ubiquitous on pop records.) She's a better singer than Andrea True—a decidedly low bar—but, ultimately, Marilyn's voice is pleasant.

The song lyrics are silly ("And you whisper/that I feel like/a flower/'cause I move so smooth"[203]) and the hook is unmemorable.

However, *Billboard* liked the song, calling it 'catchy' in its review. 'She sings quite nicely in a sexy little voice,' they wrote.[204] Another reviewer wasn't so kind and said the song 'sounds like an obscene phone call with a rhythm track.'[205]

Marilyn told the *Los Angeles Times* she was prepared for some negative reaction about her single. Not because of the song itself ("I'm pleased with that") but because of potential comparisons to Andrea True. Marilyn resented the implication that she was a follower; she wanted to be *the* leader when adult actresses crossed into the mainstream. Linda Lovelace opened the door, but Marilyn kicked it down. By 1977 she was the country's most significant, marginalized, celebrated, and loathed adult film star. Andrea True scored a major pop hit, but Marilyn (and Chuck) wanted it known that that wouldn't have happened without Marilyn's hard work and contributions.

"People are curious about my ability to perform," Marilyn said. "They don't know what I'm capable of doing. I have to work harder, and it's more of a challenge winning people over. [Benihana is] a record to which you close your eyes and fantasize."[206]

She called the music "sex-rock." Another article noted that Marilyn would appear on *Dinah!*, *Soul Train*, and *The Tonight Show* to promote the record. None of those appearances materialized. She did, however, appear on *Future Shock*, a syndicated variety show hosted by James Brown.

Marilyn said the reception to her record was good, but she was keenly aware of the skepticism. People seemed to ask, "What's *she* doing making a record?"

Despite a full cross-country promotional tour, including appearances on radio shows, at record stores, and DJ conventions, the song hadn't charted nationally on *Billboard*'s disco or pop charts two months after its release. Because of the suggestive moaning and groaning, Zager was convinced the song wouldn't receive airplay. There's no way to say conclusively if the song received any radio airplay. However, *Billboard* tabulated its national pop and disco charts on record sales and airplay. The fact that Benihana didn't chart on either suggests radio airplay was minimal at best.

The song got rotation in several clubs. It made some regional top twenty charts, too. It hit number twelve on Seattle's disco chart in March 1977. Seattle was one of sixteen major disco action markets identified by *Billboard*. The regional charts tracked the top songs played in discotheques, as opposed to radio.[207] Regardless, an album was never recorded for Roulette, and the record company went bankrupt soon after Marilyn's single was released.

Chuck told the *Los Angeles Times* he wasn't concerned by the single's poor chart performance. He claimed the momentum was on their side, rattling off a litany of projects for which Marilyn was being considered or courted and others she had signed, begun production on, or recently finished. None of the projects he mentioned came to fruition. He said one type of project was not being considered: another X-rated film. Despite Marilyn's protestations that her image was spicy and sexy, and she intended to keep it that way, hardcore films were not up for consideration.

"It's hard to live down that kind of reputation," Marilyn told *Filmscene* magazine. "I've been doing so many other things in the last couple of years, but so many people still remember me from those darned movies!"[208]

Finally, a break. A young Canadian filmmaker named David Cronenberg, who would go on to be a significant Hollywood presence, was casting the lead for his second feature, a horror film called *Rabid*. David Cronenberg's first feature, *Shivers*, had caused an uproar in Canada. The film drew scorn from critics but was a hit. As he did for *Shivers*, Cronenberg wrote the *Rabid* screenplay, which told the story of a man and woman badly injured in a motorcycle accident. The nearest medical facility specializes in plastic surgery and conducts experimental skin grafts on the couple. The man heals, but the woman, Rose, becomes the carrier of a virus that causes an insatiable craving for human blood. She draws it through a phallic tube that protrudes from a vagina-type opening under her left arm. Every person she infects becomes a blood-hungry monster. As she infects more people, the virus spreads across Montreal.

"When we start to think about casting, all the usual questions come to the fore," Cronenberg said. "You want an actor who you can afford, but you also want an actor whose name will induce distributors around the world to take on the distribution of your film. So you want a name. Even a low-budget horror film like *Rabid* needed a name, and that's still true today."[209]

For the part of Rose, Cronenberg had in mind Sissy Spacek. She was relatively unknown then but had earned good reviews for her work in Terrence Malick's *Badlands*. However, John Dunning, the head of Cinépix, which produced *Rabid*, didn't like Spacek's freckles or Texas accent.

Producer Ivan Reitman had heard about Marilyn's desire to break into so-called "legitimate" films and suggested her to Cronenberg.

"Look, if you don't like her, we won't use her," he told Cronenberg. "But she's a name we can afford."[210]

Cronenberg knew of Marilyn and her adult film past, but had not seen *Behind the Green Door* (he has not seen it to this day, he said). He did, however, watch *Together*, which impressed him. She was sweet, approachable, sympathetic, and "not bad as an actor," he said. He agreed to meet with her.

"She was harder looking in person, at that point, than I had hoped," he said. "Because she and Chuck Traynor had been hanging out in Las Vegas and had sort of taken on the harder, kind of vulgar aspects of Vegas life. Chuck mentioned proudly that he traded their gold-plated revolvers with Sammy Davis, Jr. That whole kind of scene was extremely foreign to me and still is. However, in talking to Marilyn, I thought that she could definitely work in the role and that she could handle it."[211]

Cronenberg knew she desired a role in a straight movie, even if it was a genre film. Unlike adult films, horror films were considered legitimate entertainment. He knew that working with Chuck would be unavoidable.

"Chuck was going to be watching over her and guarding her and protecting her, but he was also very supportive of her," Cronenberg recalled. "He was a kind of tough guy, just not my kind of guy, but he was part of the package deal. He was very supportive of the film, so it was a workable situation. And he was very professional. She was very shrewd; she was tough. She and I got along very well. It was just a very professional, sweet relationship."[212]

The shoot went well. Marilyn was always prepared, Cronenberg remembered. She even invented her own kind of method acting. In a scene where she's supposed to cry, Chuck helped her prepare by reminding her of when her cat died.

"I asked her after she did her crying scene beautifully how she managed to do that, given that she hadn't had much experience acting in a straight movie," Cronenberg said. "And she told me that Chuck said, 'Why don't you just think of Fluffy?' I didn't know anything about Marilyn's personal life, so I wouldn't have had that detail to help her."[213]

But Chuck never interfered, Cronenberg said. He hovered around her and the set, but Cronenberg sensed he was trying to protect Marilyn.

"I really always felt that Marilyn was in control of that relationship," Cronenberg said. "She didn't take any shit from Chuck and knew what she wanted. Certainly, nothing that I saw suggested that she was being manipulated by him or forced by him to do anything."[214]

Marilyn thoroughly enjoyed working on *Rabid* and remained forever grateful to Cronenberg and Reitman for the opportunity. Thanks to Cronenberg, she came away from the experience feeling more confident about her acting abilities.

"I've been in front of the camera since I was fifteen years old, so I always thought that I knew what I was doing, but he really taught me a lot," said Marilyn. "For example, when doing close-ups, most people just totally overdo it, and if you have no idea what the frame looks like, then you have no clue how close it is. So he'd actually take me behind the camera and show me exactly what the shot looked like so I could get an idea of what other people were seeing. He also told me that I was doing too much with my mouth and my eyes; I had too much of a 'horror film' look on my face. So he really calmed me down and said, 'Less is a lot more.'"[215] In August 1977, Marilyn held a press conference in San Francisco to promote *Rabid*. As one reporter wryly observed, 'With the grace and guts of a Ringling Brothers lion-tamer, Chambers took on a pack of snarling drama critics.' The critics were less interested in *Rabid* than they were in questioning her about her past films.

'The ex-porn queen never lost her cool or quit smiling. She graciously carried on like a stewardess aboard a doomed flight,' the *San Francisco Examiner* noted.[216]

"It's all right,' she sighed when the two-hour confrontation was concluded. 'I

David Cronenberg's horror film *Rabid* earned Marilyn positive notices for her acting in 1977. *Tom Sweeney.*

love defending myself."[217]

The press peppered her with questions about censorship and the First Amendment. Did First Amendment rights apply to, say, child pornographers? She struggled to find a suitable, well-worded answer. Of course, it was an inferior form of entertainment and terrible for the children, but she'd never met one and couldn't vouch for any deleterious effect, she said. She added that politicians, most of whom were very hypocritical, were rushing to jump on the anti-child pornography bandwagon—even though it's been around for years. It was a cringe-worthy response.

She was appalled, however, when actor Harry Reems was put on trial for simply appearing in *Deep Throat*, and *Hustler* publisher Larry Flynt was charged with obscenity in 1976. Both instances were violations of First Amendment rights, she said.

"I never in my wildest fantasies imagined that an actor could be prosecuted for a role he was playing," she said. "That means it could happen to anybody— Jack Nicholson or Jane Fonda. And if you're not allowed to read *Hustler*, or if someone said you can't read that..."

She trailed off. Chuck piped in: "Hitler said that!"[218]

It was an awkward attempt to compare arrests in the US for breaking obscenity laws with the government censorship practiced by a maniacal dictator who ultimately was responsible for the deaths of up to ten million people.

Marilyn told reporters she was through with X-rated films but would never denigrate them. Her real fantasy, she said, was to work with Roman Polanski or Ingmar Bergman. Following Chuck's instructions, there were some scattered untruths in her answers, such as claiming she lived alone. Her comments on being exploited by participating in pornographic films also likely came directly from Chuck:

"People always question me about women's lib," she told reporters. "They say, 'Why do you like being treated like a sex object?' Well, that's what women are for. We're put here to be attractive to men. Man is the stronger sex. I enjoy being submissive. My life is run by males. I could even quit my career if the right man asked me to."

It's a stark contrast from the ambitious young woman who defiantly turned down a powerful Hollywood producer's request that she be his mistress and belong to him just seven years before. The same woman who, after *Green Door* hit, said, "I'm not a total sex object or a dumb blonde. I'm an actress."[219]

However, in the same article, the reporter noted Marilyn's business savvy, writing that she was 'no dummy. She asked for, and got, a percentage of each

THE NEW MARILYN CHAMBERS

Mitchell Brothers film.' What the reporter didn't include was that Marilyn also received a percentage of *Rabid*, *Le Bellybutton*, her disco song, her two books, and virtually every project she worked on after *Green Door*.

After *Rabid*, Marilyn returned to the Union Plaza Hotel and Casino in Las Vegas, the same venue that had staged *Mind with the Dirty Man*. This time, it was to perform one of her most challenging roles: Bobbi Michelle, the talkative, anxious, pot-smoking young actress in Neil Simon's hit comedy *Last of the Red Hot Lovers*.

The original Broadway production opened in 1969 and ran for more than 700 performances. The Union Plaza production, featuring Marilyn, opened on October 11, 1977, with two shows nightly.[220] Like *Dirty Man*, *Red Hot Lovers* was produced and directed by Maynard Sloate and scheduled for an indefinite run. (It ended after six months.)[221] Marty Brill portrayed Barney Cashman, a married, middle-aged man who wants to join the sexual revolution before it's over. He attempts (and fails) to seduce three different women. Jane Keane, with whom Marilyn worked on *Dirty Man*, essayed two roles in the production.

"This is fun, absolute fun," Brill said. "I really enjoy the character, and with Jane and Marilyn playing their parts so superbly, the audiences can relate to every situation."[222]

Keane received the highest praise, described by critic Vic Field as 'brilliant in the development of her two roles. First, as the acerbic, snappy, middle-aged woman who wants an affair with no strings attached (like getting to know each other), and then as the insecure woman with a low opinion of people and their intentions. It is Miss Kane who meets the dramatic challenges of the play.'[223]

Marilyn received special notice as well, adding a 'contemporary appeal' to the comedy. 'She is effective as the pert, bouncy, pot-smoking youthful conquest who doesn't shut up long enough to have an affair. Collectively, all characters provide an entertaining panorama of old and new ethics. Especially appreciative of the presentation are those audience members who can relate to twenty years of marriage, and that happens to be the median demographic at the Union Plaza.'[224]

The 'choice of Marilyn Chambers by producer-director Maynard Sloate for the kicky Bobbie [*sic*] Michele was as good a gamble as seven straight passes,' *Variety* wrote. 'Chambers is a natural for the role.'[225]

Las Vegas Sun columnist Joe Delaney wrote, 'Marty Brill, Jane Kean, and Marilyn Chambers [do] full justice to the comedy writing genius of Neil Simon in 'Last Of The Red Hot Lovers,' a fine four-horse parlay at the Union Plaza.'[226] He singled out Marilyn as 'a funny composite of all the kooky females in the world, ideally cast, light years beyond her 'Ivory Snow' and 'Green Door' days.'[227]

Two promising opportunities presented themselves in 1978. The first was a meeting with actor Jack Nicholson. His next film, *Goin' South*, was a dark comedy-western set in the 1860s. Nicholson plays a horse thief sentenced to hang who agrees to marry a frontierswoman and use the marriage loophole to save his life. Not only was the film to star Nicholson but he was set to direct. He was casting for the role of his wife and invited Marilyn to meet with him. Her hopes were dashed almost immediately. Nicholson's friend Art Garfunkel joined the meeting despite having no role in the film. The men dangled a role in the film, then 'asked her for cocaine and wanted to know whether she really got off during *Green Door*, angering her to the point that she stormed out midway through the interview.'[228]

The second opportunity was for a film by Paul Schrader. By 1978, Schrader was one of the premier writer-directors in Hollywood. His original screenplay for Martin Scorsese's *Taxi Driver*, released in 1976, brought him international acclaim. An original script, co-written with his brother Leonard and titled *Blue Collar*, was Schrader's first directorial effort. It starred Richard Pryor and Yaphet Kotto and hit theaters in 1978. Critics hailed it and it became a box office smash. Schrader directed his next film, again based on one of his original screenplays.

Originally titled *Pilgrim*, the film follows a pious, sexless man whose teenage daughter runs away from home and gets trapped in the grungy, grimy business of making porn films. The father goes to extreme lengths to find her, hiring a private investigator and even impersonating an adult film casting director. Along the way, he meets Niki, a porn star and prostitute connected to many people in the business. She agrees to help him and becomes a kind of surrogate daughter.

Schrader changed the film's title to *Hardcore*. George C. Scott was set to play the lead. Chuck arranged for Marilyn to audition for the role of Niki. This was the most promising opportunity since *City Blues*. The role for which she would audition was that of a porn star, and the film had top-tier talent, including an Academy Award-winning lead actor, and a Hollywood studio backing it. Even if the film was a dud, her part was the kind to get noticed, and her work on a mainstream film alone would likely improve her chances of making others. Some filming would also be in San Francisco's North Beach neighborhood. With Marilyn's close association with the Bay Area, it seemed she'd be a natural fit for the role.

Alas, she wasn't. At least to the filmmakers.

"Sorry, we can't use you," the casting director said.

"But why?" she asked, genuinely curious and increasingly annoyed.

"Because we're looking for a porn star."

"But I *am* a porn star!" she protested. "I'm the biggest porn star there is."

THE NEW MARILYN CHAMBERS

"You're too wholesome."

"And that's *why* I'm the biggest porn star," she said. "What kind of porn star are you looking for anyway?"

"Someone not as wholesome-looking."

Marilyn was crushed. It seemed they wanted a Hollywood version of what producers believed the public perceived a female porn star to look like: strung out on drugs, down on her luck, hard-looking, unkempt, with heavy makeup slathered across an only marginally attractive face. They didn't want the girl next door. They wanted the girl everyone whispered about.

"It was perhaps the most disheartening thing of my career," Marilyn said. "I'm very glad I wasn't in it. What would it have been like if I had been there? I dress like I'm going to an elegant place, not as if I were going to walk the 42nd Street sidewalk."[229]

Perhaps there were other reasons why the filmmakers didn't want Marilyn Chambers for the role. But that was the reason she was given—and it bothered her until the day she died.

"What the hell does a porno queen look like?" she asked. "The world of adult films and entertainment is not seamy and seedy like it is made out to be in 'Hard Core' [*sic*]. It's a totally honest business, and the people involved are intelligent, good people."[230]

MARILYN GAVE A PRESS preview of her new one-woman dramatic play *Sex Surrogate* on Sunday, March 11, 1979, at the Jolly Trolley Casino. In attendance was Las Vegas Assistant City Licensing Director Howard Crow. He was there to see if the show's full and partial nudity violated a local ordinance that prohibited an indecent, immoral, or lewd performance. If, in his opinion, the play violated the ordinance, Marilyn would have to appear at least partially clothed, specifically covering the pubic region, for the play's duration—or not appear at all. After the performance, Crow recommended to Richard Mauer, Las Vegas city attorney, that the nudity could stay.

"Basically, it's okay from what we saw if they keep the same format," Mauer told the *Las Vegas Sun*. "Some things you can be nude for, some things you can't."[231]

Neither Mauer nor Crow specified by what measure it was decided if there was something "you can be nude for." Similar to the myriad obscenity cases involving *Green Door*, what was considered "indecent, immoral or lewd" usually came down to the interpretations of as few as one person.

Beginning with *Sex Surrogate*'s official premiere date of March 16, Mauer said a city representative would attend every play performance "to ensure that it does not violate the ordinance." The show, the Jolly Trolley Casino's premier attraction, was scheduled for an indefinite run. Marilyn performed the fifty-five-minute show three times a night, appearing fully nude for just two minutes.[232]

Dramatically, the one-woman show was the most demanding Marilyn had ever attempted. She played a sex surrogate named Kim, whose job is to help men with their sexual hang-ups via therapeutic, one-to-one sexual encounters. Not only did Marilyn portray Kim, but she also acted out five male patients. At the end of each performance, she would answer questions from the audience. The reviews were excellent.

'Marilyn Chambers seems to need no support, either physically or on stage,' Barry D. Levin wrote in *Vegarama*. 'It's an adult show with an adult theme, treated in an adult way. Marilyn Chambers shatters the twenty-year Las Vegas strip prohibition against total nudity. [She] shatters it with grace, style, and a strong sense of comic timing.'[233]

Sandy Zimmerman wrote in *This Week in Las Vegas*, 'Marilyn is perfect for the part, her beautiful body the stuff that male fantasies are made of. Her portrayal is superb.'[234]

About two months after it opened, Las Vegas Mayor Bill Briare proposed an ordinance prohibiting the display of the pubic area in any establishment with a city liquor or gaming license. The Jolly Trolley was just inside the city limits. If the ordinance were formally brought before the city's commissioners and passed, Marilyn would not be allowed to appear fully nude.

Marilyn and Chuck took the proposal of the so-called "fig leaf ordinance" personally. Chuck charged that Briare was specifically out to get Marilyn; he vowed Marilyn would testify against the law before the Las Vegas Board of City Commissioners and that several "big names" in entertainment would also lend their support. He declined to name them. Briare scoffed at the idea that the ordinance was aimed at Marilyn's performance, saying, "A convention city like Las Vegas just does not need this sort of image."[235]

Briare also claimed he didn't want the play's nudity to encourage the flourishing of any pornography-related businesses in Las Vegas because it would attract organized crime. The mayor was either naive, blithely unaware of the history of the city over which he governed, or simply playing politics. It was well known that organized crime not only helped establish Las Vegas as a gambling and entertainment destination but remained ingrained in the city. Furthermore, there were numerous burlesque shows on the Strip, including some featuring bare-breasted women. The ordinance would not affect the burlesque shows, but it would affect *Sex Surrogate*.

Except for some shows in nearby North Las Vegas, *Sex Surrogate* was the only show on the Strip—and the only one featuring a celebrity—that contained full nudity in certain parts of the show. There was no proliferation of shows featuring full-frontal nudity that moved into Vegas on the heels of *Sex Surrogate*.

"The law is merely an extension of the city's ban on totally nude dancing and is intended to prevent raunchy naked performances from proliferating in the city under the guise of being legitimate stage performances," Briare said.[236]

Indeed, Deputy District Attorney James Bartley told the *Las Vegas Sun* that plays such as *Sex Surrogate* were "already illegal under county law." He added that "local governments can put any conditions they want on privileged liquor and gaming licenses."[237]

The Jolly Trolley possessed a liquor license. That was one reason for scrutinizing the show. However, it's unclear why the play went through an approval process by the city attorney and was allowed to run uninterrupted for nearly two months if it was already considered illegal.

One has to question Briare's motivation and timing. The year of 1979 was a mayoral election year. Briare was nearing the end of his first four-year term and was up for re-election. Although Las Vegas was a largely liberal city, it had a small, highly influential faction of ultra-conservative residents, particularly Mormons. The proposed ordinance could be viewed as an attempt by Briare, a Democrat, to court the conservative vote and help secure his re-election.

Briare confessed he never saw *Sex Surrogate*. Instead, he fell back on an old conservative trope. "She obviously has some talent," the mayor conceded. "It's just a shame that she is being exploited."[238]

Chuck was adamant that nudity was essential to the play. "Though the mayor doesn't want to accept it, nudity is part of today's entertainment," he said.[239]

Briare chuckled at the remark and said: "I'm not trying to analyze them—they shouldn't analyze me."[240]

On May 16, Briare formally introduced the ordinance at a city commission meeting. The next day Marilyn held a luncheon at the Uptown Kiwanis Club at the Fremont Hotel.

'Wearing a blue print dress, the tanned and muscular Chambers said she has received offers of assistance from prominent groups, including the Playboy Foundation,' wrote *Sun* reporter Chris Woodyard.[241] She echoed Chuck's claim that major celebrities and entertainers were on board to help fight the nudity ban but declined to name any of them.

"I'm not sure the mayor knows what's behind the green door, and I'm not sure

I'm the one who should tell him," she told the all-male audience.[242]

The plan to fight the ordinance was preliminary, as the board might not pass it. Either way, the considerable attention generated by its proposal increased ticket sales and changed the audience's demographic. The mostly young male crowd was now composed of "elite couples up to age 60 who want to see what the big flap is about," she observed. She quipped that hitting the road in a play "banned in Vegas" might not be bad for business.

'Despite the hoopla,' the *Sun* noted, 'the pert actress said she wants to leave the legal hassles to her manager.'[243]

"I don't really like to become involved because I don't think an actress has a place in politics," she declared in a statement likely fed to her by Chuck.[244]

Two days before the Las Vegas City Commission was set to vote on the ordinance, Marilyn, Chuck, and members of the Libertarian Party protested during a press conference in front of City Hall. Marilyn reiterated that she believed the ordinance directly attacked her and her performance.

"It is obviously aimed at me," she told reporters. "I'm the only show on the Strip that has total nudity." Covering up would "ruin the therapeutic value of the show," and closing the show would put her and twenty-six others out of work.[245]

Several alternatives were discussed, including a mink patch worn over the pubic area to resemble pubic hair. However, the ordinance would also outlaw simulating genitalia, so that idea was scratched—and Marilyn refused to wear a G-string. It was considered to replace the nude scenes with blackouts accompanied by a voiceover describing a particular sexual technique. That idea didn't work either. It was nude or nothing.

Chuck said he would seek a court-ordered injunction if the ordinance passed. Rick White, the vice chairperson of the Libertarian Party of Nevada, called the ordinance "another example of government infringment [*sic*] on the rights of the American people to exercise freedom of choice."[246]

On June 6, 1979, a public hearing was held to vote on the ordinance. Marilyn and Chuck were joined by the play's author Mel Goldberg, two professional nude dancers unaffiliated with *Sex Surrogate*, and several residents who opposed the ordinance. They were in the minority.

"In the entertainment capital of the world—here of all places—why limit artistic ability?" Marilyn asked the commissioners. "It's a hypocritical view."[247]

She challenged ordinance supporters to move to Utah if they disliked Las Vegas-style entertainment. Goldberg defended his work as a serious piece of art that "is in no way, shape or form nude entertainment."

Adeline Bartlett, representing Nevadans Against Pornography, praised the ordinance and encouraged the commissioners to pass it.

"I'm glad to see people in the community stand up for morals, good sense, decency, good taste, and a decent community to raise a family in," she said.[248]

Carol Carlson, of Southern Nevada Pro-family Coalition, claimed Las Vegas "offers a great deal of entertainment that is dealt with offensively," as well as advertisements promoting nudity, which she claimed were "an intrusion on family life and work to the detriment to the youth of the community."[249]

The commissioners agreed. The ordinance passed in a vote of 5-0 and would go into effect at midnight on Friday, June 8, 1979—just two days later. That it typically took ten to fourteen days for a law to take effect suggests a certain amount of political railroading regarding this one. Marilyn was furious and vowed to continue performing.

"I may even do the whole play nude," she fumed.

An angry pro-ordinance resident yelled outside the city hall chambers at Marilyn, "You ought to be run out of town, and I'd like to be the one to do it!" Marilyn didn't respond to the woman directly but was heard mumbling about "the hypocritical Mormons who run this town" and "people across the country will laugh—a play banned in Las Vegas."[250]

Howard Crow, who had attended the show's press preview just three months earlier, and approved of the nudity in the play, once again vowed to station city employees at the Jolly Trolley to make sure it complied with the new law. If it were found to violate the law, its liquor license would be revoked. Vic Lockwood, director of public relations, advertising, and entertainment for the casino, said the establishment would comply but noted the show's producers and casino executives were still deciding how to handle the new law without ruining the integrity of the performance.

"The play will not lose its value, but we will make a serious attempt to make the play more sexually arousing," he declared, adding that the new script changes would make the play "more thunderous with more verbal allusions and atmosphere."[251]

City officials "apparently are not concerned with provocative or erotic language; they are concerned with the pubic area," he said. "And Marilyn Chambers is highly capable of stirring prurient interests."

Despite her initial refusal, it was decided Marilyn would wear a G-string. Howard Crow attended the 1:00AM show on Saturday, June 9, to ensure the show complied with the law, which went into effect at 12:01AM. Marilyn wore her G-string, and no announcements were made during the show that patrons offended by the new law should complain directly to the Mayor's office.

But the damage was done. Five days after the ordinance was enacted, the *Las Vegas Review-Journal* wrote that the show had 'suffered a 50 percent loss in business because its star no longer appears totally nude.' Lockwood agreed. He said the loss of profits was "obviously because of lack of nudity. We're searching now for ways to advertise something that isn't there anymore." The threat of a lawsuit was still on the table.[252]

'The suit could be based on the fact that the city originally allowed the show by not having a law, then passed the law after the show had been playing for some time,' the *Review-Journal* noted. Marilyn and Chuck could not be reached for comment.[253]

Less than two weeks after the law passed, and three months after it premiered, *Sex Surrogate* closed at the Jolly Trolley Casino.

Lockwood said the show "lost a lot of its artistic merit in the eyes of Chambers and producer Chuck Traynor. Each performance after the ordinance became more difficult for Marilyn because she felt artistically suppressed and was forced to alter the contents of the play to comply with the city ordinance."[254]

When Marilyn said at the Kiwanis luncheon that it might not be bad for business to take a "banned in Vegas" show on the road, she might have been giving a preview of coming attractions. It was already scheduled to open in September in London's West End.

Paul Raymond, dubbed "The Hugh Hefner of England" by the British press, brought the show to London and retitled it *Sex Confessions*. He booked the play at his famous theater and strip club, The Raymond Revuebar, in Soho's Walker's Court. Raymond, whose Paul Raymond Publications produced some well-known softcore men's magazines in the United Kingdom, including *Men Only* and *Club International*, also offered Marilyn a contract to write a monthly sex advice column for *Club*, the American sister publication. The agreement guaranteed that she'd appear on the cover of *Club* several times per year and in photo layouts. 'The arrival in London of Marilyn Chambers, the very famous 'Sex Queen of America,' triggered a veritable mini-revolution,' noted *Paris Las Vegas* magazine. 'So much so that the presence of a few police officers was necessary to allow the sensual American actress to move about the streets of London without too much of the inconveniences of the enthusiasm provoked by each of her appearances.'[255]

'Marilyn's nude appearance in the rain on the roof of the theatre for the benefit of press photographers caused great excitement in the Soho vegetable stalls below—and among the photographers,' reporter James Hughes-Onslow wrote.[256]

'Miss Marilyn Chambers, who is conferring on London the distinction of seeing a live sex show that was too much for the noted spiritual delicacy of Las Vegas and got her performances banned there, arrived in Britain yesterday,' wrote Dennis Barker in *The Guardian*. 'The young lady has been called America's Queen of the Sex Movies, as she graciously made contact with the first of her British subjects, principally barrow boys and wet-raincoated habitues of Soho, outside the Boulevard Theatre.'[257]

Marilyn explained to reporters why she loathed wearing a G-string in the Vegas performances after the ordinance was passed.

"As an actress, it would be very wrong of me to do that because it is a play about people's hang-ups," she said. "I'm trying to help people who have hang-ups. For me to wear a G-string would be hypocritical." Marilyn told reporters she didn't believe she had any sexual hang-ups herself. "I have a very good sex life and a very good business career," she said.[258]

Some of the show's dialogue in Goldberg's original script had to be translated from American Jewish humor to wry British comedy. It's unclear if Goldberg or other writers did this. Marilyn said the show was made "a lot hotter for London." She didn't elaborate. It was likely a suggestive comment made to entice people to see the show.

She said she was delighted in seeing nudity on UK television, something unheard of in the US. Although she said the American and British cultural attitudes towards sex seemed counterintuitive:

> The English Media have a much better attitude [than the American media], but the people are still very reserved. Bondage and discipline, for instance. In the States, everybody is into living out their fantasies. That's healthy, even if it's sort of tongue-in-cheek. Here nobody would ever admit to wanting to be whipped or anything like that, just for the fun of it. That part is very underground, but it's there.
>
> I don't want to say that people here are sexually frustrated, but they're not as open as Americans about sex. Here it's hidden, and you don't talk about it, and in the States, people talk about it too much![259]

London was certainly more accepting of Marilyn's show (and nudity), but she still faced similar hurdles in winning over reporters, critics, and commentators. News stories dripped with condescension, sly insults, and attempts to cast her as a dumb American blonde. For example, *The Guardian* story noted that she changed outfits—from 'a dress slit up to the waist to a blouse slit down to the navel'; adjusted her nipples for the photographers, and wrote 'a sex-problems page for a magazine which self-sacrificingly gives itself to such matters.' The story ended by noting that one of Marilyn's grandmothers was one of the Daughters of the American Revolution. Someone asked Marilyn if her grandmother was "revolted."

"My grandmother doesn't quite know what my career is," said Miss Chambers, "but I feel I am helping my country."

The British tabloids even tried to create a rivalry between Marilyn and Fiona Richmond, Britain's reigning sex queen and former lover of Paul Raymond.

"Sex queens slug it out in bitchy brawl," ran the misogynistic headline of *The Sunday People*. 'PSSST! Grab your dirty raincoats, gents, and take your seat for Bra Wars, the bitchiest show in town.' ('Bra Wars' was a pathetic attempt at a *Star Wars* pun.) The reporter, Tony Purnell, claimed Marilyn and Fiona made catty comments about each other's ages, breast size, and body fitness. The newspaper gave Richmond the last word. She claimed she could easily perform the same show as Marilyn. "They just couldn't afford me," she huffed.[260]

Sex Confessions was an unqualified success, with tickets costing £5.85 (roughly £28 today). Marilyn performed two shows nightly, six nights a week, for nearly seven months. *The Sunday Times of London* wrote a polite but favorable review. 'Miss Chambers is an articulate, blue-eyed 24-year-old with clean hair, a dancer's strong calves, and large feet,' the paper noted, 'and she puts on a show in which she populates the stage with imaginary characters, so she might be compared to Ruth Draper or Joyce Grenfell[261] if either diseuse wore nothing except a gold earring and a small Hitler moustache.' The 'moustache' referred to Marilyn's pubic hair, which was shaved into the shape of a heart, not a Hitler moustache.

The *Times* continued: 'She plays, in a brisk and matronly manner, the role of a 'sex surrogate,' that is a kind of hospital nurse employed by an American shrink to administer therapy to frustrated patients. It is a very medical show.'[262]

"Nothing is fun like working in front of a live audience," Marilyn told *Elite* magazine about the play. "You get all that energy from them, and the feedback makes you adjust the performance to their mood. It's just wonderful."[263]

THERE WERE WOMEN WHO participated in adult films before Marilyn Chambers, but none had achieved the level of notoriety or sustained as lengthy a career as she did. She pioneered the idea of the porn star as a celebrity. Seven years after *Behind the Green Door* premiered, and six years after the Ivory Snow scandal, she couldn't shake the "porno star" label. No matter how many projects she completed; the quality of the work; the caliber of the talent with whom she

THE NEW MARILYN CHAMBERS

worked; the positive reviews she received; or even her admirable, courageous attempt to prove herself as an entertainer, the stories always came back to sex, porn, *Green Door*, Ivory Snow, and, tellingly, Chuck.

It wasn't entirely the fault of the press. However, it goes without saying that many of the stories about Marilyn in the seventies were appallingly sexist. She was talented, but many critics were hard-pressed to look past the adult films and give her plaudits. At first, covering a "porn star" as news was a novelty and perfectly emblematic of the seventies. The novelty of seeing an adult movie wore off quickly, but Marilyn Chambers was still newsworthy.

To their credit, Marilyn and Chuck had succeeded in establishing "Marilyn Chambers" as a notable, bankable star—no small feat. However, they couldn't quite figure out how to market "Marilyn Chambers" to the masses. Rebranding Marilyn as a legitimate entertainer while still cashing in on her X-rated past was an attempt to have it both ways.

By most accounts, Chuck was the problem.

In her first few years partnering with Chuck, Marilyn was eager, anxious, and grateful for his guidance. They shared the same dream, it seemed, of turning her into a versatile superstar. She saw the built-in skepticism of her abilities beyond adult films as a welcome challenge. She met Chuck when she was twenty-one. At that age, nothing seemed impossible. By 1979, she began to realize that her big Hollywood dream had gone sideways.

The couple made a decision. If the public expected Marilyn Chambers to be a "porn star," she'd give them a porn star like the world had never seen.

Chapter 7

INSATIABLE

███████████████

"I don't really have any friends. I don't socialize with a lot of people because of what I do. They're curious rather than wanting to be friends."
— Marilyn Chambers, 1981[1]

"TO CREATE THE PERFECT PORN star, you have to create an image of a totally uninhibited sexual creature who would be happy being anything you wanted her to be," Chuck said. "You have to make it so there are no barriers between this chick and the audience, so men will think she'd enjoy doing anything they wanted her to do."[2]

The image bled into reality, and there were virtually no barriers between Marilyn and her male fans. For example, Marilyn would offer the bellboy a blow job instead of a cash tip when staying at a hotel.

"When Marilyn said to the room service guy, 'Let me suck your dick,' it was all part of that image," Chuck continued. "The bellboy fucks Marilyn Chambers, or she blows him, and he's an instant Marilyn Chambers fan. He goes downstairs and tells all the bellboys, and pretty soon, all the bellboys are out there pimping for Marilyn Chambers."[3]

She would often do interviews in the nude.

"Sex is my commodity," she told renowned broadcaster Larry King during an appearance on his radio show. "You have your voice; you use it. I have my body. I use it. It doesn't mean any more than that to me."[4]

As King prepared to cut to a news break, Marilyn asked him on-air, "Do you want to make love during the news [break]?"

A flustered King told Marilyn it was only a seven-minute break.

"Let's do as much as we can in seven minutes," she said, disrobing.

She stood before him, completely naked. King reluctantly agreed and asked the engineer to leave the control booth. They would make love and then talk about the experience on the air. But King couldn't perform. When they returned from the break, Marilyn asked him on-air why he couldn't get excited. King said it was just too public and too weird.

"I was willing to do anything," she told him. "In fact, I like you. We could have fun."[5]

She asked him if he was free afterward, but King declined.

It was an audacious move on Marilyn's part. For a woman who preferred to be submissive, she was expressly dominating. Her outspoken, confident sexuality was so powerful and intimidating that it emasculated King. She certainly played the part of a "porn star," but she loathed the label. She was keenly aware of the phrase's negative connotation, particularly in America. She desperately wanted to be considered an actress first.

"Hollywood's concept of sex is so corrupt," she lamented. "When I was making *Green Door* with Jim and Art, I'd say, 'I can't do this scene,' and they'd come up with a beer in one hand and a joint in another and their baseball caps on backward and say, 'Sure you can! Think about being really turned on. Think of the millions of people you're going to turn on.' They made me feel really attractive and like a real actress."[6]

With virtually no viable mainstream offers, she and Chuck rejoined the world of X-rated films.

"It used to be one of my goals to star in a totally legitimate film," she told *Adam* magazine in 1980. "Well, it's not going to happen, that I can see. And I really don't care because I'm doing fine right now. I'm very happy the way I am."

To imply that she didn't care if she would ever star in a "totally legitimate film" was bogus. She yearned for the opportunity. Telling the press she didn't care, saying it out loud, was likely an unconscious attempt to get herself to believe it. Doubtless, had the opportunity to star in a mainstream film presented itself, she would have snapped it up. But it didn't. A bitterness crystalized around her heart.

BURIED IN A COLLECTION of hundreds of personal photos Chuck took of Marilyn during their relationship are three Polaroids. They're not dated, but based on Marilyn's hairstyle, they appear to be from early in the relationship, circa 1974. The photos show Marilyn engaged in sexual activity with several men. All three images seem to have been taken on the same day.

The first photo shows a fully nude Marilyn sitting on the corner of a countertop with her legs spread. A man wearing glasses and a shirt is crouched down with his face about a foot away from her vagina. He's expressionless. With his hands, he's pinching and stretching Marilyn's outer labia, which are noticeably red.

PURE

The Sexual Revolutions of Marilyn Chambers

Marilyn's eyes are shut tight, her mouth open to expose clenched teeth. Her arms, supporting her on the countertop, are tense, with her triceps exposed. She's in pain.

In the second photo, she sits similarly, this time on a man's lap. A different man kneels before her, inserting an empty glass Coke bottle into her vagina. The expression on her face is similar to that in the first photo.

The third photo shows the backside of a heavyset man. His pants are around his ankles. His red shirt is pulled up to mid-back. Only Marilyn's legs are visible, and the man is penetrating her. Other men stand around them, partially clothed.

Out of frame is Chuck, taking the photos and relishing the moments he captured on film.

The photos are not pleasant to see. It's difficult to say if Marilyn is enjoying herself. Her facial expression would indicate otherwise, but Marilyn seemed to have a proclivity for the pleasure of pain in her sex life—at least on camera and in live performances. This was never more apparent than in a series of live performances she did in San Francisco at the O'Farrell Theater in May 1978.

It was Marilyn's first time at the theater since promoting *Inside Marilyn Chambers* in 1976. She was scheduled to perform an astonishing ten half-hour shows a day for three days, with time allotted to sign autographs in the lobby afterward. On the day the shows were announced, tickets sold out in hours. Two more days were added to the schedule.

Each day five shows took place in the theater's Ultra Room, four in their Kopenhagen Lounge, and one on the main stage. The Ultra Room was a small, oval-shaped peep-show style room. The brothers opened the room in 1977, and it was an immediate success. Patrons at the stalls surrounding the outside of the room watched live sex shows inside the room, many of which featured two women. The Kopenhagen Lounge was an even smaller room, but instead of patrons being on the outside looking in, they sat on the floor inside the room while a series of sexual acts were performed before them. The room was kept dark, and patrons were given flashlights to illuminate the performers. Because the Lounge show was more intimate and accommodated fewer patrons per show, tickets were priced at twenty-five dollars (about $120 when adjusted for inflation); Ultra Room shows were twenty dollars (about $100 today); and the one daily main-stage show was ten dollars (nearly fifty dollars today). To put this into perspective, the average ticket cost for The Rolling Stones' 1978 US tour ranged from twelve dollars and fifty cents to fifteen dollars (between about sixty and seventy dollars today).

"I can't think of any other porn star who could possibly do what Marilyn did," marveled Mitchell brothers spokeswoman Rita Mandelman. "I would think it's exhausting."[7]

That's putting it mildly.

Her Ultra Room shows consisted of verbal degradation by two women; being paddled, spanked, and anally fisted; and being penetrated vaginally and anally with large dildoes. She was then hung upside down by her feet while the women took turns receiving oral sex.

All three women appeared in the Kopenhagen Lounge, and the patrons who sat inside the room could fondle and digitally penetrate each woman.

The mainstage show was tamer. Marilyn opened with her disco tune Benihana, took off her negligee, and danced in the nude. A question-and-answer session with the audience followed this. Then a fellow dancer walked onstage, attached a leash to Marilyn's labial ring, and led her offstage.

Marilyn returned to perform similar shows in February 1979; two were captured on film. *Never a Tender Moment* and *Beyond de Sade* are built around the same concept. Each short film runs for roughly thirty minutes and shows a series of explicit sadomasochistic sex scenes intercut with backstage interviews of Marilyn. The most graphic one involves a woman slowly inserting anal beads about the size of tennis balls into Marilyn's anus, then quickly pulling them out. The scene is shot in slow motion.

To help Marilyn prepare, Chuck rubbed cocaine on Marilyn's anus to numb it.

The films were considered so shocking that they were only available for purchase through Marilyn's fan club or by visiting the O'Farrell Theater.

The most striking element, particularly in *Beyond de Sade*, is the footage of Marilyn seated backstage at her vanity makeup mirror. Her hair is coiffed in an elegant updo, her makeup is minimal but effective, and she's wearing a see-through black nightie. She's topless, but her breasts are never fully exposed. She resembles someone like Rita Hayworth, Ann Sheridan, or any number of 1940s Hollywood glamour queens. It's a stunning contrast to the sweaty, nude woman who, for the previous twenty-five minutes, was penetrated with anal beads and had her nipples bitten.

"I never felt degraded as a woman doing what I'm doing," she tells an off-camera interviewer. "I just feel that it's made me a better woman, to make love better, to have sex better. There's an infinite number of fantasies and ways—things that have yet to be discovered [about] sex. And I hope to be one of the main pioneers."[8]

This juxtaposition captures why Marilyn Chambers was such an effective and powerful sexual force. She engages in sexual activity that provides great pleasure, even if it involves pain, but has a seductive elegance offstage. And she makes no apologies for it.

"Chuck taught me to be a whore in bed and a lady in public," Marilyn often said.[9]

It's this type of strength in sexuality, a forthrightness coupled with glamor, beauty, and talent, that attracts many gay men. It's a wonder why Marilyn Chambers isn't as prominently revered in the gay community as Madonna, Mae West, or Mamie Van Doren. She has many hallmarks associated with diva worship.

Daniel Harris, in his book *The Rise and Fall of Gay Culture*, puts it this way:

> Homosexuals' involvement with Hollywood movies was not only more intense but fundamentally different from that of the rest of the American public. For us, film served a deeply psychological and physical function. At the very heart of gay diva worship is not the diva herself, but the almost universal homosexual experience of ostracism and insecurity, which ultimately led to what might be called the aestheticism of maladjustment, the gay man's exploitation of cinematic visions of Hollywood grandeur to elevate himself above his antagonistic surroundings and simultaneously express membership in a secret society of upper-class aesthetes.[10]

Straight men tend to objectify, and straight women are often intimidated by other women's expressive sexuality. Through a 'fiercely fetishistic involvement with diva worship,' Harris writes, 'the star even in a sense traded places with her gay audience.' Gay men projected their frustrations, sexual or otherwise, onto the diva. In turn, the diva is 'voided of both her gender and femininity, and became the homosexual's proxy.'[11]

One critic wrote that Marilyn's 'lithe boyish figure and muscular shoulders and thighs...appeals to the hidden homosexual elements in all men and the bisexual element in everybody.'[12]

Susie Bright, a sex-positive feminist and writer, wrote that Marilyn was a 'whippet-slim fox with a boyish figure.' Bright pointed to traditional top-bottom roles, often found in gay relationships, and said Marilyn 'could bottom on camera like few others. So much cinematic power from an ironically-labeled 'submissive' position.'[13]

Bright added: 'Marilyn inhabited an unyielding, butch, yet feminine mojo—where you might imagine [her] taking on the entire [Navy] SEALS and then taunting them for more. She was Pelé-esque, but with the endgame of vulnerability and ecstasy. Her bonhomie about what was possible—it was infectious. She was so warm, witty, [and] accepting of you as you were.'[14]

Marilyn Chambers, as a gay icon, is overdue for consideration.

INSATIABLE

GODFREY DANIELS[15] GOT INVOLVED in the adult film industry in the early seventies. He had an idea to take some top-grossing X-rated films, including *Deep Throat*, *Green Door*, and *The Devil in Miss Jones*, and produce softcore versions for distribution in drive-ins and other theaters that refused to show hardcore films. On paper, the idea seemed ludicrous. Who would want to see a sex film without the sex? But Daniels trusted his instincts.

"I came up with an idea, a very simple idea, but it was revolutionary at the time," he said. "In the movie, you can make what we call a lap dissolve."[16]

According to StudioBinder, a film production software company, 'A lap dissolve, also called a dissolve, is a gradual transition in which one shot fades out as the next shot fades in. When a lap dissolve is used, both shots overlap for a moment of time. How filmmakers use this moment of overlap between two images can impact how audiences perceive the transition. This also allows the audience to make and feel a connection between two shots.'[17]

What made *Deep Throat* illegal was when Linda Lovelace took an erect penis in her mouth. Daniels edited the film to dissolve, so the act was only implied but never explicitly shown.

"It's kind of like the shower scene in *Psycho* where you think [Anthony Perkins is] stabbing [Janet Leigh] in the breast, but you don't actually ever see it," Daniels explained. "It's your imagination."[18]

A self-proclaimed risk-taker, Daniels partnered with a man to help distribute these softcore adult films, even though, by his own admission, "I had no idea what I was doing."[19]

In the case of *Deep Throat* and *Miss Jones*, the challenge was that he needed to negotiate a deal with the mafia, which controlled the films' funding, rights, and distribution. The Mitchell brothers controlled *Green Door*, although the mafia interfered with the film's distribution when the brothers rebuffed an offer to go into business with them.

Daniels met with the mafia bosses, who almost laughed him out of the office. They thought his idea was ridiculous. What could it hurt to cut a deal? However, this "dissolve" technique made the films legal to show in general movie theaters. According to Daniels, the softcore version of *Deep Throat* played in New York City for fifteen years. The mafia family with whom Daniels struck a deal went "ape shit," he said. Believing Daniels had pulled a fast one, the mafia secured and duplicated a copy of the softcore *Deep Throat*. They intended to flood theaters with duplicate copies and cut into Daniels's profits. Daniels, however, was friends with someone from another, more powerful, mafia family and contacted him.

"He said, 'I'll take care of it from here,'" Daniels recalled. "And he did. He made a phone call. They were very unhappy to hear his voice. Let me put it that way. They knew they just couldn't fuck with me anymore. And that was, as I found out much later on, my saving grace. It saved my life, pretty much."[20]

Around 1974, Daniels also struck a deal with the Mitchell brothers to re-edit *Green Door* into a modified, softcore version. "That's when I met Marilyn," he said. "She was very, very bright, smiley. You know, just really charming. She was only about twenty-two or twenty-three."[21] Marilyn had already parted ways professionally with the Mitchells, and when Daniels met her, Chuck was there. Chuck was, in fact, always there.

"They were never apart," he said.[22]

Daniels was one of the few people with kind words about Chuck: "He was a guy's guy. I liked him because he did four tours of duty in Vietnam. He was a patriot. And that's me, you know?" That's not to say Daniels was unaware of Chuck's reputation and attitude toward women. Daniels's wife disliked Chuck intensely. "[She] saw right through him," he said. "He pushed women around to do what he needed to do to his liking. And [my wife] saw how he treated Marilyn, which was not very nice. He was a little bit of a bully. More than a little bit. He was a bully."[23]

Daniels said that Chuck could be fun and friendly but turn on a dime and verbally assault Marilyn for something he perceived she did wrong.

"I never saw real love and affection from him toward her," Daniels said. "Not even in moments I was around them, [which was] quite a bit, especially when we were shooting. He was there every minute of every day, and that was fine with me."[24]

Daniels and his wife spent a great deal of time with Marilyn and Chuck, occasionally visiting their Las Vegas home. In Chuck's office was one accessory of which he was extremely proud: a candy dish. It wasn't a typical candy dish. It was made from a human skull. The cranium had been sliced off, which left a hole where the brain would be. A glass dish was made to fit the shape of the hole in the cranium. Chuck was proud of this macabre dish because, according to Daniels, Chuck himself had killed the man to which the skull belonged when he was a mercenary in Honduras.

"[He] loved to fight, loved to shoot, loved to kill," Daniels said.[25]

When Daniels asked Chuck about the dish, Chuck gleefully recounted how his group captured a Honduran man, decapitated him, skinned him, and somehow smuggled his skull back to the United States. What made it even more chilling was that the group of mercenaries took a photo with the man before and after he was killed. Chuck happily showed a copy of the photo to Daniels, who remembered recoiling at the sight.

"That sums him up pretty well," Daniels said.[26]

But the story of the grisly candy dish appeared to haunt Daniels all these decades later. He told it haltingly, in a soft voice, as though both disgusted by it and hesitant to expose his listener to the horror of it.

Daniels turned to directing films soon after he distributed the softcore versions of *Deep Throat*, *Green Door*, and *Miss Jones*. By the late seventies, he had directed a dozen exploitation pictures as well as a few hardcore films. In 1979, he signed on to direct *Insatiable*. It's not exactly clear who came up with the concept for the film. Not that it matters. The plot is tenuous. However, Marilyn and Chuck thought it the perfect vehicle to reintroduce "Marilyn Chambers, the porno star." The production budget for *Insatiable* has been greatly exaggerated over the years, with reported figures as high as a half-million. It's possible that, because the film's box office take was so high, fans and industry executives assumed it cost more than it did. According to Marty Greenwald, the film's producer and Daniels's business partner, the cost was $129,000 ($534,000 in today's money). It was unusually high for an adult film, but it wasn't the most expensive adult film ever made. That honor belonged to the Mitchell brothers, who spent a reported one million dollars ($5.6 million today) on their 1975 bomb, *Sodom and Gomorrah: The Last Seven Days*.

Some of the money was put up by "wise guys," as Greenwald described them. Marilyn was paid $50,000 ($280,000 today), and the film's earnings were split three ways: a third to Marilyn and Chuck, a third to Daniels and Greenwald, and a third to the organized crime members.

The film certainly made the most of its budget, thanks in large part to the work of cinematographer James R. Bagdonas, who would later put his experience to use on hit TV shows like *Hunter*, *Chicago Hope*, and *Modern Family*. The film is glossy, well-photographed, and makes use of its on-location shooting in London and Northern California. Even the sex scenes have a sensual quality to their photography.

Insatiable was shot in ten days in the late summer of 1979. Most of the film occurred at the historic Grand Island Mansion in Walnut Grove, California, in the Sacramento River Delta. The four-story, twenty-eight-thousand-square-foot mansion, built in the style of the Italian Renaissance, sat on fifty-eight acres. It was outfitted with a movie theater and bowling alley. Cast and crew, however, stayed at a shabby motel nearby.

Chuck insisted on cast and script approval, but Daniels and Greenwald thought the request absurd and said no. The script, written by Daniel Short, tells the story of Sandra Chase (played by Marilyn), a wealthy heiress whose parents died in an unspecified accident. She lives in a palatial estate, drives a Ferrari, travels to London to visit her aunt, and whisks friends, lovers, and acquaintances to her mansion by helicopter. That's the plot. Oh—and she has sex. Lots of it. It's essentially a series of vignettes strung together in no conceivable order or for any coherent reason. What the film lacks in plot, it makes up for in visceral carnal energy. Its sex scenes and Marilyn Chambers' return helped make *Insatiable* a box-office hit. By then twenty-seven-years-old, Marilyn was a far cry from the fresh-faced, all-American girl who went *Behind the Green Door*. She was a grown woman—tanned, toned, more beautiful than ever, and in the best shape of her life.

When the film was released in 1980, Marilyn was twenty-eight. Ever mindful that women live by the sexist double standard of aging, the publicity materials shaved two years off her age.

On the first day of shooting, Marilyn showed up for her 8:00AM call with Chuck. Her makeup was done in a late sixties style, Greenwald recalled. Her fingernails were painted with white nail polish, and she wore white frosted lipstick.

"It looked like something Chuck's mother would wear," Greenwald said. "Chuck was a mama's boy, but he'd never admit it."[27]

The look was wrong. *Insatiable* was a contemporary film, not a film set in the sixties. Daniels told her to change her look, but Chuck balked. "She looks great!" he protested. "Let's keep her like this." Marilyn remained silent. Daniels became angry and demanded Marilyn change her look, or he'd shut down the entire film. Marilyn dutifully followed Daniels's directions, and Chuck stalked off the set.

"It was actually the best day of the shoot because Chuck wasn't there," Greenwald said. "Marilyn was right on her game. She was the best, [although] she had the tendency to overact. She was very expressive. Godfrey would have to calm her down. She really liked Godfrey."[28]

On the second day of shooting, Greenwald said Marilyn showed up to the set with a black eye and her jaw nearly broken. He doesn't remember if she gave an explanation for her injuries or even spoke about them at all. In his opinion, she didn't need to; he knew who gave her those injuries. But that day, Chuck wasn't around.

"This could have been worse," Greenwald said. "He could have taken out a nine millimeter and killed her."[29]

Marilyn was crying and borderline hysterical when she arrived on the set, so she was sent to her trailer to calm down. When she composed herself, makeup was applied to cover as much of the bruise as possible. It would still show up on camera, so the day was spent shooting Marilyn from one side. Marilyn was given the next two days off to heal. She returned with Chuck on the fifth day in better condition and better spirits. During filming, there would be more verbal assaults and physical violence between Chuck and Marilyn.

One day on set, Marilyn was made up, ready to go, and wired for sound. She and Chuck began to argue, and Chuck told Daniels he and Marilyn were going into her trailer. Daniels could hear Chuck yelling at Marilyn.

"He was giving her shit real bad," he said.[30]

Remembering that Marilyn was wired for sound, Daniels instructed his soundman to keep the microphone on and the sound machine running. Then he eavesdropped on their argument.

"Honestly, I couldn't tell you today what it was about," he said. "It was probably nothing about nothing, but he was really giving her shit. It was one of those things where he was barking at her like, 'Fuck you!' He made her cry. And she came back to work, cleaned up her face, and we went back to work."[31]

Actor Richard Pacheco, who appeared in a scene with Marilyn, said it was not pleasant to be around the couple. During his day on set, the atmosphere was tense. Marilyn and Chuck had been arguing and feuding for several days.

"The crew was taking bets on the side of when he was going to hit her," Pacheco said. "There was a poll going on. They were all putting down money. I didn't understand any of that, and I wasn't a part of it. When you work with the top, you want to do good work. I tried to do the best I could and stay out of the way of trouble. On the set of *Insatiable*, she wasn't allowed to hang out with us. She had to be off by herself."[32] Greenwald said he didn't like spending time with Chuck, whom he described as "always at the other end of a lit fuse." As Greenwald was a writer and businessman whose job was ensuring the production ran smoothly, Chuck viewed him differently, Greenwald believed. Daniels had characteristics, professionally and personally, to which Chuck aspired. This might explain their mostly harmonious relationship.

"I was always obsequious around Chuck because I was always afraid he would come unglued," Greenwald said. "Godfrey once said to me, 'You did everything but lick that guy's asshole.' I told him, 'You rely on me to get things done.' But I looked at Chuck, the way he behaved, and thought: he must have a small dick."[33]

Marilyn and Chuck's relationship with Daniels and his wife was unusual. They rarely socialized with colleagues, even on set. However, the couples spent a lot of time together outside of work.

"[Chuck] kind of tried to make me be above that—whether that was good or not," Marilyn recalled. "Obviously, it was good because he always wanted to create a fantasy where I was kind of untouchable to the people that I was around, but on the screen, very touchable. When I would meet my fans, I was very touchable. The people that we worked with, we didn't really socialize too much with them because then they would know too much about me and find out I was a real normal person."[34]

More to the point, it was a way for Chuck to exert complete and absolute control over Marilyn.

LINDA LOVELACE MADE SEVERAL attempts at crossing over to the mainstream when she left Chuck. Every project failed miserably. By 1975, she had all but disappeared from the public eye. Her name was only mentioned in context with *Deep Throat*, which continued to be the subject of litigation, conversation, and controversy throughout the decade. Then, in early 1980, while *Insatiable* was in post-production, Linda Lovelace returned. Out of nowhere came a memoir called *Ordeal*—and it hit like a Mack truck.

Linda made several stunning allegations. Among them: that Chuck Traynor beat her and mentally abused her throughout their relationship, that she was gang raped as her initiation into prostitution, and that she was forced to make *Deep Throat* against her will. At one point, she claimed, Chuck held a gun to her head and threatened to kill her if she didn't finish work on *Deep Throat*. In fact, she claimed, all of her films had been made against her will; Chuck had dominated, intimidated, hypnotized, and brainwashed her.

The book was staunchly anti-porn, and the American media and public lapped it up. It became an instant *New York Times* bestseller. Finally, many anti-porn crusaders and feminists thought, there was proof that the adult film world was as abusive, misogynistic, and potentially life-threatening as they had always imagined. And the proof came from none other than the star of the most famous X-rated film in history.

What's more, Linda's life in 1980 had not improved much. She was married with a child and a second on the way. She and her husband lived on welfare. Her economically-disadvantaged status helped to validate feminists' claims of the debilitating and destructive effects of participating in porn. Linda Lovelace became a feminist hero.

'She is 31 now, wary, plain, nervous,' reported *The Washington Post*. 'Laughter startles; irony eludes her. She doesn't see the sleight-of-hand, the tricks that can turn a suburban cliche into a much-cherished fantasy. There is only the adamant denial of the way things seemed to be.'[35]

Surely, this resulted from having been in a porno movie, the media speculated.

"'I wouldn't want to meet Linda Lovelace,'" she told the *Post*. "'I wouldn't want to have anything to do with her. That's not the way I am at all. That wasn't me.'"[36]

Yet Linda Lovelace's name was affixed to the book's cover. Linda Boreman (her maiden name) or Linda Marchiano (her married name) wouldn't sell books. Linda Lovelace certainly would. On the one hand, that's the business of selling books. On the other, if the woman writing the book claims not to be the same Linda Lovelace whose name is on the cover, how is the reader supposed to trust her?

'She wants vindication as well, although the form it should take still seems a little vague,' the *Post* article noted. "I really have the firm belief that somebody's going to pick up the ball on this, I really do,' she says. 'I just keep my fingers crossed for that."[37]

Linda embarked on a nationwide book tour. Virtually every major print, television, and radio news outlet featured the reformed porn star. She was contacted separately by Gloria Steinem, the most well-known feminist in the United States. She expressed interest in bringing more attention to Lovelace's story. Steinem accompanied Linda on parts of her book tour, including a television appearance on *Tomorrow* with Tom Snyder.

Gloria Leonard, one of the most respected adult actresses, publisher of the adult magazine *High Society*, and tireless advocate for free speech and the adult film industry, scoffed at both the book's publication and Steinem's association with Lovelace.

"*Cosmopolitan*, back in the day when Gloria Steinem was still part of it, once did a cover story of a headless woman," Leonard said. "She was just nude from the neck down, holding flowers over her breasts—and the cover line was something like: 'Erotica vs. Pornography: Do you know the difference?' I thought, 'Here they are pooh-poohing it and making hay out of it, but they have it as their cover story. They're selling it and exploiting it themselves! Well, I'm just doing the same thing. And who are you or any other female to consider my choice of what I want to do any less valid than your choice?' It only causes more dissension. It's not going to unify women."[38]

She added: "Nobody really paid a whole lot of attention to *Ordeal* when it came out, you know, in terms of credibility. I mean, this was a woman who never took responsibility for her own shitty choices—but instead blamed everything that happened to her in her life on porn."[39]

PURE *The Sexual Revolutions of Marilyn Chambers*

Journalist Hart Williams conceived the term "Linda Syndrome" to describe someone, usually a woman, who disavows their porn past to obtain credibility and acceptance from the mainstream. Carolyn Bronstein, feminist and author of the book *Battling Pornography: The American Feminist Anti-Pornography Movement, 1976-1986*, used a different term: "rape culture."

'We live in a society where females are treated as sexual objects, and sexual violence is common,' Bronstein wrote in *The Atlantic*. 'Rape is accepted as a fact of life for girls and women, a nuisance that simply won't go away.'[40]

Just as many people refuted Linda's claims. People on the *Deep Throat* set said there was no gun. They never saw any abuse, either. Co-stars claimed Lovelace enjoyed making adult films and was a willing participant—including in the infamous *Dog Fucker*, in which a canine penetrates her.

Even the book's co-author Mike McGrady was dubious.

"Oh yeah, I had a lot of trouble believing it at first," he said. "See, I was one of the many local columnists who had interviewed her when *Deep Throat* came out, and from all I could see, she was a willing participant—and I had met Chuck Traynor at that time as well."[41]

Linda took two lie detector tests, both of which McGrady attended. "She passed with flying colors," McGrady claimed. "Linda cannot lie—as near as I can tell—and get away with it. The story itself was horrifying, and you might've thought, as I did, that when you have one of the lead celebrities tell a tale of great sex and violence, it'd be easy to sell. But the truth is I was turned down by thirty-three publishers."[42]

The book was finally picked up by publisher Lyle Stuart, probably best known for publishing the controversial 1970 book *The Anarchist Cookbook*, an instruction manual for the average person to create homemade explosives, booby traps, and engage in hand-to-hand combat, among other things.

Chuck denied all of Linda's allegations. They were "so ridiculous I can't take them seriously," he said before adding, "You'd think she would at least be grateful for a few moments of glory, even if they didn't last."[43]

Chuck was in London when Sammy Davis, Jr. sent him a manuscript of *Ordeal*. Marilyn read it to Chuck. They received a call from Hugh Hefner's secretary. Hefner was upset about the book, particularly the parts about Hefner and parties at the Playboy mansion. Chuck, Sammy, and Hefner met to discuss possibly suing Linda for libel. Chuck and Sammy were miffed that Linda described a scene in her book in which she was deep-throating Sammy and maneuvered the situation, so Sammy ended up performing oral sex on Chuck.

"Sammy and I never had sex," Chuck said flatly. "Sammy said, 'I don't know where any of this shit came from. You think we should sue 'em?' I said, 'No, because if we sue 'em, it's gonna go into litigation—that's publicity. Think about it. That book could be in litigation for years—and sell millions and millions of copies. And we ain't gettin' a penny.'"[44]

Marilyn recalled an interview she did in Seattle with a reporter who told her he wanted to speak with her alone. "Chuck wasn't around at the time," she said, "but the reporter thought he'd be hanging over me like John Derek telling me what to say. The man handed me a piece of paper and told me he had just gotten off an airplane with Gloria [Steinem]. He said Gloria had a hundred questions for me. On the paper was a phone number for battered and abused women. Ha! I wanted to show the paper to Chuck. The reporter freaked out because he thought Chuck was going to beat me up."[45]

Marilyn said she was insulted by the reporter's gesture.

"Because of the whole Lovelace screw-up, I've had to push a lot harder," Marilyn said. "I've had to be more determined to become a success."[46]

In Marilyn's defense of Chuck, she said every bit of credit for her success was due to him. In one interview, she went so far as to say, "I know I'm stupid, and I need somebody to show me the way."[47] It was an infelicitous, inaccurate self-assessment. Marilyn wasn't stupid. She was a bright woman with a quick wit. She would have benefitted from an agent and manager more experienced than Chuck, who could also act as a guide and mentor.

"[I]f [Linda] didn't enjoy being a sex symbol, that's tough," Marilyn told *Us* magazine. "She could learn to live with it, but that wouldn't sell books, would it? By denouncing the porn industry, Linda's become the idol of the people who once hated her. She's become a parody of the image Chuck worked so hard to create. She's stooped so low she's joined up with Gloria Steinem, and you know what women's libbers are. They're just frustrated women who can't get laid. That's why they're bitching all the time."[48]

Linda's association with Steinem brought greater attention to the book. Soon, other prominent feminists, such as Susan Brownmiller, supported Linda. Andrea Dworkin, the radical feminist who launched the group Women Against Pornography, also joined the cause.

"When Linda came out and denounced the 'business' and then was hanging with Gloria Steinem, it got nuts," Marilyn said. "People would hand me notes saying Gloria Steinem wants you to call her. She knows you're being forced to do this. And Gloria Steinem wrote in her book about me how she knew I was forced into it and that I was being hypnotized. I was thinking, you know what, that's bullshit."[49]

She continued: "That woman never even met me! How dare she assume I wasn't doing what I wanted to! I think *she* should be using her vibrator a lot more."[50]

Linda followed *Ordeal* with another book titled *Out of Bondage*. Again, she used the name Linda Lovelace to sell the book. It was co-written with McGrady, and Steinem penned the introduction. The book describes what Linda endured following the publication of *Ordeal*. As Clarence Petersen wrote in his review for *The Chicago Tribune*: 'Steinem looms large as [Linda]'s mentor, friend and ally in the war against sex films. Apart from the suggestion that porn star Marilyn Chambers may now be similarly enslaved by Traynor, Steinem and [Lovelace] fail entirely to show that this type of relationship is widespread in the X-rated film industry.'[51]

Out of Bondage barely made a blip on the radar. It wasn't a bestseller and the public had moved on. And in the end, Linda felt she had been used by the same feminists who supported her.

"When I look back at all the feminists and Women Against Pornography—I kind of feel like they used me, too," she said. "Because when I came out and said what I said, you know, about being a victim, too, it supported everything they had been saying, and it was coming from the horse's mouth. They needed me; that was good. But if I ever needed anything, they weren't really there. Between Andrea Dworkin and Kitty MacKinnon, they've written so many books, and they mention my name and all that, but financially they've never helped me out. When I showed up with them for speaking engagements, I'd always get five hundred dollars or so. But I know they made a few bucks off me, just like everybody else."[52]

There's no question Linda Lovelace was a victim. She endured physical, verbal, and emotional abuse at the hands of Chuck Traynor. However, the bitter claims that nearly everyone she encountered took advantage of her—including those who presumably tried to help her—begs the question: at what point is an adult human being responsible for their own choices?

"*INSATIABLE* WAS MY FAVORITE film," Marilyn said. "I looked the best. I felt the best. I felt the sexiest. It was like the prime of my life right there. That was a time where you saw me being totally sexual. Everything was going my way, and I just felt sexy, and I felt happy."[53]

The film was released by Daniels's company Miracle Films, which carried the sublimely tongue-in-cheek tagline: "If it's a good film...it's a Miracle!"

INSATIABLE

While promoting *Insatiable*, her big-budget return to X-rated films in 1980, Marilyn was besieged with questions about Linda Lovelace's controversial autobiography and claims of abuse at the hands of Chuck Traynor. *Chris Jones.*

The return of Marilyn Chambers made *Insatiable* a newsworthy event. She was invited to add her handprints and footprints in cement outside the Pussycat Theater on Santa Monica Boulevard in West Hollywood, California. It was the adult film industry's version of Grauman's Chinese Theater. Nightly news stations featured the occasion. Even though it's considered a classic of the genre, it's not an especially good film. There are noteworthy production values, such as the aforementioned cinematography. It has an above-average soundtrack, Marilyn is certainly charismatic, and the other actors are nice to look at. But the acting is wooden, there's no plot, the dialogue is banal, and aside from watching pretty people have sex, it's rather dull—except for one scene.

In the film, Marilyn's character Sandra remembers the first time she had sex. The scene dissolves into a flashback in which a supposedly much younger Sandra, dressed in a pale pink nightgown, enters the room. Already in the room is a dark-haired young man dressed in a white tank top and black trousers playing snooker on a pool table. There's playful banter between them, and he removes Sandra's nightgown and lays her on her back on the pool table.

"When they say 'action,' that's when your mind control kicks in, and you're in a different dimension," Marilyn explained about filming sex scenes. "You are involved with something where you know millions of people will be seeing this, and it's just a weird feeling. You need to make this so sexy because you're not going to have another chance."[54]

To prepare herself, she sometimes fantasized about the audience. She imagined the people in the theater getting turned on as she performed on screen.

Marilyn and actor David Morris didn't need to try to make the scene sexy. Their sexual chemistry is palpable. It's one of the most erotic sex scenes ever committed to celluloid. He was handsome, lean, and muscular. He had a permanent five o'clock shadow and thick, long, dark hair. He had the central-casting look of a tough Italian New Yorker. Indeed, he bore a striking resemblance to the actor Tony Danza. (People would ask Marilyn if Danza had appeared in *Insatiable* under a different name.)

Ernie Roebuck, the *Insatiable* lighting director, had previously worked with Morris. "He was a very strange guy," Roebuck said. "Whenever he'd show up, he was always jacking off. From the time he got there, everything I ever did with him, he'd show up on the set and start jacking off—all day, every film."[55]

When Marilyn picked Morris up at the airport the day before they shot their scene together, she was instantly attracted. His machismo and dark good looks made him exactly the type of man Marilyn was attracted to. She tried to charm him, but he was uninterested. Marilyn was stung by the rebuff; it only made her want him more.

Morris always seemed to have a serious look and demeanor. It worked perfectly for the scene with Marilyn in *Insatiable*. But there were moments of levity on the set. One behind-the-scenes photo reveals Morris smiling as he tries to grab Marilyn, who holds her hands up as if to push him away.

During their *Insatiable* scene, Morris appeared to get rough handling Marilyn. At one point, he grabbed her by the back of her neck to bring her head closer to the edge of the pool table. Marilyn whacked her forehead on the side. Daniels felt Morris was getting too rough and was about to yell, "Cut!" when Chuck intervened. Chuck knew something special was happening. According to Daniels, Chuck quietly assured him that Morris was not being too rough. The filming continued without interruption.

Marilyn recalled that while filming, there was a sexual tension that permeated the room, and the crew remained motionless and silent as they peered at the couple. When the scene was completed, the crew gave Morris and Marilyn a standing ovation. The scene remained Marilyn's favorite of any she filmed.

INSATIABLE

"We didn't know if it was planned, but it helped redefine what was sexual in an adult movie," Greenwald said.[56]

"Working with Marilyn was, obviously, an honor," actor Richard Pacheco recalled. "She was not quite part of the business. She wasn't a regular. She was above the business. She was so famous, like John Holmes. She was a business unto herself."[57]

Pacheco was referring to John C. Holmes, the most recognizable actor in the adult film business. He was the male equivalent of Marilyn Chambers. *Insatiable* was the first film the two of them made together. No matter how good the movie was, pairing the two most famous adult stars would surely draw a crowd. Unlike Marilyn, Holmes never tried to break into the mainstream. Still, he was a household name, even more so than *Deep Throat*'s Harry Reems. By the time he made *Insatiable*, Holmes had starred in several hundred adult films. In 1971 he had starred as a private detective in the adult film *Johnny Wadd*. It was a massive success and spawned a series of Johnny Wadd films throughout the seventies.

The mustachioed Holmes had an average Joe quality: tall, gangly, not especially fit, and not particularly handsome. He was most famous for his large penis. While exact measurements are unconfirmed, it was generally considered to be at least thirteen-and-a-half inches. (According to the American Association for the Advancement of Science, 'the average flaccid, pendulous penis is 3.61 inches in length; the average erect penis is 5.16 inches long.'[58]) One adult actress said performing oral sex on John Holmes was like fellating a telephone pole.[59]

Holmes was asked to film two scenes with Marilyn. One would be included in *Insatiable*: the penultimate scene in which he plays her character's ultimate "fantasy lover"; the other scene, taking place in a home gym, would be included in a series of home videos being planned called *Marilyn Chambers' Private Fantasies.*

Marilyn, Chuck, and Daniels picked up Holmes at the airport.

"I was totally nervous," Marilyn said. "I'd heard so much about him. I was not afraid but just totally shy. He and I were sitting in the back seat, and we were talking, and I was just kind of looking at him in awe, going, 'God, this guy is really smart. He really is fairly articulate.'"[60]

Some interviews with Holmes made him "look like a dope," Marilyn said, but she found him kind and gentle.

"He was so not the John Holmes I thought he was going to be," she said. She imagined he'd have an ego and be aggressive with everyone. Instead, he came across as a "meek" gentleman.

"He told me that he had a sheep farm," Marilyn remembered. "He said that he was just kind of a country boy, and he was doing all this so that he could live a normal life. John never let on who he really was. He was 'John Holmes,' the façade forever. I have to really applaud him for that because he didn't ever really let anybody know who he really was, and I think that's the true meaning of a star."[61]

By 1979, Holmes was plagued by addiction. He abused alcohol, but cocaine was the real problem. In the seventies, the drug was prevalent on virtually every adult film set, and many Hollywood film sets. Marilyn did it, too, when Chuck allowed her to. According to the television show *Frontline*, the seventies saw a resurgence of cocaine use "as a recreational drug and was glamorized in the US popular media. Articles from the time proclaimed cocaine as non-addictive. The drug was viewed as harmless until the 1985 emergence of crack."[62]

Many in Holmes' inner circle began to notice a dramatic increase in his cocaine use and changes in his behavior. His drug abuse also led to problems getting and maintaining an erection. (Those were the days before Viagra and other medications were commonly used to treat erectile dysfunction.)

The final scene in *Insatiable* was filmed in a small room draped in black. The blazing lights made it almost unbearably hot. Marilyn lay on a table which was also draped in black fabric and sat in the middle of the room. Two men and a woman make love to her. When they leave, Holmes enters.

"When John and I were actually ready to do the scene, it took forever," Marilyn recalled. "He was in the bathroom. He was doing coke—like, a gram up each nostril. John comes out, and he can't get it up. It was like a big, floppy, old worm. What he would do was hold it at the base and try to squeeze some of the blood into the head. So we really had a difficult time with that. He never really got totally hard, but I think we faked it enough to make it look real."[63]

In Marilyn's final analysis of John Holmes, she could have been talking about herself: "I think he was misunderstood, not only by the public, but I think he was also misunderstood by himself. I don't think he ever really had a home life. I don't think he ever had a real personal life. He was always living on the edge, and that was his life. It's difficult to be that person 24 hours a day, seven days a week, and come down off that and be somebody else."[64]

WHEN THE *INSATIABLE* SHOOT wrapped, the crew presented Marilyn with a gift: a gold necklace with a small gold pendant in the shape of an Academy Award. She embarked on an extensive two-year promotional tour for the movie. Without naming names, she said several A-list celebrities told her how much they liked the film. Fans lined up for blocks when she made a personal appearance. At New York's Pussycat Theatre, fans waited more than an hour.

INSATIABLE

Two fans disguised themselves as New York City police officers so they wouldn't have to wait in line.

She would appear fully nude in the lobby and sign autographs for hours. Her labial ring was usually prominently exposed, she wore her belly chain, and her pubic hair was trimmed and shaped into a heart. She took many press interviews in the nude. It was always cleared with the interviewer in advance, and many reporters didn't quite know how to respond.

Some simply expected it.

"Why aren't you nude now?" one asked.

"I'd have to ask Chuck first," she replied. "He makes *all* the decisions." She left the room to confer with Chuck. When she returned, she said it was a no-go because it wasn't prearranged, and the reporter didn't bring any photographers.[65]

The interviews were as much about Linda Lovelace and her book as they were about *Insatiable*. And, as always, she was made to defend her choices.

"Do you ever think about God, sin, right, wrong?" asked Tom Snyder on his late-night talk show *Tomorrow*.

Marilyn replied that she did not, but she thought about guilt and how it was important never to feel guilty for anything she's done.

"What I've done and what I intend to do, I will do by my own will and enjoy it," she said. "I'm not worried about later."

"You mentioned fantasy. Let me try this one on you. Play 'What if'?" Tom proposed. "What if—and this is going to sound terrible—what if you die and you go to the pearly gates and Saint Peter says, 'You've done wrong, and you're not coming in'?"

The studio audience laughed nervously. Marilyn smiled, winked at Tom, and when the laughter stopped, she replied, "Well, Tom, you and I are going to go together, I think."[66]

The audience laughed and erupted into applause.

The adult and mainstream press coverage was generous and helped propel the movie into the public's consciousness. Still, Linda Lovelace loomed large. Marilyn's first-person perspective of a strong-willed, sexually shameless woman who defended Chuck starkly contrasts with the Lovelace narrative. While reporters gave Marilyn credit for a unique and successful career, snide remarks, judgmental comments, or outright cruel comments were mixed in.

'Chambers has a most lucrative career in live shows, TV, and the porn movie business,' wrote Murray Frymer for *The Chicago Tribune*. 'She and boyfriend-manager are making a tour of a few towns to promote 'Insatiable,' just like the legitimate movie stars do.'[67]

Frymer doesn't clarify what constitutes an 'illegitimate' movie star. The only implication is that if you're an adult movie star, you are somehow valued less than Hollywood movie stars. Apart from noting Marilyn was in town to promote *Insatiable*, not once did Frymer mention the movie, its story, the actors, or the scenes. Instead, it was the same old dog-and-pony show with questions about her upbringing, her parents' thoughts about her career, and where she sees sex films heading.

By this point, Marilyn was accustomed to journalists asking her questions that contained thinly-veiled barbs, even on live television. When a reporter served such a question, Marilyn, like a tennis champion, returned the shot and often won the point with a smash.

When she appeared on the local Philadelphia talk show *Whitney & Co./Live*, hosted by Jane Whitney, she was asked, "What about the people who fantasize about you in Des Moines, Iowa? Doesn't that bother you?"

Marilyn answered the question with a question. "What about the people in Philadelphia who fantasize about you?"

"Don't you ever get tired of sex?"

"No, do you?"

After a long pause, Whitney said, "This is the first time anyone has ever stopped me on the air."[68]

It was her delivery that made Marilyn so effective in answering questions like those. She was perpetually composed and free of agitation, and employed a deceptively vulnerable voice, all breathy sexiness, that belied the strength underneath.

"I think [*Insatiable*] appeals to ladies too because it's just not as embarrassing as they would expect, or the way films in the past would be," Marilyn told Diane Haithman of the *Detroit Free Press*. "I could be wrong, but the good part about this movie is that the sex is hot, but it doesn't dominate the whole film...it's not just a male's point of view; it's not just a male fantasy anymore."[69]

Haithman saw a preview of the film before interviewing Marilyn. She left after twenty minutes because she was too embarrassed to endure a sex film.

"I don't see anything about sex that is obscene," Marilyn told Haithman. "There are a lot of things that are pornographic to me, but not sex."[70] Violence, she argued, is far more obscene than a film containing scenes of two people making love.

Having read *Ordeal*, Haithman pointed to a "nagging suspicion" that Marilyn was being forced to perform against her will, just like Linda Lovelace.

'All her manager, Chuck Traynor, had to say was, 'Hi, I'm Chuck,' and I hated him,' she wrote.[71]

INSATIABLE

So much for journalistic objectivity. After speaking with Marilyn, Haithman admitted there was no coercion. Marilyn said there was no force involved, and Haithman agreed.

'There's no shy, terrified girl under the thumb of a cruel manager here,' Haithman wrote. 'She seems joking, flirtatious, mischievous. She boldly rejects the only excuse society holds out to her for her misdeeds.'[72]

"Nobody's going to break me down to say I've been forced to do this and that and the other thing," Marilyn said. "It's a crock of you know what, as far as I'm concerned. And I think it's sad a person like Linda Lovelace has to make excuses for her failure or getting out of the business."[73]

Although *Insatiable* was a box-office hit, the reviews were mixed.

'Well, despite the fanfare, Marilyn Chambers might have stayed behind her green door if *Insatiable* is the best she has to offer,' wrote Robert Ashfield in *Mr.* magazine. 'Not that it's her fault. She has talents, besides the obvious ones, and she is still attractive[.]'[74]

Robert A. Masullo, critic for *The Sacramento Bee*, didn't like the film, but he reserved his harshest comments for Marilyn.

'Chambers is, I have always thought, a rather strange choice for a sex goddess,' he wrote in his review, which appeared under the headline, 'Marilyn Chambers has gotten older, not better.' '[S]he is not a beauty. Her mouth and nose are too large; her eyes, ordinary; her hair, dull, and her figure makes one think of a lumber yard. Now, at 28, she comes across as tired and bored. 'Insatiable?' A better title might have been: 'Exhausted.'[75]

On the other hand, Al Goldstein of *Screw* raved about the film.

'Superstar Marilyn Chambers could not have made a more auspicious return to porn than that represented by her first sex flick in four years, *Insatiable*,' he wrote. 'It is an absolutely devastating piece of erotica, reaching new heights of technical excellence and offering the American public the kind of quality sexual material they have long demanded.'[76]

Some reviewers praised Marilyn but thought the film to be tripe.

'Marilyn has a clean-cut charm and built-in personality that transcends routine porn and which, with a good movie, can be used to advantage to regain her room at the top,' wrote Alex Horne in *At Home Magazine*. '*Insatiable* is not it. The movie, besides degrading women, is a pretentious and dreary vehicle for someone as talented as Marilyn Chambers, who does her best to save it.'[77]

To say the film degraded women is confounding. Although Marilyn wanted to please—and keep—her male fan base, *Insatiable* was marketed to women, a rare gesture in the world of adult films. Indeed, in interviews, Marilyn urged women and young couples to see the film.

Before *Insatiable*, few adult films were told from a woman's point of view. *Resurrection of Eve* showed the transformation of a sexually repressed woman to one who was sexually reborn. However, in most adult films—particularly those produced in the seventies with a male audience in mind—there's almost always an element of violence towards women. Kidnappings, hostage situations, and rape were distressingly common plot devices. *Behind the Green Door* featured such a device.

There's no violence in *Insatiable*. The women are always in control. In particular, Marilyn's character, Sandra, makes no apologies for being a woman of great sexual edacity. She thrives on it, a vampiress whose thirst for physical intimacy is never satisfied.

'From a feminist perspective, it is easy, of course, to dismiss this notion of power, to see Sandra's apparent satisfaction in insatiability and masochism as the height of false consciousness and alienation from any real source of power or pleasure for women,' wrote film scholar Linda Williams in her book *Hard Core: Power, Pleasure and the "Frenzy of the Visible"*. 'But to do so is to foreclose the possibility of seeing women as subjects of sexual representation, for however we, as gendered individuals with individual sexual tastes and preferences, may judge this film's sexual acts, *Insatiable* does construct its female protagonist as a subject, and not just an object, of desire.'

Williams argued that *Insatiable* was focused 'on the new problem of pleasing the woman and of constructing her pleasure from her own point of view.' Marilyn's character was 'in complete knowledge and control of the means to her pleasure.' She didn't need a man to bring this out. Sex is both pleasure and power, and her character suffers no consequences because she knows and welcomes the idea of being a desired subject.

'The ravishment [in *Insatiable*] is all about finding the sexual number that will permit the woman the most pleasure,' wrote Williams. 'At the end, [she] calls out for 'more, more, more,' even though she has already 'had' a great deal. Rather than give her more, the film simply ends with the end title, that is also its advertising slogan: 'Marilyn Chambers is Insatiable.' Instead of the end of desire in the satisfaction of the climax, a new kind of satisfaction is offered: climax's infinite prolongation.'[78]

At the Adult Film Association of America's Fifth Annual Erotic Film Awards, *Insatiable* picked up a nod for best picture, and Marilyn, as expected, was nominated for best actress. The title song, Shame on You, performed by Marilyn in the film, was nominated for best song. She sang the tune at the event, held on June 9, 1981, at the Hollywood Palladium.[79] Marilyn was certain she would be honored as best actress. Her big-budget return to X-rated films was a resounding success. She may never win an Oscar, but her adult film peers would assuredly recognize her, she thought. After all, she was one of the main reasons erotic films were even part of the public consciousness.

The film won no awards, and Marilyn walked away empty-handed. (Samantha Fox picked up best actress for *Tramp*.)

"Let me tell you, it was a quiet night, oh boy," recalled Daniels, who accompanied Marilyn and Chuck to the event. "And we went from there to Hefner's Playboy Mansion. He had a big party for the award night. She was not a happy camper."[80]

THE THEATRICAL RELEASE OF *Insatiable* coincided with two entertainment industry milestones: the arrival of home video and the emergence of cable television. Twentieth Century Fox was the first major Hollywood studio to license their titles to a video duplication company in 1977.[81] The films were produced in two formats: videocassette and Betamax. A videocassette recorder (VCR) or Betamax player, respectively, was required to view the films. Initially, the titles were intended for rental only. Hollywood executives didn't believe a consumer would want to purchase a copy of a film to watch repeatedly. They were wrong. Consumers were eager to own copies of their favorite films. Those who could afford a film had to fork over between seventy and one hundred dollars per title (between $265 and $365 in today's money), an astronomical amount compared to the average movie ticket price of two dollars and twenty-three cents (about eight dollars today). VCRs and Betamax players cost as much as $1,400 to own in 1980 (about $5,000 today).[82]

By 1980, nearly every major Hollywood studio had entered the video rental market. So, too, did the adult film industry. The home video boom was a defining moment of the eighties, particularly in the United States. Video rental stores were the Starbucks of their generation, seeming to pop up overnight on every street corner.

For example, in a Los Angeles video store, copies of recent films like *Smokey and the Bandit* and classics like *Casablanca* sold for between thirty-five and fifty dollars (between $125 and $175 in today's money). X-rated films like *Insatiable* went for $100 ($350 today) or more. Marilyn had a theory about why adult films were so popular on home video.

"People are willing to pay $100 for an X-rated film because they can see it in the privacy of their own homes with their husband or wife or boyfriend or

After her one-woman show *Sex Surrogate* was banned in Las Vegas for its full-frontal nudity, Marilyn brought it to London, where it played for seven months. *Photographer uncredited*.

girlfriend and be turned on by them," she told Vernon Scott of United Press International. "It eliminates taking the chance of being seen at the box office of a porno theater while buying a ticket for another thing. Some people are worried about their reputations. A judge trying a porno case in his court doesn't want to be seen waiting in line at a porno theater."[83]

Marilyn also pointed to the excitement of the forbidden. It was a callback to when she was promoting *Green Door* in the porno chic days.

"If the controversy wasn't there, X-rated cassettes wouldn't sell," she added. "As long as people are willing to pay $100 for them, they'll keep selling."[84]

Insatiable was one of the first X-rated films released to the home video market. It became the best-selling video of any genre from 1980 to 1982.[85]

"It was the perfect movie for the birth of video," Greenwald said. "Two hundred ten thousand copies of the video sold in the first month [of release]. It grossed ten million dollars, and we netted about three or four million."[86] (In today's money, the gross is more than $35 million dollars, and the net is between $10.6 and $14 million.)

The profits were split between Daniels, Greenwald, Marilyn, and Chuck, and the organized crime members who had invested in the film. So successful was its release to home video that Greenwald and Daniels tried to buy out the "wise guys." They didn't tell Marilyn and Chuck of their plans.

"They trusted us because [they knew] we kept very tight control on the books," Greenwald said.[87]

The "wise guys" did not agree to a buyout. Moreover, they were miffed that Daniels and Greenwald would try to squeeze them out of any money.

"Godfrey told me months later how badly we got fucked," Greenwald lamented. "The mafia had sold another three hundred thousand bootlegs illegally and made ten to fifteen million dollars." (Between $32.5 and $48.7 million in today's money.) They finally told Marilyn and Chuck. The news sent Chuck into a rage. He became hellbent on suing the mafia. "We told him he was out of his mind," Greenwald said.[88] Marilyn fully embraced the home video boom and launched a series of films made specifically for the home video market entitled *Marilyn Chambers' Private Fantasies*. She saw the potential of home video and sensed it wasn't a fad. She knew it would become ubiquitous in every household. She regularly attended major conferences and industry trade shows like the Consumer Electronics Show to promote the videos. Attendees waited up to an hour to meet her and get an autograph. At an appearance at the Video Software Dealers Association conference, as many attendees flocked to meet her as they did to actresses Joan Collins and Jane Fonda.[89] Six volumes of *Private Fantasies* were released over three years, the first in 1983. It was filmed at the same time as *Insatiable* in the same mansion, with a bowling alley in the basement. Greenwald said Marilyn would tell him her fantasies, and he'd write a short script. The more outrageous stunts were, naturally, concocted from Chuck's imagination. A scene in the first film takes place in the Grand Island Mansion's bowling alley.

"Chuck sort of directed the thing, and I did the technical work," Daniels said. "He said, 'Ah, I've got an idea!' And he comes back with a bowling pin."[90]

Marilyn fellated the bowling pin then Chuck got the idea to insert it into her vaginally. ("It probably wasn't the most romantic thing that was ever put inside of her," Daniels quipped.[91]) After recording some footage, Marilyn attempted to remove the pin. It was stuck. Daniels tried to remove it gently, but it proved too painful. He applied some petroleum jelly to her vagina to try to loosen it. He thought about calling the paramedics but couldn't figure out what to tell them when they arrived. Everyone went into a state of panic except Chuck. He was watching the scene unfold, doubled over from laughter. Finally, after slowly and gently maneuvering the pin and applying gobs of petroleum jelly, the pin came out with a giant 'pop.' (Daniels keeps the pin, an Ivory Snow box, and a photo of Marilyn on a small shrine he has in his office.) A scene in the mansion's gymnasium with John Holmes was included in the first installment, too. In it, Marilyn displays her prowess as a gymnast, then Holmes enters, and they have sex. The plan was for Marilyn to deep-throat Holmes. Ernie Roebuck pulled Holmes aside and asked if he thought she could do it.

"Absolutely not," Holmes said. "I've never had anybody do it."[92] Marilyn repeatedly tried to deep-throat Holmes. Because his penis was not fully erect, it would get stuck in her throat.

"It's gathering up in there," she'd say after an attempt.

"It was getting to the point of being ridiculous," Roebuck said. "Godfrey Daniels wasn't going for it, and it just wasn't going to happen. But she would not give up. Then Chuck appears out of nowhere. They step outside. You'd hear a little smack. You'd hear a little thud."[93]

A tear-stained Marilyn reappeared in the room. Chuck followed behind her.

"OK, what's next?" she asked with a phony smile glued to her face.[94]

The cast and crew didn't say anything or acknowledge what they had just heard. Everyone moved on to the next shot.

Home Video magazine featured Marilyn on the cover of their January 1981 issue and hailed her as the "Video Sex Goddess." The clever cover image showed a nude Marilyn covered in videotape reels.

The availability of adult films helped propel home videos to the masses. But as X-rated films flooded the market, their revenue share dropped, and soon, Hollywood film video sales outpaced it. 'Following the popularity of video cassettes has been a trend of uncensorship [*sic*],' one newspaper reporter wrote:

> Movies cut and hacked to pieces for their theatrical release are being restored to their original, intended versions on videotapes. Why would they be cut if the scenes are going to be added back when it hits video? The Motion Picture Association of America (MPAA), which oversees the rating of all theatrical films, have this huge, ugly horror that they sometimes slap on a film. The *X* rating has become a sure sign of death for a film.
>
> The big mistake was the MPAA's error in not copyrighting the *X* as they had with the *G*, *PG*, and *R* ratings. By not doing this, they lost control (if they ever had it), and the porno industry welcomed this wonderful advertising gimmick. Soon after, the meaningless but magnificent audience attracter triple-*X* rating began adorning movie posters. Herein lies the deathtrap for non-pornographic films with an X rating. Most non-porno theaters will not show these films, and the majority of television stations and newspapers refuse their advertising. But with video, [censored and uncensored versions] are available, thus giving true movie lovers a chance to see their favorite films as intended.[95]

There were, however, two things Marilyn didn't like about video. The first was the quality of reproduction. Tape was cheap and easy to produce, but the picture quality lacked the luster and fine grain of the thirty-five-millimeter film used in cinema. So she insisted that all of her films, even those made especially for the home video market, be shot on thirty-five-millimeter film and transferred to videotape. It was a much more costly process, but she was still the reigning adult actress, and these videos were guaranteed moneymakers.

The second thing she didn't like about the home video boom was the inevitable closure of adult movie theaters. For more than a decade, the only way to see an X-rated film was in a movie theater. Home video would change that completely. Now viewers could enjoy adult films in the privacy of their own homes—"brown-bagging it," as she called it. Videos could even be ordered from men's magazines and catalogs, so the shame or embarrassment of entering and exiting adult theaters was quickly on its way out. There would always be a need for strip and sex clubs, though, with or without showings of adult films. She and Chuck decided to shift from films to strip club appearances as their main source of revenue. Anyone could watch Marilyn Chambers on video, but seeing her in person was an event.

PURE
The Sexual Revolutions of Marilyn Chambers

One more reason to stay home in the eighties was cable television. The subscription service offered viewers a seemingly endless selection of stations beyond the big three networks and public television. Some were specialized, like MTV, which launched in 1981 and showed only music videos by popular artists. Cable television also introduced the twenty-four-hour news cycle with the Cable News Network (CNN). Viewers could get premium channels like Home Box Office (HBO) and SHOWTIME for an additional fee. Unlike network television, the Federal Communications Commission did not regulate cable TV.[96] These premium channels allowed movies to air unedited.

Marilyn saw this as an opportunity. She tried unsuccessfully to launch a premium cable station called Marilyn Chambers Television (MCTV). The intention was to show hardcore films with the explicitness intact. Between movies, Marilyn and other adult industry veterans would interview performers, adult bookstore owners, sexologists, and sex workers and provide a private peek into adult filmmaking. It would have been a lucrative opportunity for Marilyn. She co-owned percentages of her films, and repeated airings would have earned her a steady stream of residuals. Alas, it was not to be. The idea of airing X-rated films on television, even if it was a premium station, was met with resistance from the public, and the idea was shelved.[97]

In 1980, there were sixteen million cable subscribers in the US. The number doubled in just five years. By the end of the decade, fifty million Americans subscribed to cable TV.[98]

Many people in the media castigated both the home video and cable television markets for, they believed, pandering to the public with pornography. It seemed there was no middle ground. The media were just as discouraged and angered by the newfound ability to view adult material in the privacy of one's home as they were about seeing an adult film in a theater.

"Shame on all TV sets that are now rated X," ran a headline about the issue. This headline was featured in a 1981 column by Bob Greene for *The Chicago Tribune*. Greene described how he called upon a friend to help set up a newly purchased VCR. (It *was* tricky technology back then.) The friend obliged and even brought a VHS tape to test it out:

> Within a few seconds, he had determined that all the wiring was hooked up correctly. He saw my eyes bugging out at what was going on on my TV screen and offered to leave 'Insatiable' for me to view through my new recorder. Which I did.
>
> Since the beginning of the television age, the home TV screen has been the one pristine holdover from a more conservative era. No matter that society has

been liberalized and loosened up; as long as the networks were constrained by government regulation, the home TV screen would never feature a naked body or an obscene word—never mind the steamy gyrations like something in 'Insatiable.'[99]

Nudity and vulgar language were the only two things with which Greene found offense. Violence, it seemed, was perfectly acceptable.[100]

'[A]fter viewing 'Insatiable' on my living-room set, I find I cannot look at television in the same way I used to,' Greene continued. 'For a few days, I was ashamed to admit this to anyone; I thought...I was some sort of classic degenerate. Marilyn Chambers and her friends are attractive people, but I'm not sure I want them in my home. The situation is bound to get worse; with cable TV on the way, the opportunities for home sleaze are going to increase, and before long, the days when the TV set was the last bastion of wide-eyed innocence will be only a memory.'[101]

By the end of 1981, Marilyn was exhausted. The US promotional tour of *Insatiable* was grueling, but she was pleased the film was a hit. She didn't have time to rest. Among other ventures, she was preparing to take *Insatiable* to the UK and Australia; she signed on to do another X-rated feature; the Playboy Channel wanted to record her one-woman show, *Sex Surrogate*, as a television special for their premium cable network; pre-production began on an R-rated film for cable television; she was in discussions for a dramatic television series; and she was months away from turning thirty.

Maybe all of the work would distract her from the exigent realization that her abusive relationship with Chuck was nearing its end.

Chapter 8

UP 'N' COMING, DOWN 'N' OUT

ARILYN BROUGHT *INSATIABLE* TO BOTH the United Kingdom and Australia in 1982. According to newspapers, neither country had ever publicly screened an X-rated film, not even *Deep Throat*.[1] To comply with film censors in both countries, certain scenes had to be removed or obscured using cinematographic tricks. This made the film's slight eighty-minute running time even shorter. Marilyn was a no-show at a London press conference in February for the film. The press speculated that she was protesting the censored hardcore footage.[2]

'The fact that the British Censor has passed *Insatiable* at all has taken Wardour Street moguls by surprise,' wrote Peter Haigh in *Film Review* magazine, referring to the street that was London's center for film production in the twentieth century. 'Of course, it goes without saying that the film gets an X Certificate. Its British distributors, Amanda Films, claim that it is without a doubt the most explicit sex movie ever passed for the legitimate cinema circuits.'[3]

Eric Braun, in *films* magazine, alerted readers to the Censor's alterations. 'It is only fair to warn you that we are only permitted to enjoy Ms. Chambers and her female pals massaging their stocking tops and whatall,' he wrote. 'As soon as anything male is about to rear its macho head, we slide into split screen, cut back to stocking tops again, or simply come up against a great black barrier masking the offending object.'[4]

Although Marilyn wasn't well-known in Australia, her visit in April 1982 was greeted with much curiosity. She was given a lavish press conference in Sydney. Shortly after she entered the room, she shocked reporters and photographers when she removed her silver fox fur coat and stood before them, stripped to the waist. She graced the cover of the Australian edition of *Playboy*, a rare instance of an adult star appearing on the cover. Despite the publicity, the reviews for the film were lukewarm at best.

UP 'N' COMING, DOWN 'N' OUT

'The film retreats to a sort of symbolic castration process every time a man doffs his pants, perhaps to appease the censor's rules but in any event discriminatory since it deprives the women in the audience of a visual metaphor to which, in all equality, they are entitled,' wrote one Australian reviewer.[5]

When Marilyn returned to the US, she picked up some work at a few nightclubs to perform her strip show. One of the clubs was Main Attraction in San Ysidro, California, about fifteen miles south of San Diego. A local newspaper, *National City Star-News*, did a front-page feature about Marilyn's appearance.

Marilyn told reporter Joe H. Cabaniss that she was disappointed the club insisted she wear a G-string during her act. '"I like to get my clothes off right away," she says matter-of-factly. She is looking forward to her next engagement in Cleveland, she said, because she will be allowed to perform completely in the nude.'[6]

In addition to common questions about her films, her sex life, Chuck, and Linda Lovelace, Cabaniss also asked Marilyn how she would like to be remembered: "As a sexy lady who enjoyed her work to the utmost and never regretted anything—not even for a minute," she told him. "I would like to grow old gracefully, like Grace Kelly. I don't want to be doing dinner theaters when I'm 50. I'm gonna be happy sailing down the Mediterranean on my yacht when I'm 40."[7]

It was an innocuous story, not unlike the countless others about Marilyn that had appeared in newspapers throughout the decade, but it touched a nerve. For the next three weeks, the publication's editors ran letters from readers who lambasted the newspaper about the 'offensive and embarrassing' article. Many readers believed the story was in 'very poor taste.'[8]

'We think that your gratuitous front-page article on a pornographic movie star is completely out of place in what should be a family-oriented, community newspaper,' wrote Pat and Art McCoole of Chula Vista, California. 'Not only was the article morally offensive, but it could not even be excused as being newsworthy or community-related.'[9]

Lloyd E. Ellis, a doctor of theology from Chula Vista, said feature articles about people like Marilyn Chambers pointed to society's ills. 'Why should these evil, wicked ones receive so much publicity?' he asked.[10]

But the most common complaint from readers was that a story about Marilyn Chambers would almost certainly harm any children who happened to see it.

Finally, after weeks of angry letters, one reader had had enough.

'I'd like to remind those people that The Star-News is not a 'family' newspaper,' wrote Desiree Stanfill of Chula Vista:

It's a community newspaper, and there are a lot more people in this community than just parents and kids. For those who think nude performances on stage, such as Marilyn's, are disgusting—the human body is beautiful. It's the attitudes about it that are disgusting. It was quite refreshing to read about someone who actually enjoys her work, after weeks of whining, griping teachers. Parents, if you're really concerned for your kids, worry about the example their teachers have been setting for them. Thank you, Star-News, for providing a different and thought-provoking article.[11]

IN 1982, MARILYN AGREED to star in a television adaptation, for the Playboy Channel, of the play *Sex Surrogate*, the multi-character performance she'd had a hit with in Las Vegas and London three years prior. She would act out all of the characters, just as she had done on stage, only there wouldn't be a live audience. The filming was on a single set with three cameras, standard for television production. Marilyn was intimidated by the three-camera setup. She had appeared on countless television shows, but never as an actress, and was afraid she'd look at the wrong camera. Another thing worried her: it had been more than two years since she had last performed the show. Although she rehearsed and had a copy of the script, she was concerned that each character's performance and the nuances were long forgotten.

She needn't have worried. Her muscle memory kicked in when it came time to shoot, and the material felt as fresh as when she performed it countless times in Las Vegas and London. The show aired on the fledgling cable television station and was later released on home video.

Whoever had the foresight to commit the performance to film and preserve it did viewers a favor. It was a career-defining performance for Marilyn and gave a taste of what she could do if given the proper material. The script may not win any writing awards, but it deftly mixes light comedy and drama. Marilyn proved she was adept at both.

It was, she said years later, "The best thing I've ever done."[12]

It's demanding for a single actor to command the audience's attention for seventy-five minutes, but Marilyn manages it beautifully. While she appears fully nude, it's neither her body nor the simulated sex that makes the performance worth watching. It's her overall performance. For more than an hour, you forget you're watching Marilyn Chambers, the adult film star; instead, you're watching Marilyn Chambers, the actress. It's no meager accomplishment, especially knowing this was ten years after *Behind the Green Door*. Apart from *Rabid*, her comedic and dramatic performances were largely relegated to the stage and, sadly, not preserved on film.

It's also heart-wrenching. Here was an actress of considerable talent. She was clearly capable of doing more than what was written in the script. With the right direction and her intuition as an actress, she added complexity and color to the characters. However, because she did adult films, she wasn't allowed to showcase her artistic talents in more mainstream-friendly, Hollywood-produced fare. When she came close, such as in *City Blues*, the fates had a different plan. *Rabid* and *Sex Surrogate* remain the only visual records of what might have been.

At least one critic thought as much. 'Chambers...came across on the screen as engaging, graceful, funny, very much in control of her roles and erotic as hell,' wrote Jon Grissim in *The San Francisco Examiner*. 'The woman can act.'[13]

The airing of *Sex Surrogate* did well on The Playboy Channel, and, in September 1982, production began on what was marketed as the first adult-oriented soap opera. Mel Goldberg, who originally wrote *Sex Surrogate*, adapted and expanded it to thirteen one-hour episodes. The show dealt with sexual situations and contained both strong language and full-frontal nudity (except for the men). However, there was no hardcore sex. Marilyn signed on to star in the series. She would play the sex surrogate, but other actors would play her clients.

The show's title was inexplicably changed to *Love Ya' Florence Nightingale*—apostrophe included. The phrase comes from a line spoken by one of the sex surrogate's patients. Out of context, it makes no sense, is unmemorable, and gives no indication of what the show is about. A casual viewer, unfamiliar with the program, scanning the pages of *TV Guide* or their local newspaper, might think it was an adult-themed soap opera about a late nineteenth-century statistician-turned-nurse. What could be sexier? *Sex Confessions*, the title used for the London iteration of the play, would have been better.

Anything would have been better than *Love Ya' Florence Nightingale*.

It was the early days of cable television, and there was great demand for content. Producers were also excited about the possibility of re-editing the episodes into twenty-six half-hour shows and selling them for network TV, syndication, and the home video market. There were reports several episodes could be edited together to make a feature-length film. Marilyn would be financially secure from the residuals if the show was a hit and ran for several seasons.

'Despite the racy concept, exec producer Josef Shaftel promises a 'very classy, highly erotic' program based on 'human problems solved on human terms'—not anything pornographic,' wrote *Variety*. 'Subject matter has been thoroughly

PURE *The Sexual Revolutions of Marilyn Chambers*

Marilyn relaxes on the set of her dramatic soap opera, *Love Ya' Florence Nightingale*, which ran for one season on cable television in 1982. *L.A. Herald Examiner/Rob Brown.*

researched, and the program will deal seriously and accurately with all types of sexual dysfunction, according to Shaftel."[14]

The project was privately financed, and Shaftel, whose previous television work included *The Untouchables*, relied on this as he felt it gave him greater control over the project and its exploitation.

"I've produced $50,000,000 worth of films, all financed ahead of time," he told *Variety*. "Too many people in this business have no business making decisions, and this is a way to maintain control of my product."[15]

Although this was episodic television, Shaftel promised "little movies" with each episode, and single-camera filming techniques typically reserved for films.

Although most daytime and evening soap operas had adult themes—including network stalwarts like *General Hospital* and *Dynasty*—none was "as conceptually sexual as the 'Nightingale' project. 'Nightingale' also has a chance to revolutionize the fledgling adult soap industry by bringing an easily recognized, bankable star to the cast."[16]

In a two-part series, the *Los Angeles Times* posed the questions of just how much sex is too much for paid TV, and if adult-themed soaps and paid TV could work.[17]

'For the past several months, by coincidence, two dramatic series for pay TV have been taping next door to each other at the Sunset Gower Studios in Hollywood, taking different approaches to [the] potentially controversial question [of: just how sexually explicit will it be?],' the *Times* wrote. 'One, [*A New Day in Eden*,] represents a rather cautious attempt to move into the unexplored TV territory of sexuality and eroticism; the other is a bold leap into the genre starring none other than Marilyn Chambers, queen of the X-rated movie circuit.'[18]

For better or worse, the *Times* called *Nightingale* 'probably the most sexually explicit programming ever produced specifically for U.S. television.' The first episode featured—*gasp!*—Marilyn in the shower, nude from the waist up during the credits sequence; three scenes later, she's shown fully nude; and later, there is a lovemaking scene in which she and her male partner engage in simulated sex acts. Some forty years after it debuted, these scenes would barely register as sexually explicit, let alone warrant an entire article in the *Los Angeles Times*. Even in 1982, these scenes were relatively benign. There was and continues to be more graphic footage of violent crimes, terrorist attacks, and other atrocities on network nightly news than on a television station a viewer is paying to see. Once again, America's spurious propriety became a touchstone for much consternation. And, as she had been nearly a decade prior, Marilyn Chambers was at its center.

"It's very exciting," Marilyn told the Associated Press. "We film at the old Columbia Studios, and I have Rita Hayworth's dressing room. I enjoy myself because, basically, I play Marilyn Chambers. I usually play me, the all-American girl."[19]

A touch of old Hollywood glamor never failed to impress Marilyn, and she was the closest thing the adult film industry had to a Hayworth-style beauty queen. She also never gave up hope that a Hollywood break might present itself. She was mostly resigned to the fact that she'd always be a "porn star" in the eyes of the public and media, but it never hurt to remind them that she commanded the same type of treatment as Rita Hayworth. She quickly pointed out, "I'm a highly-paid actress."

And yet, she states that she's usually hired to play herself, which doesn't lend itself well to being considered for roles of greater complexity. It also speaks to the idea that "Marilyn Chambers" was a character unto herself. She was Marilyn Chambers, the all-American girl, but that's the same Marilyn Chambers who was viewed as an X-rated sex queen, not an actress. Had she rebranded herself back to Marilyn Briggs and put an end to "Marilyn Chambers," it might have helped. However, she was a decade into playing the "Marilyn Chambers" role twenty-four hours a day, and the character and the woman had merged. The strands of the two personalities were finely woven into a delicate pattern. A sudden tear could cause irreparable damage to her psyche.

"I am absolutely bowled over with her versatility as an actress," executive producer Shaftel told the *Times*. "She has warmth and sexuality; she can be funny; she cries. If she didn't have that background (in X-rated films), I swear she could do as well (in the acting profession) as other actresses."[20]

Marilyn was much more modest. She enjoyed acting, she told the *Times*, but she didn't consider herself versatile because she always played herself. The series allowed her to act more than other projects, but she knew people didn't seek her out for her acting abilities.

"I can never be Katharine Hepburn," she told the *Times*, in a callback to director Nicholas Ray's instinctual assessment of her ability. "People have to stick with what they do best."[21]

Although the reality of being a forever adult film star had sunk in, there was always hope that she could shake the label and show people, especially critics, that she was capable of much more. This series could do it, and she knew it, but at thirty, she was reaching that unfortunate—and misogynistic—expiration date that beset nearly every woman in show business.

'The concept of a dramatic series about sexuality is not as startling as it seems initially,' *The Los Angeles Times* noted. 'Aired in conjunction with conventional fare such as, say, 'Dallas' or 'Diff'rent Strokes,' the program would be a shocking contrast. But on a pay-TV channel, where unedited R-rated movies are commonplace—and where even X-rated films may be shown—the series would appear entirely compatible.'[22]

Both Shaftel and Marilyn saw the series as having educational value.

"'Soap' (the former ABC show) was pretty racy if you read between the lines," Marilyn offered. "Here, you don't have to read between the lines."[23] When asked what particular value sexually explicit TV programs have, Marilyn answered bluntly: "Money." For her, that is. 'She feels no compulsion to explain it, and certainly not to justify it,' the *Times* wrote. She said she wouldn't have a problem if children watched the show but acknowledged that it was not made with children in mind.

The Australians and the English laugh at us (Americans) because we always say, 'What about the children?' Forget the children. If you say, 'You can't watch this,' that's the first thing they're going to turn on when you walk out of the house.

UP 'N' COMING, DOWN 'N' OUT

To me, seeing someone's head blown off in a movie or television—or even the news—is far more detrimental to a child's mind than a beautiful love scene.

People always ask me what I'm going to do if I have children. 'What are you going to tell them? How are you going to explain your past?' I'll tell them the truth. I don't ever feel guilty.[24]

Although the *Los Angeles Times* piece talked about her X-rated film career—and called her a "porno queen" in the opening sentence—the caption for the picture of Marilyn accompanying the article referred to her simply as an "actress." Theretofore, nearly every caption called her a "porno star," "porn actress," "X-rated actress," or similar descriptor. For once, a major newspaper described her in the way she had craved for more than a decade: an actress.

"I've been accepted, I feel, by my peers," Marilyn said. "To me, that's the most... well, it gives me shivers to think about it. I find that people like Burt Reynolds and Marion Ross—you know, the mother in TV's *Happy Days*—and other stars like that, they come up to me and say, 'Oh, Marilyn, I think you're so lovely, and I'm one of your biggest fans!' And you know, like, I'm really *their* biggest fan! So, yeah, I'm accepted now. It's been a long time coming, if you'll pardon the expression."[25]

She told this to a reporter from *Knave* magazine at the 1983 Cannes Film Festival. Several episodes of *Nightingale* had been hastily stitched into a feature-length film and screened there. Marilyn attended the festival to promote the film and series and help sell it to international distributors. The reporter marveled at the number of people who approached Marilyn simply to fawn over her. They congratulated and gushed about how much they loved her and her films—especially older women.

'In all truth, and certainly in all my years of watching the porno game, it is an amazing sight,' the reporter wrote. 'Pensioners (almost geriatrics) congratulating the porno queen on pussy power!'[26]

Newspapers across the country picked up the *Los Angeles Times* piece. Ten years after *Green Door* premiered, Marilyn still had the power to command notable mass media attention. The novelty of an erotic soap opera was intriguing. After filming six one-hour episodes, the series was sold to seventeen cable outlets and premiered in February 1983. The Playboy Channel bought the series two months later, making it the highest-profile outlet to air the show. Depending on the cable channel, the series aired as thirteen one-hour or twenty-six half-hour episodes.

Viewers hoping to find the series in their newspaper TV listings might have had difficulty figuring out which channel to watch. It turns out *Love Ya' Florence*

Nightingale was a clunky title to print. Many newspapers listed it simply as *The Marilyn Chambers Show*, which sounds more like a talk show than an episodic erotic soap opera. Her one-woman *Sex Surrogate* special was still airing regularly, adding to the confusion.

In *Florence Nightingale*, Marilyn played Kelly Carson, a sex therapist who helps male clients overcome their sexual insecurities. She's also studying for her PhD. Her job is complicated because her boyfriend (David Winn) is uncomfortable with her occupation. He's a little jealous and embarrassed to tell others what she does for a living.

The series was shot on a budget, and it looks like it. The acting is often awkward, particularly from Winn. Still, there are some effective moments. One episode deals with a client becoming a stalker. Marilyn offers up some nice touches, like the penultimate scene where the stalker is led by police officers out of Marilyn's office. As he passes her, she instinctively steps to the side, away from him. Her facial expression conveys the right amount of relief and persistent anxiety.

Despite respectable ratings and being cited by Playboy Channel viewers as their favorite program, the series was not renewed. No explanation was ever given. The tapes were locked away in a vault, never again to be seen by the general public.

IT'S DIFFICULT TO SAY with certainty when things started to go wrong with Marilyn and Chuck. Publicly, Marilyn still sang his praises and defended him whenever someone brought up Linda Lovelace. Privately, things were a mess, but no one can remember why. Perhaps more to the point, no one was allowed to know why. Chuck kept Marilyn away from her family as much as possible. Marilyn still wasn't speaking with her sister, Jann. The couple had few friends besides Godfrey Daniels, his wife, and Sammy Davis Jr. Marilyn was busier than ever with work, juggling numerous projects.

Many who knew Marilyn before and after Chuck are still bewildered as to why she stayed with Chuck. "Why didn't she just leave him?" was a commonly asked question. Unfortunately, it's not that simple.

According to the National Coalition Against Domestic Violence, 'A victim's reasons for staying with their abusers are extremely complex and, in most cases, are based on the reality that their abuser will follow through with the threats they have used to keep them trapped: the abuser will hurt or kill them...they will harm or kill pets or others, they will ruin their victim financially—the list goes on.

UP 'N' COMING, DOWN 'N' OUT

The victim in violent relationships knows their abuser best and fully knows the extent to which they will go to make sure they have and can maintain control over the victim.[27]

In an ongoing attempt to bolster their finances—and perhaps to avoid tax hits—Marilyn and Chuck opened a firearms store in Las Vegas and invested in area real estate. Nothing much came of either venture.

When Marilyn wasn't working, she and Chuck spent time horseback riding, hunting, skydiving, or enjoying the desert around their home near Las Vegas. They rarely engaged with each other sexually. Chuck was a voyeur and enjoyed watching Marilyn have sex with men and women. Sex was their commodity, but it was infrequent between the couple. Still, for many years they were happy and enjoyed each other's company. They were more like a father and daughter than a husband and wife. They could relax and forget about "Marilyn Chambers," the character, business, and product when alone. These times were few. Marilyn worked constantly, and Chuck was always with her.

"No matter how hard I worked, there never seemed to be enough money," she said.[28]

At least that's what Chuck told her. She entrusted all financial business to him and never asked any questions.

In 1982, for the first time since they met, Chuck allowed Marilyn to travel alone. She had a gig in New York City and planned to visit her parents in Westport. She hadn't been this liberated since she made the trek to San Francisco a decade prior. What made it better, she discovered, was that Chuck wasn't there. She was unhurried and unrestrained.

The man hired to be her limousine driver and bodyguard for the stay was Robert D'Apice, who went by Bobby. He was exactly Marilyn's type: a beefy, dark-haired hunk. There was an unassailable magnetism between the two. She slept with him that night but knew this wouldn't be a one-night stand. She wanted to get to know him better—and she did.

The affair with D'Apice emboldened Marilyn. It was time to finally end it with Chuck, and she knew it.

Chuck picked her up at the Las Vegas airport when she returned. The first thing he noticed was the smell of alcohol. Normally, she couldn't drink without his permission, so he accused her of doing so. She readily admitted she had. Then she told him to stop at the first convenience store he could find. He did, and she hopped out of his truck. When she returned, he noticed a pack of cigarettes in her hand. She wasn't allowed to smoke without his permission either. He fumed. Marilyn took out a cigarette and lit it in the car.

A newly confident Marilyn looked at Chuck and said, "Things are going to be different around here. I'm leaving. I'm leaving as soon as we get home."[29]

Chuck was defiant. He told her there was no way she was leaving. He knew he needed her more than she needed him. However, he had spent the better part of a decade convincing her it was the other way around. Nonetheless, when they returned home, Marilyn packed a bag and left.

She moved in with Daniels, the director of *Insatiable*, and his wife for six weeks. She tried to balance her despondency by reconnecting with old friends and surrounding herself with loving pals.

"She had a group of girls that were not in the business," Daniels recalled. "They lived up in the [Hollywood] Hills, and they hung out quite a bit. My wife went with her a few times."[30]

Marilyn had always been a drinker. When she married Chuck, her intake decreased because he wouldn't allow it. During their separation, Daniels noted that Marilyn drank considerably more, often first thing in the morning, and smoked pot. When Daniels's wife was cleaning the bedroom where Marilyn stayed, she found an empty bottle of whiskey hidden behind the bed. Even though Daniels and his wife weren't drinkers, he was sorry that Marilyn was compelled to hide it.

"She didn't need to do that," he said.[31]

After some time apart, Marilyn and Chuck reconciled enough for Marilyn to move back home temporarily. She wrote Daniels's wife a note when she left:

Dearest Wendy,

I've got to go - so sorry I can't see you before you leave -
Remember I love you! You're the absolute best -
Take care & most of all have fun!

Smile for me -

Love you,
Marilyn

For months, Marilyn and Chuck fought, reconciled, and fought again. They finally agreed to live separately. Marilyn remained in touch with D'Apice, her limo driver fling from New York. Chuck had already taken up with a younger woman: a seventeen-year-old budding model named Crissa "Bo" Bozlee. Eventually,

UP 'N' COMING, DOWN 'N' OUT

D'Apice moved in with Marilyn in Las Vegas. "Bo" moved in with Chuck.

"Why Bo? After Marilyn left, Bo was just there," Chuck said. "If you keep 18-year-olds around you, you stay young."[32]

Chuck remained Marilyn's manager. He still accompanied her to personal appearances and interviews, although his imminent physical presence was paling. Money was more important to Chuck than Marilyn's feelings. He believed he created the "Marilyn Chambers" character and, therefore, was entitled to compensation for the work she did as "Marilyn Chambers." It was the same stance he took with Linda Lovelace. "Marilyn Chambers" was his intellectual property, he believed, regardless of the work she did to inhabit the character. Marilyn, the woman, was merely his physical property. Both belonged to him, he thought.

She also remained his wife in the eyes of the law. The couple were separated but not divorced. They struck a deal. Chuck would remain her manager for five more years and retain fifty percent of everything Marilyn earned. Then she was on her own.

AFTER NEARLY FORTY YEARS of marriage, Ginny and William, Marilyn's parents, informed their three children that they were getting divorced. As usual, the couple resisted going into a detailed explanation of why they were finally splitting for good. William had continued his affair with the married neighbor who accompanied him to Marilyn's Riverboat show in 1974. The woman and her husband had been close friends with the Briggs and often went golfing with them. When the woman's husband died, she and William got closer. It's unknown if they were having an affair while the woman was still married.

Ginny never let on whether she knew about any of the affairs. Any suspicions were confirmed one Halloween when the woman phoned Ginny at home.

"Do you know where your husband was?" asked the woman. Ginny could tell the woman had been drinking. "Do you know who he was with?"

"No, I don't," Ginny replied.

"Well, he's been here with me!" the woman snapped.

"OK, thank you very much for telling me," Ginny calmly said and hung up the phone.

A short time later, William arrived home. Ginny told him she had just spoken to the woman.

"She said you two are a couple," she told William. "When were you planning to tell me?"

He thought for a moment, then said, "Probably never."

He was quite content to be married to Ginny while seeing another woman. He saw no reason to get a divorce. The woman with whom he was having an affair was not satisfied with this arrangement. She wanted William to marry her.

Ginny paused to absorb what her husband of thirty-eight years had just said. She was almost emotionless when she replied in an even tone, "Okay, we're getting a divorce."[33]

"I think he was shocked [by] her response," Jann said. "I don't know why he was shocked. I thought, and I said this to them, 'After thirty-eight years, couldn't you have figured out something to at least stay together?' I was very, very angry. Marilyn was angry like I was, but she [had] other stuff going on at that time. She wasn't really as close to them at that point as I was."[34]

Ginny moved to Washington State to be closer to Jann and her grandchildren. William stayed in Westport.

"That was shocking to all of us," Bill recalled. "I don't know what happened there. I think they drifted apart somehow in a lack of communication. They weren't together anymore, even if they [were] living in the same house. So it was a mutual kind of thing. The next time I saw my dad, he was sitting in the backyard reading a paperback, and the house seemed like it was in a little bit of disrepair. And he seemed pretty down."[35]

Ginny never let go of their connection. She frequently called him to check in and say hello.

"She kept that lifeline open," Jann said. "Because I think, in her heart, she wanted to be back with him. And in her heart, she also knew that he would need someone again, like her."[36]

The divorce was finalized in 1982.[37] William moved in with the woman he was seeing. They never married.

MARILYN TOLD REPORTERS SHE was attracted to men who were "masculine" and "macho."[38]

"Flashy dressers don't impress me," she said, "nor does the bullshit talk aimed at turning my head. I like the silent but deadly types."[39]

She found exactly that, and then some, when she met D'Apice.

D'Apice shared similar characteristics with Chuck. Perhaps none more so than primacy. Both men felt compelled to dominate Marilyn and control every aspect of her life. She perceived this as strength. Both men assaulted and emotionally abused Marilyn; they considered her their personal property. Each had hair-trigger tempers, but only D'Apice possessed jealousy. If Marilyn went to bed with another man while married to Chuck, he perceived it as business and branding the "Marilyn Chambers" character. D'Apice did not.

Marilyn once described her relationship with D'Apice as "violent, insane, [and] sex-addicted."[40] Despite this, she regularly told close friends that he was the love of her life.

Her liberation from Chuck helped her to develop a bit more self-awareness. This sentience proved just as harmful as it was insightful. For a decade, she had been entirely dependent on Chuck. She was virtually incapable of managing her career, and he was still technically her manager and husband.

It was a period of self-discovery. She wriggled her way out of the confines of "Marilyn Chambers," the character, but was left with a woman she barely knew. Her legal name was Marilyn Traynor, but who was that? She no longer desired the Traynor surname. This left Marilyn Briggs—a person, and personality, lost to time. While with D'Apice, she began 'to realize the overpowering need to be taken care of by a man.' But she was unsure how to handle this realization and was ruled by the terror of being alone, and perhaps suffering more violence at the hands of D'Apice. As she bluntly stated in the treatment for her unpublished memoir, '[I have] no self-esteem.'[41]

In a pitiful self-assessment, she told a friend, "I know I'm not any great beauty. I have some qualities about me that people obviously find to be attractive, but I don't make believe that I'm like one of these supermodels."[42]

With Chuck gone, she was free to drink as frequently as she liked; her intake increased. She started abusing cocaine. By 1983 she was engulfed in addiction.

AFTER WRAPPING *FLORENCE NIGHTINGALE,* Marilyn began working on her next X-rated film, *Up 'n' Coming.* It would be shot as a straight hardcore feature as well as an R-rated version that could be sold to cable television. The softcore version, retitled *Cassie,* would contain sex scenes, but they'd be shorter and include angles obscuring penetration or male genitals. The lack of hardcore shots would be padded out with longer dramatic scenes.

"It was Marilyn's idea to do *Up 'n' Coming,*" recalled Marty Greenwald, who again served as producer. Daniels returned to direct. When discussing ideas for the film's plot, Marilyn said, "I want to be an up-and-coming star."[43]

"Godfrey said, 'That's a great title. Marty, write a script,'" Greenwald said. "We shot on thirty-five-millimeter film. We were actual filmmakers. Godfrey and I really liked films. We knew the labs in L.A. It was a tight-knit society. Marilyn and Chuck were never really involved in the nuts and bolts [of the filmmaking process]."[44]

PURE

The Sexual Revolutions of Marilyn Chambers

When *Up 'n' Coming* began production, Marilyn's physique changed. She was still lithe, toned, and tanned but had undergone significant breast augmentation. Her natural, petite breasts suited her five-foot-seven-inch frame, but as more women got breast implants at the dawn of the video age, she felt the need to follow suit. By the nineties, the unnaturally-sized, silicone-enhanced, big-breasted look ruled. Marilyn's implants made her breasts perfectly round. They were lower on her body, and the enlargement increased her cleavage, giving her chest an unnatural, caved-in look.

It wasn't just her breasts that had changed. Her face was harder. Her natural beauty was intact, but it was a frangible physiognomy. It made sense. She had worked non-stop for a decade. However, this wasn't merely a hardness that came with the natural aging process or a grueling work schedule. It was the face of a woman burnt out on living, one who made a valiant attempt to mask the habitual dolor.

Up 'n' Coming is an *All About Eve*-meets-*Valley of the Dolls* camp extravaganza, if an unintentional one. It's Marilyn's best X-rated film. Marilyn plays Cassie Harland, a country singer on the rise who'll use all the seductive, sexual techniques she knows to advance her career and replace the reigning but fading and drunk country queen Althea Anderson, played by Lisa De Leeuw. The film is De Leeuw's all the way. She's a delight to watch, acting with the right amount of sincerity and scenery chewing. The plot meanders a bit—and the final confrontation between Marilyn and De Leeuw is laughably overacted—but taken strictly as camp, it's more than entertaining.

The film allowed Marilyn to showcase her singing. She had sung before—her cabaret act, her disco single, and *Le Bellybutton*—but she committed to the project this time. One of the things that had made *Insatiable* special was its soundtrack. It featured original rock songs and romantic ballads, and it worked. Gone was the clichéd "bow-chicka-bow-bow" background music so associated with porn of the era. The theme song for *Insatiable*, Shame on You, was a pop ballad sung by Marilyn over the opening credits—and the credit was prominently displayed on the posters and in press materials. She does a fine job on the vocals, and the hook is catchy. Miracle Films released the song as a promotional single, but it didn't take off.

Music was an integral part of the plot of *Up 'n' Coming*. To prepare, Marilyn put together a country and western band called Haywire. The band Haywire performed in Vegas to warm up and gauge audience response in the months leading up to the film's production. They played several dates in the summer of 1982 at Carollo's Country, an off-Strip watering hole, restaurant, and dance hall in Paradise Valley.

UP 'N' COMING, DOWN 'N' OUT

Variety was impressed with the show. 'Marilyn Chambers has gone country with a vengeance,' the magazine wrote in its July 1, 1982 review. 'Chambers roars into town weekends...during which she comes off as a believable vocalist. She should have no trouble selling with this group behind her.'[45]

The review called the band an 'effervescent combo, which specializes in country, rockabilly, and rock, with plenty of western tossed in the mix. It's a versatile group, and with Chambers fronting, the sessions really cook.'

The songs were a combination of original compositions, written mainly by band member Will Rose, and covers like Juice Newton's hit Queen of Hearts.

'In her pseudo-buckskin outfit with plenty of cleavage and fringes exposing full thighs, she is never still a moment, writhing, bumping, and grinding away while pealing forth her words in tune and with bombast,' the *Variety* review continued. 'Chambers considers it a compliment when she can get a floor filled with dancing customers, and she pulls up many couples while hard at her own work. This is no modest country bumpkin gal. Chambers does surprise, however, in her eagerness to capture all the essence of the genre. Customers are country/western-oriented and cheer Chambers along with no prejudice or hoorays for her porn connection and notoriety.'[46]

She might have taken on her role as a country music singer too forcefully. She developed polyps on her vocal cords and required surgery. Her voice was noticeably raspier and hoarse when it came time to shoot *Up 'n' Coming*.

Chuck visited the film set infrequently. Colleagues noticed a very different Marilyn when he wasn't around.

"When he wasn't there, she was much looser and a little bit more demanding," Daniels recalled. "Whereas when Chuck was there, he did the demanding so she didn't have to. Now she had to speak up for herself and what she wanted, which was fine."[47]

However, her demands were sometimes problematic for co-stars.

Her leading man in the film was played by Herschel Savage, a handsome, prolific actor whose most notable film was *Debbie Does Dallas* (1978).

At one point, Marilyn was fussing so much about lighting and camera angles that it was as if she were directing the scene herself. Fed up, Savage barked: "Oh, Marilyn, shut the fuck up!" Her head snapped back around, and she stared at him. The crew became quiet and edgy. After a tense moment, Marilyn smiled and let out a giant laugh. Savage smiled back, and the crew eased.[48]

"She was very fragile and insecure," Greenwald remembered. "She needed someone to micromanage her. Chuck really controlled her life. She wouldn't have a red apple or green apple until Chuck told her which one to eat. He was abusive. He hit her. I saw it. It was sort of pathetic. She used to always look out of the corner of her eye."[49]

Greenwald contends that Chuck was a man with no boundaries who controlled anyone he could.

"He had dogs fucking his wife!" he exclaimed, referring to the notorious Linda Lovelace loop. "It's fucked up. I grew more and more to understand that Chuck was a maniac. Marilyn would cry; they fought all the time."[50]

Greenwald also noted that Chuck made sure anyone and everyone, especially those on set and around Marilyn, would see the gun he had strapped to his ankle. Greenwald claimed that Chuck would backhand Marilyn across the face and shove her so hard she'd almost fall over.

"Chuck made sure you knew he was in charge," Greenwald said. "His attitude was, 'I'm Chuck Traynor, my old lady is Marilyn Chambers, and we're going to do what we want.'"[51]

As her manager, Chuck got Marilyn gigs and press coverage. He helped to enhance her image as a glamour queen. He might have done as much damage to her career as he helped it with his polarizing personality, pathological lying, and abusive behavior. Marilyn was loosening herself from Chuck's grip, and he knew it.

During an interview with Delaware's *The Morning News* in 1983, Marilyn wondered aloud about what made her successful: "Maybe the reason I've done so well is that I'm a touchable fantasy, not like [actress] Bo Derek, who can't talk to anyone without [her husband] John [Derek] being around. Chuck's not here telling me what to say. I have a mind of my own. I want to be really accessible."[52]

It was a stunning admission, especially as the reporter noted earlier in the article that Chuck was in the room during the interview. Marilyn was sharing her thoughts with the reporter, but she also made a direct statement to Chuck.

She also made another revealing and solemn admission during the March 1983 Hollywood premiere of *Up 'n' Coming* at the Pussycat Theater.

"I'm something like the queen of B movies," she told Jack Mathews of Gannett News Service. "For me to do a movie with Burt Reynolds, sure, that would be wonderful. But it's something I don't count on anymore. I came close a couple of times. I had contracts sitting in front of me for major movies, then the next day, the producer's wife or someone didn't want me involved. It's silly to fight that. I'm at the top of the ladder of my profession. It may be a different ladder, and it may not be as high as those others, but hey, I'm working. A lot of people aren't."[53]

UP 'N' COMING, DOWN 'N' OUT

JOHN HOLMES HAD BEEN involved in a plot that left four gang members murdered in California's Laurel Canyon in 1981. Although acquitted of charges, he spent 110 days in prison for contempt of court. The filmmakers and Marilyn thought it would be a coup to get Holmes for a scene that could be inserted at the end of *Up 'n' Coming*. Holmes agreed. He went to work on the film the day he was released from prison. There was a noticeable change in his demeanor when he got on the set.

"He'd become way more introverted," Marilyn recalled. "He was always introverted, but he became more so. His intellectual side had sprung out. He obviously had time to think about stuff, read, and find out who he was. He really became almost a Zen-like person. He had become a different person, and obviously, the drugs weren't as important. He wasn't loaded out of his mind—just really, really quiet."[54]

In the film, Holmes played a powerful music industry executive who could help Cassie's career. The final scene involved a group session with Marilyn, Holmes, Herschel Savage, Richard Pacheco, and Lili Marlene.

"That was an interesting day," Pacheco recalled.

Holmes hadn't arrived yet. The call for the four of us (me, Marilyn, Herschel, and Lili) was early morning. And the first shot was the blowjob scene with Marilyn and Lili. And that scene went really well, and I was done. Holmes showed up after that and kept to himself. This was the day he had gotten out of jail, which was just weird. I remember it was very cold, and we were all shivering because we were naked, and Holmes was sitting in the corner naked by himself. I remember one of the crew whispered to another, 'Well, that's what prison will do for you,' because he was comfortable sitting there by himself.

Then he and Marilyn went to work. [The film] was, ironically, [shot] at the home of a proctologist in Marin County. There was a balcony over the living room. The balcony was where they had set up the food. I was done working, and I was hanging around the set, but I decided to have lunch before I went home. And I started to hear these screams. And it's Marilyn screaming. They're incredible screams. So I go to see what's going on, and Holmes is fucking her in the ass with that little league baseball bat that he has for a penis. And Marilyn is doing like a yogic breath of fire. Her face is just electric. It's amazing. It was the visual experience of speaking in tongues. I couldn't believe it. It was red hot, red fucking hot. I had just come, and here I am, getting a hard-on. I watched the sex, just transfixed, and at the end, I thought, 'That is the best sex scene I have ever seen. I can't wait for the film to come out!' And I'm telling people for six months about how great this scene is. But when the movie came out, they missed it. Instead, they showed shots of his dick going in her ass, but the scene was all in her face. They just blew it.[55]

While not nearly as successful at the box office as *Insatiable*, *Up 'n' Coming* did well on home video, generating about seven million dollars in revenue (more than $21 million in today's dollars). The R-rated version, *Cassie*, did well on home video and played on cable television for several years.

"I liked *Up 'n' Coming*," Greenwald said. "It gave Marilyn another dimension and a chance to show her abilities."[56]

As Delaware's *News Journal* put it: 'No triple-X-rated-film star is better known, or probably has made more for herself or the industry, than Marilyn Chambers.'[57]

'THEY SAID IT COULDN'T be done, but with the release of her first starring role in an R-rated feature, 'Angel of H.E.A.T.,' Marilyn Chambers has proven to be the only actress to successfully transcend X-rated features to all aspects of the entertainment industry,' read the press materials for the film. It wasn't entirely true. The action comedy, originally called *The Protectors*, wasn't the first R-rated feature in which Marilyn starred. That honor belonged to *Rabid*. In *Angel of H.E.A.T.*, Marilyn played the role of Angel Harmony, one of the agents for The Protectors, an organization out to stop a mad scientist who aims to take over the world with robots that look like humans and that only he can control. The film is as silly as that single-sentence description reads.

However, it allowed Marilyn to flex her acting and actual muscles. There were several action sequences involving martial arts and diving; Marilyn found those sequences the most exciting thing about filming. She also performed most of her own stunts.

"I got to train with this really cool guy who was like this unbelievable [martial arts] master up in Lake Tahoe," she said. "It was freezing cold up there, but it was fun. One thing I had to do [in the film] was dive into Lake Tahoe. I had to wear this arctic wetsuit with a hood, so I had to dive in from the boat and swim to shore. I remember diving into this water, and it was so fucking cold my head froze! I couldn't lift my arms! I thought I was going to drown. Seriously, that was the scariest thing I had ever been through. But, being the trouper that I am, I did it."[58]

By the time it was released, the title had changed from *The Protectors: Book #1* to *Angel of H.E.A.T.* While always intended for television, the film played in

UP 'N' COMING, DOWN 'N' OUT

pitifully few movie theaters during the summer of 1983. It was mostly shown on TV, where it played frequently for several years, and was released to home video. "It was fun to make, but *Angel of H.E.A.T.* was basically people using my name to exploit and draw attention to a film," Marilyn lamented. "I was hoping it would draw attention to me too, but you still need a good script and director."[59]

Just as Hollywood cranks out sequels to their biggest hits, so, too, does the adult entertainment industry. Marilyn teamed up again with Godfrey Daniels and Marty Greenwald for *Insatiable II*, which further chronicled the sexual escapades of Sandra Chase. Production started in early 1984. It was fraught from the beginning.

Juliet Anderson played Marilyn's female foil. Anderson was something of an anomaly in the X-rated business. She began her career in the late seventies at the age of thirty-nine. She had gained a following playing a character called "Aunt Peg" in a series of hardcore films. She was forty-six at the time she made *Insatiable II*.

Anderson did not like Marilyn.

"She had a very nasty attitude from day one," Anderson recalled. "She walked into the set—she strode in and pushed everybody aside and said, 'Get out of my way, I'm Marilyn Chambers.'"[60]

When Anderson approached Marilyn to tell her how happy she was to meet her, she claimed Marilyn retorted with the same remark: "Get out of my way, I'm Marilyn Chambers."

In another interview, Anderson claimed that when she introduced herself, Marilyn "just said: 'Shut up, you bitch—I'm MARILYN!', and walked out the room. Those were her first words! That was it!"[61]

"She had bodyguards, security guards who came with her," Anderson said. "She was very spoiled. I never would have chosen to do another film with her. I wasn't alone; other people said to me, 'Don't take it personally. That's just the way she is.'"[62]

To the credit of both women, any animosity between them isn't noticeable on screen.

Daniels remembered that Marilyn did, indeed, play the star bit—but not with him.

"I did see it just as an overall feeling I got from her," he said. "Again, this is after *Insatiable*, and I would say she was tired of doing [adult films]."[63]

In addition to her hardened attitude, possibly a consequence of her ongoing drug addiction, Marilyn made incessant demands. She insisted, for example, that D'Apice, her lover, be cast in *Insatiable II*.

D'Apice, who was billed as Bobby Dee, was not an actor. Daniels was none too pleased about casting him. He didn't like the man, and having never appeared in adult films, D'Apice was unfamiliar with the process and the preparation it took. It was believed by some, including Daniels, that D'Apice might have been affiliated with organized crime. To be on the safe side, Daniels made a phone call. "The last fucking thing I'm going to do was put a wise guy's son in the movie," Daniels said. "Have the guy tell me, 'Hey, motherfucker, why didn't you call me?' Well, I called him. I was still a motherfucker, by the way, but at least I wasn't going to be a dead motherfucker."[64]

The rest of the cast, notably Anderson, was also annoyed by Marilyn's insistence on casting D'Apice.

"He'd never been in a film before—which was completely against the way things were done," Anderson said. "A man may be a good lover, but he has to [be] able to get it up and keep it up—'keep the wood,' they call it—and come on command. This takes a particular skill for men to be able to do this. But she wouldn't make the movie unless this man could star with her."[65]

While Marilyn was doing her hair and makeup for a scene, Daniels asked Anderson to come on set, get on the bed, and become acquainted with D'Apice. She was worried that Marilyn might enter the room unexpectedly and throw a fit. Daniels assured her that wouldn't happen. Anderson said:

> This guy was really, really nervous, so I started joking with him and making him feel at ease and told the [crew] to turn the lights out. We just talked a little bit, and I found out about what he did in life like a real person—and found that he was not Marilyn's lackey. He felt really comfortable with me, and I was hugging and kissing him, saying, 'You're gonna be absolutely fine!'
>
> So then we came to do the scene, and there were no rehearsals. They just blocked it, and then you go ahead and shoot it—that's the way it was done. The scene called for me to be with this man on the bed and for Marilyn to join us. So we started fooling around, and she tried to get him hard—and she couldn't do it! She was whispering in his ear, 'C'mon, baby, mmm... ahhh.' The cameras were rolling, and we only had a certain amount of time to do it, but he couldn't get it up. So I went down and started sucking his cock and licking his balls, and he got the biggest hard-on. Marilyn looked at me with daggers—she absolutely hated me! But, and I give her credit for this, she was a fine actress.[66]

It wasn't just the scene with Marilyn and Anderson that made D'Apice nervous. During his one-on-one scene with Marilyn, he had difficulty maintaining an erection. Eventually, another man, referred to in the business as the "stunt cock," was brought in to do close-ups of many penetration shots.

Insatiable II, released in April 1984, doesn't have much to recommend it. Daniels said he hardly remembered directing the film at all. The pool table scene from *Insatiable* was recycled for the sequel. It was an explosive scene, but its inclusion felt like a cop-out, as though the filmmakers were trying to pad the second film's thin running time. The only scene of note is one in which Marilyn's character explores some of her pain-and-pleasure fantasies. She's paired with Jamie Gillis, one of his generation's most prolific adult actors. The scene involves consensual rough play, including slapping, restraints, and biting. Gillis dripped hot candle wax on Marilyn's nipples and vagina. At one point, he inserts the bottom of a lit candle into her vagina. (The X-Rated Critics' Organization awarded the encounter "Best Kinky Scene" at its 1985 ceremony.)

"There were other actresses—Jane Hamilton, Annette Haven—who looked like they were involved in the sex. I never got that kind of warmth from Marilyn," Greenwald said. "[Her scenes] were rougher. Marilyn always seemed, because she was bigger than life, [that] she almost became a caricature of herself. Every move she made, she calculated in her head. There were far better actresses. I never got aroused when I watched a Marilyn Chambers scene—but we were friends. There were few people in the industry I became friends with. I was close to Marilyn. I would have been a lot closer had it not been for Chuck."[67]

Greenwald said the film's budget was under $100,000 (nearly $300,000 today). Marilyn was paid her standard $50,000 fee (close to $150,000 today). As Chuck was still her manager, he took his cut, too. The film collected about five million dollars in revenue ($14.5 million in today's money), mostly from home video. It was Marilyn's last film to receive a theatrical wide release.

During a stop in Chicago for a promotional tour of *Insatiable II*, Marilyn spoke with columnist Bob Greene. (He was the same columnist who'd lamented Marilyn's appearance, in *Insatiable*, on his newly-wired-up video system.) He met Marilyn in her suite at the Ambassador East Hotel.

'She spoke rapidly and seemed to have a case of the sniffles,' he wrote, a not-so-subtle suggestion that she had been doing cocaine.[68]

Greene was astonished that a woman famous for making adult films would be put up in such a lavish hotel and made a point to tell her that.

'I said that in the '40s and '50s, actors and actresses like Humphrey Bogart and Marilyn Monroe used to be put up in these same V.I.P. suites when they passed through Chicago,' he wrote. 'Didn't she think it was ironic that she was getting the same treatment on the mere strength of her having performed sexual acts in front of a movie camera?'[69]

Ever accustomed to backhanded compliments, Marilyn answered his question bluntly.

"It's not that ironic," she said. "A 'Dirty Harry' movie is acting, and 'Insatiable' is acting. I'm just a different kind of actress."[70]

She continued, "When people meet me, they never treat me with disrespect. Women especially are nice to me. I'm not a threat to them like Marilyn Monroe must have been. She tried to be more of a mystery. She was more coy; she put on more of a façade. People sensed she was naughty, but you never knew how naughty. Me, you know exactly how naughty I am."[71]

THE YEAR OF 1985 started well enough. Marilyn reconciled with her sister. Chuck was still her manager, but he was (mostly) out of her day-to-day life. She was in a relationship with a man, D'Apice, whom she desperately and dangerously loved.

In January, she was asked to appear at the opening for an adult bookstore called Ms. Kitty's in Spokane, Washington, and record a segment about it for The Playboy Channel. This particular adult bookstore was newsworthy because it was owned and operated by a man named John Bauer. He was a forty-eight-year-old former Roman Catholic Priest who still wore his priest's collar and said his spiritual mission was "alleviating sexual repression." He had been kicked out of the priesthood in 1970 for speaking openly about his homosexuality. He had taught social work at the Montana State University before he opened the first Ms. Kitty's store in his hometown of Bozeman, Montana, in 1981. The Spokane store was the third Ms. Kitty's location. Bauer had invited Marilyn for the store's grand opening to give the occasion some star quality.[72]

More than a decade into the business, reporters asked Marilyn what her parents thought of her career.

"They were appalled," she told *The Spokesman-Review* at a press conference for the store opening. "(My mom) didn't know how to react. It's not the type of thing you go brag to your friends about."[73]

Indeed, she did not. The day before the store's opening, Marilyn visited her mother and sister about 300 miles away in Puyallup. Ginny, still grieving the divorce, was in especially bad humor that day. When Marilyn told her mother about her gig at the bookstore, Ginny replied tersely, "I can't imagine why anybody would want *your* autograph." Marilyn didn't reply, but Jann reminded their mother that "Marilyn Chambers" was a celebrity.

"I don't want to hear it," Ginny said. "I don't want to know about it."[74]

UP 'N' COMING, DOWN 'N' OUT

On Tuesday, January 29, 1985, Marilyn returned to San Francisco's O'Farrell Theater with a new live show. She was scheduled for four shows a day for five days. The first few nights were so successful that a fifth show was added to the weekend performances. Nearly every show sold out during its run. D'Apice accompanied her and acted as her bodyguard. Marilyn's cocaine use had increased dramatically since she had separated from Chuck. At first, it was an act of independence and rebellion. Now she was in the throes of addiction. Being around the Mitchell brothers didn't help. They were frequently loaded on coke and liquor, especially Art.

Her show was called "Feel the Magic"—and she meant it. As in previous shows, Marilyn would engage in a striptease, sometimes sing a song, and always end up nude. Then she would go out into the audience, and men were allowed, even encouraged, to touch her body, including digital penetration. Drenched with perspiration, she would gyrate wildly with an intense sexual abandon that was both erotic and terrifying.

Everything went off without a hitch until the last day. The penultimate performance was scheduled for midnight on February 2. Shortly after it began, four plainclothes vice squad officers from the San Francisco Police Department stopped the performance 'after observing Chambers engaging in what they called 'sexual contact' with about 20 customers.'[75]

A stunned, nude Marilyn was escorted offstage—some claim she was carried—and arrested. D'Apice, who tried to stop the officers, was also taken into custody.[76]

"They had the nerve to crowd into my dressing room and ask why I wasn't wearing any underwear," Marilyn huffed.[77]

She had to convince the police to allow her to change before she was taken to jail.

"They said, 'You mean you don't want to go down there nude?'" she said.[78]

Handcuffed and wearing nothing but her silver fox fur coat, Marilyn was taken to the city jail, where she was booked and charged with committing a lewd act in a public place and for soliciting prostitution, both misdemeanors. D'Apice was also booked and charged with interfering with the arrest and carrying a loaded handgun. He posted a $5,000 bail and was released at 2:53AM. Marilyn posted a $2,000 bail and was released at 3:44AM. She stayed in jail for nearly an hour longer than D'Apice because the officers on duty lined up to take photos with her in the jail cell and collect her autograph. The officers, who addressed her as "Miss Chambers," acted like shy little schoolboys as they waited patiently, one by one, to memorialize the bizarre occasion.

"It was like a zoo," she said.[79]

Marilyn and her attorneys, Tom Steel and Emily Graham, held a press conference the next day at the O'Farrell Theater to address the arrest and allegations. She apologized to the police, her fans, and San Francisco residents "for offending them" but denied the charges.

"I've never been arrested in my life for anything, ever, so this is kind of a big shock for me, not only as a performer but as a human being," she said calmly. "I don't know if I'll be back with my act. Well, maybe it's up to my fans."[80]

Marilyn also made a point to apologize to her mother specifically. She addressed the cameras directly, "Mom, I'm not a prostitute." She added, "She just got over the X-rated films."[81]

She also wondered aloud if the number of police officers involved in the arrest was necessary. "The force...that took me to jail was appalling," she scoffed. Steel, one of her attorneys, accused authorities of using Marilyn as a political pawn in a struggle over adult businesses.

Marilyn insisted she did nothing wrong during her show.

"These people have been my fans for years, and it's a thrill for them to touch me up close," she said. "There's nothing illegal if I'm not taking money."[82]

San Francisco Police Lieutenant William Groswird disagreed. The twenty-dollar admission fee (nearly fifty-eight dollars in today's money), he said, constituted an exchange of money for sex. Marilyn's lawyers advised her not to describe what transpired during the show. Steel said, "There was some touching involved, and that's what they're calling lewd conduct."[83]

She was arraigned in San Francisco Superior Court on Monday, February 4.

Marilyn's arrest made national headlines. She was *Entertainment Tonight*'s top story and featured in *People* magazine. Jim Mitchell was already one step ahead, thinking of the publicity and dollars this would generate for the theater.

"The Ivory Snow girl arrested for prostitution in San Francisco," he said. "It's awesome."[84]

Although the night of her arrest was supposed to be the final day of Marilyn's five-day run at the O'Farrell, the Mitchell brothers knew a good publicity angle when they saw it. With news of the arrest ricocheting across the Bay Area and throughout the national media, Marilyn returned the next evening for several shows. The lines stretched around the block. The San Francisco Police Department made no arrests.

The Mitchells had dealt with police busts since they opened the O'Farrell Theater in 1969. When *Green Door* became a hit, they were largely left alone. Many officers were also patrons, and the theater was a popular tourist

Marilyn awaits her trial in Cleveland Municipal Court on charges of pandering for prostitution in December 1985. It was one of several high-profile arrests that year. Behind Marilyn's left shoulder sits her boyfriend and bodyguard, Robert D'Apice. Marilyn described their tumultuous relationship as "insane and sex-addicted." *The Plain Dealer/Ralph J. Meyers*

destination. Nevertheless, two key city officials had had enough of the Mitchell Brothers' debaucherous offerings: San Francisco Mayor Dianne Feinstein and Police Chief Cornelius "Con" Murphy.

Several days after Marilyn's arraignment, the San Francisco police again raided the O'Farrell Theater. This time, officers held a warrant that authorized them to search for 'all writings, materials, drawings, photographs, computer printouts, microfilms, files, diagrams, bills, statements, memoranda, and records...tending to establish the performances and appearances of Marilyn Chambers at the aforementioned premises from Ja. 28 through Feb. 2, 1985.'[85]

Steel, Marilyn's lead attorney, called the three-hour search a "fishing expedition" and "paper chase" in a "desperate attempt by the vice squad to build a case for the D.A."[86]

"This is an absurd abuse of police power and a ridiculous misallocation of police resources—sending a dozen officers in here in order to prove that Marilyn Chambers did, in fact, perform here last week," Steel said. "All of San Francisco knows that."[87]

Marilyn's arrest touched a nerve with San Franciscans but not in the way the police, Mayor Feinstein, or Chief Murphy had hoped. Residents were angry that their tax dollars had funded the undercover sting operation—and at a venerable business, the significance of which to the city had only increased in the fifteen years since it had opened—all to arrest a woman performing a show for paying customers. It didn't matter if the show was sexually suggestive. Every patron in attendance was an adult who paid the admission and wanted to be there. The fact that it took multiple police officers to wrangle the five-foot-seven, 115-pound Marilyn, who didn't resist arrest, struck many as use of excessive force.

Even the police commissioner, Jo Daly, was incensed. She demanded to know if Murphy had been aware of the raid in advance and if Feinstein had authorized it. Both said they hadn't.

"I got 51 phone calls about this," Daly fumed. "The most touching was from a 79-year-old native of San Francisco who lives in the avenues and is scared to walk to the store and doesn't go out at night. She acknowledged that California passed consenting-adults-sex legislation 10 years ago, not because it approved of it, but because the people of the state truly believe the police have better things to do."[88]

Daly was particularly upset about the reports that more than a dozen officers participated in the raid.

"If (Chambers) is convicted of prostitution," she added, "I'll eat these words."[89]

News of the arrest reached a fever pitch when outspoken, flamboyant columnist Warren Hinckle wrote a scathing piece in the *San Francisco Chronicle* called "The Cops and Marilyn Chambers." Hinckle thought the arrest was absurd and that the police had embarrassed the city. He claimed twenty-five to thirty officers stormed the theater to arrest Marilyn.

'The Chambers bust was a grand hour for San Franciscan's finest,' he wrote wryly. 'I think the cops who busted into the theater [that] night had another agenda. I think they wanted to score some ink, and Marilyn Chambers was the biggest score in town. The cops have a nervous eye on legislation going before the Board of Supervisors today that would end the police power to license adult theaters.'[90]

Supervisor Richard Hongisto noted that the only complaints about adult theaters, including the O'Farrell, came from police, not from so-called concerned and offended citizens. Hongisto suggested the regulation of theaters should be left to the Fire Department, whose responsibility was to keep any establishment safe to occupy without passing judgment on the show.

'Even if Hongisto wins today,' penned Hinckle, 'you can be certain the boys from vice will be busily finding another pretense for saving the city from such a menace

UP 'N' COMING, DOWN 'N' OUT

as Marilyn Chambers. As S.J. Perelman once said, a dirty mind never sleeps.[91]

On February 4, the San Francisco Board of Supervisors repealed the Police Department's power to license adult theaters and businesses.[92]

Hinckle again harangued the police in his column published on Monday, February 11. Two days later, he was arrested opposite the *Chronicle* building. Three police officers were sent to pick him up on three misdemeanor warrants: a late automobile registration, having an unlicensed dog, and perhaps the most ludicrous, walking his basset hound, Bentley, without a leash. Hinckle paid the fines totaling $178 ($513 today) and was released.

It was another embarrassing miscalculation by Chief Murphy, and it reflected poorly on Mayor Feinstein.[93] San Francisco residents were infuriated. They wrote letters to the *Chronicle* and other newspapers, and phoned their supervisors, the police chief, the police commissioner, and the mayor's office to complain. Nearly $200,000 of taxpayer money (more than $575,000 in today's money) was spent in the O'Farrell Theater bust.[94]

The arrest also struck a chord in the gay community, members of which were already accustomed to—and resented—police harassment. Many of them, reeling from the devastation of the AIDS crisis and city officials' recent forced closure of the bathhouses, felt the police were being weaponized against them. Hinckle spoke at a monthly meeting of the Alice B. Toklas Lesbian/Gay Democratic Club, and his sentiment about law enforcement was shared by the crowd.

"The San Francisco Police Department is getting out of control," he said to loud cheers. Yet he charged that the gay community had "not been critical enough of the police department."[95]

"I hear some Gays saying, 'If they punish Marilyn, it's not my issue,'" he told the group. "But this should be an issue for Gays when the cops go into the Mitchell Brothers' Theatre. Until this town gets undivided, there will be no progress. I know that if Harvey Milk were alive, he would be livid over this Mitchell Brothers thing."[96]

Jerry Jansen of the Committee to Preserve Our Sexual and Civil Liberties wrote an open letter to Hinckle in the *Bay Area Reporter* after his appearance:

> The Committee to Preserve Our Sexual and Civil Liberties wishes to thank you for appearing at the Alice B. Toklas meeting and emphasizing the need for Gay men to be aware that the attacks on sexual and civil liberties by the current city administration are an attack on all of our freedoms. We have made known to the Police Commission and relevant authorities that we condemn...[the] use of police to intimidate straight bookstores, to politically prosecute you and Marilyn Chambers, and to use surveillance files to intimidate Gay political organizations.

Unless Gay men are willing to stand for freedom of all—be it Marilyn Chambers or the baths—no one's freedom is safe.[97]

On Monday, February 11, the San Francisco District Attorney's Office before a Municipal Court judge declined to press charges against Marilyn. The D.A.'s office left open the possibility to charge her if further investigation warranted it. That never happened.[98] As *The San Francisco Examiner* noted several weeks after the arrest, 'Chambers's public exploits have earned her a cherished niche in the city's Barbary Coast soul.'[99]

"I DON'T WANT TO continue making X-rated films if they don't mean anything," Marilyn told *The San Francisco Examiner* in 1985. "I'd love to do a film that had serious acting, good writing, and good directing, but you can't really hope for that."[100]

Marilyn made about $250,000 annually (more than $578,000 today), primarily from live performances and film residuals. The San Francisco arrest gave her an unexpected publicity boost. Her controversial "Feel the Magic" show was booked at several more theaters in the US and Canada. Despite the bookings and their financial influx, Marilyn began to realize it was time to leave the adult film world, at least as an actress. The AIDS epidemic was raging with no end in sight, so the health risks of X-rated acting far outweighed the financial benefits. Moreover, Marilyn was ready to settle down and have a family. Now thirty-three, she knew that she'd soon age out of the industry, and that her time to conceive a child was diminishing. She knew one thing more: she would not have a child with Chuck Traynor.

They filed for divorce in 1985. He remained her manager and business partner, but the marriage was over. Near the end, their relationship was acrimonious. One day Marilyn left Chuck an eight-by-ten glossy color photo of herself. The photo shows her kneeling in a bubble bath with a vase of red roses behind her. She's nude, but only her breasts are exposed. A pouty, sensual expression fills her face. She wears a simple gold necklace, and her hair is up, adding a touch of glamour to a palpably erotic photo. It's classic Marilyn Chambers.

The inscription read:

Chuck,

you blew this piece of ass –

UP 'N' COMING, DOWN 'N' OUT

good luck with the next one –
you got what you deserve –
Your (5th or is it 6th?) ex-wife,

Marilyn

P.S. Trust is a disappointing thing

The message is somewhat cryptic. They kept their relationship and its complications concealed. Apart from the despair at the dissolution of their marriage, it's not unlikely Marilyn was angered by the fact that Chuck had already taken up with someone nearly half her age, and that he was grooming her to be the next "Marilyn Chambers."

The night before their divorce was finalized, Marilyn wrote a three-page letter to her soon-to-be ex-husband.[101] On Chambers/Traynor Enterprises letterhead, she scrawled:

Dear Chuck,

Well, now that it's over between us, <u>really</u> over, there are a couple of things I must say.

At one (or maybe two) point[s], I thought we might be able to realize that we really were meant for each other. I never have, and probably never will, have that special raporé [sic] with any man ever again in my life. It's tragic, in a way, that we blew it, but in retrospect, it's all for the best. Bo is <u>great</u> for you, and I'll always keep wondering if Bobby's great for me. Whatever. Thanks for the best 11 years of my life and for having the patience in teaching me everything I know and making me the woman I've become – which I feel is a hell of alot [sic] better than I ever would've been without you. You know I'll <u>always</u> <u>love</u> & <u>adore</u> you with all my heart and will <u>always</u> till the day I <u>die</u> be there for you. You're a <u>very</u> special man, and I'm saying "I Do" to this divorce with a terrible personal sadness. You're someone whom I could always turn to in times of sorrow & happiness, and I shall miss that extreme personal interaction we've always taken for granted. I only pray we can still be friends (as I consider you the best I'll <u>ever</u> <u>have</u>) and look out for each other.

No sense in being maudlin, but I shall miss the title of being Mrs. Charles Everett Traynor. You can always count on me personally & of course, businesswise. I'll always still be the same old "<u>Mare</u>" (Not the old gray kind!), so let's not change our communication. Also, please tell your mother of the divorce. I can't bear to tell her it's finally happened.

I'm writing this the eve before I go to court - when the judge declares our divorce final, I shall remove my wedding ring, never to wear it again on the same finger. But have it resized to wear forever on my right hand as a reminder of my love & gratitude for all you'll <u>always</u> <u>mean</u> to me. Hate to sound sad, but I am because this is an end to an extremely important era. It's kind of like a death in the family. Don't mind me if I act upset for a couple of days 'cause this <u>is</u> <u>final</u> and traumatic. I promise to keep my sadness to myself, but I want you to know I'll <u>always</u> love you and really do regret, at times, the reasons for our breakup.

Please know I truly think a lot of Bo and wish you all the luck in the world. In your best interests, I suggest you rip up this letter so she'll never have reason to resent me & my eternal love for you - my husband of 11 years -

Goodbye my dear husband - may you always find happiness & lots of <u>young</u> <u>chicks</u>!!!

Love you honey,

Marilyn xxx

It is hard to know how someone as emotionally detached as Chuck might respond to such a vulnerable, heart-rending note. Still, it must have resonated. He kept it neatly folded in its original envelope for the rest of his life and never took Marilyn's suggestion to rip it up.

Marilyn reflected on the marriage two years later in GQ magazine. She largely blamed herself for its failure, and pointed to a perceived inability to please Chuck. She believed this shortcoming stemmed from a driving need for her father's approval:

All my life I have tried to please my father, but I never could. Then I tried to please Chuck, Uncle Chuckie, I call him, but I knew I didn't. There's something in me that doesn't please men. I don't know. Maybe that's why I worked so hard at it all these years. Maybe that's why I always need a man to take care of me. To be Daddy's girl. That's the way it was for me with Chuck[.] [A]ll I want from Chuck [is] his blessing. I just want to be a good wife and have kids someday.[102]

The divorce also signaled the end of the "Marilyn Chambers" era. She continued to ask herself, "If I'm no longer 'Marilyn Chambers' or Marilyn Traynor, who am I?"

UP 'N' COMING, DOWN 'N' OUT

She had no idea.

She hoped to find a new version of herself through her relationship with D'Apice.[103] He replaced Chuck not only as a lover and companion but as a gatekeeper. In addition to acting as Marilyn's bodyguard, he screened every phone call and interview request and managed every appearance. Theirs was a relationship of recurring cruelty and violence fueled by daily cocaine use. Marilyn developed an unhealthy, codependent infatuation with him. The violence reached a new extreme one night during the winter of 1985.

'We'd been fighting over money,' Marilyn wrote in the treatment for her unpublished memoir. 'He spent a lot of it. So did I, but the cash he was spending was mine, which really pissed me off. That night I let him know how much it bothered me by verbally abusing him and giving him a bunch of shit like: 'You're just using me!' or, 'It's all about money to you, isn't it, asshole?' Then he threw me on the bed, pulled a roll of bills out of my purse, and began shoving them in my mouth to the point where he was choking me. I felt like I was going to die because I couldn't breathe. To him, this was the ultimate humiliation—to take me out by stuffing money down my throat.'[104]

The irony of this sort of possible death was not lost on her.

'I could see the headlines: 'Marilyn Chambers deep-throated to death with her own wad!'' she quipped.

However, the gravity of the situation was all too real, and she knew D'Apice had taken it too far.

'I knew I was going to die or relent and marry him,' she wrote. 'What a choice! I didn't want to do either. I wanted to be free of him, but I didn't know how. I couldn't believe there were places I could call and say, 'Help me; I can't get away from this guy!' I mean, I'm Marilyn Chambers. You think they're going to buy that? I was stuck in my own personality. Mired in my own image. Trapped!'[105]

There were good times between the couple, she insisted. However, they 'were such volatile, passionate, lusting, highly-sexed individuals that it was like fire on top of fire, and we were burning all the time. There was no relief.'

They needed to take a break, but they could still date.

'See, I could never totally let go,' she wrote. 'That's how stupid I was.'[106]

She insisted that it was the sex that kept her coming back to him. She didn't believe she could have it any better than with him. Nevertheless, she moved out of their shared duplex into a fully-furnished Las Vegas penthouse. Her personal belongings, D'Apice, and their two dogs were still at the duplex. She and D'Apice continued 'their sick little relationship,' as she described it. They'd fuck and fight a couple of times a week.

'The only difference,' she pointed out, 'was that we weren't living together.'[107]

It wasn't until years later, when she had gotten clean and sober, that she had realized she was a prisoner of her past and 'the image I created for myself.' For fifteen years, she had played the role of Marilyn Chambers, the ivory sex goddess. There was no alternative plan, no plan B. She lacked the insight to discover her authentic self away from her image. She used drugs and alcohol to figure it out and to escape the persona. They didn't work.

While Marilyn was dating D'Apice, she was introduced to a woman named Peggy McGinn. McGinn's ex-husband was close friends with D'Apice. He thought he might be able to impress McGinn, whom he was courting at the time, by introducing her to a celebrity. But McGinn grew up in Hollywood, and meeting celebrities was unremarkable. However, she and Marilyn formed an instant bond and remained close friends for nearly twenty-five years.

Marilyn confided in McGinn about the violence she suffered at D'Apice's hand. McGinn never witnessed it but said Marilyn took and kept photos documenting wounds D'Apice had inflicted on her, but she never did anything with them.

"Why she kept wanting to go back to it, I can't really even explain that," McGinn said, referring to Marilyn's relationship with D'Apice. "Other than they were both addicts at the time. You know, she actually chalked it up to him being Italian. And I said, 'Bullshit!'"[108]

McGinn told Marilyn repeatedly the violence didn't stem from D'Apice being Italian.

"It's because he's an animal," McGinn said. "He's an abuser, and you have to teach people how to treat you."[109]

Despite McGinn's protestations, Marilyn replied, "I can handle it. I'll kick his ass; I'm a tough broad."

"And she wasn't a 'tough broad,'" McGinn said. "She may act like it, but she's not."[110]

Still, Marilyn was able to continue her performance schedule, even if she was playing "Marilyn Chambers," the character. On Friday, December 13, she took the stage at Cleveland's New Era Burlesk for her "Feel the Magic" show. Shortly after the performance began, she was arrested. As with the O'Farrell Theater, she'd performed there repeatedly over the years. As with the San Francisco bust ten months prior, she was taken into custody by ten police officers who observed a nude Marilyn 'having sexual contact with a member of the audience.' Police Sergeant Roger Dennerll said police were responding to a complaint that the show was 'obscene.' Fourteen men, including several patrons and two of Marilyn's bodyguards, were also picked up.[111]

UP 'N' COMING, DOWN 'N' OUT

Marilyn was charged with promoting prostitution and was held overnight in City Jail before being released on a $1,000 bond. Again, Marilyn denied the allegations.

"I did the same show I've been doing for the last six years," she said. "Police just happened to be in the audience."[112]

The following Monday, December 16, Marilyn was convicted of pandering obscenity in Cleveland Municipal Court. She pleaded no contest, had to pay a $500 fine (nearly $1,400 in today's money), and was given a thirty-day suspended sentence.[113]

On Super Bowl Sunday, 1986, Marilyn went over to the duplex to see D'Apice before he left for a business trip to Sacramento. She had already been getting wasted for most of the day. Her day began with beer and pot. When her energy lagged, she'd break out the cocaine.

'I knew I had a drinking problem,' she wrote. 'I really needed to do something about it, but I had absolutely no support from Bobby, or anybody else for that matter. Yet he always told me I had a problem, but I was in such big-time denial I would ignore him because he drank and took drugs too.'[114]

D'Apice ignored her when she arrived at the duplex. He sat on his newly-purchased couch and smoked a cigarette. Marilyn noticed the couch right away. She wondered if he had used her money to pay for it. It wasn't just the couch she noticed. D'Apice had rearranged some of the furniture as if to stake a claim on the place. This irritated her. He went into another room to watch the football game.

She wandered around the place, looking at the photos and mementos on the wall.

'Despite my dazed state, I distinctly remember looking at the walls and feeling really sad because my whole life was up there,' she said.[115]

Arranged neatly in a frame were six medals she won in diving competitions. She had given her father every medal, and they sat in his desk drawer for years. She regularly bugged him to put them in a frame. He finally did, and they looked beautiful behind the glass against the gold-bordered black velvet. The one that stuck out, though, was the silver medal. It was the same silver medal she had presented to her father, who had responded, "Why didn't you get first?"

The medals hung near an end table. The photo of her as a three-year-old wearing her new Mary Jane shoes and holding a stuffed dog was in a frame on the table. It was taken the same day as the family photo when she had chopped off her hair. She looked at the girl in the picture and remembered her sadness that day and her detachment from the rest of her family.

She flipped through her high school yearbook next. D'Apice let out a whoop and a holler when his favorite team scored a touchdown or made a strategic play. Each time she heard him, anger surged through her.

A photo from Marilyn's first professional modeling shoot was tucked into one of the yearbook pages. She was eighteen when the photo was taken and already living in New York. After the shoot, the photographer invited her back to his place. Immediately after they made love, he said he wanted to take a picture just as she looked.

'My hair was all disheveled, the false eyelashes were crooked, and my makeup was smeared,' she wrote. He handed her a denim jacket, turned up the collar, and opened the front. 'Very sexy yet innocent at the same time,' she thought.[116]

He took her up to the roof of the apartment building and continued photographing her.

'These pictures were some of my very favorites,' she wrote. 'They represent a time of innocence, of the beginning of something unknown. I had stars in my eyes and great expectations for myself.'[117]

As she floated around the duplex, she grew increasingly morose. She grabbed another beer from the kitchen and lit up a joint. She thumbed through photos of her and Doug. It had been so long since they split up that she had forgotten what he looked like. There were wedding photos and ones of the trip to Cannes for *Green Door*. She thought of the Mitchell brothers, the enjoyment they all shared in showing their film, and the reception from the audience.

'That adulation only served to reinforce my illusions which, by this time, were virtually indistinguishable from my hallucinations,' she wrote. 'I was so young and gullible and naive, filled with wonderful thoughts of how this was the start of a really great thing.'[118]

She found a box with more photos. These were all with or taken by Chuck. Marilyn was surprised D'Apice hadn't thrown this box away. He didn't want any ghosts of former lovers in their home. Funny, she thought, that there were no pictures of her and Chuck's wedding.[119] There were plenty of her and Sammy, though. The pictures of her and Sammy reminded her of the framed photo of Marilyn Monroe she had prominently displayed on another end table. The photo had been given to her by Milton Greene, a friend of Sammy's, who took innumerable photos of the fabled star. Marilyn, who had once been dubbed "The Marilyn Monroe of Porn," never considered herself a big Monroe fan. This photo was different. It captured something with which she identified. It showed Monroe leaning against a wall with her dress falling off her shoulder.

'The picture was self-prophetic in a way,' Marilyn wrote. 'Even though I admired her, I didn't want to end up like her. But it was the same type of career—

UP 'N' COMING, DOWN 'N' OUT

the drugs, the alcohol, the fame, and the husbands and being a sexual creature. I could relate to it.'[120]

More prominently displayed around the duplex were photos of Marilyn and D'Apice. In some, she thought, they genuinely looked happy, but the pictures didn't tell the whole story. She flopped down on the couch, lit a cigarette, and stared at the photo of Marilyn Monroe. She wondered whether Monroe shared similar feelings to the ones she had that day. Another relationship was coming to an end, and she had to make a decision. She had to figure out who she was.

'Is this all there is?' she asked herself. 'Is this what happens when you become rich and famous, and the money comes, the money goes, along with the boyfriends and the husbands? Will I ever be happy? Fulfilled? Will I ever have babies? Will I ever have a normal relationship with a man? Is this fantasy a reality?'[121]

Maybe the reality was a fantasy. Maybe everything was one gigantic hallucination. It would help explain some of the more outrageous things that had happened to her. She craved an explanation and a resolution. She yearned to be a mother, too, but it was becoming clear D'Apice didn't want children.

D'Apice came into the room carrying a briefcase. He was heading to his job as a bodyguard at a strip club. Then he was taking a business trip with his boss to Sacramento. Marilyn didn't believe the part about the trip. She was sure he was screwing one or more of the strippers and was using the trip as a cover. They started fighting, which quickly escalated and then turned into fucking. The same old pattern.

Around 6:00PM, Marilyn stubbed out her cigarette in the ashtray on the sofa. Then she left the duplex while D'Apice stayed behind to make final preparations for his trip. She went to a bar for a drink and returned to her penthouse. When she got there, the phone was ringing. It was D'Apice calling from the strip club. He apologized again for having to leave. He promised to be back as soon as possible. She said she hoped so because the dogs were still at the duplex, and she didn't want them left alone for too long. He said he'd let them out for the night before he left.

When the call ended, she left the penthouse and scored some coke. Then she walked into the Nevada desert to search the night sky for UFOs. She liked to believe there might be other life forms in the universe. It always fascinated her. If extraterrestrials from advanced civilizations existed, maybe they could help sort out some of her problems. She certainly didn't know how to help herself or where to start.

She walked back to her penthouse. When she returned, she sat on the floor and pulled out her books about the cosmos and theories on aliens. She had been up for two days and continued to snort cocaine. It made her jittery, but more than that, it made her paranoid. She moved all the furniture up against the door and barricaded herself inside. She retrieved her handgun, sat on the floor, and thought about suicide.

'I knew I didn't have the backbone to do it, but I also knew I didn't have the guts to get clean either,' she recalled.[122]

Her mind raced back to D'Apice and what she believed he was doing that very minute with any number of other women. She suspected he would bring some of the club's strippers back to the duplex—*their* duplex—to fuck them. And she was determined to catch him in the act. Around 2:00AM, she called the strip club, and they informed her that he had left about an hour before. She phoned their home and got a busy signal. He must have taken the phone off the hook, she thought. That was all the proof she needed that he was cheating.

Too strung out on coke to think straight, and knowing an explosive and violent scene awaited her if she busted in on D'Apice and another woman, Marilyn went to one of her favorite local bars. She downed double-shot Bloody Marys. She gambled and scored more cocaine. She kept calling their home and received the same busy signal. Finally, around 5:30AM, she decided to head over there.

'Every fiber in my body is screaming for sleep, but my burned-out brain overpowers them all, and I haul my ass into the Cadillac and drive over to Bobby's, bent on justifying my delusions.'[123]

She pulled up to the house, which was obscured from the street. She exited the car and walked around to the side of the house. All of the furniture was scattered across the front lawn. It was blackened and charred. Plywood had been nailed over the windows. Marilyn couldn't comprehend what she was seeing. Was this a hallucination, she wondered? Then she saw the note taped to the front door: 'Please call us right away—LVFD [The Las Vegas Fire Department].'[124]

Marilyn gently pushed the door, and it opened. The smell of smoke and fumes hit her first. She coughed and caught her breath. As the morning air flowed into the home through the open door, the smoke cleared enough for her to see the hellscape before her. Flames had ravaged everything. Her first thought was her two dogs. She ran through the kitchen. There was glass all over the floor. The fire had been so hot it had blown out the windows. She reached the backyard and found her Dobermans, Freeway and Rocky, cowering in a corner surrounded by glass.

The nightmarish reality began to set in.

'I looked at the charred wall and saw a Daliesque vision of Hell,' she said. 'My medals had melted down the wall, looking as if they'd been etched by some demonic hand.[125]

The photographs she had perused just hours before were warped, curled by the heat, singed around the edges. Others were water damaged. Nothing was salvageable.

D'Apice kept an array of firearms and ammunition in the apartment. All of it had exploded in the conflagration. Every appliance was melted.

Marilyn carried the shivering, terrified dogs to her car and drove them to a friend's home. She returned to the site of the fire and the blistered remnants of her life. A neighbor had made her way to the wreckage and told Marilyn she had called the fire department when she'd seen the flames coming from the home. The fire started in the living room, specifically on the couch. Then Marilyn remembered the cigarette butt. She thought she had stubbed it out in the ashtray, but, evidently, it hadn't completely gone out, and must have fallen between the cushions.

When D'Apice finally arrived, the two just sat and cried.

'I knew it was the end of an era, the end of the old Marilyn Chambers,' Marilyn wrote. 'And he knew he was out: out of his house, out of the relationship, and out of my life.'

'For myself, I was humiliated and devastated,' she added. 'But most of all, I was lost. Everything that was me was gone as I shuffled through the disaster, kicking aside the parched ruins of my life. And then something caught my eye in the withered pile. I picked it up, wiped the soot away, and gazed through my tears one last time at the scared little girl in her brand new Mary Janes holding on to that stuffed puppy for dear life.'[126]

Chapter 9

FAKING IT

"You have to recognize that you can only stay up there for so long. And then you have to say, 'Thank you and good night.' And then, that's it. In a way, you never leave the top if you do it that way. Knowing how to make it is only half the job. Knowing when to leave is just as important."
— Marilyn Chambers, 1975[1]

T AROUND 9:00PM ON FRIDAY, June 6, 1986, Harley Curtis and Robert Kavanaugh paid the ten-dollar fee at Jason's Tavern, a strip club in Windsor, Ontario, Canada, to see Marilyn Chambers in the flesh. A club staffer told the two men that they'd have to wait downstairs in the club's bar until there was space in the lounge. The men ordered a few drinks; Kavanaugh drank two-and-a-half bottles of beer, and Curtis drank almost three. The two spent about thirty-five dollars, including tips, and each left a full beer on the table until they could move to the lounge around midnight.

The two men were among 300 patrons in the standing-room-only club. They were standing about thirty feet from the stage. Shortly after midnight, Marilyn entered and opened the show with a song. As she sang, she moved about and seductively removed her clothes. The crowd cheered approvingly. Kavanaugh took note of their response and all the "hooting and hollering."

After she finished her song, a prerecorded dance track boomed over the club's sound system, and Marilyn began dancing and removed her top. The crowd responded enthusiastically. Marilyn 'wrapped herself around a vertical brass pole on stage and pulled on her breasts. [S]he moved off the stage and into the crowd where she pushed her breasts into the face of a stage-side patron.'[2]

Neither Kavanaugh nor Curtis could see the patron, but they wanted to. They were trying to take note of every detail and every person in the club. Both men were constables with the Windsor police department and were operating undercover. Both had heard Marilyn's shows could be considered lewd and obscene and primed themselves to arrest her if necessary.

The officers observed as Marilyn stretched herself out across the lap of another patron. After she removed her G-string, Marilyn turned her back to the audience and bent forward.

Curtis, one of the officers, said it was impossible to remember everything that happened during the performance. "There was too much action," he said. "She was doing too many things. I don't remember everything."[3]

Curtis admitted he was probably the only patron at the club who found the performance distasteful.

Marilyn was arrested.

"The officers determined she was giving an indecent theatrical performance because of the way she was gyrating," said Staff Sgt. John Abbey. Marilyn posted the bail of $500 (nearly $1,400 in today's money) and was released.[4]

Marilyn hadn't planned to make an appearance that night. She did it as a favor to Chuck. After their divorce in 1985, they stayed in touch. At first it was out of necessity; Chuck was still her manager. But they continued speaking and remained friends.

Chuck had called Marilyn and asked her to appear at Jason's Tavern because he was molding his new girlfriend, Crissa "Bo" Bozlee, into "the new Marilyn Chambers." He wanted "Bo" to open for Marilyn and learn from her. Marilyn agreed. It was also an easy way to pick up an extra $15,000 (approximately $42,000 today).

A trial was set for January 29, 1987. Chuck convinced Marilyn to return to Jason's Tavern for additional performances during the trial period. He thought her appearances would make a great test case for Canada's nude-dancing law.

"Whichever way it goes, it'll be called 'the Marilyn Chambers law,'" Chuck speculated. "That'll be neat."[5]

The trial featured testimony from constables Curtis and Kavanaugh.

Police contended Marilyn removed her clothing to "an aerobics-style dance." The most serious of the allegations was that she was touching audience members during her performance, and they, in turn, were touching her in a sexualized way. Police testified that the patrons seemed pleased with her performance, which the constables claimed pushed the bounds of decency. The first part of the trial wrapped in January. It resumed on February 25, with Marilyn taking the stand to defend her actions.[6]

"Any show I do, I try to make a little sexy because that's what I'm known for," she told the court. "It's more of a tease. It's intended to stimulate the audience in an erotic fashion. I hate to use the [phrase] sexually arouse. That's kind of crass. I'd say I lightly titillate them."[7]

Marilyn denied touching her breasts, claiming she puts her hands near them but not on them. The pole, she said, was a prop and gave her something to do with her hands. She did make a licking motion toward the pole, but the police were mistaken, she said, when they claimed she wrapped her body around it. And she did not touch any member of the audience. She acknowledged her reputation as an erotic performer but made a point to note she had starred in legitimate films and learned choreography from the same person who taught Ann-Margret.

Despite the word-of-mouth reputation and the notoriety of her previous arrests, Marilyn's performances were often benign.

'The men are shy, reticent, as most men are when they confront her,' writer Pat Jordan wrote about Marilyn's January performance at Jason's Tavern. 'Men unfailingly treat her like a lady in her presence, but then, out of earshot, they make coarse comments. The men here [at the performance], however, are perfect gentlemen. They ask her a few innocuous questions as if in awe of her. Marilyn Chambers is nostalgia for these older men. She represents the sex of their youth, long gone, after years of marriage.'[8]

Marilyn's defense attorney, Robert Ducharme, said the police officers who attended the performance stood at the back of the tavern, so they could not fully see the performance. While some of the officers' details matched, Ducharme charged, they "had different recollections of other crucial areas of the performance."

Marilyn's recollection was much more credible, he argued. Ducharme also reminded the court that Jason's was a private club only open to adults. Assistant Crown attorney Tim Zuber said Marilyn's performance had no artistic merit. "Its only purpose was to titillate, in a fairly obvious and indecent way," he charged.

At one point, the judge asked a constable to demonstrate what Marilyn did on stage instead of describing it. The constable placed his hands on his buttocks and attempted to bend over. His bulging gut stopped him.

"I could, Your Honor if I was built like her," the constable said. The men in the courtroom laughed. The women in the courtroom, including the prosecutor's wife and court clerk, were stone-faced and glared at Marilyn.[9]

"It gets to you after a while," Marilyn sighed. "Being arrested and fingerprinted just because you're giving people pleasure. It's so degrading. You begin to wonder if you're as bad as people say."[10]

Finally, more than a year after Marilyn's arrest, Judge Saul Nosanchuk ruled in her favor. He said she "did not exceed contemporary community standards of morality" during her performance. The judge determined that because Marilyn was covered—however scantily—she did not meet the Criminal Code definition of "nude."[11]

Following the acquittal, an op-ed in *The Windsor Star* by Gord Henderson lambasted the police for wasting tax-payer dollars on a 'futile thirteen-month pursuit.'[12]

Marilyn had another reason to celebrate: her parents remarried. The woman with whom William was living and having an affair died unexpectedly. Neither Ginny nor William had let go of their connection, and the couple rebuilt the relationship. William moved to Washington State to be with Ginny. Bill, Jann, and Marilyn all noticed an improvement in their parents' moods.

FOLLOWING ANOTHER HIGH-OCTANE PERFORMANCE of her controversial "Feel the Magic" show in Cleveland in 1986, Marilyn met reporters Kathy Kennedy and Patti Thomas from *Connection Magazine* at a nearby restaurant.

'Marilyn Chambers is upfront with her feelings; she is tough and has learned to cover her sensitivity,' Kennedy wrote. 'Her vulnerability came out when we asked her if she planned to have children. She answered quite glibly, "Oh, sure, see mommy in *Behind the Green Door*, come on, give me a break. People make choices in life. You really can't have it all."'[13]

She paused momentarily to reflect on what she had just said.

"It's hard," she continued. "I have lots of peer pressure and family pressure to get married, have children, but first of all, you have to find a man who makes more money than you do, and he has to be secure. I mean, the 'Mr. Chambers' [thing] and all! You really can't have it all—money, great sex, a career, a family. I have no regrets. My life has been fine. Who knows?"[14]

She didn't know. Perhaps she meant to ask, "What happened?" or "What's next?"

The pressure to have children did not come from just peers and family. Marilyn had known in her heart that she was ready to be a mother. Chuck had never wanted children; he'd forced her to have at least one abortion. ("I thought about having kids at 18 but decided I didn't want to leave anything to anyone," Chuck told *GQ* magazine in 1987. "I just want to be cremated and made into douche powder for nude dancers."[15]) Neither did D'Apice evince interest in being a father. When Marilyn learned that D'Apice had a new girlfriend and had adopted the woman's children, she was incensed.

After the fire destroyed the duplex Marilyn had shared with D'Apice, one of

Marilyn's women friends invited her to travel to Los Angeles to live with her for a bit and decompress. The friend also wanted to fix Marilyn up with her cousin Bill Taylor. Marilyn wasn't big on blind dates and wasn't sure she was ready to date so soon after splitting from D'Apice, but, she thought, maybe it would take her mind off him. In fact, part of the reason she agreed to the blind date was to spite D'Apice.

To Marilyn's great surprise, she actually liked Bill when the two of them met. He was handsome and charismatic. On their first date, he told her he had been clean and sober for three years. She knew she had to get clean, and here was a man doing the work to maintain sobriety. She told Bill about the fire and about her relationship with D'Apice, highlighting their drug abuse. He understood. She could sense he was genuinely compassionate. But there was something else she needed to tell him.

"My married name is Marilyn Traynor," she said. "I've been divorced for more than two years, but that's my legal name. Most people know me as Marilyn Chambers."

After a moment, Bill said, "Who's Marilyn Chambers?"

She was flummoxed.

"Marilyn Chambers," she repeated. *"Behind the Green Door, Insatiable,* Ivory Snow."

Bill just looked at her quizzically.

"Are you telling me you've never heard of Marilyn Chambers?"

He had not.[16]

Despite the blow to her ego—"I was crushed," she said[17]—the couple continued to date. She hadn't completely gotten over D'Apice, and smarted every time she thought of him adopting that woman's children, but Bill was charming and kind-hearted. Unlike D'Apice or even Chuck, Bill had steady employment. He owned a trucking company and made good money. Maybe this relationship was more substantive than she originally thought.

She didn't realize just how deep her feelings for Bill ran until he called her one day to break some bad news. He couldn't continue to see her, he said. She figured he would say he couldn't see a "porn star." That wasn't it. He told her she needed to get clean and sober first. He cared for her deeply but couldn't risk his sobriety if she continued using. Surely, she had to understand that.

She didn't understand it. "Go fuck yourself!" she yelled. She slammed down the phone. A seething rage surged through her. Without thinking, she kicked a nearby steel door with her left foot. It was with such force that her knee dislocated and her leg broke in three places.

FAKING IT

She was delighted to see Bill walk into her hospital room. He visited her every day after he learned what had happened. D'Apice made one trip from Las Vegas to Los Angeles to see her. His visit meant next to nothing. She wondered whether he had used her money to make the trip.

During one of Bill's visits, she told him, "I've been doing a lot of thinking. Once my leg heals, there are two things I need to do. The first is to stop drinking and using—period. I'm ready to get help. And the second thing is, I never want to live in Las Vegas ever again."[18]

She left the hospital and stayed at Bill's. There was some business to take care of in Las Vegas. When she felt better, she got into a car and drove from Los Angeles to Vegas. She met D'Apice and told him it was over. She gathered her few pitiful possessions that had survived the fire. On February 15, 1986, she drove from Vegas for the last time. When she returned to Los Angeles, she moved in permanently with Bill and entered a twelve-step program. On January 17, 1987, they married.[19]

"I was shocked because I hadn't even met him yet," said Peggy McGinn, Marilyn's close and longtime friend. "Then we went out there and visited her. I stayed the weekend. And she seemed wonderful. She was in the [twelve-step] program, just doing great."[20]

Bill's job at the trucking company allowed the newlyweds to live comfortably. The couple moved to a tract house in Moreno Valley, California, roughly sixty-five miles east of Los Angeles. This was an adjustment from Marilyn's lavish lifestyle for nearly fifteen years. In a way, she welcomed it. It gave her time to focus on her sobriety and being a housewife. The couple also discussed having children.

The switch from movie star to suburban housewife was well-timed. The year of 1987 marked the end of the five-year agreement Marilyn had made with Chuck. He could no longer collect fifty percent of her earnings. However, she remained friends with him and the two spoke often on the phone. She continued to write her monthly sex advice column for *Club* magazine, which she had started in 1980, and collected royalties on her films. Now they belonged to her. And she still commanded as much as $15,000 for her strip shows. But she knew those couldn't last much longer thanks, in part, to her recent knee injury.

In 1988, she did four live strip shows at some of her favorite nightclubs in the US and Canada. Naturally, she began at the O'Farrell Theater. So much had happened since her arrest there three years earlier. Then, she'd been consuming huge amounts of cocaine and alcohol. Her marriage with Chuck had ended. D'Apice was playing an overpowering part in her life. In short, she'd been spiraling toward death. Now, she was clean, sober, happily married to a wonderful man, free of D'Apice, and on friendly terms with Chuck.

'Ms. Chambers has not entirely shaken off her treatment at the hands of San Francisco cops,' wrote Warren Hinckle in the *San Francisco Examiner*.[21]

That gave her all the more reason to make this new show even more titillating. Billed as a "water show," it opened with Marilyn taking a shower onstage. She bathed herself with Ivory Soap, then let the audience dry her off. Bill initially struggled to accept that his new bride was an adult film star. Marrying a celebrity was one thing, but the area of entertainment for which she was best known was different, to say the least. He wasn't jealous; she no longer had sex on film. However, besides performing live shows, she occasionally posed nude for *Club*, often in explicit poses.

"I used to love the order of going on the road, of doing each show at a certain time," Marilyn told *GQ* magazine. "But now that was an intrusion into my order as a housewife. Cooking and vacuuming were a joy to me for the first time. I love taking care of my husband. It's more fun to make real love to one man than the fantasy of making love to 500."[22]

Bill watched some of her X-rated films with her. The more he saw her on film, the more he understood that sex was just part of the business. Then he found himself falling for "Marilyn Chambers." He became a fan. This added a layer of complexity to their relationship. It was flattering, but she wanted and needed him to love Marilyn Taylor, not Marilyn Chambers.

THE ADULT FILM INDUSTRY was slow to respond to the AIDS crisis. Throughout the seventies and into the eighties, condoms weren't required or even considered by participants—in gay or straight hardcore features. Yes, tests for venereal diseases were common, and Marilyn had insisted on them since filming *Green Door*. But filmmakers could no longer ignore the burgeoning AIDS epidemic.

The mysterious disease, which affected a disproportionate number of gay men, was first reported by the mainstream press in July 1981. At first, medical experts thought it was a rare form of cancer.

'The cause of the outbreak is unknown, and there is as yet no evidence of contagion,' wrote reporter Lawrence K. Altman for *The New York Times*. 'But the doctors who have made the diagnoses, mostly in New York City and the San Francisco Bay area, are alerting other physicians who treat large numbers of homosexual men to the problem in an effort to help identify more cases and to reduce the delay in offering chemotherapy treatment.'[23]

The disease was already known within the gay community, particularly in San Francisco, Los Angeles, and New York, before the *Times* article appeared.

FAKING IT

The US federal government agency Centers for Disease Control and Prevention (CDC) had published an article about the infection—which seemed to be a rare, virulent type of pneumonia—nearly a month prior, on June 5, 1981. The Associated Press, *Los Angeles Times*, and *San Francisco Chronicle* reported on the CDC's article, but the public ignored the stories. The gay press picked it up, though. The *Bay Area Reporter*, a free, weekly gay-community newspaper distributed in bars, newsboxes and gay-area stores, ran a story on July 2 about "Gay Men's Pneumonia." The term was replaced with "gay cancer."[24]

By May 1982, the presence of the disease was declared to have reached epidemic proportions. It had a name: Gay-Related Immune Deficiency (GRID). The name only deepened the public perception and misconception that the disease was limited strictly to the gay community. In his two terms as President, from 1981 to 1989, Ronald Reagan and his ultra-conservative administration did little to curb the epidemic. Nor did he use the presidential bully pulpit to agitate for federal funding to support AIDS-care organizations or treatment research. In September 1982, the CDC changed the name of the disease to Acquired Immunodeficiency Syndrome (AIDS).

Five years passed before Reagan even said the word "AIDS" publicly. By then, more than 50,000 cases had been reported in the US, with a death rate of eighty-two percent. Deaths would top 100,000 before the end of 1989. The total number of cases and deaths is likely higher. The human immunodeficiency virus (HIV) destroyed a person's immune system, leaving them vulnerable to opportunistic infections. Having two of those qualified a person for an AIDS diagnosis. In the early years of the epidemic, before the development and distribution of effective treatments, getting an AIDS diagnosis was tantamount to receiving a death sentence.[25]

It wasn't until 1986 that the first safe-sex, condoms-required adult film appeared. Ironically, it was the Mitchell brothers' *Behind the Green Door: The Sequel*. Marilyn did not appear in the film.

That same year John Holmes tested positive for HIV. He kept the diagnosis to himself and traveled to Italy to make his final two pornographic films. The production company, Paradise Visuals, was unaware that Holmes was HIV-positive. He chose not to tell his onscreen partners and engaged in unprotected sex. The disease had already begun to ravage his body, and Holmes knew he was dying. When asked about his gaunt appearance, he told people he had colon cancer. On March 13, 1988, Holmes died from AIDS-related illnesses at the age of forty-three.

"His eyes were open," said Laurie Rose, Holmes's wife, whom he had married a little more than a year before he died. "[I]t looked like he had looked up to Death and said, 'Here I am.' It was the most peaceful look I ever saw in my life."[26]

PURE

The Sexual Revolutions of Marilyn Chambers

News of his death infuriated and terrified those in the adult film industry. There was no vaccine for the disease. The first drug to treat HIV infection, azidothymidine (AZT), was approved by the Food and Drug Administration (FDA) in March 1987. It was difficult to obtain. It was also toxic and caused severe side effects. AIDS remained a death sentence, and Holmes had engaged in unprotected sex knowing he had the disease.

Just as Rock Hudson became the most prominent Hollywood celebrity to die from AIDS in 1985, Holmes was now the face of AIDS for the triple-X industry.

When Marilyn heard of Holmes' death, she was petrified. Although it had been five years since she'd had sex with Holmes, medical experts believed that HIV could incubate in the human body for as long as ten years before a person tested positive for it. As a recently married woman ready to start a family, learning about Holmes, and considering her past connections to him, jeopardized her lifelong dream.

"I was freaking out, like, 'Oh, my God, *Shit!* What am I going to do?'" she recalled. "I was tested every six months for ten years after that."[27]

Marilyn told the *Edmonton Journal* in 1987 that she was "not going to be making any more X-rated films." (The paper, rather untactfully, said the epidemic was "killing" the industry, not necessarily taking into account that the disease was literally doing that to people within it.) "I live in fear that I might get it from some past experience," she told the paper. "The AIDS scare is creating a pretty monogamous society, and I think that's great."

As usual, the male reporter asked if she had any regrets about her past.

"I'd do it all again," she replied. "I was treated fairly well."

She noted, however, that drugs and alcohol proliferated in the industry, and other stars weren't so lucky.

"Fortunately, I made it through it," she said. "Two months ago, I celebrated my seventeenth month of sobriety."[28]

IN THE SUMMER OF 1989, Marilyn signed a deal with Private Screenings. The production company would produce several softcore direct-to-cable and direct-to-video feature films starring Marilyn. Nudity was required, but no hardcore sex, which was a relief. There were suggestions that the films might be picked up for international or theatrical distribution. The offer came at a fortuitous time for Marilyn. Newly married, clean, sober, and ready to start a family, the films gave Marilyn steady, lucrative employment, and it helped keep her name in the press. She was surrounded by younger models on their way up, and she was at an age

FAKING IT

where she was ready to impart some wisdom to these young women.

Marilyn's association with Private Screenings dated back several years. In 1982, Satori Productions, Inc., which owned Private Screenings, spun off the unit. Investment banker Fred Schoenberg, head of Schoenberg, Hieber, Inc., managed the offerings and scheduled a meeting with brokers at the exclusive, members-only New York Stock Exchange Luncheon Club inside the New York Stock Exchange building.[29]

Marilyn was scheduled to appear at the luncheon, in late April 1982, to entice brokers and add a little star quality. When word got around that Marilyn would attend, the conservative *New York Post* ran a story, and the Luncheon Club slammed the door. It also demanded that Schoenberg hand in his membership. He declined. Schoenberg rescheduled the pitch to brokers and held it at the headquarters of the New York Society of Securities Analysts. Marilyn's schedule prevented her from attending, 'but just the rumor that Marilyn Chambers would be present changed the normally sparse gathering into the largest crowd' the Securities Analysts headquarters had seen in years.[30] The first film Marilyn did for Private Screenings was *Party Incorporated*, originally titled *Party Girls. Party Incorporated* is the most inventive of all the Private Screenings films she made. Marilyn plays Marilyn Sanders, a wealthy, suddenly-widowed socialite who learns that her late husband has left her deep in debt and owing a large sum of back taxes to the government. To pay off her debts, she forms a company, Party Girls, which throws get-togethers featuring throngs of beautiful young women. It's a silly concept, but in many ways, it's a precursor to reality television. Marilyn's character invites a camera crew into her home to chronicle her everyday life. Nearly every participant breaks the fourth wall, including the director, script girl, and sound man. There are shots of viewers at home watching the scenes as they unfold. She even sings two songs directly to the camera, and the scenes are edited like music videos.

It's a comedy, and while it's not especially funny, there are some humorous moments. Beautiful, well-endowed women and buff, shirtless men cavort freely. In one scene, Marilyn appears topless, revealing that she'd had yet more breast augmentation procedures. If nothing else, it's fun, mindless entertainment.

Marilyn did a whirlwind publicity tour for *Party Incorporated*, which included a trip to the Cannes Film Festival to find financiers to help bring the films to the big screen. No such deals were ever made.

As home video became more ubiquitous and accessible to the general consumer in the eighties, direct-to-video films increased in popularity. They were cheap to make (and often looked that way), and although they never played theatrically, they provided video stores with much-needed products. Because of the low production costs and often exorbitant prices for VHS tapes—*Party Incorporated* sold for eighty dollars when it was released (nearly $200 today)—they usually earned money.

It was something of a novelty for a celebrity to push a direct-to-video film. Critics and industry observers considered them even less artistically valid than made-for-television movies. Millions would likely see traditional made-for-TV movies played on network television. D-list actors, who appeared in direct-to-video films simply for a paycheck, often kept the titles off their resumes. It was even more surprising that major talk shows and radio programs booked actors to promote a direct-to-video and direct-to-cable feature.

Marilyn Chambers was different. She was still a recognizable name and still carried a degree of controversy. She also owned a percentage of the film's profit, so it behooved her to shill it wherever she could.

She landed some plum gigs to promote the movie, including *Larry King Live* on CNN, the wildly popular daytime talk show *Live with Regis and Kathie Lee*, Howard Stern's radio show, and countless newspaper and magazine interviews.

"[The film] wasn't something I went out and looked for or was hungry for," she told *Newsday*. "I'd just gotten married, and I decided I was going to hang back. I wanted to work, but I didn't want to do X-rated films, and I had some money coming in and wasn't desperate or anything. It's just how things work out in life; just amazing. Somebody up there likes me, I think."[31]

She continued, "It didn't really matter what the films were about. Of course, the money was of importance. And (so was) the fact that I was going to do films again and be seen on video and cable."[32]

Even at the age of thirty-seven, the idea of "legitimate acting" was not far from Marilyn's mind. If *Party Incorporated* was successful, it could be an opportunity to do additional non-X acting.

'Perhaps the most pressing social value [*Party Incorporated*] holds is that it allows this once salacious star a chance to start over—clean,' the New York *Daily News*'s Alan Mirabella wrote.[33]

Marilyn told Mirabella, "For a while, I wasn't feeling secure, but then I met my husband, and he changed my life. He's a guy who loves me for me."[34]

It was a statement that echoed many she told reporters over the years about Chuck and Doug. However, her marriage to Bill was different. She was older now, and while her husband's approval was critical, she rarely spoke about her need for Bill's approval. Bill was self-sufficient. Neither was he a father figure like Chuck. And Marilyn, for the first time in her life, didn't have to be the sole breadwinner. Nor must she try as hard to live up to her sex-goddess image. She certainly had moments of insecurity, but for once, in this marriage, she could breathe, evolve, and turn into Marilyn Taylor. Syndicated columnist Mike Cidoni noted in his piece about Marilyn's new venture: 'Chambers' new spin on her old career hasn't gotten much support from Hollywood's hottest shots. She says big studios such as Universal Pictures aren't banging her door down. Not yet. "But it's changing," [she says]. "The networks used to be worried about hiring me and then have me turn around to another X-rated film. Now they know better. I've got a lot of things in the works. A lot of maybes."'[35]

When Cidoni noted that Jane Fonda, Meryl Streep, and other highbrow acting counterparts needn't worry about any competition from Marilyn, she cheerily interjected, "You mean *today*! But they better start looking over their shoulder 'cause I'm comin." It's a sweet and endearing yet piteous statement.[36]

Acting issues aside, it was hardly a surprise that AIDS figured prominently in most interviews.

"I found the people in X-rated flicks to be pretty hygienically together, but the AIDS thing came out when nobody was aware of it, and there's nothing you can do to retrace your path there," she told *The Chicago Tribune*. "I was offered a lot of money to do another X-rated film, a lot more than my normal asking price, which was $100,000. But I'm not willing to die for it."[37]

Newsday called Party Incorporated 'so tongue-in-cheek, it's charming,'[38] and *Variety* generously complimented Marilyn's performance, though it called the film 'merely okay.' 'Chambers has fun with a self-absorbed role that would have been tailor-made for Mae West,' the magazine noted.[39]

Several direct-to-video and direct-to-cable features followed, including *Breakfast in Bed*, *The Marilyn Diaries*, *Bedtime Stories*, and *New York Nights*. In nearly all of them, Marilyn played a character named Marilyn. They all followed a similar pattern: Marilyn's characters were generally the older, more experienced mentors to small groups of younger, naked women (often models) who have troubles with men. They were all softcore, tits-and-ass flicks, with Marilyn generally appearing partially nude with only her breasts exposed.

"When I work for Private Screenings, they use me for my name but also because I can do things in one take," Marilyn said. "They don't have time to screw around and do ten takes or something. We do, like, twenty-five pages of dialogue a day! It's a breakneck speed, which really doesn't allow for creativity. It's really boom-boom-boom. You're not really aware of what you're saying or doing—you're just *doing* it."[40]

Like *Party Incorporated*, *The Marilyn Diaries* was shopped around at Cannes for potential theatrical distribution. *Variety*, once again, singled out Marilyn for praise. '[The] only excuse for this genially frilly softcore comedy is to witness the grace and good humor with which ex-porn star Marilyn Chambers moves into middle age,' it commented. 'She still looks in sufficiently solid shape to survive this inane outing.'⁴¹

Although the films progressed from terrible to even worse, their near-constant, after-hours airings on US cable television stations like Cinemax and SHOWTIME introduced Marilyn Chambers to a new generation of viewers. Sons and daughters of baby boomers were coming of age in the early nineties. Marilyn's films, which played well into the early 2000s, served as an introduction to erotic material to these young adults—just as her appearances in *Green Door* and *Eve* twenty years prior became their parents' first-time experience with X-rated films.

Marilyn appeared as an actress in about half a dozen Private Screenings productions. For the rest of the productions, she would bookend the film as a hostess and do the voiceover work. She heard from many fans of her X-rated work that they were disappointed she turned to softcore, but, as she said, the films "paid the bills." Still, by the mid nineties, the films' titles became increasingly witless: *Lusty Busty Fantasies*, *Little Shop of Erotica*, and *Incredible Edible Fantasies*. Appearing in them, even as hostess, made her cringe.

"I started doing these wrap-around segments for movies and things like *Lusty Busty Fantasies*. I'm not proud of that stuff," she said.⁴²

The best of the bunch, and Marilyn's favorite, was *Desire*. In it, she plays a demanding, over-the-top soap opera actress who's nasty to all her coworkers. It allowed Marilyn to show her flair for comedy and have fun overacting. She does a serviceable job in most Private Screenings films, but the scripts are terrible. The script for *Desire* was not *Casablanca*, but she palpably relishes the role.

It was during the production of *Desire* that Marilyn began fertility treatments. They worked. In late 1990, she became pregnant.

ON THURSDAY, FEBRUARY 28, 1991, San Francisco Bay Area residents woke to the shocking news that Art Mitchell had been gunned down in his own home the night before. His brother Jim was held on a first-degree murder charge. The news soon reverberated across the country. Fratricide remains a rare type of killing, one not well understood by psychiatrists or law enforcement.⁴³ What was understood was that Jim went to his brother's home in Corte Madera, California, allegedly to confront Art about his increasingly heavy drug use and reckless

FAKING IT

behavior. What wasn't understood was why Jim took a .22 caliber rifle with him and why he fatally shot his brother. "Marilyn was at my dad's funeral," said Liberty Bradford, Art's daughter. "And she was eight months pregnant. This woman huffs and puffs her way to the podium. Her hair was short, and no one really knew who it was. She said, 'Hi, I'm Marilyn Chambers,' and everybody shifted and sat up in their chairs. And she said, 'Art would love it if I went into labor right now.' We were all laughing because it was so true."[44]

After a lengthy trial, which captured local and national attention, Jim was convicted of voluntary manslaughter on February 27, 1992—exactly one year after he shot and killed his brother. Two months later, he received a sentence of six years in prison, to be served at San Quentin, north of San Francisco.[45]

Although Marilyn did not testify at the trial or speak on either brother's behalf, she was besieged with requests to participate in articles, books, documentaries, and television shows about them. She appeared in episodes of hit shows like *E! True Hollywood Story* and *Forensic Files*, among others. Two separate books about the crime were published in 1993. Marilyn participated extensively in one of them, *Bottom Feeders*, penned by reporter John Hubner. The book was optioned by Robert De Niro's production company, Tribeca Films, for a screen adaptation. Marilyn was hired as a consultant and met with De Niro to discuss the project. He wanted to produce and star in the film, but only with Jim's permission. He asked Marilyn if she would visit Jim in prison to try and convince him. She agreed.

She visited Jim at San Quentin. She described him as a "beaten man."[46]

"I know why you're here, Mar," Jim said. "You know I love you, and I'm glad you came to see me, but I'm not interested."[47]

"He said, 'You know, I don't want anyone to capitalize on this,' and he kept calling it 'the tragedy,'" Marilyn recalled. "He said, 'I don't give a flying fuck who's doing it. I don't care if fucking Robert De Niro is doing it. I will never speak to anyone about this—ever.'"[48]

Marilyn told Jim she understood. "I felt stupid for bringing it up," she said.[49]

She told De Niro that Jim wasn't interested, and the project was shelved.

ON MAY 13, 1991, Marilyn gave birth to her daughter, McKenna Marie Taylor, an event Marilyn would later say was the most important of her life.

For the first time, her life was filled with joy. No mainstream movie role, no amount of male adulation, nor any parental approval could compare to the moment Marilyn became a mother. She had survived drugs and alcohol, abusive relationships, and the cutthroat entertainment business and still managed to make an indelible mark on popular culture. She was happily married, clean and sober, and finally, a mother.

"The best thing that ever happened to me was being a mom," she'd often say in interviews. And she meant it.

Bill and Marilyn's home became the spot for neighborhood kids to play as McKenna grew. She baked treats and wanted to be part of every aspect of McKenna's life—from PTA meetings to school pick-ups and drop-offs. It was an idyllic life almost too good to be true.

McKenna now happily recalls the backyard pool at the Moreno Valley house. "My mom and I would swim—skinny dipping, actually," she said. "She told me all about her imaginary friend that she had when she was a kid. It was a boy, and he had a really weird name. And I remember being in the pool, looking at the sky, and talking to her about her imaginary friend. That's probably my earliest memory. I did have one imaginary friend, [but] I can't remember anything about mine. For some reason, I remember talking to her about hers."[50]

Marilyn's sobriety was important to her, as was that of others in the twelve-step programs where she found—and offered—support.

"[S]he helped a huge number of people," Bill Briggs said of his sister. "That was her thing. One after another, people talked about how Marilyn saved their life. And she took a lot of kids under her wing. They saw her as a glamorous figure, but she made sure they didn't get involved in the seamier side of life, as she had."[51]

The programs meant so much that she got a vanity plate for her car that read LUVNA.[52]

Then Bill relapsed.

"I think that destroyed her," McGinn said. "Then we were talking morning, noon, and night. She was calling me in the morning to give me a report, calling me at noon [asking], 'What do I do? What about McKenna? I gotta get her to a sitter. I gotta get him to a meeting.' And she was trying to fix him, fix him, fix him. That went on for a year. Then he got sober."[53]

A year later, he relapsed again. He totaled at least three cars. One of the accidents happened in the morning and was witnessed by neighbors and their children, including McKenna. Marilyn was humiliated. Bill agreed to enter a drug-and-alcohol rehabilitation program. That left his trucking business without a person in charge. McGinn speculated in an interview that Bill's company had been annually earning roughly a million dollars. But his relapses had caused the company to stumble. Marilyn suspended her professional obligations and opportunities to step in and salvage it.

"Now Marilyn is saving the company," McGinn said. "She knows shit about trucking, [but] she brought that company back from bankruptcy."[54]

She was a quick study and sweet-talked the clients. When clients asked about Bill, she told them he had had a hernia or kidney operation.

"If you know Marilyn, she will not lie," McGinn said. She added that when she'd visit Marilyn at work, she would watch "her sit in that office and lie to these customers. And she'd hang up the phone and shake like a dog that just got out of a pool. And she'd say, 'It makes me sick to do this, but I have to. We have to pay our mortgage and eat.'"

The words of Bill's ultimatum from several years prior swirled in her mind. He told her he couldn't see her unless she got clean. The words enraged her at the time, but they resonated now. She knew what he had meant. She couldn't stay married to him unless Bill got sober—and stayed sober. She also had to be a mother and didn't want McKenna exposed to Bill when he was loaded. She was tired of telling the girl that daddy was sick but would be better soon, because it was a lie.

"I can't rescue him anymore," she told McGinn. "I gotta cut myself off."

"And that's how it ended," McGinn said. "She couldn't do it anymore—and stay sober. She had her own sobriety to take care of."[55]

The couple divorced in 1994. Bill kept the Moreno Valley house, and Marilyn got custody of McKenna. Mother and daughter moved to Palmdale, about eighty-two miles northwest. Three or four months after Bill left rehab, he moved to Santa Clarita. Marilyn moved there, too, so shuttling McKenna between the two homes would be easier and provide the three-year-old with stability.

It took about a year for Marilyn to bring Bill's trucking company back from bankruptcy. While she tended to that, she took herself off the market for other opportunities. People stopped calling Marilyn Chambers. When Bill left rehab, he wanted to reinstate himself as sole owner of his trucking company. Even though Marilyn saved the company from going under and helped it thrive, he said he didn't want or need her help. Nor was she entitled to any part of the business. It was still technically in his name, not hers. "Every single person she's ever made money for screwed her, I'm telling you," McGinn said. "And it pisses me off."

In 1995, Marilyn auditioned for a role on an episode of the hit sitcom *Married...with Children*. Shannon Tweed got the part. However, that same year Marilyn received the rare opportunity to make a cameo appearance on another primetime network television sitcom. *Women of the House*, a spinoff of the popular show *Designing Women*, starred Delta Burke as a United States House of Representatives member. CBS ordered thirteen episodes of the sitcom, and the first eight aired. The show, however, was critically panned and did not click with viewers. CBS canceled the series after episode eight. Marilyn's episode was number nine. Three additional episodes had already been filmed. (The show was canceled before the thirteenth episode was filmed.) Fortunately, cable television station Lifetime picked up the remaining four episodes and aired them on September 8, 1995. And yet, it was another example of an opportunity that was on track to give Marilyn one of her biggest audiences in decades, and, at the last minute, it was relegated to a network with a much smaller viewership.

The episode in which she appeared, "Women in Film," was rather somber for a sitcom. Burke's character attends a congressional hearing on the violence against women depicted in films and on television. During the hearing, a host of prominent female stars appear as themselves and "testify" before the congressional committee to discuss their personal experiences as women in show business. Carol Burnett, Roseanne Barr, Shirley Jones, and Rita Moreno are among them.

Marilyn appeared refined, dressed in a dark blazer and skirt with her hair in an updo.

"I've been blackballed by the mainstream film industry, which I find very violent because I was a porn star," Marilyn tells the committee. "Under the current rating system, it's more socially acceptable to cut off a woman's breast than to kiss it."[56]

MARILYN'S HOME WAS DECORATED with a few mementos from her career. There was an Ivory Snow box on display as well as a framed *Le Bellybutton* poster. Photos, held in place by magnets, covered the refrigerator, including one of Marilyn and Robert De Niro. When McKenna was around ten, she made the connection that the woman in these photos, "Marilyn Chambers," was her mother. When McKenna asked about it, Marilyn explained that she was an actress. But she thought her daughter was still too young to learn the more explicit details of her career.

McKenna often saw "Marilyn Chambers" when she flipped through a *TV Guide*. She'd ask to watch the films. Marilyn hesitated.

"But I want to see you act," McKenna would protest.

Finally, Marilyn relented. "OK," she said, "but only certain parts."[57]

The pair would settle in on the couch. An excited McKenna would watch her famous mother on television—mostly the Private Screenings films—and a nervous Marilyn readied the remote control to mute certain scenes and cover her daughter's eyes.

Marilyn and Bill kept in touch. Over time, a post-divorce acrimony dissolved, to be replaced by friendship.

"It took a while, a few years, for all of us to find our footing and how to navigate it," McKenna said of the separation. "Then it was totally amicable. We had shared birthday parties. I don't ever remember having separate birthday parties, with one birthday party with my mom, [and] one birthday party with my dad."[58]

Marilyn was thrilled that Bill maintained his sobriety. She hoped if he was able to stay in the program, that they could reconcile and remarry. But it wouldn't happen. Bill met a woman in the twelve-step program he attended; a year later, he married her.

For Marilyn, the combined strain of the divorce, financial worries, and parental duties, coupled with her mixed feelings about Bill's new relationship, created an immense amount of stress. Eventually, she once again turned to drugs and alcohol to dull the pain and ease her mind.

"I remember having a distinct feeling of knowing and being uncomfortable with the drinking," McKenna said, who was about ten-years-old. "Not because I would see her drinking or chugging beer or anything like that. But I started to pick up on cues when she was drunk."[59]

When McKenna asked Marilyn if she'd been drinking, Marilyn would say she hadn't. McKenna knew better. "I could smell wine on her breath," McKenna said. She began spending more time at her father's and stepmother's house. They were sober, and her school was closer to their home. Being around two sober people reinforced McKenna's intuition that her mother was not sober.

However, McKenna was the most important person in Marilyn's life. Marilyn didn't want to jeopardize their relationship or lose custody of her.

When McKenna was about ten-years-old and staying with her father, she received a phone call. It was her mother.

"I wanted to let you know that I'm going to a meeting, and I'm getting sober," Marilyn told McKenna.[60]

McKenna was thrilled, and Marilyn once again began attending twelve-step meetings.

"I think those first couple of years when my dad moved in with my stepmom, that was hard for her," McKenna said. "Then you're having to share your kid with another woman. And [my stepmom] had a bigger family, so I would do things with them. There are so many things that I look back on and think, 'God, that must have been so fucking hard.'"[61]

PURE
The Sexual Revolutions of Marilyn Chambers

Holidays, like Christmas, were especially difficult for Marilyn. McKenna would celebrate with her father, stepmother, and a large extended family. Then she would visit her mother, and it was just the two of them. McKenna loved it, but, in hindsight, she realized the loneliness her mother experienced.

"I probably think too much about it," McKenna said. "You know, she felt alone. That makes me really sad because I probably could have done more to make her not feel like that. Now that I'm a mother, I just can't imagine how she felt about certain things."[62]

AFTER THE DIVORCE, MARILYN dated a few men, but none seriously. Many of the men she dated exhibited similar characteristics to Chuck and D'Apice.

McGinn, Marilyn's friend, had a thirty-year career as a family law mediator, which gave her an insight into what she dubbed Marilyn's "Svengali-ism." "She had this thing [of being with] men who wanted to control her and made her feel a certain way," McGinn said. "She was just attracted to it. And the worse they treated her, the more she loved him."[63]

Marilyn didn't disagree.

"I chose men who were violent and very sexy, but I could never choose the proper mate," she said. "That doesn't go for the last guy I had my child with, but we had our problems. There's drugs; there's alcohol; there's all kinds of stuff involved in any relationship that I've ever had."[64]

Although Bill treated her well—and may have been the only man to do so—his relapses, new sobriety, and remarriage took him from Marilyn's life. Other boyfriends came and went. The person Marilyn shared the closest bond with, akin to a marriage, was McGinn. As Marilyn felt more insecure and anxious after the divorce, she began to rely more heavily on McGinn. It was the closest dependent relationship she'd had since Chuck. They wouldn't just converse as friends and mothers. Marilyn wouldn't make a move without McGinn's approval.

McGinn explained that Marilyn had a kind of insecurity about nearly everything. "The only word I can think of is indecisive," McGinn said. She and Marilyn would speak every night at 8:30PM, seven days a week if they were not together. "And there were questions about everything. Everything from, 'Should I sign this contract?' to 'Did you look at [the contract]?' to 'What kind of jeans [should I] buy McKenna for Christmas?' It was just frantic."[65]

McGinn continued, "These men that made decisions for her gave Marilyn comfort in some strange way. And then it was me. In the last ten years of her life, I was probably the closest person to her besides her daughter."[66]

FAKING IT

THE HIT FILM *BOOGIE Nights*, released in 1997, revitalized public interest in the golden age of pornography. The main character, played by Mark Wahlberg, was inspired by John Holmes. Marilyn disliked the film. She said it wasn't an accurate representation of the industry as she experienced it.

"I absolutely don't get it," she said. "It wasn't anything that I knew. I couldn't really deal with it at all. Maybe that was what the porn business was, but I was with Chuck Traynor."[67]

Marilyn's oft-stated intention never to return to X-rated films—that part of her life was over after a good run, she thought—took a hit when a lucrative, three-picture deal appeared. In 1999, Marilyn signed with VCA, a premier adult film production company. Her primary motive was money. The salary would provide a much-needed source of revenue. She could even squirrel some of it away for McKenna's college tuition. Her secondary motive was safety. Each production required condom use by all performers. Former adult film star Jane Hamilton, also known as Veronica Hart, would direct all three films. Having a female director and someone who knew the industry so well encouraged Marilyn.

Marilyn and Hamilton worked together as actresses in the early nineties, completing two Private Screening films. Because both women acted well, they'd finished a non-sex scene in record time. As women in the industry, they'd developed mutual respect and camaraderie. Marilyn had been so impressed with her co-star, she'd suggested they pair up for a *Cagney & Lacey*-style detective show, although nothing came of it.

It wasn't the first time the two had met. When Hamilton was an aspiring actress in the seventies, she briefly met Marilyn at a party.

"Marilyn Chambers was it; she was the 'it' girl," recalled Hamilton. "[It] was like, 'Oh, my God, it's Marilyn Chambers!' You know, that kind of thing. I went to a dinner, and I think she was with Chuck Traynor at that time. She had all the hullabaloo around her and everything. It was just like, 'Wow!' I wasn't jealous of her, but I really looked up to her. And I thought, 'Oh, my God, wouldn't that be great to be that successful and do something you love?' Because she was it."[68]

When VCA wooed her back, Marilyn negotiated a nice deal for herself.

"She was the only star that I know that actually got a royalty on her movies," Hamilton said. "I don't know the amount, but that was unheard of."[69]

Russell Hampshire, the founder of VCA, informed Hamilton that Marilyn Chambers would be returning to X-rated films, and he wanted her to direct. Hamilton was ecstatic.

"She was just doing it for the money, let's be honest," Hamilton said. "She got a really good deal, I think, from Russell. Maybe not as much as she deserved. But

Marilyn struck a three-picture deal with VCA Studios in 1999. Although she heavily promoted the films, the reviews were brutal. *VCA Studios Publicity*.

FAKING IT

it definitely was good with the kickback on all the DVDs or videos being sold."[70]

The first film was titled *Still Insatiable*, in a nod to Marilyn's classic X-rated feature. When news broke about the forty-seven-year-old Marilyn's return to the industry, every major adult actor and actress wanted to be in the film. VCA contract players were required to be in the film, and none balked at the opportunity to work with Marilyn Chambers. Hamilton coordinated an omnium gatherum of adult stars from numerous generations.

Nonetheless, Marilyn struggled with the decision to return to adult films. She was incredibly self-conscious about her appearance. Fifteen years had passed since her last X-rated feature, *Insatiable II*, and seven years since she had last appeared nude in a Private Screenings film. Having given birth and gained weight, even another breast enlargement procedure couldn't wholly bolster her confidence. She also knew what her fans expected of her—and what they hoped to see. She knew she couldn't look as firm, sun-kissed, and limber as she had in *Insatiable*. She was also well aware of the ageist double standard for a woman in show business, especially one who was rightly considered a sex goddess.

She thought, perhaps, she could show women (and men) in their mid forties that sex could still be enjoyable and give credence to the adage that women hit their sexual peak over the age of forty.

"She was no kid at that time," Hamilton said. "She was an older woman. And as we age, our bodies are certainly different than our twenty- or thirty-year-old selves. I think that part of it was very difficult for her."[71]

Hamilton surrounded Marilyn with crew members she thought Marilyn would get along with, including hair and makeup artist Lee Garland.

"Between the care we put into her wardrobe and everything, I think it was okay for her," Hamilton said.[72] She wanted Marilyn to feel as comfortable and sexy as possible. More than two decades later, as she recounted the making of the film, it sounded as though Hamilton was still trying to convince herself that she was successful in this endeavor. Hamilton revered Marilyn as an actress and industry pioneer, loved her as a friend, and knew she was deeply concerned about her appearance.

"The acting for her was a breeze," Hamilton said. "That was no problem. I think that was fun for her. We spent some money on those shows; they weren't just little one-day wonders. And I hope that she was happy with the outcome. It was great for the guys to be able to work with the legend.

"I certainly tried to make good movies. As a director, I had my artistic vision. And believe me, we really think of it as art."[73]

PURE

The Sexual Revolutions of Marilyn Chambers

On the first day of filming, Hamilton spotted a familiar face: Chuck Traynor. Marilyn had asked him to come down to help ease her anxiety.

Hamilton knew that Marilyn and Chuck had maintained a friendship after their divorce. "She had such a connection to him, and she loved him so much," Hamilton said. "He looked over the contracts. He was completely businesslike. She didn't mind being told what to do by somebody she had complete faith in, and that was Chuck Traynor to her."[74]

Chuck was only on set for a day or two. In addition to making Marilyn feel comfortable, he wanted to ensure the atmosphere was right and that Hamilton was trustworthy.

"When he figured out I would always try and make her feel comfortable," Hamilton said, "I would always treat her with respect, and [I] wasn't going to try and take advantage of her, [that] we would somehow work it out to get what she needed and what I needed, and that we were going to work together—then he just kind of said, 'Oh, you're okay.' And he never came back to set again."[75]

Still Insatiable was the first of the three films. Instead of continuing the storyline of Sandra Chase, Marilyn's character in the first two *Insatiable* films, *Still Insatiable* nonsensically opted for a new plot and characters altogether. The script, written by Legs McNeil, was a riff on the largely forgotten 1998 film *Bulworth*, a political satire starring Warren Beatty. Marilyn plays Charlotte Ballworth, a conservative senator who campaigns on an anti-pornography stance. After privately watching some of the films she's vocally opposing, she gets aroused and engages in sexual activity.

Marilyn does a serviceable job but looks uncomfortable and self-conscious throughout—particularly in the sex scenes. She wore a bustier which exposed her breasts but covered her stomach.

'Obviously, this is not the Marilyn Chambers of *Behind the Green Door*,' *Adult Video News* noted in its four-star review. 'Though she seems to enjoy her four robust sex scenes, and she'll be the reason that this will be one of 1999's biggest hits, the rest of the erotic segments give this high-budget story its flair.'[76]

The film's highlight is a brief scene in which Senator Ballworth converses with three uptight, ultra-conservative women played by Georgina Spelvin, Gloria Leonard, and Hamilton. It's a nice ironic touch to have four industry stalwarts cheekily skewering their images by playing women so vehemently opposed to pornography.

"You know, frankly, I don't know how any woman could allow themselves to be so degraded having sex in front of a camera," Leonard's character snipes. "I mean, they must all be forced into it, don't you think?"

Still Insatiable was given a big build-up before its release to VHS and DVD

Marilyn attends a home entertainment convention in 1999 to promote *Still Insatiable*, her first X-rated film in fifteen years. *Celebrity Photo Agency.*

PURE
The Sexual Revolutions of Marilyn Chambers

in the summer of 1999. A billboard on the Sunset Strip in Hollywood heralded the return of America's girl-next-door to the world of X-rated entertainment. The reviews were mixed. Some were just downright mean.

One male critic's brutal take read: 'Marilyn looks old and fat and tries to cover herself using the modified, extended cummerbund method in all scenes but is unsuccessful in dispelling the idea that you might need a forklift to turn her over.'[77]

Marilyn returned to the O'Farrell Theater in late July 1999 for a three-night stint. The theater was celebrating its thirtieth anniversary, and her appearances helped promote *Still Insatiable*. It had been eleven years since her last performance there and the first since Art Mitchell's death. After having served three years of his six-year San Quentin sentence for killing his brother, Jim Mitchell had been released on October 3, 1997.[78] He had been given three years probation. He had returned to the theater to assume some managerial duties.

Marilyn was greeted warmly by her long ago adopted city. Mayor Willie Brown declared Wednesday, July 28, 1999, "Marilyn Chambers Day" in the city and county of San Francisco.[79] Brown praised Marilyn's artistic presence, vision, and energy. It was a bittersweet, befitting homecoming to one of the most provoking pop culture icons the city had produced.

"San Francisco was my mother's Hollywood," McKenna said. Receiving the honor from where she got her big break "must have been thrilling, and a mirror image of how much she could influence not only people but also an entire city."[80]

Marilyn told the *San Francisco Chronicle* that she intended to perform at the theater several times over the next three years—until she turned fifty.

"I've got to pull out all the stops as far as my career goes," she said. "I've got to take these next three years and do the best I can to make some money."[81]

The money, she told the *Chronicle*, was largely for McKenna. Marilyn told the paper that she fretted when McKenna entered her teens in the early 2000s because she thought classmates might tease her when they discovered her mother was Marilyn Chambers. She said she wanted to provide her daughter with a sexual moral compass.

"In a world that's so sexually bizarre, she needs a moral role model," Marilyn said, adding that she had never allowed boyfriends or dates to spend the night at the house where she and McKenna lived. "She does not deserve for her mom to live out her screen image at home. That would not be fair to her."[82]

In the same interview, Marilyn ruminated about what would happen in her career when she turned fifty in 2002.

"I'm really into computers," she said. "I can run a company to the utmost. I'm a great businesswoman, and that's what I want to do. I can't be in front of the camera, but I can always be Marilyn Chambers."[83]

DVD was relatively new and fast replacing VHS. Marilyn didn't own the copyright for any of her films. Now that she had returned to X-rated films, it seemed the perfect time to release her older titles in the new physical media format. Someone was bound to make money off Marilyn's name, but it wasn't her. Although she participated in some of the DVD bonus features, like feature-length commentary, she wasn't paid a dime for a single DVD sale. It was likely considered that the release of her classic film would spur sales of her new films. Her fans were more interested in watching the younger Marilyn Chambers. (A 2007 reissue of *Insatiable* sold thousands of copies, which only increased after Marilyn's death.[84])

Dark Chambers, the second of three films for VCA Productions, was released in August 2000. The reviews were slightly more friendly. 'Marilyn [is] better in her four scenes, in fact, than…her previous comeback tape,' noted *Adult Video News*.[85]

The last of the three films, *Edge Play*, was released a year later.

'Rumor has it that this is Marilyn Chambers' last (no, really) adult feature, and if so, the blonde veteran of the porn wars is going out with a bang,' *Adult Video News* wrote of the film in its four-star review. '*Edge Play* is Chambers' best show to date, with plenty of hot sex and the proverbial 'cast of thousands.' (Well, maybe not actual thousands, but that party scene near the end has more extras than anybody in this biz can shake a stick at.)'[86]

In both films, she's surrounded by male and female contract players, most of whom appear to be in their late twenties or early thirties. All of them are youthful, buff, or perky-breasted. By contrast, Marilyn's age showed. Only in *Dark Chambers* was she reunited with one of her former co-stars, Herschel Savage, who appeared in *Up 'n' Coming*. (Ron Jeremy, who filmed a scene with Marilyn for her *Private Fantasies* series in the mid eighties, appeared in a non-sex role in *Still Insatiable*.) It would have been interesting, perhaps more erotic, and certainly nostalgic, if Marilyn had been paired with more of her former male co-stars. In that respect, she deserves enormous credit for appearing in the VCA films. It's possible that many of her former male co-stars had also gained weight and wouldn't have dared to appear naked and vulnerable in front of the cameras.

The criticisms did not go unnoticed by Marilyn, and the attempts to debase her were, unfortunately, successful.

"It hurts so bad," Marilyn told the *Riverfront Times* in 2001. "They're mocking you, telling you [to] go put your clothes back on. I can't allow that to happen. It's stupid. But they're right. Enough is enough. I'm tired. I'm tired of the bullshit. I don't mean to sound so bitter. I'm getting too old. I felt like I should have never done the last movies I've done."[87]

PURE *The Sexual Revolutions of Marilyn Chambers*

ON MAY 28, 2000, William Briggs, Marilyn's father, died. He was seventy-nine-years-old.[88] Five months later, Ginny, William's wife and Marilyn's mother, died. She was seventy-seven.[89] Neither obituary mentioned their divorce or separation. Marilyn had spent time in Washington State with her sister, Jann, caring for their parents in their final days. Although her parents never accepted Marilyn's career choices nor provided the approval she once so desperately craved, she found forgiveness in her heart before they passed. The anger and hurt weren't worth holding onto, she thought. She was a mother now; she understood some of the difficult choices her parents had faced while raising her.

The time she and Jann spent together was healing, too. With McKenna spending most of her time at her father's, Marilyn was already thinking about empty nest syndrome. Now that her relationship with her sister was on the mend, and they shared their grief about their parents, Marilyn considered moving to Washington State when McKenna went off to college.

Jann remembered when Marilyn came to Washington for one of her son's weddings: "We were coming back [from the wedding], and she was driving back with me and my best friend to California. I had the tape of ABBA's *Mamma Mia!* And we sang the whole tape all the way home for, like, five hours. We just kept replaying it, the three of us singing all the songs. She was sitting in the front seat with me. I just remember looking over at her; she looked so happy, just belting it out, window open. And we're driving or flying down the highway. We were having a really good time as sisters. That was good."[90]

GRIM NEWS GREETED MARILYN on her fiftieth birthday: Linda Lovelace had died. She was fifty-three. She had been in a car accident on April 3 and suffered massive injuries. Marilyn had heard about the accident and Linda's need for a liver transplant. She sent Linda's family some money. Marilyn, who always believed in the supernatural, found it unsettling that the woman whose likeness and shadow from which she could never escape had perished on her birthday. She took it as a bad omen.

The year of Linda's death coincided with the thirtieth anniversary of *Deep Throat*. Linda's oft-told tale was rehashed and reexamined. What was her legacy? Was she the victim of an abusive husband and a heartless industry? A feminist hero? A sexual icon? Maybe it didn't matter.

A year before she died, Linda had returned to the same industry she'd excoriated. She posed for the adult magazine *Leg Show*. She also made several convention appearances. She happily signed *Deep Throat* memorabilia as "Linda

FAKING IT

Lovelace," the same name she desperately tried to forget and simultaneously keep in the public consciousness.

Three months to the day after Linda's death, Chuck Traynor died of a heart attack in Chatsworth, California. It's almost as if, even in death, Chuck refused to let go of Linda Lovelace. Whereas Linda's death warranted news coverage from major media outlets, Chuck's death wasn't even given an obituary in a local newspaper.

Despite their intemperate and often violent relationship, Marilyn never wavered in her reverence for Chuck, even after his death.

Still grieving the loss of her parents, she decided to earn a certification as a home health aide and nursing assistant. Chuck had never allowed Marilyn to attend college. She wanted to take a few classes in Las Vegas, when they lived there in the seventies, but he felt the idea of a college-educated "Marilyn Chambers" would turn off her male fans. It might be coincidental that she waited until Chuck's death to further her education. Once she earned her certification in 2003, she volunteered to work with end-of-life patients and the elderly in hospice care. She considered returning to college full-time to earn her degree in nursing, just like her mother had done, but decided against it. She told a reporter that she didn't have the energy for it—or the money.[91] Now that her X-rated film career was officially over, and she no longer made films for Private Screenings, Marilyn needed to pick up work where she could find it. Residuals from Private Screenings helped, but they didn't provide enough to sustain a reasonable living, nor to pay the rent, insurance, and other bills, never mind raising a pre-teen daughter.

She took a series of odd jobs. She worked at an animal food company, hauling bags of feed. She adored animals, but worried people would recognize her. Her brother, a car salesman for nearly his entire adult career, helped land her a job at a local dealership. McKenna said her mother felt ashamed and embarrassed taking these jobs. At one particularly low point, Marilyn went door-to-door in her trailer park and asked neighbors if she could clean their homes for pay.

Marilyn often wondered what had happened to all the money she'd made as "Marilyn Chambers." She should have asked Chuck more questions about how he was investing—and spending—her money. However, it seems unlikely he would answer her truthfully, if at all. For five years after they split, he took fifty percent of her earnings. When she dated D'Apice, he'd spent a lot of her money. At the time, she was supporting an expensive cocaine addiction. Other funds were handed over to the legal teams she'd hired following her arrests. When she married Bill, she still made money but he made more. Following their divorce, she was left with more questions than answers about her financial situation.

She made appearances at ComiCon and other celebrity autograph conventions. These were lucrative opportunities for one or two days' work, but the days were long and grueling. The one thing she loved was interacting with fans.

"She enjoyed the money," McGinn said, "and the adoration. I mean, who's going to turn that down? They did obsess over her."[92]

She occasionally produced X-rated films and released a series of *Marilyn Chambers' Guide To...* DVDs on subjects like oral sex and dirty dancing. She was the hostess and provided the voiceover.

Bill, whose company was valued at millions, paid Marilyn only $100 a month in child support. McGinn liked Bill very much, but she saw her best friend struggling financially. She suggested to Marilyn that she take Bill to court. Marilyn said no. She understood the logic of McGinn's suggestion, but she hated the idea of taking her ex-husband to court.

"Marilyn had so much pride," McGinn said.[93]

McGinn persisted and told Marilyn that if she felt bad about taking extra money from Bill, to put it in savings or spend it on something McKenna wanted. Marilyn relented and she sued Bill. In court, Marilyn kept apologizing to Bill and the judge. McGinn, who'd accompanied her friend, took Marilyn aside and told her to stop. There was nothing to be sorry for, she said. Marilyn and Bill ended up settling. He agreed to pay $700 a month.

"My dad and stepmom were pretty well off," McKenna said. "My dad was able to give me so much more than my mom monetarily. And I know that really affected her poorly. She told me a few times, 'This is hard for me that you can get this, and I can't give this to you.' But she never made it a thing because I could tell she didn't want me to feel bad."

Still, McKenna was angry at her mother for taking her father to court. At the time, she thought it unnecessary and embarrassing.

"I wish I could talk to her about it now because I totally get it," she said.[94]

IN 2004, MARILYN TEAMED up with boxing and gambling industry magnate Charles Jay in a quixotic bid for the White House.[95]

Charles Jay made his living in the sports betting business. In 1996 he promoted a boxing match for pay-per-view television in the Miami-Fort Lauderdale area. The match took place during a celebrity autograph convention. The expectation was that the celebrities who appeared at the convention would also attend the fight. One star never showed up: Marilyn. Jay was miffed. The next day his friend Jim Stinson called and invited Jay to dinner. Marilyn would join, too, Stinson said.

FAKING IT

"To hell with her!" Jay replied. "She stiffed us last night."[96]

With a little coaxing, Jay relented and decided to join them. The trio dined out and then went to a couple of bars. As Jay and Marilyn talked, she complimented him on his business savvy and how he interacted with people. It occurred to him that she might have thought he was a famous businessman.

"I'm not famous," he told her. "*You're* famous."

She corrected him. "No, I'm not famous; I'm *infamous.*"

"I never forgot [that]," Jay recalled. "But I think she wasn't giving herself enough credit."[97]

As the evening drew to a close, Stinson said he was ready to turn in.

"What I didn't realize is that Jim was trying to fix us up," Jay remembered. "And we stayed by each other's side for the next eight days."[98]

Marilyn flew back to L.A. but returned to Florida a few weeks later for Jay's birthday. She gave him some sex toys. The two dated for a time. They even discussed working on some projects and recorded a pilot show for a radio program called *Chuck & Chambers*. However, Marilyn didn't just want to collaborate with Jay; she wanted him to take control of her affairs.

"Honestly, I believe...she may have expected that I would get involved in her business a little," he said. "And I wasn't very interested in that. I didn't want to have a Chuck Traynor-type of relationship. In other words, I didn't want to control her like that. I didn't want to mix business with personal. It's not an unusual way to feel."[99]

Jay wasn't certain if his lack of interest in taking control was a major cause of tension in their relationship.

"She underpriced herself," Jay stated. "And I think maybe there was a little bit of—it wasn't a lack of self-esteem, it was a lack of confidence. [It was] a lack of saying, 'Hey, I know my worth.' And this is where she could have had a real agent, not just a guy who tried to help her out; somebody who was actually an entertainment agent that could have helped her along the way."[100]

The couple broke up after several months of dating. There was a period of estrangement, but they reconnected and became friends. Then Jay decided to get into politics. Jay won the presidential nomination on the Personal Choice Party ticket with Marilyn as his running mate. She agreed to the longshot bid as long as she didn't have to participate in any debates.

The pair secured enough signatures to be added to the ballot in Utah.

"We're trying to get on the ticket in five other states," Marilyn explained. "I've never been into politics because I've never felt that an actress needs to spout her political beliefs—but I'm not a reluctant candidate. When Charles Jay asked me if I wanted to do this, I thought he was kidding. Once my name and biography were on the site, I thought I better get going."[101]

The Personal Choice Party, in its constitution, sought to limit government involvement in citizens' personal life. The party believed that as long as people weren't "hurting anyone else," they had the right to choose how to spend their time, wealth, life, and honor.

'The purpose of government is to prevent us from harming others and to prevent others from harming us,' their constitution reads. 'That is all we should expect or allow [the] government to do. It is not the job of [the] government to stop us from harming ourselves or to make us help others. That is our responsibility as individuals.'[102]

Added Marilyn: 'The candidates with the Personal Choice Party have the freedom to [compose] their own platforms, and mine is built on the right to have your personal choices. Americans are supposed to have the Constitutional right to partake in whatever activities they want to, without restrictions. That's not quite how the country's being run. They use their power to decide what American citizens can or can't do or what they can and can't say.'[103]

Marilyn and Jay campaigned on several issues, including abolishing the Federal Communications Commission; legalizing same-sex marriage nationwide; and maintaining the integrity of the Constitution's Second Amendment, which gives Americans the right to bear arms.

'I used to own a gun shop in Las Vegas called The Survival Store,' Marilyn said. 'It's a good thing for people to register their guns, but there are criminals that can do that, too. I need a gun in my home if somebody breaks in. I want to be able to shoot them. I also want to be able to protect my country.'[104]

Despite making the ballot in Utah, she was not courting any Mormon votes.

'Personally, I don't approve of polygamy,' she said. 'It's been around for years, but it always seems to be a group of men having power over women and children. The men have the power to do whatever they want. It's not about equal rights.'

She continued: 'I'm very serious about standing up for the rights of others. When people talk about freedom of speech, very rarely do they concern themselves with standing up for the freedom of others. I spoke to this agent who thought I was making a mockery out of the system. Maybe I'll get some attention from this, but it's not a joke.'[105]

Jay thought Marilyn's involvement in the campaign was more helpful than harmful. Her notoriety gave the campaign some exposure. Jay said he was inundated with requests for campaign buttons—but only because her picture was on it.

FAKING IT

One thing that can't go unsaid here is that Marilyn, in addition to being well-known, is also a very strong presence in terms of her identification with the First Amendment, Freedom of Speech issues," he said. "It would be well argued that her work and her existence in the adult entertainment business probably had a lot to do with leading it to where it is today, which is a rather mainstream business. She was a real pioneer in that regard. She's been involved in a lot of Freedom of Speech issues in the past. In terms of all the candidates running this year, she is the strongest in identifying and advancing the First Amendment. So, there is a political usefulness to her involvement as well that I think can't go unrecognized.[106]

The pair weren't able to make it onto any other state ballots. On election day, the Jay-Chambers ticket finished sixth in the presidential balloting in Utah with 946 votes.[107] George W. Bush was elected to a second term as President.

After the election, Jay moved to Beverly Hills. Marilyn helped him look for an apartment. Jay hoped the pair would get back together romantically, but they never did.

MARILYN'S DRINKING DIDN'T ENTIRELY keep her from performing tasks or fulfilling duties, but it adversely affected her relationships—including with McKenna. Sometimes, Marilyn's daughter was simply too angry at her mother's drinking to show up for get-togethers on Marilyn's court-appointed visitation days.

"I was so mad at my mom," McKenna recalled. "And I remember her crying, and I can only imagine now how embarrassed she probably was because I'm pretty sure she was drinking."[108]

When McKenna entered high school, she spent most of her time at her father's house, down the street from the school. However, her father relapsed several times and was in and out of rehab. Unlike Marilyn, Bill's addictions all but destroyed his ability to function.

"I kind of just took care of myself," McKenna said. "My mom would say, 'Why don't you come and stay here?' And I would still [say], 'I'm just gonna stay in my house.' I didn't know what my dad's rehab really meant, but I think I was pushed to be a parent [to myself], even when I didn't have to be. I was independent, which is a regret that I have of not spending more time with my mom when I could have."[109]

When McKenna was a teenager, Marilyn told her about her career. McKenna remembered being slightly embarrassed at first but not overly shocked or upset. Regarding her career, Marilyn told her daughter, "You can ask me *anything.*"

Marilyn became the go-to expert for McKenna's friends if they had questions about sex or relationships.

"She was an open book," McKenna said. "Anytime a friend had a question, my mom would say, 'OK, c'mon, let's go talk about it.' They could ask her anything."

Marilyn said of McKenna: "She's a great kid, and we tell each other that we love each other all the time. We have a very special and amazing relationship. She understands me and realizes that that whole film business was but just one small fragment of what makes up the total of who and what I am."[110]

Bill's relapses and rehab stints proved a breaking point for his still-sober wife, who divorced him when McKenna was sixteen-years-old.

"I was devastated," McKenna remembered. "Even though my life was very dysfunctional, it was functionally dysfunctional. My mom got along with her. I have this family, right? And when they divorced, that was just, like, 'Are you fucking kidding me?'"[111]

McKenna loved spending time with sober Marilyn. The girl was never sure of whether her mom was sober or not, so often did she enter and exit twelve-step programs. If Marilyn wasn't sober, McKenna was uncomfortable and angry.

Bill's situation grew far more dire. As a drug user, every relapse damaged his body. Both Marilyn and McKenna began to psychologically prepare for his death.

"My mom would come and stay with me," said McKenna. "She never said the words, but I could tell by her engagement with me and conversations that she was trying, in her head, to prepare for that to happen."[112]

"I'LL STILL GET CALLS from [agencies] such as William Morris, and we get to the point where we're going to sign, and they say, 'We don't know what to do with you,'" bemoaned Marilyn. "The thing about my career is that I've always played myself. That's always been a problem. None of these roles have been a big stretch for me. They didn't do my career any good."[113]

Marilyn picked up a few small roles in ultra-low-budget independent films. The most significant was that of a no-nonsense Rhode Island police officer in a black-and-white crime drama called *Solitaire*. There was no nudity, innuendoes, or references to Marilyn Chambers, the sex star.

Filming in New England was a homecoming for her; it allowed her to visit and reconnect with people she knew, and she loved the role.

"She said she always fantasized about playing a cop," remembered Frank Durant, who co-wrote and directed the film.[114] He originally approached her about another project before sending her the script for *Solitaire*. She accepted the role and flew to Rhode Island for a few days of filming.

"She could make you blush with her stories, but she was so down-to-earth, very engaging, very humble," said Durant. "That was one of her superpowers."[115]

Her name added credibility and star power to the young writer-director's film, and when word got out that Marilyn Chambers was making a movie in Rhode Island, the media, onlookers, and well-wishers visited the set to catch a glimpse of the superstar. Still, Durant remembers, one or two bystanders didn't want to meet or engage with her because of her past in adult films.

Durant spent several days getting to know Marilyn and recalls that she prided herself on being a good mother. When asked if she wanted her daughter to become Marilyn Chambers, Jr., she said, "Over my dead body."

She wanted to ensure everyone was at ease on the set and took her role seriously.[116]

"She was very patient with me and the young actors," recalled Durant, who was thirty at the time the film was made. "It takes a special kind of actor to take directions from a young kid, but she really cared and got what the writing was about. She had a raw talent. She was very simple, in a good way. She didn't want to come across as complicated."[117]

In early 2009, Marilyn flew to New York to audition for the play *The Deep Throat Sex Scandal*, about the making of the infamous film and its aftermath. She read for the role of Shana Babcock, the best friend of Linda Lovelace.

"She killed it," David Bertolino, who wrote the play, told *The Daily Beast*. "I think she knew she could act, but I think she wanted to prove it to the general public. She was phenomenal. I had goosebumps."[118]

Bertolino also said Marilyn told him he judged Chuck too harshly in the script and requested some changes to cast him in a more favorable light.

Marilyn got the part. McGinn, her longtime friend, helped her finalize the contract. Later, McGinn recalled that Marilyn was more nervous about leaving McKenna in California than about appearing onstage. McGinn reminded her that she was doing this project for McKenna, and that McKenna would be starting college in the fall. The play was scheduled to open in late April 2009, but Marilyn had one non-negotiable in her contract: she had to be in California to attend McKenna's high school graduation.

"She said, 'If it means I lose the part, I lose the part,'" McGinn said. "She had to be there."[119]

The producers agreed, and Marilyn returned to California in early April to memorize her lines, prepare to return to the stage for the first time in nearly thirty years, and see her only child graduate high school.

PURE *The Sexual Revolutions of Marilyn Chambers*

MARILYN HAD A PRECISE evening routine.

Shortly before 7:00PM, she'd pour herself a glass of chardonnay, sit on the couch, and light a cigarette. At 7:00PM, she'd call McKenna, and then she'd call McGinn. After the calls ended, she went to sleep. She talked to her daughter and friend multiple times daily, but the evening calls were always part of the habit.

On Saturday, April 11, 2009, Marilyn spoke to McGinn around 5:00PM and then drove to a Rite Aid in Van Nuys to pick up an Easter card for McKenna as well as some items for her Easter basket. Easter Sunday was the following day. A timestamp on the Rite Aid receipt read 6:51PM. Marilyn drove home. Around 8:00PM, neither McGinn nor McKenna had heard from Marilyn.

McGinn called her and left a message, "I guess you fell asleep."

Shortly before 10:00PM, a neighbor called and left a message. Marilyn's dog had been barking incessantly.

"Marilyn, I love you," the neighbor said, "but please shut up your fucking dog!"

The dog never barked when Marilyn was home, only when she wasn't there. But Marilyn's car was in the driveway. The neighbor assumed Marilyn was home. When the dog continued barking, the neighbor phoned again.

"Please, Marilyn, the dog is going non-stop inside your house. Can't you hear that?"

McKenna spent most of Easter Sunday at her father's house. She'd left multiple voicemail messages for her mother but still hadn't heard from her. It was highly unusual, but she didn't think anything was wrong. Around 10:30PM on April 12, McKenna drove to Santa Clarita. She wanted to spend what was left of the holiday with her mother. She also planned to review plans for her graduation celebration. She arrived and knocked on the door. There was no response. Inside, the dog barked incessantly. McKenna walked to the neighbor's home and retrieved a spare key.

After using it to enter her home, she discovered Marilyn's lifeless body on the living room floor. She rushed over and tried to wake her. She cried and screamed. The neighbor heard McKenna and called 911. The police officers found no evidence of foul play. It appeared Marilyn had fallen, although there was no obvious trauma to her head, face, or body. Her legs were already in a state of rigor mortis and showed signs of lividity. Some blood pooled near her left hand. The tip of her index finger had bite marks. The dog had sensed that something was wrong and had bitten the finger to get her attention. When Marilyn didn't respond, the dog started barking.

McGinn believes Marilyn died on Saturday, April 11. A glass of chardonnay remained untouched, and a lit cigarette had burned down to one long ash. It seemed Marilyn had returned from Rite Aid, poured her usual glass of wine, lit a cigarette, and was about to make her regular evening phone calls to McKenna and McGinn when she suddenly died.

The paramedics told McGinn that they were required to list the date and time that they found the body. Marilyn's official date of death was April 12.

At first, it was thought that Marilyn had died of a massive heart attack. She had not been in ill health. She didn't even have a cold. The autopsy showed that the cause of death was "hemorrhage (bleeding) around the brain due to a ruptured cerebral artery aneurysm, also known as a berry aneurysm." A medical examiner found traces of hydrocodone-acetaminophen (Vicodin) and citalopram (Celexa) in her system. The toxicology report showed that neither drug contributed to her death, and there was no evidence of drug or alcohol toxicity.[120]

Marilyn Taylor was fifty-six-years-old.

EPILOGUE

"I've had to start over many times in my life." — Marilyn Chambers, 2008[1]

MCKENNA CALLED HER FATHER TO tell him what happened. He was in rehab. She begged him to stay there.

"You're the only parent I have now," she said. "And I need you to stay sober. Don't come out. Please stay sober!"[2]

Suddenly, seventeen-year-old McKenna, who had been planning for her senior prom, high school graduation, and college, had to plan funeral services for her mother.

"Peggy, I'm prepared for my dad's death, but now my mother?" McKenna asked McGinn.[3]

McGinn helped. The critical thing for her was to keep things as normal as possible for McKenna. When McKenna said she wanted to skip her prom, McGinn insisted she go.

"Marilyn and I made a pact that if anything ever happened to either one of us, we'd watch out for the others' kids," McGinn said.[4]

Marilyn was cremated, according to her wishes. McGinn, her daughter, and McKenna were with Marilyn's body inside the crematorium. They watched as Marilyn's physical remains made their final journey into the glaring, brutal flames.

"She was in a box," McGinn said. "It had her date of birth and death written on it with a Sharpie. It said her weight was 150 pounds. I crossed it off and wrote 112. I took thirty-eight pounds off. That's a true friend."[5]

Marilyn's siblings came to Santa Clarita.

"I felt so bad because all of these plans we had recently made weren't going to happen," Jann remembered.[6]

Two memorial services were held. One was private for family and friends. The second was a public memorial. The latter was held at Zuma Beach in Malibu on

EPILOGUE

April 22, 2009—what would have been Marilyn's fifty-seventh birthday. Marilyn's ashes were scattered there.

"I can't remember if it was the evening before the funeral or the evening of the funeral, but McKenna and a bunch of her friends wanted to go out," Jann said. "I said, 'Please don't go. Just don't go out tonight. I just don't think it's a good thing to do.' And I know she was really pissed at me. What right did I have to say that? But I just thought that she should be around family. Well, later, I realized she probably needed to be with her friends. Looking back on it, I know she really resented that, and I felt bad about it."[7]

Bill left rehab to attend the private service. He was gaunt and yellow from multiple relapses. Two medical attendants accompanied him. He left rehab once more to attend McKenna's high school graduation. After graduation, he was officially released from rehab. He died of a heart attack six months later.

McKenna received a life insurance policy from her mother. No will was found. A few days after Marilyn died, her mobile home was burglarized and ransacked. Some papers went missing from a filing cabinet, and jewelry had been taken. Marilyn's brother, Bill, smashed Marilyn's computer hard drive to bits in an apparent attempt to keep whatever files Marilyn had on her computer private. McGinn still has the pieces.

Several people shared untold stories of Marilyn's generosity at the private service.

"There must have been at least ten people that said, 'I got a check in the mail for two thousand dollars because I mentioned a surgery or my kid couldn't go to camp,'" McGinn said. "That's probably why she died broke. People were important to her. That's what she cared about."[8]

News of Marilyn's death made headlines worldwide. McGinn, who acted as spokesperson and tended to Marilyn's legal affairs, was inundated with calls from reporters at virtually every major television network and newspaper. *The New York Times* obituary noted Marilyn's 'photograph as the mother of a newborn on a laundry soap package, and whose performance as a fantasy-fulfilling wanton in a pornographic movie evoked stunningly contrasting portrayals of womanhood.'[9]

Richard Corliss, *TIME* magazine's famed film critic, wrote, 'Chambers never realized her dream of starring in mainstream movies; for the next three decades, she anchored dozens of hard- and soft-core movies. Spanning the entire era of above-ground erotic films, Chambers was the queen mum of porn.'[10]

Those in the adult industry paid their respects. Marilyn was honored at the 2010 Legends of Erotica event in Las Vegas. In attendance were McGinn, her husband, Jane Hamilton, and David Bertolino, the producer of the play in which Marilyn was set to appear.[11]

"Marilyn Chambers was the first leading lady of the adult film industry," said fellow adult actress and free speech advocate Gloria Leonard. "She brought something to these films that nobody ever had before. It was a certain enthusiasm, a certain energy, and spirit that you knew that this girl was having a good time doing what she was doing. There was no faking it with Marilyn. I got into this business probably a couple of years after she did, and although there weren't a whole hell of a lot of role models around, she certainly set a standard that a lot of girls in this business, [and] a lot of the women now, aspire to."[12]

Writer and sex-positive feminist Susie Bright, who had befriended Marilyn in her later life, penned a touching tribute.

'I totally fell for her,' she wrote. 'That grin of hers. Marilyn's instant expression of earthy satisfaction. It was like a combination of Huck Finn, The Miss America Pageant, and the first great fuck you ever had all rolled into one.'[13]

However, Bright was upset by the way Marilyn's death was characterized in the media.

"It's not too strong to say I was devastated by some of the public and editorial reaction to her death," Bright said during her podcast. "There was a great deal of feeling that she was just some, I don't know, 'Oh, some slut died. Yes, I suppose pornography ruined her. What was she known for? Oh, well, this is what porn does to people.' And I have to say, all of that blather is a complete lie and really disrespectful to who she was, why she is memorable, her legacy, and the circumstances of her career and older age."[14]

McKenna went to college and adjusted to life without either parent. Having experienced trauma at such a young age, she could have quickly gone down a path of destruction. However, Marilyn and Bill raised a bright, generous, and thoughtful daughter.

Now happily married, McKenna and her husband became parents in April 2023 when their daughter Willa Lyn was born. The name is a tribute to McKenna's parents, William and Marilyn.

McKenna is protective of both her parents, but particularly her mother. She watched how hard her mother had worked, and felt the disappointment when deals fell through. Even when Marilyn was alive, people continued to make money using her name. Compilation DVDs featuring scenes from classic X-rated films, including Marilyn's, were mass-produced. Marilyn didn't earn anything from them. In the early 2000s, someone purchased the domain marilynchambers. com and sold photos of Marilyn without her permission. It took her nearly six

EPILOGUE

years in the legal system to gain control of the domain. After she died, someone sold the domain. A quick Internet search for Marilyn pulled up dozens, if not hundreds, of her videos—all pirated.

"I have to get through this life," Marilyn told a reporter two years before she died. "It's either screw the day...and be a totally bitter, resentful woman who's just furious because everyone's making money off of me, or I can say I have to move on. I can equate it with someone who worked for me who stole all of my jewelry; every single bit of it that I had been collecting since my early twenties. It took me about fifteen years not to hate these people. They were never arrested. It's the kind of thing [that] just engulfed me. It's very difficult to let go. You can also parallel it to what was stolen from me by being a porn star, my adulthood. You know, from the years eighteen to forty. It was stolen from me, but I allowed it. I did it. I own up to it.

"Life is too short to be bitter and angry and hateful. It's not worth it. When it's over, it's over."[15]

Marilyn Taylor's revolution is complete. The revolution of Marilyn Chambers is far from over. Just as the earth revolves around the sun, so does Marilyn Chambers' impact whirl around the ecliptic plane of our popular culture—both blazing hot and pure as the driven snow.

Appendix

FILMOGRAPHY

The Owl and the Pussycat (1970)
R | 96 mins | Romantic Comedy | Released: November 3, 1970
Director: Herbert Ross; **Writer:** Buck Henry (Based on the play *The Owl and the Pussycat* by Bill Manhoff); **Producer:** Ray Stark; **Cast:** Barbra Streisand, George Segal, Robert Klein, Roz Kelly, Marilyn Briggs (credited as "Evelyn Lang"); **Cinematographer:** Andrew Laszlo, Harry Stradling; **Editor:** Margaret Booth, John F. Burnett; **Production Company:** Rastar Productions, Inc.; **Distributed by:** Columbia Pictures.[1]

Together (1971)
X | 72 mins | Sexploitation | Released: December 1971 [January 19, 1972 (New York, NY)]
Director: Sean S. Cunningham; **Writer:** Sean S. Cunningham; **Producer:** Sean S. Cunningham, Myrna Karger; **Cast** (uncredited): Marilyn Briggs, Maureen Cousins, Sally Cross, Jan Peter Welt (narrator); **Cinematographer:** Roger Murphy; **Editor:** Wes Craven (Jan Peter Welt, uncredited); **Production Company:** American International Pictures (AIP), Sean S. Cunningham-Roger Murphy Productions; **Distributed by:** Hallmark Releasing. **Also Released As:** *Sensual Paradise*; *Kama Sutra Today*.[2, 3]

Behind the Green Door (1972)
X | 72 mins | Adult Drama | Released: August 1, 1972 (San Francisco)
Director: Jim and Art Mitchell; **Writer:** Jim Mitchell, Art Mitchell, Bill Boyer (Based on an anonymous short story); **Producer:** Jim and Art Mitchell; **Cast:**

FILMOGRAPHY

Marilyn Chambers, George S. McDonald, Johnnie Keyes; **Cinematographer:** Jon Fontana; **Editor:** Jon Fontana; **Production Company:** Jartech, Inc., Cinema 7 Film Group; **Distributed by:** Mitchell Brothers Film Group.[4]

Resurrection of Eve (1973)

X | 85 mins | Adult Drama | Released: September 13, 1973 (San Francisco and New York)
Director: Jon Fontana and Art Mitchell; **Writer:** Jon Fontana and Art Mitchell; **Producer:** Jim and Art Mitchell, A.R. Benton; **Cast:** Marilyn Chambers, Johnnie Keyes, Matthew Armon, Mimi Morgan; **Cinematographer:** Jon Fontana; **Editor:** Mark Bradford, Jon Fontana; **Production Company:** Anatuna, Inc., Cinema 7 Film Group; **Distributed by:** Mitchell Brothers Film Group. **Note:** Sometimes incorrectly identified as *The Resurrection of Eve*. The article "The" does not appear in the screen credits or in official press materials.[5]

Inside Marilyn Chambers (1976)

X | 75 min | Adult Documentary | Released: January 23, 1976 (San Francisco)
Director: Art Mitchell; **Writer:** none credited; **Producer:** Jim and Art Mitchell; **Cast:** Marilyn Chambers, Johnnie Keyes, George S. McDonald, Tyler Reynolds; **Cinematographer:** Jon Fontana; **Editor:** none credited; **Production Company:** Cinema 7 Film Group; **Distributed by:** Mitchell Brothers Film Group.[6]

Rabid (1977)

R | 97 min | Horror | Released: April 8, 1977 (Canada), July 6, 1977 (United States)
Director: David Cronenberg; **Writer:** David Cronenberg; **Producer:** Ivan Reitman (exec.), André Link (exec.), John Dunning, Don Carmody, Danny Goldberg; **Cast:** Marilyn Chambers, Frank Moore, Joe Silver, Howard Ryshpan; **Cinematographer:** René Verzier; **Editor:** Jean Lafleur; **Production Company:** Dunning/Link/Reitman Productions, Cinépix Film Properties (CFP), Cinema Entertainment Enterprises, Canadian Film Development Corporation (CFDC), Famous Players; **Distributed by:** Cinépix Film Properties (Canada), New World Pictures (United States); **Also Released As:** *Rage*.[7, 8]

Never a Tender Moment / Beyond de Sade (1979)

X | 28 min / 27 min | Adult Short | Released: 1979
Director: Jim and Art Mitchell; **Writer:** uncredited; **Producer:** Jim and Art Mitchell; **Cast:** Marilyn Chambers, Tana Rabonson, Erica Boyer;

PURE

The Sexual Revolutions of Marilyn Chambers

Cinematographer: uncredited; **Editor:** uncredited; **Production Company:** Cinema 7 Film Group; **Distributed by:** Mitchell Brothers Film Group.[9, 10]

Insatiable (1980)

X | 77 min (71 min in U.K. and Australia) | Adult Drama | Released: May 23, 1980 (United States), February 1982 (United Kingdom), April 8, 1982 (Australia) **Director:** Godfrey Daniels; **Writer:** Daniel Short; **Producer:** Marty Greenwald; **Cast:** Marilyn Chambers, Jesie St. James, John C. Holmes, Serena, John Leslie, Richard Pacheco, David Morris, Mike Ranger, Joan Turner; **Cinematographer:** James R. Bagdonas; **Editor:** Joe Diamond; **Production Company:** Miracle Films; **Distributed by:** Miracle Films (United States), Amanda Films (United Kingdom), Blake Films (Australia).[11, 12]

Sex Surrogate (1982)

R | 61 min | Drama-Comedy | Released: 1982 **Director:** Al Rossi, Gary Legon; **Writer:** Mel Goldberg; **Producer:** John Ward; **Cast:** Marilyn Chambers; **Cinematographer:** Steve Ferguson, Don Cirillo, Bob Campbell; **Editor:** Sarah Legon; **Production Company:** Heritage Enterprises, Inc., TPL Productions; **Distributed by:** Heritage Enterprises, Inc., TPL Productions. **Note:** This filmed adaptation of Marilyn's one-woman show was recorded for broadcast on The Playboy Channel in 1982. It was released on home video in 1988 by New Star Video.[13]

Electric Blue the Movie (1982)

R (18) | 96 min | Adult Documentary | Released: March 1982 (United Kingdom) **Director:** Adam Cole; **Writer:** uncredited; **Producer:** Tony Rower (exec.), Roger Cook (exec.), Adam Cole; **Cast:** Marilyn Chambers, Joanna Lumley, Desiree Cousteau, Randy Feelgood; **Cinematographer:** uncredited; **Editor:** uncredited; **Production Company:** Scripglow; **Distributed by:** Tigon Film Distributors Ltd. **Note:** Movie is a collection of clips from the popular U.K. *Electric Blue* video magazine series.[14]

My Therapist (1983)

R (18) | 85 min | Drama-Comedy | Released: January 1984 (United Kingdom) **Director:** Al Rossi, Gary Legon; **Writer:** Mel Goldberg; **Producer:** Josef Shaftel (exec.), John Ward; **Cast:** Marilyn Chambers, David Winn, Buck Flower, Roger Newman, Milt Kogan; **Cinematographer:** Robert Dracup; **Editor:** Estate Films Inc., Tommy Monroe; **Production Company:** TPL Productions; **Distributed by:**

FILMOGRAPHY

TPL Productions. **Note:** This feature-length film comprises several episodes of *Love Ya' Florence Nightingale* edited together. It received home video releases in the U.S. and the U.K. but played briefly in U.K. theaters in early 1984.[15]

Up 'n' Coming (1983)

X | 96 min | Adult Drama-Musical | Released: January 3, 1983
Director: Godfrey Daniels; **Writer:** Marty Greenwald, Jim Holliday; **Producer:** Marty Greenwald, Godfrey Daniels, John Harvey; **Cast:** Marilyn Chambers, Lisa De Leeuw, Herschel Savage, Richard Pacheco, Cody Nicole, John Lazar, Tom Byron, John C. Holmes; **Cinematographer:** Jack Remy; **Editor:** Lawrence Avery, Bob Hollywood; **Production Company:** Miracle Films, Key International Pictures; **Distributed by:** Miracle Films. **Also Released As:** *Cassie*.[16]

Angel of H.E.A.T. (1983)

R | 93 min | Action Comedy | Released: March 1983
Director: Myrl A. Schreibman; **Writer:** Helen Sanford, Myrl A. Schreibman; **Producer:** Hal Kant (exec.), Myrl A. Schreibman, Anthony Kant; **Cast:** Marilyn Chambers, Mary Woronov, Stephen Johnson, Milt Kogan, Remy O'Neill; **Cinematographer:** Jacques Haitkin; **Editor:** Barry Zetlin; **Production Company:** Studios Pan-Imago; **Distributed by:** Levy Films. **Note:** Originally called *The Protectors, Book #1*.[17]

Insatiable II (1984)

X | 76 min | Adult Drama | Released: April 25, 1984
Director: Godfrey Daniels; **Writer:** Manny Haten; **Producer:** Godfrey Daniels, Marty Greenwald; **Cast:** Marilyn Chambers, Juliet Anderson, Paul Thomas, Jamie Gillis, Shanna McCullough, Bobby Dee; **Cinematographer:** Jack Remy; **Editor:** B.J. Cutter; **Production Company:** Miracle Films, Essex Entertainment; **Distributed by:** Miracle Films, Essex Distributing.[18]

Party Incorporated (1989)

R | 80 min | Comedy | Released: May 1989
Director: Chuck Vincent; **Writer:** Craig Horrall, Edd Rockis, Chuck Vincent (story); **Producer:** Gary P. Conner (exec.), Ernest G. Sauer (exec.), Chuck Vincent; **Cast:** Marilyn Chambers, Kurt Woodruff, Christina Veronica, Kimberly Taylor, Kurt Schwoebel; **Cinematographer:** Larry Revene; **Editor:** James Davalos; **Production Company:** Platinum Pictures, Private Screenings; **Distributed by:** New World Video. **Note:** Originally titled *Party Girls*. Released on video in some parts of the world under that title.[19]

Breakfast in Bed (1990)

R | 76 min | Drama | Released: April 1990
Director: Ernest G. Sauer; **Writer:** Don Shiffrin, Gary P. Conner (story); **Producer:** Ernest G. Sauer (exec.), Timothy J. Bernard, Don Shiffrin, Gary P. Conner; **Cast:** Marilyn Chambers, Michael Rose, Courtenay James, Angela Schreiber, Mark Stolzenberg, Annie O'Donnell, Gary Vermillion; **Cinematographer:** Larry Revene; **Editor:** Jim Finn; **Production Company:** Private Screenings; **Distributed by:** Private Screenings.[20]

The Marilyn Diaries (1990)

R | 91 min | Drama | Released: May 1990
Director: Eric Drake; **Writer:** Don Shiffrin, Gary P. Conner (story); **Producer:** Ernest G. Sauer (exec.), Gary P. Conner, Don Shiffrin; **Cast:** Marilyn Chambers, Tara Buckman, Michael Rose, Sean Westin; **Cinematographer:** Larry Revene; **Editor:** Jim Finn; **Production Company:** Private Screenings; **Distributed by:** Private Screenings.[21]

Bedtime Stories (1993)

R | 81 min | Drama | Released: January 1993
Director: Ernest G. Sauer; **Writer:** Mike MacDonald, Gary P. Conner (story); **Producer:** Ernest G. Sauer (exec.), Paul Borghese, Gary P. Conner; **Cast:** Marilyn Chambers, Brian Carpenter, Camille Donatacci, Richard Cascioli, Isabelle Fortea; **Cinematographer:** Larry Revene; **Editor:** John Rogers; **Production Company:** Private Screenings; **Distributed by:** Private Screenings.[22]

New York Nights (1994)

R | 89 min | Drama | Released: October 1994
Director: Ernest G. Sauer; **Writer:** Mike MacDonald, Gary P. Conner (story); **Producer:** Tanya York (exec.), Ernest G. Sauer (exec.), Paul Borghese, Garry P. Conner; **Cast:** Marilyn Chambers, Julia Parton, Susan Napoli; **Cinematographer:** Larry Revene; **Editor:** John Rogers; **Production Company:** Private Screenings; **Distributed by:** Private Screenings.[23]

Bedtime Fantasies (1994)

R | 90 min | Drama | Released: June 1994
Director: Eric Drake; **Writer:** Michael MacDonald; **Producer:** Ernest G. Sauer (exec.), Gary P. Conner; **Cast:** Marilyn Chambers, Richard Cascioli, Tyra Smith, Kimberly Taylor; **Cinematographer:** Larry Revene; **Editor:** Jim Finn; **Production**

FILMOGRAPHY

Company: Private Screenings; **Distributed by:** Private Screenings.[24]

Bikini Bistro (1995)

R | 84 min | Comedy | Released: January 1995
Director: Ernest G. Sauer; **Writer:** Matt Unger, Gary P. Conner (story), Matt Unger (Story); **Producer:** Ernest G. Sauer (exec.), Brian Zadikow, Paul Borghese; **Cast:** Marilyn Chambers, Amy Lynn Baxter, Isabelle Fortea, Joan Gerardi, John Altamura; **Cinematographer:** Spike Marker; **Editor:** John Rogers; **Production Company:** Private Screenings; **Distributed by:** Private Screenings. **Note:** Released on home video April 4, 1995.[25]

Desire (1997)

R | 84 min | Drama-Comedy | Released: August 1997
Director: Ernest G. Sauer; **Writer:** Ken Dashow, Gary P. Conner (story), Ken Dashow (story); **Producer:** Ernest G. Sauer (exec.), Gary P. Conner, Debi A. Mauro; **Cast:** Marilyn Chambers, Amy Lynn Baxter, Steve O'Brien, Colleen Cooper, Steve St. John, Barbara Joyce, Michael Stevens, Tammy Parks; **Cinematographer:** Michael Watkins; **Editor:** Bill Buckendorf; **Production Company:** Private Screenings; **Distributed by:** Private Screenings.[26]

Still Insatiable (1999)

X | 141 min | Adult Drama-Comedy | Released: September 4, 1999
Director: Veronica Hart; **Writer:** Legs McNeil, Jay Allen Sanford; **Producer:** Chanze, Jane Hamilton; **Cast:** Marilyn Chambers, Stacy Valentine, Kylie Ireland, Juli Ashton, Julian, Georgina Spelvin, Gloria Leonard, Veronica Hart, Ron Jeremy; **Cinematographer:** uncredited; **Editor:** Hugh Briss, Veronica Hart; **Production Company:** VCA Pictures; **Distributed by:** VCA Pictures.[27]

Dark Chambers (2000)

X | 120 min | Adult Drama | Released: June 2000
Director: Veronica Hart; **Writer:** Richard DeWitt; **Producer:** Chanze, Veronica Hart; **Cast:** Marilyn Chambers, Herschel Savage, Asia Carrera, Erica Boyer; **Cinematographer:** Dino Ninn, Barry Wood; **Editor:** Veronica Hart, L. Ron Kenobi; **Production Company:** VCA Pictures; **Distributed by:** VCA Pictures.[28]

Edge Play (2001)

X | 143 min | Adult Drama | Released: August 2001
Director: Veronica Hart; **Writer:** Coni Sir; **Producer:** Jane Hamilton; **Cast:**

PURE *The Sexual Revolutions of Marilyn Chambers*

Marilyn Chambers, Keisha, Brooke Hunter, Kim Chambers, Tyce Buné, Jamie Gillis, Kylie Ireland; **Cinematographer:** uncredited; **Editor:** Al Dente; **Production Company:** VCA Pictures; **Distributed by:** VCA Pictures.[29]

Nantucket Housewives (2006)
X | 116 min | Adult Comedy | Released: August 2006
Director: Bud Lee; **Writer:** George Kaplan, Derek Wood (story); **Producer:** Derek Wood (exec.), Marilyn Chambers, Billy Hendrix; **Cast:** Kirsten Price, Brooke Haven, Kelly Kline, Jenaveve Jolie, Sativa Rose, Marilyn Chambers, Ron Jeremy; **Cinematographer:** Jack Remy; **Editor:** D3; **Production Company:** PTF Studios; **Distributed by:** Damaged Productions.[30]

Stash (2007)
Unrated | 80 min | Comedy | Released: April 27, 2007
Director: Jay Bonansinga; **Writer:** Jay Bonansinga; **Producer:** Jay Bonansinga, Peter Miller (exec.), Lance Catania, Ken Nilsson, Tracy Burns, Gene Cosentino, Walter Maksym (exec.), Terrence Rogers (exec.), Jonathan Sheinberg (exec.); **Cast:** Tim Kazurinsky, Marilyn Chambers, Brian King, Will Clinger, Jim Carrane, Mary Kay Cook; **Cinematographer:** Lance Catania; **Editor:** Lance Catania, Kenneth Nilsson; **Production Company:** X RAY Productions Inc.; **Distributed by:** Gravitas Ventures (United States), Pegasus Entertainment (United Kingdom).[31]

Solitaire (2008)
Unrated | 106 min | Crime Drama | June 14, 2008
Director: Victor Franko; **Writer:** Frank Durant, Vin Fraioli; **Producer:** Frank Durant, Vin Fraioli, Rand Alan Sabatini; **Cast:** Marilyn Chambers, Nick Jandl, Alex Fraioli, Short Sleeve Sampson, Anthony Goes; **Cinematographer:** Christian de Rezendes; **Editor:** Christian de Rezendes; **Production Company:** Prince Caspian Productions; **Distributed by:** Rand Alan Studios.[32]

Porndogs: The Adventures of Sadie (2009)
Unrated | 82 min | Comedy | Released: December 5, 2009
Director: Greg Blatman; **Writer:** Greg Blatman; **Producer:** Greg Blatman, Gene Trent, Felice, Thomas Harrigan; **Cast (voices only):** Marilyn Chambers, Ron Jeremy, Too $hort, Dustin Diamond, Heidi Fleiss, Paul Rodriguez, Tera Patrick, Evan Seinfeld, Paul Ogata; **Cinematographer:** Pat Shepherd; **Editor:** Greg Blatman; **Production Company:** Watermark Pictures; **Distributed by:** Watermark Pictures. **Note:** The film was released after Marilyn's death.[33]

NOTES AND SOURCES

████████████████████████

"TO JS" DENOTES AN interview with the author.

Inflation totals for U.S. dollars were calculated using the U.S. Bureau of Labor Statistics' Consumer Price Index (CPI) Inflation Calculator. This data represents changes in the prices of all goods and services purchased for consumption by urban households in the U.S. https://www.bls.gov/data/inflation_calculator.htm

Inflation totals for British pounds were calculated using the Bank of England's Inflation Calculator. The calculator uses the Consumer Price Index (CPI) as this is the measure used by the Government to set the Bank of England's target for inflation. https://www.bankofengland.co.uk/monetary-policy/inflation/inflation-calculator

INTRODUCTION

1. U.S., Sons of the American Revolution Membership Applications, 1889-1970, Volume 137 (Louisville, Kentucky: National Society of the Sons of the American Revolution). Microfilm, 508 rolls. Ancestry.com.
2. Vernon Scott, "Marilyn's just an average successful 26-year-old porno star," United Press International. [*Sandusky*

Register (Sandusky, Ohio), June 4, 1980, C-8.]
3. Marilyn Chambers with Andrew M. Finley, *The Hard Way* (Unpublished Book Treatment, 1991), 1-2.
4. Jill C. Nelson, *Golden Goddesses: 25 Legendary Women of Classic Erotic Cinema, 1968-1985* (Duncan, OK: BearManor Media, 2012) 136.

PROLOGUE

5. John Hubner, *Bottom Feeders: From Free Love to Hardcore–the Rise and Fall of Counterculture Heroes Jim and Artie Mitchell* (New York, NY:

Doubleday, 1993), 306-307.
6. *Golden Goddesses*, 167.
7. *Golden Goddesses*, 137-138.

CHAPTER 1: THE SHOW-OFF

1. *Playboy Video Magazine, Vol. 4* (Collector's Edition). (1983). [VHS]. Playboy Video.
2. Dan Woog to JS, December 16, 2022.
3. Jann Smith to JS, March 21 and 28, 2022.
4. Dan Woog to JS.
5. Marilyn Chambers, *Marilyn Chambers: My Story* (New York, NY: Warner Books, 1975), 25-26.
6. Jann Smith to JS.
7. *My Story*, 23.
8. Jann Smith to JS.
9. Dan Woog to JS.
10. Tom Connor, "The Story of M.: Connecticut's Porn Star," *Connecticut Magazine*, September 2009.
11. Bill Briggs to JS, March 12, 2022.
12. Pat Jordan, "Inside Marilyn Chambers," *GQ—Gentlemen's Quarterly*, September 1987, 441.
13. *The Hard Way*, 10.
14. *The Hard Way*, 11.
15. Jann Smith to JS.
16. *The Hard Way*, 12.
17. Jann Smith to JS.
18. Ibid.
19. Ibid.
20. Robert Hilburn, "The Spin-Off of Marilyn Chambers," *Los Angeles Times* (Los Angeles, CA), April 3, 1977, 80.
21. Jann Smith to JS.
22. Ibid.
23. Ibid.
24. *My Story*, 24.
25. Jeanne Davis, "Local girl swaps swimsuit for show biz glamour," *The Westport News*, March 22, 1974, 31.
26. Liz Boyd to JS, January 4, 2023.
27. Ibid.
28. Ibid.
29. Ibid.
30. *My Story*, 27.
31. Liz Boyd to JS.
32. *My Story*, 23.
33. Marilyn Chambers, "The Club Lady Advisor: Marilyn Chambers," *Club Magazine*, Vol. 6, No. 5, June 1980, 72-73.
34. *Connecticut Magazine*, September 2009.
35. Ibid.
36. *Insatiable* (30th Anniversary Edition). (2009). [Two-disc collector's edition on DVD]. Dynasty Group Distribution, LLC. Special feature: In-depth interview with Marilyn Chambers.
37. *Connecticut Magazine*, September 2009.
38. Ibid.
39. Ibid.
40. Ibid.
41. *My Story*, 45.
42. *Bottom Feeders*, 180.
43. Legs McNeil and Jennifer Osborne; *The Other Hollywood: The Uncensored Oral History of the Porn Film Industry* (New York, NY: HarperCollins, 2005), 22.
44. *My Story*, 47.
45. Richard L. Lewis, "Visits Movie Set, Gets Role (?) in Film," *Fond Du Lac Commonwealth Reporter* (Fond Do Lac, WI), November 20, 1970, 21.
46. *My Story*, 79.
47. *The Other Hollywood*, 24.
48. *My Story*, 79.
49. Alecia Swasy, *Soap Opera: The Inside Story of Procter & Gamble* (New York, NY: Times Books, 1993), 113.
50. *The Other Hollywood*, 26.

CHAPTER 2: THE PROPOSITION

1. "Robert Klein," *Later with Bob Costas*, November 22, 1989, Season 2, Episode 52, NBC Productions.
2. Ibid.

NOTES AND SOURCES

3. Kenneth Turan and Stephen F. Zito, *Sinema: American Pornographic Films and the People Who Make Them* (New York, NY: Praeger Publishers, 1974), 174.
4. *My Story*, 48.
5. *My Story*, 51.
6. *Fond Du Lac Commonwealth Reporter*, 21.
7. *The Other Hollywood*, 83.
8. Robert Taylor, "It's Heartbreak All the Way, Kid," *Oakland Tribune* (Oakland, CA), November 22, 1970, 2-EN.
9. Robert Sylvester, "Dream Street," *Daily News* (New York, NY), November 20, 1970, 74.
10. *Fond Du Lac Commonwealth Reporter*, 21.
11. Michael Chaiken, "Editing Mailer: A Conversation with Jan Welt and Lana Jokel," *The Mailer Review* (University of South Florida and The Norman Mailer Society, Vol. 3 No. 1, 2009)
12. Jan Welt to JS, October 22, 2022.
13. David Konow, *Reel Terror: The Scary,*

Bloody, Gory, Hundred-Year History of Classic Horror Films (New York, NY: St. Martin's Publishing Group, 2012), 130.
14. *Marilyn Chambers: The Mr. Skin Interview*, November 11, 2004, Mr. Skin; SK Intertainment, Inc. https://www.mrskin.com/marilyn-chambers-the-mr-skin-interview---1051
15. Edgar Driscoll, Jr., "'Together' filmmaker: it's sexy, not dirty," *Boston Evening Globe* (Boston, Massachusetts), September 14, 1971, 36.
16. James Harwood, "Film Review: Together," *Daily Variety*, December 29, 1971, 8.
17. *Sinema*, 175.
18. Army Archerd, "Just For Variety," *Daily Variety*, January 6, 1972, 2.
19. Marilyn Chambers, *Still Insatiable*, Spoken word compact disc, USA Music Group, 1999.
20. *Los Angeles Times*, April 3, 1977, 80.
21. *Sinema*, 175.
22. *My Story*, 71.

CHAPTER 3: "NOW CASTING FOR A MAJOR MOTION PICTURE"

1. "Herb Caen in 50 quotes," April 4, 2016. *Tony Quarrington*. https://tonyquarrington.wordpress.com/2015/01/04/herb-caen-in-50-quotes/
2. Mark Harris, "The Flowering of the Hippies," *The Atlantic*, September 1967.
3. Ibid.
4. Amy Graff, *50 things people who grew up in 1970s San Francisco will remember*, July 19, 2019, SFGATE; Hearst Communications, Inc. https://www.sfgate.com/living/article/1970s-San-Francisco-memories-history-culture-12860729.php (Original work published 2018)
5. Greg Keraghosian, *Meet the man who made San Francisco the porn capital of America 50 years ago*, February 1, 2020,

SFGATE; Hearst Communications, Inc. https://www.sfgate.com/characters/article/San-Francisco-porn-capital-de-renzy-1970-14998797.php
6. "KPIX Eyewitness News," December 2, 1970, CBS5 KPIX-TV.
7. Greg Keraghosian, SFGATE.
8. Ibid.
9. William Murray, "The Porn Capital Of America," *The New York Times* (New York, NY), January 3, 1971.
10. *My Story*, 73.
11. *My Story*, 73.
12. Liz Boyd to JS.
13. Chicopee High School Yearbook 1963 (Chicopee, Massachusetts), 40.
14. Commonwealth of Massachusetts, Department of Public Health, Registry of Vital Records and Statistics,

Massachusetts Vital Records:
Index to Births, 1941-1945, Burbank-
Deflumeri, Volume 142 (Charlestown,
Massachusetts: New England
Historic Genealogical Society, 1995
[Preservation Photocopy]), 211.

15. "Newlyweds to reside in San
Francisco," *The Westport News*
(Westport, CT), November 29, 1972,
Section Two, 8.

16. Ibid.

17. *My Story*, 75.

18. *My Story*, 76.

19. *My Story*, 77.

20. *My Story*, 77.

21. Jim Gibbons, "This is the girl-next-
door?" *The Spectator*, August 1-7, 1980,
8.

22. *My Story*, 74.

23. *Bottom Feeders*, 162-163.

24. *Bottom Feeders*, 167.

25. *Bottom Feeders*, 175.

26. *The Other Hollywood*, 82.

27. *The Other Hollywood*, 83.

28. *Bottom Feeders*, 166-167.

29. *Bottom Feeders*, 178-179.

30. Frank Hoffmann, *Analytical Survey
of Anglo-American Traditional Erotica*
(Bowling Green, Ohio: Bowling Green
University Popular Press, 1973), 66.

31. Ibid, 145.

32. Ibid.

33. Phyllis and Eberhard Kronhausen, *The
Sex People: Erotic Performers and their
Bold New Worlds* (Chicago, Illinois:
Playboy Press, 1975), 149.

34. David McCumber, *X-Rated: The
Mitchell Brothers: A True Story of Sex,
Money, and Death* (New York, NY:
Pinnacle Books, 1996 [1992]), 57.

35. "Green Door" by Bob Davie and
Marvin J. Moore, published by Alley
Music Corp and Green Door Music,
BMI (Work ID: 508318).

CHAPTER 4: BEHIND THE GREEN DOOR

1. George S. Mcdonald, *Dirty Movies*
(Unpublished Manuscript, 1975: The
Rialto Report, 2018), 304. https://
www.therialtoreport.com/2018/05/20/
george-mcdonald-2/

2. Ibid.

3. Ibid.

4. Steven V. Roberts, "Pornography in
U.S.: A Big Business," *The New York
Times* (New York, NY), February 22,
1970, 1.

5. *X-Rated*, 59.

6. Earl Wilson, *Show Business Laid Bare*
(New York, NY: Signet Books, 1973), 103.

7. *DOPE 061: Michael Aldrich*, Internet
Archive (December 1, 1987). Internet
Archive. https://archive.org/details/
DOPE061

8. William Rotsler, "Marilyn Chambers,
The Girl from Behind the Green Door,"
The Golden Age of Erotic Cinema:

1959-1972 (Digital Parchment Editions,
2015 [1973]), Part 2, Chapter 9.

9. *The Golden Age of Erotica*, Part 2,
Chapter 9.

10. "Twentieth Century Foxy: Film,"
*Pornography: A Secret History of
Civilization*, Episode 4, directed by
Chris Rodley, aired November 2, 1999,
on Channel 4 Television Corporation
(UK).

11. *Inside Marilyn Chambers*, directed
by Art Mitchell (San Francisco, CA:
Cinema 7 Film Group, 1975), DVD.

12. William Rotsler, "Johnnie Keyes, Black
Stud!," *The Golden Age of Erotic
Cinema: 1959-1972* (Digital Parchment
Editions, 2015 [1973]), Part 2, Chapter
10.

13. *After Porn Ends 2*, directed by Bryce
Wagoner (Hollywood, CA: WeBros
Entertainment, 2017), Streaming.

14. Linda Williams, *Porn Studies* (Durham

NOTES AND SOURCES

and London: Duke University Press, 2004), 299.

15. *After Porn Ends 2.*

16. Peter Warren, "Golden Age Icon Johnnie Keyes Dies," *AVN*, June 4, 2018. AVN Media Network. https://avn.com/business/articles/video/golden-age-icon-johnnie-keyes-dies-779191.html

17. *DOPE 061: Michael Aldrich*, Internet Archive (December 1, 1987). Internet Archive. https://archive.org/details/DOPE061

18. Linda Williams, *Hardcore: Power, Pleasure, and the "Frenzy of the Visible"* (Berkeley, CA: University of California Press, 1989), 158.

19. *My Story*, 13.

20. *My Story*, 16.

21. *Dirty Movies*, 314.

22. *Bottom Feeders*, 181.

23. *Inside Marilyn Chambers.*

24. *My Story*, 16-17.

25. George McDonald: The First Adult Film Star – Podcast 54 (September 6, 2015). The Rialto Report. https://www.therialtoreport.com/2015/09/06/george-mcdonald/

26. *Show Business Laid Bare*, 94.

27. *Inside Deep Throat*, directed by Fenton Bailey and Randy Barbato (Los Angeles, CA: Universal Studios, 2005), DVD.

28. *Inside Deep Throat.*

29. Ralph Blumenthal, "Porno Chic," *The New York Times* (New York, NY), January 21, 1973, 28.

30. Sanjay P. Hukku, "Plotting Sex: Pornography's *Performatistic Screen*," (Berkeley, CA: University of California Press, 2014), 116.

31. John Morthland, "Porn Films: An In-Depth Report," *TAKE ONE*, Vol. 4 No. 4, July 11, 1974, 12.

32. *The Other Hollywood*, 69.

33. "Anonymous Sources," (n.d.). Associated Press. https://www.ap.org/about/news-values-and-principles/telling-the-story/anonymous-sources

34. *The Other Hollywood*, 61.

35. Al Goldstein, "The Blonde Bombshell of Blue Movies: An Intimate Interview with Marilyn Chambers," *SCREW*, No. 245, November 12, 1973, 7.

36. *The Other Hollywood*, 73.

37. *Fluffy Cumsalot: Porn Star Names Revealed*, directed by Nathan S. Garfinkel (Vancouver, British Columbia, Canada: United Nathan Productions, 2003), Streaming.

38. *Bottom Feeders*, 193.

39. *Bottom Feeders*, 196.

40. John L. Wasserman, "A Porno Film That Looks Better," *San Francisco Chronicle* (San Francisco, CA), October 2, 1972, 42.

41. Ibid.

42. Variety Staff, "Behind the Green Door," (n.d.), *Variety*. Variety. https://variety.com/1971/film/reviews/behind-the-green-door-1200422840/

43. Roger Ebert, "Behind the Green Door," (December 11, 1973). Roger Ebert. https://www.rogerebert.com/reviews/behind-the-green-door-1973

44. Arthur Knight, "Dirty Movies," *Saturday Review*, September 30, 1972, 84.

45. Horace Freeland Judson, "Skin Deep: How to watch a pornographic movie," *Harper's*, February 1975, 42-49.

46. Ibid.

47. Al Goldstein, "Fellini with a Hardon," *SCREW*, No. 216, April 23, 1973, 19.

48. Ibid.

CHAPTER 5: "99 ⁴⁴/₁₀₀% PURE"

1. John Grissim, "Anyone's Daughter: A candid interview with Marilyn Chambers," *California Living Magazine*, March 24, 1985, 22.

2. *My Story*, 25.

3. *The Sex People*, 172.

4. *The Sex People*, 171.

5. *My Story*, 23.

6. Ibid.

7. *The Sex People*, 171.

8. Ibid.
9. Ibid.
10. Liberty Bradford to JS, February 6, 2023.
11. Tony Crawley, "Marilyn's Box," *Game*, Vol. 3 No. 7, July 1976, 24-25.
12. Ibid.
13. David Oestreicher, "Mrs. Clean is a Porno Cutie," *Daily News* (New York, NY), May 3, 1973, 4.
14. *Soap Opera*, 113.
15. Meredith Bradford to JS, February 6, 2023.
16. *Bottom Feeders*, 219-220.
17. Harry Stein, "Cannes, this side of paltry paradise," *Richmond Mercury* (Richmond, Virginia), Vol. 1 No. 40, June 13, 1973, 13.
18. NBC NEWS Archives, Getty Images, May 29, 1973.
19. Author Unlisted, "For Purity, Inside and Out: Ivory to Scrub Marilyn's Face," *Daily News* (New York, NY), February 5, 1974, 4C.
20. United Press, "In a Lather Over That Soap Box," *The San Francisco Chronicle* (San Francisco, CA), May 30, 1973, 3.
21. *Sinema*, 173.
22. Martin Tolchin, "Supreme Court Tightens Rule Covering Obscenity, Gives State New Power," *The New York Times* (New York, NY), June 22, 1973, 1.
23. United States Supreme Court, *Miller v. California*, 413 U.S. 15 (1973).
24. Ibid.
25. The conviction was overturned a year later, on June 24, 1974, when the U.S. Supreme Court found that the State of Georgia had gone too far in classifying material as obscene in view of its prior decision in *Miller v. California*.
26. Michael F. Mayer, "Film as Business: Back to obscenity," *TAKE ONE*, Vol. 4 No. 6, July-August, 1973, 34.
27. Ibid.
28. The right to view pornography in private is not absolute. Possessing or viewing child pornography is still considered illegal.
29. William B. Lockhart, et. al., *The Report of the Commission on Obscenity and Pornography*, September 1970, 27.
30. Richard Nixon, "Statement About the Report of the Commission on Obscenity and Pornography," October 24, 1970. *The American Presidency Project*. https://www.presidency.ucsb.edu/node/240090
31. Unidentified television interview, August 3, 1973.
32. Robert Berkvist, "...And What About the Peeps?," *The New York Times* (New York, NY), December 9, 1973, Section D, 15, 44.
33. Ibid.
34. Ibid.
35. KRON-TV (San Francisco, CA), June 6, 1973, Nexstar Media Group, Inc. https://diva.sfsu.edu/collections/sfbatv/bundles/227867
36. *X-Rated*, 67.
37. *The Golden Age of Erotic Cinema*, Part 2, Chapter 9.
38. Al Goldstein, "Conversation with Marilyn Chambers," *Oui*, Vol. 3 No. 2, February 1974, 70.
39. *My Story*, 90.
40. William Rotsler, "Orgy," *Cinema Blue*, 1973, 47-49.
41. *My Story*, 87-88.
42. *My Story*, 84.
43. John Morthland, "Porn Films: An In-Depth Report," *TAKE ONE*, Vol. 4 No. 4, July 11, 1974, 15.
44. Advertisement, *Berkeley Barb*, Volume 18, Issue 26, January 11-17, 1974, 32.
45. Anthony Gambino (ed.), "Naked City," *SCREW*, No. 252, December 31, 1973, 23.
46. Advertisement, *The Record* (Hackensack, New Jersey), January 21, 1974, A-17.
47. Scott Cohen, "Marilyn Chambers: 99 $^{44}/_{100}$% Pure," *Andy Warhol's Interview*, September 1973, 9.
48. *Show Business Laid Bare*, 97.

NOTES AND SOURCES

49. *SCREW*, No. 245, November 12, 1973, 4-5.
50. "Hugh Hefner, Rollo May, Grace Slick and Jefferson Airplane, Sally Kempton, Susan Brownmiller," *The Dick Cavett Show*, March 26, 1970, Season 3 Episode 8, ABC.
51. *The Naked Feminist*, directed by Louisa Achille (Parklands, Dulwich Hill, Australia: Lush Lily Productions, 2004), Streaming.
52. The adult film industry remains one of the few in which women make significantly more money than men—as much as five hundred twenty-five percent more, according to some estimates. Bernie Alexander, "5 Things You Didn't Know: Adult Films," September 2, 2007, *AskMen*. Ziff Davis Canada, Inc. https://www.askmen.com/entertainment/special_feature_150/150_special_feature.html
53. Rich Moreland, *Pornography Feminism: As Powerful as She Wants to Be* (Winchester, UK: Zero Books, 2015), 48-49.
54. *The Naked Feminist*.
55. Author Unlisted, "Rapping with Marilyn: A Conversation With That Shocking Ms. Chambers," *SHOW*, Vol. 3 No. 6, September 1973, 45.
56. Ibid.
57. Bill Kelly and Michael Caton, "Marilyn Chambers: Smalltown sweetheart makes good," *Los Angeles Free Press* (Los Angeles, CA), Vol. 12 Issue 550, January 31, 1975, C.
58. Jane Hamilton to JS, April 11, 2023.
59. *SHOW*, 44.
60. *Sinema*, 174.
61. Gerard Van der Leun, "Motherhood Comes to the Sordid Soaps," *CITY*, Vol. 1 No. 2, June 6, 1973, 26.
62. Associated Press, "Students See 'Nudie,' Talk to Porn Queen," *Los Angeles Times* (Los Angeles, CA), October 5, 1973, Part 1, 27.
63. Ibid.
64. *Sinema*, 168.
65. *Sinema*, 176.
66. *Sinema*, 176.
67. *Sinema*, 177.
68. *The Sex People*, 150.
69. Ibid.
70. *Bottom Feeders*, 241.
71. *The Other Hollywood*, 116.

CHAPTER 6: THE NEW MARILYN CHAMBERS

1. Jeff Goldberg, "Marilyn's Recording Chambers," *ROCK*, Vol. 2 No. 2, March 1977, 33.
2. *My Story*, 125-126.
3. *My Story*, 124.
4. *My Story*, 125.
5. *My Story*, 125.
6. *My Story*, 126-127.
7. Fred Robbins, "Marilyn Chambers is Insatiable," *Porn Stars*, Vol. 2 No. 1, February 1981, 30.
8. Donna Rockwell, Psy.D., "Fame is a Dangerous Drug: A phenomenological glimpse of celebrity," (n.d.), PsychAlive. https://www.psychalive.org/fame-is-a-dangerous-drug-a-phenomenological-glimpse-of-celebrity/
9. Donna Rockwell, Psy.D. and David C. Giles, "Being a Celebrity: A Phenomenology of Fame," *Journal of Phenomenological Psychology*, No. 40, October 2009, 203.
10. Norman Gaines to JS, August 28, 2023.
11. Norman Jackson, "Marilyn Chambers Opens Up," *Man's World*, Vol. 22 No. 9, September 1976, 17.
12. *My Story*, 130.
13. Lionel Chetwynd, "Interview: Marilyn Chambers," *Genesis*, Vol. 2 No. 6, January 1975, 48.
14. Jim Lowe, "Marilyn Chambers' Secret

Sex Fear...," *Police Gazette*, Vol. 180 No. 11, November 1975, 7.

15. Al Goldstein and Peter Brennan, "Linda Lovelace & Marilyn Chambers," *Man's World*, Vol. 20 No. 6, December 1974, 41-42.

16. Ashley West, "Deep Throat @ 50: Svengali - The Chuck Traynor Story: Part 1," The Rialto Report, June 19, 2022. The Rialto Report. https://www.therialtoreport.com/2022/06/12/chuck-traynor-2/

17. Ancestry.com, "U.S., Social Security Applications and Claims Index, 1936-2007," Ancestry.com Operations, Inc., 2015. Original data: Social Security Applications and Claims, 1936-2007.

18. *My Story*, 139.

19. The Rialto Report, June 19, 2022.

20. *My Story*, 143.

21. Florida Department of Health, *Florida Divorce Index, 1927-2001*. (Jacksonville, FL: Florida Department of Health, 2005), 326.

22. The Other Hollywood, 5.

23. The Rialto Report, June 19, 2022.

24. The Other Hollywood, 15.

25. The Rialto Report, June 19, 2022.

26. John Lombardi, "Marilyn Chambers: The Ivory Goddess Hits Las Vegas," *Rolling Stone*, May 8, 1975, 40.

27. Colin Dangaard, "Jury Acquits Two Of Pot Possession," *The Miami Herald* (Miami, FL), September 11, 1971, 12-B.

28. The Other Hollywood, 17-18.

29. The Other Hollywood, 18.

30. The Other Hollywood, 19.

31. The Other Hollywood, 31.

32. The Other Hollywood, 31.

33. The Other Hollywood, 33.

34. The Other Hollywood, 33-34.

35. The Other Hollywood, 34.

36. The Other Hollywood, 34.

37. *My Story*, 150.

38. The Other Hollywood, 35.

39. Linda Lovelace with Mike McGrady, *Ordeal* (New York, NY: Berkeley Book, 1981 [1980]), 108.

40. *Ordeal*, 109.

41. Ibid.

42. The Other Hollywood, 48-49.

43. The Other Hollywood, 58.

44. *My Story*, 127.

45. *My Story*, 130.

46. *My Story*, 133.

47. *My Story*, 135.

48. *My Story*, 136.

49. *My Story*, 136.

50. *Bottom Feeders*, 237-238.

51. Markham Heid, "Is hypnosis real? Here's what science says," *Time*, March 2, 2023. https://time.com/5380312/is-hypnosis-real-science/

52. Ivan Tyrrell, "The uses and abuses of hypnosis," July 25, 2022, *Human Givens Institute*. https://www.hgi.org.uk/resources/delve-our-extensive-library/ethics/uses-and-abuses-hypnosis

53. Al Goldstein and Peter Brennan, "Linda Lovelace & Marilyn Chambers," *Man's World*, Vol. 20 No. 6, December 1974, 35-36.

54. Norman Jackson, "Marilyn Chambers Opens Up," *Man's World*, Vol. 22 No. 9, September 1976, 18.

55. Timothy Green Beckley, "Porn Star Marilyn Chambers: 'A Woman Gets Better As She Gets Older,'" *Man to Man*, Vol. 26 No. 1, March 1976, 68.

56. *Man's World*, 36.

57. *Ordeal*, 20.

58. *Ordeal*, 84.

59. *Ordeal*, 84.

60. *Ordeal*, 85.

61. *Man's World*, 36.

62. Allan Starr, "Marilyn Chambers in Live Burlesque," *Mr. Magazine*, Vol. 18 No. 7, July 1974, 41.

63. Susan Greatorex, "Burlesque draws X-movie stars," *The Herald-News* (Passaic, NJ), December 5, 1973, 2.

64. Associated Press, "Porn star cleans up act with eye on club circuit," *The Berkshire Eagle* (Pittsfield, MA),

NOTES AND SOURCES

December 6, 1973, 11.

65. Jim Willse, "'Ivory Snow Girl' Not Quite 99 and 44/100 Percent Bare on Stage," *Philadelphia Inquirer* (Philadelphia, PA), December 7, 1973, 6-B.

66. "Rain to end tomorrow," (n.a.), *The Herald-News* (Passaic, New Jersey), December 5, 1973, 2.

67. *Mr. Magazine*, 42.

68. *Mr. Magazine*, 50.

69. Harry Maravel, "'Skin and Grin' girl sues," *The Herald-News* (Passaic, NJ), January 29, 1974, 2.

70. "March 7 court date scheduled on burlesque star's charges," *The Herald-News* (Passaic, NJ), February 13, 1974, 16; John J. Miller, "Memo From John J. Miller," *San Francisco Sunday Examiner & Chronicle* (San Francisco, CA), February 17, 1974, 18.

71. Pat Clark, "Marilyn Sues Two for 12G Unpin Money," *Daily News* (New York, NY), January 29, 1974, 7-C.

72. United Press International, "About People: Marilyn to Sing," *The Dubois County Daily Herald* (Jasper, IN), March 6, 1974, 18.

73. Charles McHarry, "On the Town," *Daily News* (New York, NY), February 20, 1974, 57.

74. *Rolling Stone*, 39.

75. Ibid.

76. *My Story*, 195-196.

77. Norman Gaines to JS, August 28, 2023.

78. Ibid.

79. Mark Potts, "PG Hones a Strategy for the Future," *The Washington Post* (Washington, DC), July 26, 1987. https://www.washingtonpost.com/archive/business/1987/07/26/pg-hones-a-strategy-for-its-future/fd7c2559-ec73-44f3-adc1-48adcf20e9f5/

80. *Good Night, America*, Episode 8, August 1, 1974, ABC.

81. Judy Bachrach, "Getting Marilyn's Act Together," *San Francisco Sunday Examiner & Chronicle* (San Francisco,

CA), March 17, 1974, 2.

82. Robert Taylor, "Stage and Screen," *Oakland Tribune* (Oakland, California), August 28, 1973, E35.

83. Judy Bachrach, "Getting Marilyn's Act Together."

84. *My Story*, 199-200.

85. James Davis, "Li'l Chambers Music Goes Long Way," *Daily News* (New York, NY) March 13, 1974, 38.

86. Earl Wilson, syndicated column, *Florida Today* (Cocoa, FL), March 18, 1974, 5D.

87. Richard Branciforte, "Marilyn Chambers: From Ivory Snow Girl to Riverboat Queen," *Good Times*, March 13-26, 1974, 21.

88. Norman E. Gaines, Jr., "Marilyn Chambers's Singing Debut," *Columbia Daily Spectator* (Columbia University, New York, New York), April 3, 1974, 7.

89. David Tipmore, "Chambers: Straight & strained," *The Village Voice*, Vol. 19 No. 11, March 14, 1974, 58.

90. Alec Grant, "Mr. Lovelace Finds a New Linda...And She's a Wow with the Women!," *Titbits*, No. 4614, August 8-14, 1974, 4.

91. Don Randi with Karen "Nish" Nishimura, *You've Heard These Hands: From the Wall of Sound to the Wrecking Crew and Other Incredible Stories* (Milwaukee, WI: Hal Leonard Books, 2015), Chapter 11, ebook edition.

92. *My Story*, 197.

93. Lynn Fallon, "99 44/100 Pure: Marilyn Chambers," *Swingle*, July 1974, 40.

94. Gwendolyn Seidman, Ph.D., "Why Some of Us Seek Dominant Partners," *Psychology Today*, May 8, 2015, Sussex Publishers, LLC. https://www.psychologytoday.com/us/blog/close-encounters/201505/why-some-us-seek-dominant-partners

95. Joey Sasso, "Broadway Is My Beat," *The Daily Record* (Long Branch, NJ), April 6, 1974, 11.

96. Dick Maurice, "Our Man On Broadway,"

Greater Oregon (Albany, OR), April 19, 1974, 3.

97. "Chambers Music," *Daily News* (New York, NY), March 5, 1974, 50.

98. George Lazarus, "Procter & Gamble sketches new packaging plan," *Chicago Tribune* (Chicago, IL), April 29, 1974, Section 3, 8.

99. Tom Shales, "Commercials Now 'Big Break' For Actors," *The Cincinnati Enquirer* (Cincinnati, OH), January 2, 1976, A-4.

100. Otile McManus, "Doors start opening for Marilyn Chambers," *Boston Evening Globe* (Boston, MA), June 4, 1974, 21.

101. The only record of a *Flooring Magazine* that could be located is a publication serving Australia and New Zealand. It didn't launch until 1981.

102. Bernard Cornfeld (1927-1995) was a controversial figure in the American mutual fund industry. In 1965, the Securities and Exchange Commission accused Cornfeld and his company, Investors Overseas Services, of violating American securities laws. He was charged with defrauding employees of Investors Overseas Services by selling them stock in the faltering company. He spent eleven months in a Swiss jail before being freed on bond. He was later acquitted of the charges. (*The New York Times*, March 2, 1995.) https://www.nytimes.com/1995/03/02/obituaries/bernard-cornfeld-67-dies-led-flamboyant-mutual-fund.html

103. Larry Fields, "Marcia a Fading Rose?" *Philadelphia Daily News* (Philadelphia, PA), June 11, 1974, 27.

104. Gloria Steinem, *Outrageous Acts and Everyday Rebellions, Second Edition* (New York, NY: Henry Holt and Company, 1995 [1983]), 276.

105. Larry Fields, "The Spades Are Coming," *Philadelphia Daily News* (Philadelphia, PA), July 12, 1974, 33.

106. Lawrence A. Light, "Soapbox Porno Queen Wows Pavio's Audience," *Courier-Post* (Camden, NJ), July 12, 1974, 31.

107. Lionel Chetwynd, "Genesis Interview: Marilyn Chambers," *Genesis*, Vol. 2 No. 6, January 1975, 86.

108. Charles McHarry, "On the Town," *Daily News* (New York, NY), September 30, 1974, 47.

109. Bill Mahan, "Actress Leaves Porno Flicks," *Valley News* (Van Nuys, CA), October 31, 1974, 94.

110. "'Ivory Snow' Girl Returning to Plaza," *Las Vegas Sun* (Las Vegas, NV), July 20, 1975, 14.

111. Jules Tasca to JS, January 31, 2022.

112. Ibid.

113. Ibid.

114. Ibid.

115. "Union Plaza Star At Odds Over Nudity," *Las Vegas Sun* (Las Vegas, NV), January 28, 1975, 4.

116. Ibid.

117. Ibid.

118. Nevada State Health Division, Office of Vital Records, *Nevada Divorce Index, 1968-2005* (Carson City, Nevada: Nevada State Health Division, Office of Vital Records).

119. Nevada State Health Division, Office of Vital Records, *Nevada Marriage Index, 1966-2005* (Carson City, Nevada: Nevada State Health Division, Office of Vital Records), Book 452.

120. Sammy Davis, Jr. and Jane and Burt Boyar, *Why Me? The Sammy Davis, Jr. Story* (New York, NY: Farrar, Straus and Giroux, 1989), 280.

121. Baron Wolman, "Interview: Sammy Davis, Jr.," *Gallery*, January 1974, 43.

122. *Why Me?*, 300.

123. *The Other Hollywood*, 119-120.

124. Tracey Davis with Dolores A. Barclay, *Sammy Davis, Jr. My Father* (Los Angeles, CA: General Publishing Group, Inc., 1996), 185.

125. *Gallery*, 37.

NOTES AND SOURCES

126. *The Hard Way*, 18-19.
127. "Plaza 'Sleeper Of Year,'" *Las Vegas Sun* (Las Vegas, NV), August 8, 1975, 10.
128. "Final Curtain For 'MWTDM,'" *Las Vegas Sun* (Las Vegas, NV), September 19, 1975, 46.
129. Michael Perkins, "Portrait of a Porno Princess," *The Best of Screw*, No. 10, Summer 1976, 54.
130. Ibid.
131. Ibid, 55.
132. Dick Valentine, "The Auto-Erotic Biographies Of Harry Reems & Marilyn Chambers," *FLICK*, Vol. 1 No. 5, February 1976, 15-16.
133. Charles Jay to JS, April 22, 2023.
134. Xaviera Hollander to JS, April 17, 2013, email.
135. Ibid.
136. Jann Smith to JS.
137. Ibid.
138. Ibid, and email from Bill Briggs to JS, August 24, 2023.
139. Liz Boyd to JS.
140. Jann Smith to JS.
141. Bill Briggs to JS.
142. "Hustler Interview: Chuck Traynor," *Hustler*, Vol. 1 No. 7, January 1975, 98-99.
143. Jann Smith to JS.
144. Ibid.
145. Laura Green, "Marilyn Chambers comes out from behind the green door (Or the confessions of a porn film star)," *The Miami News* (Miami, FL), September 12, 1975, 6.
146. Ibid.
147. Kevin McKean, Associated Press, "'Green Door' Slams on Film Panel," *San Francisco Chronicle* (San Francisco, CA), January 28, 1976, 43.
148. Ibid.
149. "It was friendlier behind the green door," *St. Petersburg Times* (St. Petersburg, FL), January 30, 1976, D-1.
150. Kevin McKean, Associated Press, "Women's Film Panelists Irked By Porn Actress," *Lubbock Avalanche Journal* (Lubbock, TX), January 29, 1976, 14-C.
151. Robert Taylor, "The New Image of a Sex Star," *Oakland Tribune* (Oakland, CA), February 17, 1976, 14.
152. Red Leeks, "Marilyn's Back," *Partner*, Vol. 1 No. 12, May 1980, 78.
153. Advertisement, *San Francisco Examiner* (San Francisco, CA), January 23, 1976, 29.
154. Charles A. Fracchia, "Movin' On With Marilyn," *KNIGHT*, Vol. 11 No. 9, January 1977, 28-30.
155. Meredith Bradford to JS.
156. Wayne Wilson, "Porno Queen Plays The Percentages," *The Sacramento Bee* (Sacramento, CA), January 29, 1976, 6.
157. Ibid.
158. Ibid.
159. "Letters From The People: Sad Story," *The Sacramento Bee* (Sacramento, CA), February 7, 1976, 14.
160. "News in Brief: Southland," *Los Angeles Times* (Los Angeles, CA), August 24, 1976, 2.
161. Globe Wire Services, "Names and Faces," *Boston Evening Globe* (Boston, MA), August 19, 1976, 2.
162. Associated Press, "Nudie trial is halted," *Austin Daily Herald* (Austin, MN), August 21, 1976, 2.
163. United Press International, "About People: No Encore," *Suffolk News-Herald* (Suffolk, VA), March 16, 1978, 2.
164. Tom McElfresh, "Cereal Actor Builds 'Bellybutton' For Soap Package Gal," *The Cincinnati Enquirer* (Cincinnati, OH), December 7, 1975, H-3.
165. Elizabeth L. Wollman, *Hard Times: The Adult Musical in 1970s New York City* (New York, NY: Oxford University Press, 2013), 174.
166. "Names and Faces," *Detroit Free Press* (Detroit, MI), March 26, 1976, 12-D.
167. William Glover, "Sex star happy with reputation," *The Lima News* (Lima, OH), April 11, 1976, C14.
168. Ibid.

169. Ibid.
170. Michael Musto, "XXX: Marilyn Chambers Stands Revealed to All," *Columbia Daily Spectator* (Columbia University, NY), April 14, 1976, 5.
171. Ibid.
172. Ibid.
173. *Hard Times*, 171.
174. "People," *TIME*, March 29, 1976. TIME. com. https://content.time.com/time/subscriber/article/0,33009,918163,00.html
175. *Hard Times*, 172.
176. Edmund Gaynes to JS, August 16, 2014.
177. Earl Wilson, Syndicated, *Reno Evening Gazette* (Reno, NV), April 8, 1976, 23.
178. *Efrom Allen's Underground TV Show* (New York, NY), airdate: April 4, 1976, Worldwide Television Enterprises.
179. Ibid.
180. *Hard Times*, 174.
181. Ibid.
182. Ibid.
183. *Man's World*, September 1976, 16.
184. Jan Welt to JS.
185. Addison Verrill, "Ray's 1st Pic In 13 Years Co-Stars Porn's Chambers," *Variety*, April 21, 1976, 10.
186. Ibid.
187. Patrick McGilligan, *Nicholas Ray: The Glorious Failure of an American Director* (New York, NY: ItBooks, an imprint of HarperCollins Publishers, 2011), 484.
188. *Nicholas Ray*, 484.
189. Variety Staff, "Nick Ray 'Blues,'" *Variety*, August 11, 1976, 3.
190. Ibid.
191. Jay Cocks, "Director in Aspic," *TAKE ONE*, Vol. 5 No. 6, January 1977, 21.
192. *Golden Goddesses*, 144.
193. *My Story*, 121.
194. Mitch Morrill, "Marilyn Chambers: the facts behind the fiction," *Los Angeles Free Press* (Los Angeles, CA), Vol. 12 No. 32 (577), August 8-14, 1975, C.
195. Ibid.
196. Ibid.
197. Ibid.
198. *Los Angeles Times*, April 3, 1977, 80.
199. Will Tusher, "On the Music Beat: A Little Chamber Music," *Variety*, November 19, 1976, 14.
200. James Arena, *First Ladies of Disco: 32 Stars Discuss the Era and Their Singing Careers* (Jefferson, NC: McFarland & Company, Inc., 2013), 50-51.
201. Ibid.
202. Ibid.
203. "Benihana," by Barbara Ann Soehner and Michael Zager, published by EMI Full Keel Music, Louise/Jack Publishing, Inc., ASCAP; EMI Longitude Music, Sumac Music, BMI (Work ID: 320214273).
204. Billboard Staff, "Billboard's Top Single Picks: First Time Around," *Billboard*, February 5, 1977, 68.
205. "Stevie Wonder stunned by law," *Daily Facts* (Redlands, CA), February 7, 1977, 10.
206. Ed Harrison, "Ex-Porn Star Goes Vocal," *Billboard*, April 9, 1977, 4.
207. "Billboard's Disco Action," weekly song charts, (n.a.), *Billboard*, March 26, 1977, 46.
208. Mitch Morrill, "Marilyn Chambers: Adult Film Star to Recording Artist," *Filmscene*, 1977, 36.
209. David Cronenberg to JS, January 4, 2022.
210. Ibid.
211. Ibid.
212. Ibid.
213. Ibid.
214. Ibid.
215. Jen Vuckovic, "13 Minutes with Marilyn Chambers," *Rue Morgue*, Issue 39, May/June 2004, 18.
216. John Stark, "Porn queen steps up to a role with more bite," *San Francisco Examiner* (San Francisco, CA), August 26, 1977, 13.
217. Ibid.
218. Judy Stone, "The Horror of Chambers—(Marilyn, That Is)," *San Francisco Chronicle* (San Francisco,

NOTES AND SOURCES

CA), August 27, 1977, 36.

219. "Inside Marilyn Chambers: 99 & 44/100's% pure profit," *Cinema X*, Vol. 3 No. 2, 1973, 38.

220. "'Red Hot Lovers' Debuts At Plaza," *Las Vegas Sun* (Las Vegas, NV), October 11, 1977, 25.

221. Bill Willard, "Les Vegas Strip," *Variety*, March 20, 1978, 30.

222. "Suitor's Acting A-1," *Las Vegas Sun* (Las Vegas, NV), November 11, 1977, 22.

223. Vic Field, "'Bedroom comedy' has good actors," *Valley News* (Van Nuys, CA), October 20, 1977, Section 3, 8.

224. Ibid.

225. "Night Club Reviews: Union Plaza, Las Vegas, Las Vegas, Oct. 20. 'Last of the Red Hot Lovers,'" *Variety*, October 26, 1977, 78.

226. Joe Delaney, "On & off the Record," *Las Vegas Sun* (Las Vegas, NV), December 2, 1977, 24.

227. Joe Delaney, "On & off the Record," *Las Vegas Sun* (Las Vegas, NV), October 14, 1977, 22.

228. Bruce Rushton, "Porn again," *Riverfront Times* (St. Louis, MO), June 6, 2011. Riverfront Times. https://www.riverfronttimes.com/news/porn-again-2471638

229. *Paris Las Vegas International*, No 13, M 3267, News Ramdam Suplement, (n.d.), 18.

230. Ron Englert, "Interview with Marilyn Chambers," *Hooker*, Vol. 1 No. 1, November 1980, 17.

231. "City OKs Chambers' Nude Act," *Las Vegas Sun* (Las Vegas, NV), March 13, 1979.

232. "Porno Queen Raps Proposed Ban On Nudity," *Las Vegas Sun* (Las Vegas, NV), June 5, 1979.

233. Barry D. Levin, *Vegarama* (Press kit materials for *Insatiable*, 1980).

234. Sandy Zimmerman, *This Week in Las Vegas* (Press kit materials for *Insatiable*, 1980).

235. Associated Press, "Mayor to force

cover up," *Big Spring Herald* (Big Spring, TX), May 11, 1979, 12-A.

236. Alison Harvey, "Marilyn's Manager Decries 'Coverup," *Las Vegas Sun* (Las Vegas, NV), May 11, 1979.

237. *Las Vegas Sun*, May 11, 1979.

238. "Las Vegas Mayor Wants Chambers To Cover It Up," *Variety*, May 21, 1979, 14.

239. *Las Vegas Sun*, May 11, 1979.

240. *Las Vegas Sun*, May 11, 1979.

241. Chris Woodyard, "Star Fights To Keep Nude Show," *Las Vegas Sun* (Las Vegas, NV), May 18, 1979, 15.

242. *Las Vegas Sun*, May 18, 1979.

243. *Las Vegas Sun*, May 18, 1979.

244. *Las Vegas Sun*, May 18, 1979.

245. "Porno Queen Raps Proposed Ban On Nudity," *Las Vegas Sun*, June 5, 1979.

246. *Las Vegas Sun*, June 5, 1979.

247. Jeff Adler, "Porno Queen Chambers To Fight Las Vegas Ban On Nudity," *Las Vegas Sun* (Las Vegas, NV), June 7, 1979, 1.

248. *Las Vegas Sun*, June 7, 1979.

249. *Las Vegas Sun*, June 7, 1979.

250. Bill Willard, "Las Vegas Strip," *Variety*, June 11, 1979, 16.

251. Ann Kofol, "Porno Queen Bares Design For Cover-Up," *Las Vegas Sun* (Las Vegas, NV), June 9, 1979.

252. Mark Dent, "Clothing's back on, profits off," *Las Vegas Review-Journal* (Las Vegas, NV), June 14, 1979, 6A.

253. *Las Vegas Review-Journal*, June 14, 1979.

254. Jeanne M. Hall, "Marilyn Chambers' show closes," *Las Vegas Review-Journal* (Las Vegas, NV), June 22, 1979, 14A.

255. "Marilyn Chambers cache bien son jeu!," *Paris Las Vegas*, (n.d.), 15.

256. James Hughes-Onslow, "People and places in and around town," *What's On In London*, September 28-October 4, 1979, 16.

257. Dennis Barker, "A regal cure for hang-ups," *The Guardian* (London, England,

UK), September 20, 1979, 4.

258. *The Guardian*, September 20, 1979.

259. Kemsley, "Alternative London Interview: Marilyn Chambers," n.d.

260. Tony Purnell, "Bra Wars! Sexy queens slug it out in bitchy brawl," *Sunday People* (London, England, UK), September 23, 1979, 5.

261. Ruth Draper (1884-1956) and Joyce Grenfell (1910-1979) were American and British actresses, respectively,

who specialized as dramatic storytelling monologists, also called diseuses.

262. *The Sunday Times of London*, "Marilyn Chambers Now Doing Her Bit On London Stage," *Santa Cruz Sentinel*, December 10, 1979, 18.

263. R. Allen Leider, "An Interview with Marilyn Chambers," *Elite*, Vol. 7 No. 2, February 1981, 38.

CHAPTER 7: INSATIABLE

1. Dave Feller, "Tip of the Tongue: Marilyn Chambers," *VELVET TALKS*, Vol. 3 No. 9, September 1981, 8.

2. *Bottom Feeders*, 305.

3. *Bottom Feeders*, 305.

4. Larry King with Peter Occhiogrosso, *Tell It to the King* (New York, NY: Jove Books, 1989 [1988]), 68-69.

5. Ibid.

6. *Bottom Feeders*, 306-307.

7. Clark Peterson, "Letter from San Francisco: Ultra Chic," *The Best of SCREW*, No. 23, Fall 1979, 66.

8. *Beyond de Sade*. Directed by Art Mitchell and Jim Mitchell, Cinema 7, Inc., 1979, VHS.

9. *GQ*, 438.

10. Daniel Harris, *The Rise and Fall of Gay Culture* (New York, NY: Hyperion, 1997), 10.

11. *The Rise and Fall of Gay Culture*, 12.

12. Robert Ashfield, "Why Marilyn Chambers is Insatiable," *Mr. Magazine*, Vol. 24 No. 2, December 1980, 58.

13. Susie Bright, "Remembering Marilyn Chambers—1952-2009," *Susie Bright's Journal*, April 13, 2009. https://susiebright.blogs.com/susie_brights_journal_/2009/04/still-insatiable-the-legacy-of-marilyn-chambers.html

14. Ibid.

15. Although his real name is easily found online, Mr. Daniels, who's

never spoken on the record about his relationship with Marilyn and Chuck, requested to be credited with the pseudonym he used during his years as an adult film director.

16. Godfrey Daniels to JS, October 30, 2021.

17. Kyle DeGuzman, "What is a Lap Dissolve — Film & Video Editing Techniques," April 3, 2022. *StudioBinder*. https://www.studiobinder.com/blog/what-is-a-lap-dissolve-definition/

18. Godfrey Daniels to JS.

19. Ibid.

20. Ibid.

21. Ibid.

22. Ibid.

23. Ibid.

24. Ibid.

25. Ibid.

26. Ibid.

27. Marty Greenwald to JS, November 9, 2021.

28. Ibid.

29. Ibid.

30. Godfrey Daniels to JS.

31. Ibid.

32. *Insatiable* [DVD]. Directed by Godfrey Daniels, 1980. Wild Side Films (French Edition).

33. Marty Greenwald to JS.

34. *Golden Goddesses*, 145.

NOTES AND SOURCES

35. Lynn Darling, "The 'Ordeal' of being Linda Lovelace," February 19, 1980, *The Washington Post*. https://www.washingtonpost.com/archive/lifestyle/1980/02/19/the-ordeal-of-being-linda-lovelace/a1cdda9b-7ac1-4b60-b7cf-6f1162433d67/

36. Ibid.

37. Ibid.

38. *The Other Hollywood*, 266.

39. *The Other Hollywood*, 267.

40. Carolyn Bronstein, "Why the New Movie About 'Deep Throat' Could Be Important," January 7, 2013, *The Atlantic*. https://www.theatlantic.com/entertainment/archive/2013/01/why-the-new-movie-about-deep-throat-could-be-important/266850/

41. *The Other Hollywood*, 265.

42. *The Other Hollywood*, 266.

43. *The Washington Post*, February 19, 1980.

44. *The Other Hollywood*, 269.

45. Craig Modderno, "Marilyn Chambers: The Passionate Pushover," *Oui*, Vol. 10 No. 10, October 1981, 110.

46. Gregg Kilday, "Inside Marilyn Chambers: The X-Rated queen finds new life as a video superstar," *HOME VIDEO*, Vol. 2 No. 1, January 1981, 27.

47. "Porn queens battle: Chambers scolds Lovelace for kiss-and-tell," September 26, 1980, *Us*, [*Winnipeg Free Press* (Winnipeg, Manitoba, Canada)], 23.

48. Ibid.

49. Robert Steven Rhine, "Miss Marilyn Chambers: 'I Am What I Am,'" *Girls and Corpses*, Vol. 2, Summer 2008, 46.

50. *GQ*, 438.

51. Clarence Petersen, "Paperbacks: Out of Bondage," *Chicago Tribune*, January 17, 1988, Section 14, 4.

52. *The Other Hollywood*, 439.

53. *Golden Goddesses*, 151.

54. *Golden Goddesses*, 150.

55. *Insatiable* [DVD]. Directed by Godfrey Daniels, 1980. Wild Side Films (French Edition).

56. Marty Greenwald to JS.

57. *Insatiable* [DVD]. Directed by Godfrey Daniels, 1980. Wild Side Films (French Edition).

58. David Shultz, "How big is the average penis?" March 3, 2015, *Science*. https://www.science.org/content/article/how-big-average-penis

59. *Exhausted: John C. Holmes, the Real Story*, directed by Julia St. Vincent, Annazan Productions, 1981.

60. *John Holmes*, 174-175.

61. *John Holmes*, 175.

62. "Drug Wars: The Buyers - A Social History Of America's Most Popular Drugs," *FRONTLINE* (PBS: Public Broadcasting Service), November 18, 2015. https://www.pbs.org/wgbh/pages/frontline/shows/drugs/buyers/socialhistory.html

63. *John Holmes*, 175-176.

64. *John Holmes*, 414.

65. Craig Modderno, "Marilyn Chambers: The Passionate Pushover," *Oui*, Vol. 10 No. 10, October 1981, 108.

66. "Marilyn Chambers, Chuck Traynor, Maureen McGovern, Trevor Howard," *Tomorrow with Tom Snyder*, January 6, 1981 (rerun date), NBC.

67. Murray Frymer, "For porn star Marilyn Chambers, sex is public and that's the way she wants it," *Chicago Tribune* (Chicago, IL), September 1, 1980, Section 2, 3.

68. Larry Fields, "There's an Art to Making Movies," *Philadelphia Daily News* (Philadelphia, PA), November 17, 1980, 25.

69. Diane Haithman, "G-rated writer meets X-rated movie queen," *Detroit Free Press* (Detroit, MI), November 14, 1980, 1B, 4B.

70. Ibid.

71. Ibid.

72. Ibid.

73. Ibid.

74. Ibid., *Mr. Magazine*, December 1980, 58.

75. Robert A. Masullo, "Chambers

has gotten older, not better," *The Sacramento Bee* (Sacramento, California), July 24, 1980, E5. Masullo was one of the few journalists who reported Marilyn's accurate age of twenty-eight. The *Insatiable* press materials falsely claimed she was twenty-six.

76. Al Goldstein, "Porn-Again Marilyn," *SCREW*, No. 608, October 27, 1980, 23.
77. Alex Horne, "At Home's X-Rated Video Review: Insatiable," *At Home Magazine*, Vol. 2 No. 6, 1981, 12.
78. Linda Williams, *Hard Core: Power, Pleasure, and the "Frenzy of the Visible,"* (Berkeley, CA: University of California Press, 1989), 176-179.
79. Ashley West, "AFAA Award ceremonies: A Pictorial History, Part 2 (1981-1984)", *The Rialto Report*, September 16, 2018. The Rialto Report. https://www.therialtoreport.com/2018/09/16/afaa-adult-film-awards/
80. Godfrey Daniels to JS.
81. Frederick Wasset, *Veni, Vidi, Video: The Hollywood Empire and the VCR* (Austin, TX: University of Texas Press, 2001), 95.
82. Mark J. Perry, "Christmas Shopping for a VCR/DVD: 1981 Vs. 2009," December 19, 2009, *AEI*. American Enterprise Institute. https://www.aei.org/carpe-diem/christmas-shopping-for-a-vcrdvd-1981-vs-2009/
83. Vernon Scott, United Press International, "The appeal of X-rated cassettes," *San Francisco Examiner* (San Francisco, CA), April 4, 1981, A6.
84. Ibid.
85. *Hard Core*, 175.
86. Marty Greenwald to JS.
87. Ibid.
88. Ibid.
89. Randi Henderson, "Sex and the VCR," *The Sun* (Baltimore, MD), August 29, 1985, C1.
90. Godfrey Daniels to JS.
91. Ibid.
92. *Insatiable* [DVD]. Directed by Godfrey Daniels, 1980. Wild Side Films (French Edition).
93. Ibid.
94. Ibid.
95. Tom Gibson, "X ratings a deadly force on theatrical films," April 20, 1989, *The Captain's Log* (Newport News, VA, Christopher Newport College), 2.
96. "The FCC and speech," August 31, 2022, *FCC*. Federal Communications Commission. https://www.fcc.gov/consumers/guides/fcc-and-speech
97. William Couey, "Marilyn Chambers Channel could be offered in valley," *Daily Press* (Victorville, California), August 6, 1987, A-5.
98. "Cable Television, Systems and Subscribers statistics, 2000 USA Census numbers," (n.d.). https://allcountries.org/uscensus/925_cable_television_systems_and_subscribers.html
99. Bob Greene, "Shame on all TV sets that are now rated X," *Chicago Tribune* (Chicago, IL), August 31, 1981, Section 2, 1.
100. In 2002, Greene was forced to resign from the *Chicago Tribune* after twenty-four years when he admitted to a sexual relationship with a high school student fourteen years prior.
101. Ibid.

CHAPTER 8: UP 'N' COMING, DOWN 'N' OUT

1. Dougal MacDonald, "'Insatiable' has no idea but a definite purpose," *The Canberra Times* (Canberra, Australia), May 19, 1982, 31.
2. "Sexpot film star whips detergent firm into a lather," *The Guardian* (London,

NOTES AND SOURCES

England, UK), February 20, 1982, 11.

3. Peter Haigh, "Peter Haigh's Pictures & People," *Film Review*, Vol. 32 No. 1, February 1982, 4.

4. Eric Braun, "Reviews: Insatiable," *films*, Vol. 2 No. 5, April 1982, 36.

5. *The Canberra Times*, 31.

6. Joe H. Cabaniss, "Porno queen enjoys working in nude," *National City Star-News* (National City, California), March 14, 1982, A-1.

7. Ibid, A-10.

8. "Dear editor... 'Porno queen' article stirs up some readers," *National City Star-News*, March 18, 1982, D-10.

9. Ibid.

10. "Dear editor... 'Porno queen 'article points up society evils," *National City Star-News*, March 28, 1982, C-10.

11. "Dear editor... 'Porno queen' story has this writer's backing," *National City Star-News*, April 4, 1982, D-8.

12. *Still Insatiable*, CD.

13. Jon Grissim, "Anybody's Daughter," *San Francisco Sunday Examiner and Chronicle* [*California Living* magazine (San Francisco, CA)], March 24, 1985, 24.

14. Tom Bierbaum, "Prod'n Begins On Adult Soap Starring Marilyn Chambers," *Variety*, September 27, 1982, 1.

15. Ibid, 10.

16. Tom Bierbaum, "Prod'n Begins On Adult Soap Starring Marilyn Chambers," *Variety*, September 27, 1982, 10.

17. Before it was more commonly referred to as "cable television," the new service of additional channels at cost was called "paid television," "pay TV," or "fee-vee."

18. Lee Margulies, "Marilyn Chambers Takes Sex To The TV Screen," *Los Angeles Times* (Los Angeles, CA), November 26, 1982, Part VI, 1, 26.

19. Jerry Buck, Associated Press, "Marilyn Chambers turns her talents to TV,"

News-Journal (Pensacola, FL), May 8, 1983, 6.

20. *Los Angeles Times*, November 16, 1982, 26.

21. Ibid.

22. Ibid.

23. Ibid.

24. Ibid.

25. "Marilyn Chambers Comes Again," *Knave*, Vol. 15 No. 11, 1983, 33-34.

26. Ibid.

27. "Why Do Victims Stay?" *National Coalition Against Domestic Violence (NCADV).* (n.d.). National Coalition Against Domestic Violence. https://ncadv.org/why-do-victims-stay

28. *Bottom Feeders*, 307.

29. *Bottom Feeders*, 307-308.

30. Ibid.

31. Ibid.

32. *GQ*, 440.

33. Jann Smith to JS, Ibid.

34. Ibid.

35. Bill Briggs to JS.

36. Jann Smith to JS.

37. *Connecticut, U.S., Divorce Index, 1968-1997*, Database. Connecticut Department of Public Health, Hartford, Connecticut.

38. Robin Fredericks, "Marilyn Chambers Talks Dirty," *Swank*, Vol. 30 No. 5, June 1983, 31.

39. Marilyn Chambers, "State of the Nation," *Club*, Vol. 10 No. 7, August 1984, 72.

40. *The Hard Way*, 32.

41. Ibid.

42. Charles Jay to JS, Ibid.

43. Marty Greenwald to JS.

44. Ibid.

45. Variety Staff, "New Act Reviews: Marilyn Chambers & Haywire," *Variety*, July 1, 1982, 10.

46. Ibid.

47. Godfrey Daniels to JS.

48. Herschel Savage to JS, August 19, 2013.

49. Marty Greenwald to JS.

50. Ibid.

51. Ibid.
52. Harry F. Themal, "Looks, sex were doors to stardom," *Sunday News Journal* (Wilmington, DE), March 27, 1983, F2.
53. Jack Mathews, Gannett News Service, "Marilyn Chambers Knows Success," *The Cincinnati Enquirer* (Cincinnati, OH), March 17, 1983, C-13.
54. *John Holmes*, 325.
55. Richard Pacheco to JS, March 12, 2013.
56. Marty Greenwald to JS.
57. Harry F. Themal, "Looks, sex were doors to stardom," *Sunday News Journal* (Wilmington, DE), March 27, 1983, F1.
58. Hugh Gallagher, "Marilyn Chambers: Angel in Heat," *Draculina*, No. 45, January 2004, 8-9.
59. *Mr. Skin*.
60. *Golden Goddesses*, 521.
61. Ashley West, "Juliet Anderson: An Unpublished Conversation with the Original Cougar," May 22, 2022, *The Rialto Report*. The Rialto Report. https://www.therialtoreport.com/2022/05/22/juliet-anderson/
62. Ibid.
63. Ibid.
64. Godfrey Daniels to JS.
65. "Juliet Anderson: An Unpublished Conversation with the Original Cougar," *The Rialto Report*.
66. Ibid.
67. Marty Greenwald to JS.
68. Bob Greene, "Porn queen for the '70s," *Wisconsin State Journal* (Madison, WI), May 29, 1984, Section 2, 4.
69. Ibid.
70. Ibid.
71. Ibid.
72. Rebecca Nappi, "X-rated mission: Notorious star defends value of porn career," *The Spokesman-Review* (Spokane, WA), January 17, 1985, 16.
73. Ibid.
74. *Golden Goddesses*, 162.
75. "They felt too much 'magic,'" *San Francisco Examiner* (San Francisco, CA), February 2, 1985.
76. "People: Star jailed," *Akron Beacon Journal* (Akron, OH), February 4, 1985, 2.
77. Warren Hinckle, "A dog's life," *San Francisco Examiner* (San Francisco, CA), June 23, 1988, A-3.
78. Don Lattin, "Chambers bumps into cops, finds The City a grind," *San Francisco Sunday Examiner & Chronicle* (San Francisco, CA), February 3, 1985, B10.
79. Warren Hinckle, "A dog's life," *San Francisco Examiner*.
80. Enquirer News Services, "The Nation: San Francisco," *The Cincinnati Enquirer* (Cincinnati, OH), February 5, 1985, A-2.
81. Associated Press, "Arrest shocks porn star," *The Press Democrat* (Santa Rosa, CA), February 5, 1985, 4A.
82. Ibid.
83. Birney Jarvis, "What Worries Marilyn: Porn Star Hates Telling Mother About Arrest," *San Francisco Chronicle* (San Francisco, CA), February 5, 1985,
84. Warren Hinckle, "The Cops and Marilyn Chambers," *San Francisco Chronicle* (San Francisco, CA), February 4, 1985, 4.
85. J.L. Pimsleur, "Vice Squad's Encore Visit To Porn Theater," *San Francisco Chronicle* (San Francisco, CA), February 9, 1985, 2.
86. Ibid.
87. Ibid.
88. Cathy Castillo, "Porn Star Arrest Angers Official," *San Francisco Chronicle* (San Francisco, CA), February 8, 1985, 7.
89. Ibid.
90. Warren Hinckle, "The Cops and Marilyn Chambers," *San Francisco Chronicle*.
91. Ibid.
92. "San Francisco won't press charges against Chambers," (n.a.), *Reno*

NOTES AND SOURCES

Gazette-Journal (Reno, Nevada), February 12, 1985, 4A.

93. Daniel J. Silva, "Sex scandals, other controversies plague S.F. cops," *UPI*, April 7, 1985. United Press International, Inc. https://www.upi.com/Archives/1985/04/07/Sex-scandals-other-controversies-plague-SF-cops/2454481698000/

94. Warren Hinckle, "San Francisco Vice Busts Don't Come Cheap," *San Francisco Chronicle* (San Francisco, CA), February 15, 1985, 6.

95. Will Snyder, "A Man and His Dog Win Over Alice," *Bay Area Reporter* (San Francisco, CA), March 14, 1985, 5.

96. Ibid.

97. Jerry Jansen, "Letters: Freedom for All," *Bay Area Reporter* (San Francisco, CA), April 4, 1985, 8.

98. "D.A. Shelves Case Against Porno Star," *San Francisco Chronicle* (San Francisco, CA) February 12, 1985, 3.

99. John Grissim, "Anyone's Daughter," *San Francisco Sunday Examiner & Chronicle* [*California Living*, supplement (San Francisco, CA)], March 24, 1985, 20.

100. Ibid.

101. Nevada State Health Division, Office of Vital Records, *Nevada Divorce Index, 1968-2005* (Carson City, Nevada: Nevada State Health Division, Office of Vital Records).

102. Pat Jordan, "Inside Marilyn Chambers," *GQ—Gentlemen's Quarterly*, September 1987, 441.

103. In 2007, D'Apice was sentenced to 41 months in prison for extorting monies from patrons at the Crazy Horse Too strip club in Las Vegas through force and violence. D'Apice was a shift manager at the club from 1998 to 2006. https://www.justice.gov/archive/usao/nv/news/2007/02152007.html

104. *The Hard Way*, 7.

105. Ibid.

106. *The Hard Way*, 8.

107. *The Hard Way*, 9.

108. Peggy McGinn to JS, June 20, 2023.

109. Ibid.

110. Ibid.

111. Associated Press, "Porn star arrested," *Springfield News-Sun* (Springfield, OH), December 15, 1985, 4A.

112. Associated Press, "Bare facts," *Akron Beacon Journal* (Akron, OH), December 16, 1985, 2.

113. Associated Press, "Porn star convicted," *Galion Inquirer* (Galion, OH), December 16, 1985, 8.

114. *The Hard Way*, 21.

115. Ibid.

116. *The Hard Way*, 15.

117. Ibid.

118. *The Hard Way*, 17-18.

119. *The Hard Way*, 18.

120. *The Hard Way*, 20.

121. Ibid.

122. *The Hard Way*, 22.

123. *The Hard Way*, 23.

124. Ibid.

125. *The Hard Way*, 24.

126. *The Hard Way*, 25.

CHAPTER 9: FAKING IT

1. Stan Malinowski, "Genesis Interview: Marilyn Chambers," *Genesis*, Vol. 2 No. 6, January 1975, 88.

2. Dave Pink, "Porn queen's act described as indecent by two officers," *The Windsor Star* (Windsor, Ontario, Canada), January 30, 1987, A5.

3. Ibid.

4. Associated Press, "Porn star jailed for 'gyrating,'" *The Daily Press* (Escanaba, MI), June 10, 1986, 3.

5. *GQ*, 389.

6. "Chambers' trial resumes Feb. 25," *The Windsor Star* (Windsor, Ontario,

Canada), February 3, 1987, A5.

7. Dave Pink, "Chambers says act is not obscene," *The Windsor Star* (Windsor, Ontario, Canada), February 26, 1987, A3.
8. *GQ*, 440.
9. *GQ*, 388.
10. Ibid.
11. Nino Wischnewski, "Chambers' act wasn't indecent, Nosanchuk rules," *The Windsor Star* (Windsor, Ontario, Canada), July 17, 1987, A3.
12. Gord Henderson, "Nice work if you can get it...," *The Windsor Star* (Windsor, Ontario, Canada), July 18, 1987, A6.
13. Kathy Kennedy, *Pennsylvania Connection*, "Inside Marilyn Chambers," No. 53, 1986, 48.
14. Ibid., 55.
15. *GQ*, 389.
16. Ibid., *Insatiable* (30th Anniversary Edition). Special feature: In-depth interview with Marilyn Chambers.
17. Ibid.
18. *The Hard Way*, 33.
19. *The Hard Way*, 33-34.
20. Peggy McGinn to JS, December 13, 2022.
21. Warren Hinckle, "A dog's life," *The San Francisco Examiner* (San Francisco, CA), June 23, 1988, A-3.
22. *GQ*, 389.
23. Lawrence K. Altman, "Rare Cancer Seen In 41 Homosexuals," *The New York Times* (New York, NY), July 3, 1981, A20.
24. "Timeline of The HIV and AIDS Epidemic," (n.d.), *HIV.gov*. U.S. Department of Health & Human Services and the Minority HIV/AIDS Fund. https://www.hiv.gov/hiv-basics/overview/history/hiv-and-aids-timeline/#year-1981
25. "Snapshots of an Epidemic: An HIV/AIDS Timeline," *amfAR, The Foundation for AIDS Research*. amfAR, the Foundation for AIDS Research.

https://www.amfar.org/about-hiv-aids/snapshots-of-an-epidemic-hiv-aids/

26. Mike Sager, "The Devil and John Holmes," *Rolling Stone*, May 1989. https://web.archive.org/web/20150917214413/http://longform.org/stories/the-devil-and-john-holmes
27. *John Holmes*, 406.
28. Al Turner, "AIDS killing porn film, star says," *The Edmonton Journal* (Edmonton, Alberta, Canada), June 18, 1987, B2.
29. Associated Press, "Adult film firm stock causes stir on Wall St.," *The Daily Argus* (Mount Vernon, NY), April 24, 1982, B1; Associated Press, "Adult film company appeals to brokers," *The Journal-News* (Rockland County, NY), April 28, 1982, A6.
30. "When Chambers Speaks, People Listen," press release, Miracle Films, Inc. (Hollywood, CA), 1982. *Up 'n' Coming* press kit.
31. John Anderson, "Chambers Opens A New Door," *Newsday* (Nassau Edition, Hempstead, NY), June 25-July 1, 1989, 89.
32. Mike Cidoni, "Chambers leaves X scene for mainstream," *Richmond Palladium-Item* (Richmond, IN), July 13, 1989, 9.
33. Alan Mirabella, "Porn Queen to Ms. Clean," *Daily News* (New York, NY), May 7, 1989, 5.
34. Ibid.
35. Mike Cidoni, "Chambers leaves X scene for mainstream," *Richmond Palladium-Item*.
36. Ibid.
37. Clarence Petersen, "Porn? Rate it 'ex' for Marilyn Chambers," *Chicago Tribune* (Chicago, IL), June 2, 1989, Section 5, 8.
38. John Anderson, "Chambers Opens A New Door," *Newsday*.
39. Variety Staff, "Showing at Cannes Film

NOTES AND SOURCES

Festival: Party Incorporated (Party Girls)," *Variety*, May 10-16, 1989, 56.

40. Debbie Rochon, "Marilyn Chambers: The Naked Truth," *Scream Queens Illustrated*, No. 8, 1995, 57.

41. Variety Staff, "Cannes Film Festival Market Reviews: The Marilyn Diaries," *Variety*, May 30, 1990, 24.

42. *Mr Skin*, Ibid.

43. Dominique Bourget and Pierre Gagné, "Fratricide: A Forensic Psychiatric Perspective," *Journal of the American Academy of Psychiatry and the Law Online*, Vol. 34 No. 4, December 2006, 529.

44. Liberty Bradford to JS, February 6, 2023.

45. Associated Press, "Pornographer Gets 6 Years In Shooting Death of Brother," *The New York Times* (New York, New York), April 25, 1992, 9.

46. *The Other Hollywood*, 496.

47. *The Other Hollywood*, 497.

48. *Girls and Corpses*, 48.

49. *The Other Hollywood*, 497.

50. McKenna Taylor to JS, June 21, 2023.

51. *Connecticut Magazine*.

52. *Bottom Feeders*, 399.

53. Peggy McGinn to JS.

54. Ibid.

55. Ibid.

56. *Women of the House*, "Women in Film," Season 1, Episode 9, directed by Harry Thomason, written by Linda Bloodworth-Thomason, aired September 8, 1995 (Lifetime). Mozark Productions, Perseverance Inc., TriStar Television.

57. McKenna Taylor to JS.

58. Ibid.

59. Ibid.

60. Ibid.

61. Ibid.

62. Ibid.

63. Peggy McGinn to JS.

64. *Golden Goddesses*, 157.

65. Peggy McGinn to JS.

66. Ibid.

67. *Golden Goddesses*, 144.

68. Jane Hamilton to JS, April 11, 2023.

69. Ibid.

70. Ibid.

71. Ibid.

72. Ibid.

73. Ibid.

74. Ibid.

75. Ibid.

76. "Still insatiable," *AVN*, August 1, 1999. AVN Media Network. https://avn.com/movies/26334/still-insatiable

77. Bruce Rushton, "Porn Again," *Riverfront Times* (St. Louis, MO), June 6, 2001. Euclid Media Group, LLC. https://www.riverfronttimes.com/news/porn-again-2471638

78. Susan Sward, "Porn King Jim Mitchell Walks Out of Prison Today: Served 3 years for killing his brother," *San Francisco Chronicle* (San Francisco, CA), October 3, 1997, 1. https://www.sfgate.com/news/article/PAGE-ONE-Porn-King-Jim-Mitchell-Walks-Out-of-2826073.php

79. Matier & Ross, "Dozens of 'Maybes' Ponder Making a Run for S.F. Mayor," *San Francisco Chronicle* (San Francisco, CA), July 30, 1999, A19.

80. *Golden Goddesses*, 161.

81. Michael Dougan, "Porn star makes her return to O'Farrell," *San Francisco Examiner* (San Francisco, CA), July 25, 1999, D-6.

82. Ibid.

83. Ibid.

84. David Sullivan, "VCX Reports Massive 'Insatiable' Pre-Sales," January 12, 2007, *AVN*. AVN Media Network. https://avn.com/business/articles/video/vcx-reports-massive-i-insatiable-i-pre-sales-29569.html

85. "Dark Chambers," September 1, 2000, *AVN*. AVN Media Network. https://avn.com/movies/18336/dark-chambers

86. "Edge Play," December 1, 2001, *AVN*. AVN Media Network. https://avn.com/movies/20918/edge-play

87. Bruce Rushton, "Porn Again."

88. "Obituaries: William Henry Briggs, Jr.," *The News Tribune* (Tacoma, WA), June 1, 2000, 7.

89. "Obituaries: Virginia Richardson Isabelle Briggs."

90. Jann Smith to JS.

91. Bernard Perusse, "Rabid resurrected," *The Gazette* (Montreal, Quebec, Canada), June 5, 2004, D3.

92. Peggy McGinn to JS.

93. Ibid.

94. McKenna Taylor to JS.

95. Charles Jay to JS, April 22, 2023.

96. Ibid.

97. Ibid.

98. Ibid.

99. Ibid.

100. Ibid.

101. J.R. Taylor, "Putting The 'Vice' In Vice President," August 26, 2004, *Mr. Skin.* SK Intertainment, Inc. https://www.mrskin.com/putting-the-vice-in-vice-president---530

102. Personal Choice Party of Utah, "Constitution of the Personal Choice Party of Utah." https://web.archive.org/web/20040704015504/http://party.personalchoice.org/constitutionpcp.html

103. Ibid.

104. Ibid.

105. Ibid.

106. "Charles Jay Interview (Personal Choice Party presidential candidate)," June 8, 2020, *FamousInterview.com.* FamousInterview.com. https://famousinterview.com/political-hopefuls/charles-jay-interview-personal-choice-party-presidential-candidate/

107. "2004 Presidential election by state," October 9, 2005, *The Green Papers.* The Green Papers. https://www.thegreenpapers.com/G04/President-Details.phtml?n=JAY,CHARLES

108. McKenna Taylor to JS.

109. Ibid.

110. John Bench, "Marilyn Chambers, a Proud and Loving Mother," *LUKE IS BACK*, April 2009. LUKE IS BACK. https://www.lukeisback.com/2009/04/marilyn-chambers-a-proud-and-loving-mother/

111. McKenna Taylor to JS.

112. Ibid.

113. "Marilyn Chambers: The Mr. Skin Interview," November 11, 2004, *Mr. Skin.* SK Intertainment, Inc. https://www.mrskin.com/marilyn-chambers-the-mr-skin-interview---1051

114. Frank Durant to JS, January 8, 2017.

115. Ibid.

116. Ibid.

117. Ibid.

118. Christine Pelisek, "The True Life of Marilyn Chambers, the 'Other' Queen of Porn," *The Daily Beast*, August 19, 2013 (Updated May 28, 2020). The Daily Beast Company, LLC. https://www.thedailybeast.com/the-true-life-of-marilyn-chambers-the-other-queen-of-porn

119. Peggy McGinn to JS.

120. Raffi S. Djabourian, Deputy Medical Examiner, Autopsy Report, County of Los Angeles, Department of Coroner, May 25, 2009.

EPILOGUE

1. *Insatiable* (30th Anniversary Edition). (2009). [Two-disc collector's edition on DVD]. Dynasty Group Distribution, LLC. Special feature: Pussycat Theater footage audio commentary.

2. McKenna Taylor to JS.

3. Mark Kernes, "Peggy McGinn Remembers Marilyn Chambers," *AVN*, April 16, 2009, AVN Media Network. https://avn.com/business/articles/

NOTES AND SOURCES

video/peggy-mcginn-remembers-marilyn-chambers-312638.html

4. Peggy McGinn to JS.
5. Ibid.
6. Jann Smith to JS.
7. Ibid.
8. *The Daily Beast.*
9. Bruce Weber, "Marilyn Chambers, Sex Star, Dies at 56," *The New York Times* (New York, NY), April 14, 2009. https://www.nytimes.com/2009/04/14/movies/14chambers.html
10. Richard Corliss, "Fond Farewells: Marilyn Chambers," *TIME* (n.d.) TIME USA, LLC. https://content.time.com/time/specials/packages/article/0,28804,1946375_1946448_1947246,00.html
11. Mark Kernes, "Legends of Erotica Show Brings Out Early Porn's Best," *AVN*, January 10, 2010. AVN Media Network. https://avn.com/business/articles/video/legends-of-erotica-show-brings-out-early-porn-s-best-377789.html
12. *Insatiable* (30th Anniversary Edition). (2009). [Two-disc collector's edition on DVD]. Dynasty Group Distribution, LLC. Special feature: Audio commentary with Gloria Leonard.
13. Susie Bright, "Remembering Marilyn Chambers: 1952-2009," *Susie Bright's Journal*, April 13, 2009. Susie Bright. https://susiebright.blogs.com/susie_brights_journal_/2009/04/still-insatiable-the-legacy-of-marilyn-chambers.html
14. "Marilyn Chambers, the Sex Star Who Changed Everything," *In Bed with Susie Bright*, Episode 385, April 24, 2009. Audible, Inc. https://www.audible.com/pd/In-Bed-with-Susie-Bright-385-Audiobook/B002VCRWBA
15. *Golden Goddesses*, 164-165.

FILMOGRAPHY

1. "The Owl and the Pussycat," *AFI | Catalog.* (n.d.). American Film Institute. https://catalog.afi.com/Film/23488-THE-OWLANDTHEPUSSYCAT
2. "Together," *Collections Search | BFI.* (n.d.). British Film Institute. https://collections-search.bfi.org.uk/web/Details/ChoiceFilmWorks/150060583
3. "Together (1971)," *IMDb.* (n.d.). Internet Movie Database. https://www.imdb.com/title/tt0067862/
4. "Behind the Green Door (1972)," *IMDb* (n.d.). Internet Movie Database. https://www.imdb.com/title/tt0068260/
5. "Resurrection of Eve (1973)," *IMDb.* (n.d.). Internet Movie Database. https://www.imdb.com/title/tt0070602/
6. "Inside Marilyn Chambers (1975)," *IMDb.* (n.d.). Internet Movie Database. https://www.imdb.com/title/tt0073173/
7. "Rabid," *AFI | Catalog.* (n.d.). American Film Institute. https://catalog.afi.com/Film/56316-RABID
8. "Rabid (1977)," *IMDb.* (n.d.). Internet Movie Database. https://www.imdb.com/title/tt0076590
9. "Never a Tender Moment (1979), *IMDb.* (n.d.). Internet Movie Database. https://www.imdb.com/title/tt0195943/
10. "Beyond de Sade (1979)," *IMDb.* (n.d.). Internet Movie Database. https://www.imdb.com/title/tt0082068/
11. "Insatiable (1980)," *IMDb.* (n.d.). Internet Movie Database. https://www.imdb.com/title/tt0080927/
12. "Insatiable," *Collections Search | BFI.* (n.d.). British Film Institute. https://collections-search.bfi.org.uk/web/Details/ChoiceFilmWorks/150191972

13. *Sex Surrogate*, VHS, directed by Al Rossi, Gary Legon, 1982, Beverly Hills, CA: New Star Video, 1988.

14. "Electric Blue The Movie," *Collections Search | BFI*. (n.d.). British Film Institute. https://collections-search.bfi.org.uk/web/Details/ChoiceFilmWorks/150164006

15. "My Therapist," *Collections Search | BFI*. (n.d.). British Film Institute. https://collections-search.bfi.org.uk/web/Details/ChoiceFilmWorks/150245317

16. "Up 'n' Coming (1983)," *IMDb*. (n.d.). Internet Movie Database. https://www.imdb.com/title/tt0086518/

17. "Angel of H.E.A.T. (1983)," *IMDb*. (n.d.). Internet Movie Database. https://www.imdb.com/title/tt0085167/

18. "Insatiable II (1984)," *IMDb*. (n.d.). Internet Movie Database. https://www.imdb.com/title/tt0087475/

19. "Party Girls (1989)," *IMDb*. (n.d.). Internet Movie Database. https://www.imdb.com/title/tt0098069/

20. "Breakfast in Bed (1990)," *IMDb*. (n.d.). Internet Movie Database. https://www.imdb.com/title/tt0099178/

21. "The Marilyn Diaries (1990)," *IMDb*. (n.d.). Internet Movie Database. https://www.imdb.com/title/tt0100113/

22. "Bedtime Stories (1993)," *IMDb*. (n.d.). Internet Movie Database. https://www.imdb.com/title/tt23111578/

23. "New York Nights (1994)," *IMDb*. (n.d.). Internet Movie Database. https://www.imdb.com/title/tt0110655/

24. "Bedtime Fantasies (1994)," *IMDb*. (n.d.). Internet Movie Database. https://www.imdb.com/title/tt0128958/fullcredits/

25. "Bikini Bistro (1995)," *IMDb*. (n.d.). Internet Movie Database. https://www.imdb.com/title/tt0112503/

26. "Desire (1997)," *IMDb*. (n.d.). Internet Movie Database. https://www.imdb.com/title/tt0119618/

27. "Still Insatiable (1999)," *IMDb*. (n.d.). Internet Movie Database. https://www.imdb.com/title/tt0228900/

28. "Dark Chambers (2000)," *IMDb*. (n.d.). Internet Movie Database. https://www.imdb.com/title/tt0306713/

29. "Edge Play (2001)," *IMDb*. (n.d.). Internet Movie Database. https://www.imdb.com/title/tt0308209/

30. "Nantucket Housewives (2006)," *IMDb*. (n.d.). Internet Movie Database. https://www.imdb.com/title/tt1045635/

31. "Stash (2007," *IMDb*. (n.d.). Internet Movie Database. https://www.imdb.com/title/tt0918566/

32. "Solitaire (2008)," *IMDb*. (n.d.). Internet Movie Database. https://www.imdb.com/title/tt0478268/

33. "Porndogs: The Adventures of Sadie (2009)," *IMDb*. (n.d.). Internet Movie Database. https://www.imdb.com/title/tt1328912/

INDEX

313

PURE *The Sexual Revolutions of Marilyn Chambers*

INDEX

as 'porn star' 1, 2, 3, 7, 67,
92, 100, 132, 158, 165, 172,
174, 175, 209, 211, 246, 258,
261;
professionalism of 24, 55,
58, 61, 122, 130, 150, 153,
160, 222, 253, 263, 275;
sadomasochism and 175,
176, 177, 178, 225;
San Francisco and 31, 32,
39, 40, 41, 42, 44, 45, 82,
112, 227, 228, 229, 230, 231,
232, 247, 248, 254, 255,
266;
sex and sexuality, attitude
towards 1, 7, 19, 20, 21, 27,
29, 32, 34, 36, 46, 48, 50,
57, 58, 60, 61, 80, 88, 91, 92,
98, 99, 100, 126, 129, 131,
171, 174, 175, 177, 178, 190,
210, 211;
sexism and misogyny,
faced by 2, 3, 26, 30, 31,
88, 118, 124, 126, 127, 129,
145, 171, 173, 182, 193, 194,
195, 210, 263, 266, 267;
sexual harassment of 3,
24, 25, 26, 27, 30, 31, 35, 37,
142;
singing of 6, 15, 16, 114,
115, 117, 119, 120, 121, 122,
127, 128, 129, 151, 156, 157,
158, 218, 219, 251;
sister, relationship with 11,
15, 16, 19, 72, 73, 137, 138,
139, 140, 226, 268, 278,
279;
sobriety 246, 247, 250,
255, 256, 274;
stage name of 66, 72;
submissiveness of 3, 4,
123, 136, 140, 141, 175, 216,
271;
suicidal ideations of 240;
talent and 5, 6, 15, 16, 31,
92, 93, 94, 97, 119, 120, 121,
122, 126, 128, 129, 130, 166,
167, 172, 195, 207, 210;
television appearances of
22, 118, 119, 132, 149, 158,
206, 207, 211, 212, 223, 252,
254, 255, 257, 258;
Taylor, relationship with

see: Taylor, Bill;
transition to mainstream
entertainment 6, 91, 92,
94, 97, 114, 115, 116, 117, 118,
119, 120, 121, 122, 124, 127,
129, 132, 137, 146, 147, 149,
151, 153, 154, 155, 156, 159,
163, 164, 165, 172, 173, 175,
222;
Traynor, relationship with
see: Traynor, Chuck;
See also specific movies
Chambers/Traynor
Enterprises 233
Chapin, Douglas Joseph 42,
43, 44, 45, 50, 72, 75, 87,
93, 94, 109, 110, 112, 131,
238, 252
Charest, Micheline 141
Chicago Hope (TV) 181
Cidoni, Mike 253
Cinépix 159, 283
City Blues (unmade movie)
153, 154, 164, 207
Club International
(magazine) 170
Club (magazine) 170, 247,
248
cocaine 67, 138, 139, 142, 164,
177, 192, 217, 225, 227, 235,
237, 240, 247, 269
Collins, Joan 199
Committee to Preserve Our
Sexual and Civil Liberties
231
Cooper, Wilhelmina 22
Corliss, Richard 279
Cosmopolitan (magazine)
185
Craven, Wes 35, 282
Crawford, Joan 151, 153
Cronenberg, David viii, 6,
158, 159, 160
Crow, Howard 165, 169
Cunningham, Sean S. 32,
34, 35, 36, 282
Curtis, Harley 242, 243

Dallesandro, Joe 79
Daly, Jo 230
Damiano, Gerard 62, 66, 81,
86, 108, 109, 154
Damned, The (movie) 68

Daniels, Godfrey viii, 179,
182, 183, 199, 200, 212, 217,
223
Daniels, Wendy 214
Danza, Tony 190
D'Apice, Robert 213, 214,
215, 216, 217, 224, 226, 227,
229, 235, 236, 237, 238,
239, 240, 241, 245, 246,
247, 260, 269
Dark Chambers (movie) 267,
287
Davidson, Ben 55
Davie, Bob 53
Davis, Altovise 131
Davis, Bette 23, 153
Davis Jr., Sammy 93, 97, 120,
131, 133, 159, 186, 212, 238
Davis, Tracey 132
Dean, James 152, 153
Debbie Does Dallas (movie)
219
Dee, Bobby see also:
D'Apice, Robert 224
Deep Throat (movie) 1, 3, 62,
63, 64, 65, 66, 78, 79, 80,
81, 88, 90, 105, 109, 114, 126,
162, 179, 181, 184, 186, 191,
204, 268, 275
Deep Throat Sex Scandal,
The (play) 275
de Kermadec, Liliane 141
Delaney, Joe 163
de Laurentiis, Dino 128, 154
De Leeuw, Lisa 218, 285
Deliverance (movie) 91
De Niro, Robert 255, 258
Dennerll, Roger 236
Derek, Bo 106, 107, 220
Derek, John 106, 187
De Renzy, Alex 41, 42, 81
Dershowitz, Alan 63
Designing Women (TV) 258
Desire (movie) 254, 287
Devil in Miss Jones, The
(movie) 1, 66, 69, 79, 80,
81, 89, 114, 179, 181
de Vries, Xaviera see also:
Hollander, Xaviera 135
Dick Cavett Show, The (TV)
88
Dinah! (TV) 158
Diplomat Cabaret Theater,

315

PURE The Sexual Revolutions of Marilyn Chambers

INDEX

PURE The Sexual Revolutions of Marilyn Chambers

INDEX